T0321983

Advancements in Quantum Blockchain With Real–Time Applications

Mahendra Kumar Shrivas
Department of Personnel and Administrative Reforms (E–Governance), Government of Karnataka, Bangalore, India

Kamal Kant Hiran
Aalborg University, Denmark

Ashok Bhansali
Department of Computer Engineering and Applications, GLA University, Mathura, India

Ruchi Doshi
Azteca University, Mexico

A volume in the Advances in Data Mining and Database Management (ADMDM) Book Series

Published in the United States of America by
IGI Global
Engineering Science Reference (an imprint of IGI Global)
701 E. Chocolate Avenue
Hershey PA, USA 17033
Tel: 717-533-8845
Fax: 717-533-8661
E-mail: cust@igi-global.com
Web site: http://www.igi-global.com

Library of Congress Cataloging-in-Publication Data

Names: Shrivas, Mahendra, 1987- editor.
Title: Advancements in quantum blockchain with real-time applications /
  Mahendra Shrivas, Kamal Hiran, Ashok Bhansali, and Ruchi Doshi, editors.

Description: Hershey, PA : Engineering Science Reference, an imprint of IGI
  Global, [2022] | Includes bibliographical references and index. |
  Summary: "This research book covers various concepts of computing to
  include quantum computing, post-quantum cryptography, quantum attack
  resistant Blockchain, quantum Blockchains along with multidisciplinary
  applications and real-world use cases"-- Provided by publisher.
Identifiers: LCCN 2022020073 (print) | LCCN 2022020074 (ebook) | ISBN
  9781668450727 (h/c) | ISBN 9781668450734 (s/c) | ISBN 9781668450741
  (ebook)
Subjects: LCSH: Blockchains (Databases) | Quantum computing.
Classification: LCC QA76.9.B56 A44 2022 (print) | LCC QA76.9.B56 (ebook)
  | DDC 005.74--dc23/eng/20220705
LC record available at https://lccn.loc.gov/2022020073
LC ebook record available at https://lccn.loc.gov/2022020074

This book is published in the IGI Global book series Advances in Data Mining and Database
Management (ADMDM) (ISSN: 2327-1981; eISSN: 2327-199X)

British Cataloguing in Publication Data
A Cataloguing in Publication record for this book is available from the British Library.

All work contributed to this book is new, previously-unpublished material.
The views expressed in this book are those of the authors, but not necessarily of the publisher.

For electronic access to this publication, please contact: eresources@igi-global.com.

Advances in Data Mining and Database Management (ADMDM) Book Series

David Taniar
Monash University, Australia

ISSN:2327-1981
EISSN:2327-199X

MISSION

With the large amounts of information available to organizations in today's digital world, there is a need for continual research surrounding emerging methods and tools for collecting, analyzing, and storing data.

The **Advances in Data Mining & Database Management (ADMDM)** series aims to bring together research in information retrieval, data analysis, data warehousing, and related areas in order to become an ideal resource for those working and studying in these fields. IT professionals, software engineers, academicians and upper-level students will find titles within the ADMDM book series particularly useful for staying up-to-date on emerging research, theories, and applications in the fields of data mining and database management.

COVERAGE

- Customer Analytics
- Text Mining
- Web-based information systems
- Profiling Practices
- Data Mining
- Association Rule Learning
- Predictive Analysis
- Data Analysis
- Web Mining
- Data Warehousing

IGI Global is currently accepting manuscripts for publication within this series. To submit a proposal for a volume in this series, please contact our Acquisition Editors at Acquisitions@igi-global.com or visit: http://www.igi-global.com/publish/.

The Advances in Data Mining and Database Management (ADMDM) Book Series (ISSN 2327-1981) is published by IGI Global, 701 E. Chocolate Avenue, Hershey, PA 17033-1240, USA, www.igi-global.com. This series is composed of titles available for purchase individually; each title is edited to be contextually exclusive from any other title within the series. For pricing and ordering information please visit http://www.igi-global.com/book-series/advances-data-mining-database-management/37146. Postmaster: Send all address changes to above address. Copyright © 2022 IGI Global. All rights, including translation in other languages reserved by the publisher. No part of this series may be reproduced or used in any form or by any means – graphics, electronic, or mechanical, including photocopying, recording, taping, or information and retrieval systems – without written permission from the publisher, except for non commercial, educational use, including classroom teaching purposes. The views expressed in this series are those of the authors, but not necessarily of IGI Global.

Titles in this Series

For a list of additional titles in this series, please visit: *http://www.igi-global.com/book-series/*

Encyclopedia of Data Science and Machine Learning
John Wang (Montclair State University, USA)
Engineering Science Reference • © 2022 • 2500pp • H/C (ISBN: 9781799892205) • US $2,145.00

Applied Big Data Analytics and Its Role in COVID-19 Research
Peng Zhao (Intelligentrabbit, LLC, USA) and Xi Chen (Beijing University of Civil Engineering and Architecture, China)
Engineering Science Reference • © 2022 • 349pp • H/C (ISBN: 9781799887935) • US $270.00

Data Mining Approaches for Big Data and Sentiment Analysis in Social Media
Brij B. Gupta (National Institute of Technology, Kurukshetra, India) Dragan Peraković (University of Zagreb, Croatia) Ahmed A. Abd El-Latif (Menoufia University, Egypt) and Deepak Gupta (LoginRadius Inc., Canada)
Engineering Science Reference • © 2022 • 313pp • H/C (ISBN: 9781799884132) • US $250.00

Blockchain Technology Applications in Businesses and Organizations
Pietro De Giovanni (Luiss University, Italy)
Business Science Reference • © 2022 • 315pp • H/C (ISBN: 9781799880141) • US $250.00

Handbook of Research on Essential Information Approaches to Aiding Global Health in the One Health Context
Jorge Lima de Magalhães (Institute of Drugs Technology - Farmanguinhos, Oswaldo Cruz Foundation, - FIOCRUZ Brazil & Global Health and Tropical Medicine – GHMT, Institute of Hygiene and Tropical Medicine, NOVA University of Lisbon, Portugal) Zulmira Hartz (Global Health and Tropical Medicine – GHMT, Institute of Hygiene and Tropical Medicine, NOVA University of Lisbon, Portugal) George Leal Jamil (Informações em Rede Consultoria e Treinamento, Brazil) Henrique Silveira (Global Health and Tropical Medicine – GHMT, Institute of Hygiene and Tropical Medicine, NOVA University of Lisbon, Portugal) and Liliane C. Jamil (Independent Researcher, Brazil)
Medical Information Science Reference • © 2022 • 390pp • H/C (ISBN: 9781799880110) • US $435.00

701 East Chocolate Avenue, Hershey, PA 17033, USA
Tel: 717-533-8845 x100 • Fax: 717-533-8661
E-Mail: cust@igi-global.com • www.igi-global.com

Table of Contents

Chapter 10

Detailed Table of Contents

 Peter Nimbe, University of Energy and Natural Resources, Ghana
 Benjamin Asubam Weyori, University of Energy and Natural Resources,
  Ghana
 Jacob Mensah, University of Energy and Natural Resources, Ghana
 Anokye Acheampong Amponsah, University of Energy and Natural
  Resources, Ghana
 Adebayo Felix Adekoya, University of Energy and Natural Resources,
  Ghana
 Emmanuel Adjei Domfeh, University of Energy and Natural Resources,
  Ghana

Quantum blockchain is a distributed database that is decentralized, encrypted, and based on quantum information theory and computation. This comes as a result of the recent progress made in quantum computing and the need for quantum equivalents of classical blockchains. Algorithms, frameworks, models, tools, architectures, and databases, of which quantum blockchain is a part, are still being standardized. Recently, the growth of quantum information theory and computation has resulted in a rise in the number of research ongoing in this domain. This chapter presents an insight into quantum blockchain using the PRISMA technique with results registered and analyzed. The literature is analyzed based on some parameters or categorizations accompanied by graphical and tabular representations.

Chapter 2

Omega John Unogwu, Universidad Azteca, Mexico
Ruchi Doshi, Universidad Azteca, Mexico
Kamal Kant Hiran, Sir Padampat Singhania University, India
Maad M. Mijwil, Baghdad College of Economic Sciences University,
    Iraq

Quantum-resistant blockchains refer to cryptographic processes that are resistant to attacks via quantum computers. Present public-key algorithms depend on the difficulty of deciphering the discrete log and factorization problem of large prime numbers. Shor's algorithm can be used to break the hash signatures by quantum computers. Therefore, it is necessary for the development of a post-quantum secure signature scheme or quantum-resistant blockchain for post-quantum blockchain security. This chapter will discuss the impact quantum computers are predicted to have on public key cryptography based on the following topics: quantum computers, public key cryptography, quantum threat to PKI, Shor's and Grover's algorithms, post-quantum cryptography, and quantum-resistant blockchain.

Chapter 3

Emerging Blockchain Technology vis-à-vis Limitations and Issues:

Prantosh Kumar Paul, Raiganj University, India

Blockchain has now become blockchain technology, and this is the record of data that are encrypted, and here distributed database is required for the purpose of transaction, contract, and independent record. It is therefore a digital ledger and can be reachable in different platforms for different financial activities and services. It is supported by healthy digital currency systems like bitcoin transactions and does not depend on any third party systems. Blockchain supports the multiple numbers of shared copies, and it works in a same database. Very recently blockchain was considered as an important subfield of information technology. It is therefore treated as a tool, technique, as well as procedure for financial management. This chapter is based on existing literature on blockchain with basics and special focus on the issues and limitations. This chapter highlights the scenario of blockchain technology in India with opportunities, companies, and scenario of manpower availability and potentiality.

Sarika Khandelwal, G. H. Raisoni College of Engineering, Nagpur,
India
Shaleen Bhatnagar, Presidency University, India
Nirmal Mungale, G. H. Raisoni College of Engineering, Nagpur, India
Ritesh Kumar Jain, Geetanjali Institute of Technical Studies, India

Biometric templates must be secured with traceability, immutability, and high-trust capabilities. A variety of system models are proposed by researchers, most of which either utilize blockchains or machine learning for improved security and quality of service (QoS). The augmented sharding model is designed using light weight incremental learning framework, which assists in shard formation and management. Performance evaluation of the proposed model indicates that it is able to achieve high accuracy attack mitigation, along with low block mining delay and high throughput. This performance is compared with various state-of-the-art methods and an improvement of 10% in terms of delay and 14% in terms of throughput is achieved. Further, an attack detection accuracy of 99.3% is obtained for sybil, masquerading, and man in the middle (MITM) attacks. This text further recommends improvement areas which can be further researched for enhancing security and QoS performance of the proposed model.

Punit Sharma, Janardan Rai Nagar Rajasthan Vidyapeeth, India
Indu Sharma, Meera Girls College, India
Suman Pamecha, Janardan Rai Nagar Rajasthan Vidyapeeth, India
Kamal Kant Hiran, Sir Padampat Singhania University, India

English poet Samuel T. Coleridge wrote "O! lady, we receive but what we give? And nature alone lives in our lives." The Earth is one, but nations are not. New technology, especially blockchain paves the way toward a global village. This chapter analyses the ultimate solution to the global warming issue through the introduction of green currency based on blockchain technology to inculcate the concept of environmental protection in the next generation. We never value the free gifts of nature as the economies are driven by markets globally. Unless and until a monetary value is associated with environmental protection it's difficult to motivate the next generation to protect it. The introduction of green currency helps in creating a market. Development with the acceptance, protection, and maintenance of nature as it is is possible only through the use of advanced technologies. This chapter introduces a new concept of global green currency based on blockchain technology. This tool may ultimately present a platform as a solution to the global warming issue.

Chapter 6

Alok Singh Gahlot, MBM University, India
Ruchi Vyas, MBM University, India

Blockchain is a leading-edge innovation that gives the possibility to streamline numerous enterprises like gaming. There have been many investigations done utilizing blockchain innovation in money, wellbeing, and different areas, yet gaming is a region yet to be conquered. This chapter will explain how blockchain innovation can be utilized in games. Blockchain is known to make exceptional computerized resources that can be copied and make decentralized environments. There are two parts of blockchain innovation that can change the gaming industry. Blockchain has generally affected our ways of life somewhat recently. A word that frequently emerges while discussing blockchain is bitcoin. Current answers for planning and building decentralized blockchain applications need interoperability. Thus, blockchains and existing advancements don't incorporate well in a brought together system. The authors propose a design expecting to effortlessly connect existing decentralized advances and blockchains. Blockchain gaming is an arising diversion worldview.

Chapter 7

Chandani Joshi, Sir Padampat Singhania University, India
Chitra Bhole, Sir Padampat Singhania University, Udaipur, India & K.
J. Somaiya Institute of Engineering and Information Technology,
Mumbai, India
Naveen Vaswani, Sir Padampat Singhania University, Udaipur, India &
Thadomal Shahani Engineering College, Mumbai, India

Data collection mechanisms have become effectively advanced by leveraging the internet of things and cyber physical systems. The sensors are heavily developed with intricate details to capture data in varied forms which can be stored and used as an information base for knowledge extraction using analytics and statistical prognostication in artificial intelligence sub-branches. Storing this data with a different approach that ensures stringent security measures is done using blockchain. The loopholes that compromise the security of blockchain are quantum computing for which quantum resistant blockchain ideas are discussed. This chapter finally sheds some light on the effective approach to implement the CPS 4.0-based blockchain mechanism with detailed scrutiny.

Chapter 8

Neha Gupta, Symbiosis University of Applied Sciences, Indore, India

Blockchain and quantum technology breakthroughs are currently being debated publicly across a variety of forums. There are numerous applications and capabilities that can provide transparent, redundant, secure, accountable environments thanks to these technologies. To ensure resource-dependent high security requirements, certain cryptographic primitives and protocols can be used effectively. Quantum proofs, safe quantum solutions, and anti-quantum systems will assess any system for quantum attacks and create a secure quantum computing system. Therefore, this work intends to encourage experts from different fields to provide technology-integrated solutions that combine cost-effective and quality service, quickly, securely, and meet requirements. Researchers will be encouraged to provide helpful overviews and guidance in dealing with real-time applications from post-quantum technologies.

    Manish Dadhich, Sir Padampat Singhania University, India
    Harish Tiwari, Sir Padampat Singhania University, India

Smart cities are a futuristic urban development concept that uses ICT to enable citizens, governments, and organizations to collect and share real-time data. Q-BoC technology can provide a new level of convenience and security for communication and transactions among all of a smart city's many stakeholders. Information technology, including quantum blockchain, has been integrated to govern physical, social, and business infrastructures in today's rapidly developing smart cities. Innovative technologies and concepts such as the IoT, 5G, artificial intelligence, and quantum blockchain have become necessary for an intelligent and advanced society. In recent years, both academics and industry have demonstrated a strong interest in the revolution of smart cities. Smart cities can deliver a variety of smart functions, such as intelligent transportation, Industry 5.0, governance, Healthcare 5.0, and smart banking, to improve people's quality of life. The chapter explores the application, challenges, and opportunities for making a smart society.

    Farhan Khan, Geetanjali Institute of Technical Studies, India
    Rakshit Kothari, Geetanjali Institute of Technical Studies, India
    Mayank Patel, Geetanjali Institute of Technical Studies, India

Blockchain is a new but quickly growing technology in the world, which was developed by a pseudonymous Satoshi Nakamoto in 2009 as the cryptocurrency Bitcoin. Blockchain was un-hackable but now, due to use of quantum computers, it is possible to tamper with blockchain. As a counter to this, the researchers have come up with quantum blockchain using the principles of quantum cryptography. Today we see that the technology has given birth to many new technologies as well. One of its examples is non-fungible tokens (NFTs). These are a new sort of blockchain-based token that is unique and indivisible. They were first created in 2014. These are blockchain-based virtual assets. Since early 2021, the phenomena and its marketplaces have increased dramatically.

Preface

After the Internet, blockchain is one of the most promising new technologies with the potential to radically alter our global society. Blockchain technology is being adopted and implemented across the entire spectrum of business and industry operations, following the initial phase of bitcoin and cryptocurrencies. The solutions that guarantee trust, transparency, non-repudiation, and redundancy have been developed by application developers who have taken advantage of the characteristics of the blockchain, such as decentralization, immutability, cryptographic security, and so on. Blockchain 3.0 provides a large amount of distributed storage space with minimal effort, scalability without compromising security, assistance in integrating data from multiple sources without compromising privacy, transparency without revealing ownerships, interoperability without excessive complexity, and authenticity in provenance. Blockchain's adaptability and multidimensional capability, combined with the incorporation of AI, ML, IoT, etc., promises to have a significant, positive impact on a wide range of industries and organizations, and opens exciting opportunities to deliver a superior value proposition to customers through novel products and services.

Digital signatures, hashing algorithms, and public-key cryptography are all heavily utilised in blockchain infrastructures to create a one-of-a-kind secure and reliable application backbone. Whether it's for digital signatures or encryption, the time it takes to solve certain mathematical problems is generally used as a yardstick of the strength of the various cryptographic methods currently in use. Due to the massive amount of time required relative to the available computational power, Blockchain deployments are safe from hacking for any practical purpose. The current blockchain encryption systems, however, are vulnerable to the emerging quantum computing. The prospect of quantum computer cyber-attacks on the Blockchain network is a very real possibility soon, given the rapid pace of progress being experienced with quantum computing technology.

Members of the Blockchain community and developers are working on projects to strengthen existing distributed ledger technology (DLT) and blockchain networks so that they are immune to attacks from quantum computers. These post-quantum algorithms are based on computational problems that Shor's algorithm, Grover's algorithm, or similar ones have proven to be infeasible for quantum computers. Secure computing is achieved through the incorporation of post-quantum cryptography in cyber-physical systems, which also opens up new possibilities in fields like smart contracts, quantum blockchain, and intelligent security solutions. There is a growing consensus that the only way to protect computing and security infrastructure from the imminent threat of quantum attacks is to implement quantum-proof cryptography. Post-quantum implementations of the Blockchain can be seen in projects like Ethereum 2.0 and Ethereum 3.0. Research into quantum Blockchain has attracted a lot of attention in recent years thanks to the growth of quantum computation and quantum information theory. Although post-quantum cryptography shows great promise in many areas, there is surprisingly little written on the subject from an applied perspective. For those unfamiliar with distributed ledger technology (DLT) and blockchain, this book offers a primer on the topic, as well as an overview of the most popular post-quantum algorithms and how they ensure the long-term viability of DLT-based applications.

Quantum computing, post-quantum cryptography, quantum attack-resistant blockchain, quantum blockchains, multidisciplinary applications, and real-world use cases are all topics covered in this book. Several industry-specific problems, and their potential resolutions, are also covered in the book. This reference is perfect for computer scientists, industry professionals, academics, practitioners, scholars, researchers, teachers, and students, as it covers crucial topics like cybersecurity, data management, and the smart society.

ORGANIZATION OF THE BOOK

The book is organized into 10 chapters contributed by researchers, scholars, and professors from prestigious laboratories and educational institutions across the globe. A brief description of each of the chapters in this section is given below.

Chapter 1: Quantum Blockchain – A Systematic Review

Quantum blockchain is a decentralized, encrypted, quantum-based database. This is due to quantum computing progress and the need for quantum blockchains. Quantum blockchain is part of standardized algorithms, frameworks, models, tools, architectures, and databases. Quantum information theory and computation research has grown recently. This chapter analyses quantum blockchain using the PRISMA technique. Literature is analyzed using parameters and graphical and tabular representations.

Chapter 2: Introduction to Quantum-Resistant Blockchain

Quantum-resistant blockchains resist quantum computer attacks. Present public-key algorithms depend on the discrete log and factorization problem of large prime numbers. Shor's algorithm breaks quantum hash signatures. Post-quantum blockchain security requires a quantum-resistant signature scheme or blockchain. This chapter discusses the impact quantum computers will have on public key cryptography based on quantum computers, public key cryptography, quantum threat to PKI, Shor's and Grover's Algorithms, post-quantum cryptography, and quantum-resistant blockchain.

Chapter 3: Emerging Blockchain Technology vis-à-vis Limitations and Issues

Blockchain Technology is a record of encrypted data that requires a distributed database for transactions, contracts, and independent records. It's a digital ledger accessible on multiple platforms for financial activities and services. It's supported by digital currency systems like bitcoin and doesn't rely on third parties. Encrypted data can be breached. Blockchain works in the same database with multiple shared copies. Blockchain is a new IT subfield. It's a financial management tool, technique, and procedure. This chapter covers Blockchain basics, issues, and limitations. This chapter describes Blockchain technology in India, including opportunities, companies, and manpower availability.

Chapter 4: Design of a Blockchain-Powered Biometric Template Security Framework Using Augmented Sharding

Traceability, immutability, and high trust are required for biometric templates. Most proposed system models use blockchains or machine learning to improve security and service quality (QoS). Using a light-weight incremental learning framework, the augmented sharding model aids in shard formation and management. The proposed model achieves high attack accuracy, low block mining delay, and high throughput. This performance improves by 10% in delay and 14% in throughput compared to state-of-the-art methods. Sybil, masquerading, and MITM attacks are detected with 99.3% accuracy. This text also recommends areas for improving the proposed model's security and QoS.

Chapter 5: Green Currency Based on Blockchain Technology for Sustainable Development

This chapter analyses the ultimate solution to global warming using Green Currency based on blockchain technology to inculcate environmental protection in the next generation. As global economies are driven by markets, we don't value nature's free gifts. Until a monetary value is associated with environmental protection, it's hard to motivate the next generation to protect it. Green Currency helps Bad find a market. Advanced technologies are needed to accept, protect, and maintain nature as-is. This chapter introduces Block-Chain-based global green currency. This tool may help solve Global Warming.

Chapter 6: Blockchain in Gaming

Blockchain can streamline many industries, including gaming. Blockchain technology has been studied in money, health, and other areas, but gaming remains unconquered. This chapter discusses blockchain's use in games. Blockchain creates decentralized, copyable computer resources. Blockchain can change gaming in 2 ways. Recently, blockchain has impacted our lives. Bitcoin is a common Blockchain term. Interoperability is needed for planning and building blockchain apps. Thus, blockchains and existing innovations don't mix well. We propose a design to link decentralized advances and blockchains. Blockchain gaming is a new distraction.

Chapter 7: A Scrutiny Review of CPS 4.0-Based Blockchain With Quantum Resistance

Internet of Things and Cyber Physical Systems have improved data collection over time. The sensors capture data in various forms that can be stored and used for knowledge extraction using analytics and statistical prognostication in artificial intelligence sub-branches. Blockchain stores this data with stringent security measures. Quantum computing loopholes compromise blockchain security, so quantum-resistant blockchains are discussed. This review article explains how to implement CPS 4.0's blockchain mechanism effectively.

Chapter 8: Quantum and Blockchain for Computing Paradigms – Vision and Advancements

Blockchain and quantum technology advancements are widely discussed today. These technologies and others have created many applications and abilities to create transparent, redundant, secure, accountable, and well-organized environments. Blockchain provides a secure peer-to-peer, decentralized network with advanced cryptography primitives and protocols. These cryptography primitives and protocols ensure resource-dependent security. It inherits environmental conditions and automates solutions. Test existing blockchain networks against quantum attacks and design quantum-computing enabled secure blockchain solutions. Any system against quantum attacks, post-quantum computing, quantum-proofs, quantum-safe solutions, quantum-resistant systems, and processes must be studied.

Chapter 9: Quantum Blockchain for Smart Society – Applications, Challenges, and Opportunities

Smart cities use ICT to collect and share real-time data with citizens, governments, and organizations. This technology can improve Smart city stakeholders' communication and transactions. Quantum Blockchain is used to govern smart cities' physical, social, and business infrastructures. Intelligent and advanced societies need IoT, 5G, AI, and Quantum Blockchain. Both academia and industry are interested in smart cities. Smart cities can provide intelligent transportation, industry 5.0, governance, healthcare 5.0, and smart banking to improve people's lives. The chapter discusses smart society applications, challenges, and opportunities.

Chapter 10: Advancements in Blockchain Technology With the Use of Quantum Blockchain and Non-Fungible Tokens

Blockchain was developed by Satoshi Nakamoto in 2009 as the cryptocurrency Bitcoin. Quantum Computers can now tamper with blockchain, so researchers have created Quantum Blockchain using Quantum Cryptography. Today, technology has spawned many new technologies. Non-Fungible Tokens (NFTs) are a unique, indivisible blockchain-based token.

Mahendra Kumar Shrivas
Department of Personnel and Administrative Reforms (E-Governance),
Government of Karnataka, Bangalore, India

Kamal Kant Hiran
Aalborg University, India

Ashok Bhansali
Department of Computer Engineering and Applications, GLA University,
Mathura, India

Ruchi Doshi
Azteca University, Mexico

Acknowledgment

It is important to acknowledge the unwavering support and innumerable contributions of numerous individuals in this project's completion. Without the assistance of IGI Global: International Academic Publisher, USA, this book would not have been possible. We are grateful to the IGI Global team, particularly Angelina Olivas, Jan Travers, and Rowan Rumbaugh, for providing this great opportunity and for being extremely cooperative from the beginning to the end of this book's production. Their unique suggestions, knowledge, and promptness were key to making this book a reality.

We would like to express our heartfelt gratitude and profound appreciation to Prof. Anders Henten, Prof. Kund Erik Skouby, Prof. Reza Tadayoni, Prof. Lene Tolstrup Sørensen, Anette Bysøe, Center for Communication, Media and Information Technologies (CMI), Aalborg University, Copenhagen, Denmark and Dr. Ricardo Saavedra (Universidad Azteca, Mexico) for their continuous guidance.

We also wish to thank all reviewers, and authors for their prompt response, dedication, and quality contributions in the area of Advancements in Quantum Blockchain with Real-Time Applications.

Last but not least, the editorial team wish to express their gratitude to their respective family members Dr. Mahendra K. Doshi, Bhuvi Jain for their understanding and support throughout.

Mahendra Kumar Shrivas
Department of Personnel and Administrative Reforms (E-Governance),
Government of Karnataka, Bangalore, India

Kamal Kant Hiran
Aalborg University, Denmark

Ashok Bhansali
Department of Computer Engineering and Applications, GLA University,
Mathura, India

Ruchi Doshi
Universidad Azteca, Mexico

Introduction

When we discuss the future of computing, Blockchain and Quantum computing emerge out as the two most interesting, promising as well as controversial computing paradigm. While blockchain is already being used across industries and adoption is growing faster, quantum computing is making headlines and approaching fast towards becoming reality in the near future.

We have witnessed how the web and the Internet of information has shaped the world around us. In a similar manner the Internet of values, driven by Blockchain technology, is adding unimaginable values to every bit if life around us. Blockchain is a decentralized permission-less distributed ledger technology across peer-to-peer networks where the nodes of the network embed trust amongst themselves. Blockchain technology has revolutionized the businesses and operations across industry segments. The Inherent attributes and characteristics of the blockchain technology solves most critical issues of trust and transparency and thus makes it suitable for almost every business and industry domain. At the time when different industries are adopting blockchain and implementing it to make operations more efficient and secure, the quantum computing is evolving silently and poses a threat to the classical blockchain technology. Quantum computer uses qubits, quantum bits, rather than traditional digital bits that can solve the highly difficult computational problems with ease and at a lighting fast speed. While ttraditional computers, often called as classical computers, performs calculations on bits that are either 1s or 0s, quantum computers work on qubits. A concept of quantum physics called quantum super positioning, permits these bits to simultaneously exist in both states at the same time. Additionally, unlike classical bits, qubits can affect each other at the time of processing, through a phenomenon called quantum entanglement, that generates one, large quantum state for the whole computing system. Every time a qubit is added to the system, the number of potential computing states gets doubled and that is what makes quantum computers too powerful compared to traditional computing machines.

Apart from solving the highly complex computing intensive problems quantum computers have incredible potential to affect the cryptographic system and that's what poses a threat to the existing blockchain systems. The security, integrity, and transparency of the blockchain to a larger extent depends on cryptographic procedures. For example, digital signatures, based on public key cryptography, are used to authenticate a transaction whereas data immutability is achieved by the hashing based on symmetric key cryptography. Speed of quantum computing and quantum algorithms poses a real threat to the very foundation of the blockchain technology i.e. cryptography and hashing. It makes digital signatures used in the blockchain technology susceptible to quantum threat. The asymmetric cryptography works on the basis of mathematical relation between key pairs. A private-public key pair is generated, and private key is kept secret, whereas public key is made available to the public. This permits anybody to generate a digital signature using their private key that can be validated by anybody with the corresponding public key. This scheme is the very essence of the blockchain based BFSI industry to prove authenticity and integrity of transactions. The security of asymmetric cryptography is derived the mathematical function called a "one-way function". This function dictates that the public key can be easily derived from the private key but not the other way around. All traditional algorithms used to derive private key from the public key needs unimaginable huge amount of time to do such a computation which is not feasible for any practical purpose. However, in 1994, the mathematician Peter Shor designed an algorithm based on the quantum computing that can break the common belief regarding the security of the most common algorithms of asymmetric cryptography. This suggests that a person with a sufficiently large quantum computer could make use this algorithm to calculate the private key from its corresponding public key, and thus, forge a digital signature. And so, there is an urgent need to address the issues in the context of evolving quantum algorithms and computing.

There are two angles to look into the quantum resistant blockchain – one is to append guards to the existing already deployed systems called as quantum proofing and second is to design a quantum safe blockchain from the very scratch. One of the approaches to solve the problem is to replace the existing digital signature schemes like RSA or ECDSA with the post quantum signature schemes. We can use much bigger public/private keys or digital signatures but then it will create further issues for the scalability. Decreasing the size of the signature and public /private keys is the most critical issue in designing the quantum resistant blockchain. As per blockchain researchers the most feasible and cost-effective way of making blockchain safe against quantum attack is to replace the existing RSA or ECDSA schemes with post quantum algorithms which works on the basis of computational security. Some of the computational security schemes are lattice-based schemes, learning with errors, super singular isogenies schemes, multivariate-polynomial schemes, code-based schemes, or Merkle tree-based signature schemes. These cryptographic schemes are having solid resistance against quantum attacks in the sense that till date there is nothing which can compromise security of these schemes. The only practical issues is that are computational incentive because of their slightly larger key sizes.

A study by Deloitte states that 25% of bitcoin are at risk of being stolen in security attacks. As on January 2022, that amounts to approximately $300 billion. A quantum computer-based crypto attack can rob trillions of dollars and has the potential to throw the global markets and economy into recession and chaos. For an example and to be more specific, Shor's function, when used by a quantum computer, can solve for the prime factors that are currently concealed by elliptic-curve multiplication and is considered to be impossible to reverse. As per the data a typical classical computer requires approximately 340,282,366,920,938,463,463,374,607,431,768, 211,456 basic operations, to determine a private key associated with a public key utilizing elliptic-curve multiplication and this will take thousands of years of time. However, a quantum computer that uses Shor's function would take only 2,097,152 operations to figure out the corresponding private key and this can be achieved in just a few hours. It's only a matter of time when such powerful quantum computers will become part of mainstream computing but than it is the need of the hour to develop blockhead-based systems and solutions which are quantum safe.

This book presents a systematic review of the current situation and how different industry applications should implement blockchain for the post quantum era. It provides various industry cases, applications and research studies around the quantum proofing of the Blockchain and will help readers to understand the issues, challenges; and approaches and was forward.

Chapter 1
Quantum Blockchain:
A Systematic Review

Peter Nimbe

ⓘD https://orcid.org/0000-0002-6823-
5274
*University of Energy and Natural
Resources, Ghana*

Benjamin Asubam Weyori
*University of Energy and Natural
Resources, Ghana*

Jacob Mensah
*University of Energy and Natural
Resources, Ghana*

Anokye Acheampong Amponsah
*University of Energy and Natural
Resources, Ghana*

Adebayo Felix Adekoya
*University of Energy and Natural
Resources, Ghana*

Emmanuel Adjei Domfeh
*University of Energy and Natural
Resources, Ghana*

ABSTRACT

Quantum blockchain is a distributed database that is decentralized, encrypted, and based on quantum information theory and computation. This comes as a result of the recent progress made in quantum computing and the need for quantum equivalents of classical blockchains. Algorithms, frameworks, models, tools, architectures, and databases, of which quantum blockchain is a part, are still being standardized. Recently, the growth of quantum information theory and computation has resulted in a rise in the number of research ongoing in this domain. This chapter presents an insight into quantum blockchain using the PRISMA technique with results registered and analyzed. The literature is analyzed based on some parameters or categorizations accompanied by graphical and tabular representations.

DOI: 10.4018/978-1-6684-5072-7.ch001

INTRODUCTION

This chapter seeks to provide some insight into quantum blockchain technology by presenting and analyzing relevant literature as well as proposing a framework to address land management and administration transparency.

The goal of this chapter is to

- Identify literature on quantum blockchain
- Categorize the literature on quantum blockchain.
- Present results of categorization of literature in tabular and graphical formats.
- Compare quantum blockchain to classical blockchain.
- Propose a classical and quantum framework to address the issue of transparency when it comes to land management and administration.
- Present future directions of quantum blockchain and unanswered questions
- Outline the method and shortfalls of some of the quantum blockchain literature

Background

Blockchain is a modern technology with a lot of potential real-world applications in fields like medicine, energy, and finance. It is distributed and encrypted to prevent tampering (Kiktenko et al, 2018). The present blockchain networks depends on schemes, which are susceptible to assaults from quantum computers despite their promise in a wide range of applications. The most serious is the storage problem in blockchain systems, which arises from the fact that each node must store a copy of all blocks. Immutability is a fundamental attribute of blockchain systems, which has gained some attention in recent times. Due to their promise to offer accountability, transparency, and redundancy, blockchain technologies have been advocated for a variety of applications in recent years (Fernandez-Carames & Fraga-Lamas, 2020). Figure 1 below shows a diagram comprising the various types of blockchain technology.

Karbasi and Shahpasand proposed a solution that ensured the validity of digital data that is shared and published online such as cryptographic keys, digital certificates, and common reference strings by combining several recently developed innovations, the most prominent of which are blockchain, smart contracts, and the quantum-resistant Password-based Authenticated Key Exchange protocol over rings (Karbasi & Shahpasand, 2020).

Wu et al. introduced a couple of hash algorithms based on a lattice, with or without trapdoors, and demonstrated their applications in the redactable blockchain. Furthermore, their study proposed two ways to avoid the misapplication of blockchain's redaction functionality. They proposed a key management mechanism, which is fully distributed for the first scheme, and used the general framework to handle the redaction-misuse problem that still exists in blockchains, but they also suggested a voting strategy for their second scheme. To better comprehend their work, they demonstrated how to combine the blockchain technology with the hash with relatively slight changes to existing blockchains (Wu et al, 2021).

Figure 1. Blockchain technology
(Wegrzyn & Wang, 2021)

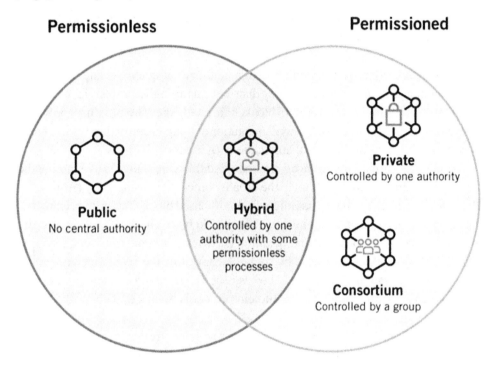

Attacks are now possible due to the algorithms proposed by Shor and Grover, and quantum computer's development and progress. Blockchains have been rebuilt to use cryptosystems that can withstand quantum attacks as a result of these algorithms, leading to quantum-resistant cryptosystems. In light of this, there was an investigation of post-quantum cryptographic systems and how they can be used in blockchains and distributed ledger technologies. As a result, their effort aimed to give future blockchain researchers and developers a wide perspective and practical instructions on post-quantum blockchain security (Fernandez-Carames & Fraga-Lamas, 2020).

Mesnager et al. suggested a threshold verified multi-secret sharing technique centered on hard problems that are post-quantum lattice-based based for verification and private communication. The proposed threshold technique was then implemented in a distributed storage blockchain (DSB) system to exchange transaction data at each block in their work. The suggested DSB system encrypts the data block with the AES-256 encryption technique before distributing it to nodes at each block, and the proposed scheme simultaneously shares the hash value and private key of the block across nodes (Mesnager et al, 2020).

Khalid & Askar reviewed the quantum blockchain and the major issues associated with the most essential post-quantum blockchain systems to provide researchers with a broad insight and advice on post-quantum blockchain security. Furthermore, signature encryption and digital blockchain signature techniques showing signs of promise are described in depth in their work concerning the usefulness and durability (Khalid & Askar, 2021).

Küfner et al. offered an instantiation of a platform for quantum-safe blockchain secure authentication that leverages key distribution through an urban fiber network as a likely answer to the quantum-era blockchain challenge. Their findings provided answers to key questions about the implementation and expansion of these blockchains in commercial and governmental applications (Küfner et al, 2012).

To solve this difficulty, Ablayev et al. adopted the natural notion of adapting the Grover quantum search algorithm to the broader blockchain technology (Ablayev et al, 2018). Sun et al. provided a paradigm for logic-based blockchain, which enhances the efficiency and power of quantum-secured blockchain. The power was boosted by including quantum protection and quantum certificate into the transaction syntax, and the efficiency was increased by the replacement of the Byzantine agreement protocol with a quantum equivalent. They were able to resolve a momentous problem in cheat-sensitive quantum bit commitment protocols thanks to their work (Sun et al, 2018).

Bennet & Daryanoosh proposed a blockchain architecture that is quantum-enabled based on a group of quantum servers. They created an interactive mining protocol that is carried out among servers and clients and employs quantum data encoded in light to eliminate the need for network infrastructure trust (Bennet & Daryanoosh, 2019). Sharma et al. identified assaults on optical networks and advocated using quantum-secured blockchain to safeguard networks from security threats. They provided an overview of blockchain technology which included security problems, and concentrated on QKD, which protects blockchain technology from quantum attacks. In addition, they included a detailed overview of quantum-secured blockchain and network architecture for future research and development of safe and trusted optical communication networks based on quantum-secured blockchain (Sharma et al, 2021).

Given the vast amount of keys and signatures utilized by lattice cryptosystems, Zhang et al. presented a way to store the whole content of public keys and signatures on an interplanetary file system by putting their hash values on the blockchain (IPFS). As a result, each blockchain block could only carry so many transactions (Zhang et al, 2021).

To combat quantum computing, Xie et al. developed a lattice signature algorithm, as well as a cuckoo filter to reduce the overhead of the verification step of the user. Finally, a decentralized blockchain network is implemented to supplant traditional centralized audits to disseminate and certify verification outcomes, hence boosting the scheme's transparency and security (Xie et al, 2021).

Li et al completed the development of a signature scheme, which could be utilized to protect the blockchain network over existing traditional channels. The keys were created utilizing the Bonsai Trees technology and the Rand-Basis algorithm, which ensures randomization while also creating lightweight non-deterministic wallets. The strategy can be demonstrated securely in the oracle model and is effectual. Their research could help to progress post-quantum biology research in the future (Li et al, 2019).

Choi et al suggested a new approach of monitoring the information veracity of Programmable Logic Controllers (PLCs) using blockchain technologies. In the context of nuclear power plants, they designed a blockchain to check the information integrity of PLCs. A novel concept called Proof of Monitoring (PoM) for information integrity of PLCs was presented to circumvent the restrictions of the application of blockchain to the nuclear power plants cybersecurity. They also employed blockchain to create a monitoring system for nuclear power plants' Reactor Protection Mechanism, which is a safety system (Choi et al, 2020).

Gao et al. developed a safe cryptocurrency method based on PQB that is resistant to quantum computing assaults. They began by presenting a lattice problem-based signature system. Secondly, they build the PQB and propose a cryptocurrency system that combines the suggested signature scheme with blockchain. The security of the cryptocurrency method and the signature scheme is capable of being simplified to the lattice short integer solution problem (Gao et al, 2018).

A blockchain-based electronic voting protocol that ensures transparency in the process of voting was suggested by Gao et al. At the same time, this approach may audit voters who are voting improperly and withstand attacks by using code-based and certificateless cryptography. Their technique was found to be suitable for small-scale elections and to have certain efficiency and security advantages when the voter number is limited after a performance analysis (Gao et al, 2019).

In the blockchain, Yin et al. developed an innovative anti-quantum transaction authentication technique. Public and private keys for lightweight non-deterministic wallets were produced from master public and private keys and this constitutes a major takeaway from their research. They present a new authentication method based on Bonsai Trees technology, which allows a lattice space to be extended to many lattice spaces with the same key. Their work laid the theoretical groundwork for blockchain's applicability in the post-quantum era (Yin et al, 2017).

The immunity and transparency of a blockchain-based cryptographic currency system was investigated using a simulation of the six-state QKD Protocol. To assure the creation of a better crypto-currency system, the process of key rate generation was examined. A mathematical model was utilized to generate the appropriate restrictions for a linear connection. At the application level, the protocol contributed to the creation of a crypto-currency system (Azhar et al, 2019).

Iovane presented a new data transmission protocol based on the BB84 protocol's quantum encryption capabilities as well as the possibilities given by distributed ledgers and blockchain. Their method allowed for the most secure transmission of keys, whether on a quantum communications channel or by using a classical standard channel and simulating quantum functionality on it using network nodes as new virtual quantum components (Iovane, 2021).

Nieto-Chaupis proposed a quantum mechanics-based formalism for simulating blockchain dynamics in an e-commerce transaction. The algorithm was tested with integer-order Bessel functions in a comprehensive blockchain-based algorithm. In simulations, the reliability of a simple blockchain model on the order of 75 was also established. Their research, on the other hand, fails to take advantage of quantum mechanics' properties to describe the complete dynamics of the bitcoin movement in huge economies (Nieto-Chaupis, 2019).

The world's first efficient asynchronous blockchain with quantum safety that uses concurrent preprocessing and an online prototype was presented by Dolev and Wang (Dolev & Wang, 2020). Sun et al. proposed an auction mechanism for a quantum blockchain and a lottery protocol. Their lottery protocol guarantees randomization, verifiability, decentralization, and unconditional security, whereas their auction protocol guarantees bid privacy and binding, decentralization, and unconditional security. Their approach could not be applied to the multi-party computation field since more elaborate quantum blockchain protocols will be devised in the future. (Sun et al, 2020).

MatRiCT was introduced as a RingCT system for blockchain secret transactions centered on post-quantum lattice assumptions. The protocol's proof length is almost two orders of magnitude lower than the previous post-quantum approach, and it scales well to huge anonymity sets, unlike the present proposal. The system or scheme can be modified to make it auditable, in which a user can choose from a list of authorities to expose her identity (Esgin et al, 2019).

To improve the security of blockchain, Gao et al. presented a unique quantum blockchain scheme. Their effort began with a proposal for a definition of quantum blockchain and a detailed description of its architecture. They established a sort of cryptocurrency dubbed a quantum coin for their research. To create the unique quantum blockchain scheme, they used quantum entanglement and DPoS. The outcomes of their theoretical research provide a scientific foundation for future applicability (Gao et al, 2020).

By demonstrating a blockchain architecture that makes use of key distribution across an urban fiber network for safe authentication, Kiktenko et al. were able to address the quantum blockchain challenge. These results tackle significant issues with the scalability and realizability of quantum-safe blockchains for business applications. (Kiktenko et al, 2018).

Li et al presented an anti-quantum blind signature system centered on the lattice assumption. The security of this scheme was enhanced through the utilization of the bimodal Gaussian distribution and other technologies amongst others, given that lattice cryptography is the major candidate algorithm in post-quantum cryptosystems and the blind signature scheme is widely utilized in electronic cash and electronic voting for creating payment systems that are untraceable, and these are more suitable for privacy preservation in blockchain-enabled systems. However, as quantum computers become more common, post-quantum cryptographic techniques will become more important, and anti-quantum lattice-based signatures will become more realistic (Li et al, 2021).

Iovane used a novel negotiation technique to propose a method to resolve the validity of a block and the assignment of a new block in the infrastructure of the blockchain. Negotiation processes centered on an extended probability environment were used to achieve block validation and assignment. However, their efforts failed to provide a widespread strategy for community development, despite the adoption of the MuReQua solution and the creation of particular research to examine the influence of the generation of keys on a significant number of requests and users (Iovane, 2021).

A quantum blockchain was developed by Banerjee et al. using multiparty entanglement of quantum weighted hypergraph states. The entanglement of the hypergraph state acts as the protocol's "chain," with the information in the classical blocks starting at a single qubit that acts as a vertex of the relevant hypergraph. Their study represented a step forward in the development of a truly secure quantum money transaction system (Banerjee et al, 2020).

A design for a quantum blockchain was proposed by Rajan and Visser. The blockchain was represented as a nonpermanent Greenberger–Horne–Zeilinger state of non-coexisting photons. The fundamental quantum advantage was revealed to be provided by time entanglement rather than spatial entanglement. This finding could open up a new area of research in quantum information science given the rise of conventional blockchains and the potential construction of a worldwide quantum network (Rajan & Visser, 2019).

QChain, a blockchain-based quantum-resistant decentralized PKI system, was proposed by An and Kim. They suggested a redesigned lattice-based GLP signature technique. The QChain signature is a GLP signature that has been enhanced to use Number Theoretic Transformation (NTT) (An & Kim, 2018).

Sun et al. created the Logic contract architecture, which is a permissioned blockchain (LC). To accomplish consensus on the blockchain, LC uses a signature scheme based on vote-based consensus algorithm and Quantum Key Distribution (Sun et al, 2019).

Vignesh et al. offered a quantum-built solution to handle the harnessing of security for a democratic application using Hyperledger Sawtooth. The focus of their research was on a voting protocol centered on Quantum Blockchain. In keeping with their modesty, their protocol offered a secret, proven, qualified, rational, and self-evaluating voting system (Vignesh et al, 2021).

The Quantum Blockchain was used to create a basic voting protocol by Sun et al. The most significant qualities and criteria of voting protocols that are secure include anonymity, non-reusability, verifiability, eligibility, and fairness, which their suggested protocol met. Currently, available technology could potentially be used to implement the protocol. To pursue their research, quantum blockchain can be applied in other domains such as quantum auctions and quantum lotteries (Sun et al, 2019).

Sun et al. extended the voting system based on quantum blockchain to the multi-candidate scenario. The essential idea was to limit multi-candidate voting to two-candidate voting by calculating the Condorcet winner of numerous candidates. Quantum blockchain, according to their research, can substantially ease the job of electronic voting while also providing a number of desirable security qualities. It is feasible to improve the protocol's effectiveness in terms of both security and democracy (Sun, 2019).

Zhu et al. developed a strategy for extending the usage of blockchain technology and quantum in Internet of Vehicles security (IoV). They utilized a blockchain architecture to demonstrate a semi-quantum system, as well as two lightweight applications for IoV with unconditional security (Zhu et al, 2020).

Karbasi & Shahpasand proposed a solution for ensuring the validity and genuineness of digital data that is shared such as digital certificates, common reference strings, and cryptographic keys by combining some recently developed innovations, the most notable of which are blockchain, smart contracts, and the quantum-resistant Password-based Authenticated Key Exchange protocol over rings (Karbasi & Shahpasand, 2020).

Blockchain, represented by Bitcoin and Ethereum, has been significantly developed and implemented due to the variety of application prospects, including IoT and digital currency. The computational complexity problem, on the other hand, has an impact on the security of present blockchain technology based on classical cryptography. This form of protection is seriously compromised as attackers' processing power develops, particularly with the advent of quantum computers. Wen et al proposed a quantum blockchain system with quantum secure communication centered on quantum SWAP test, quantum hash, and quantum teleportation. This system's security is unconditional and does not rely or depend on the attackers' computational power or resources (Wen et al, 2021).

Ikeda created a system that has considerable quantification advantages. To begin, currency transactions were conducted using quantum teleportation technology, which precludes the coin's owner from storing the original coin data after passing it. A massive problem arose in traditional circuits, thus a blockchain was built to solve it. In qBitcoin, there is no double-spending problem, and its security is theoretically assured thanks to quantum information theory. Because it takes time to create a block, qBitcoin's architecture uses a quantum chain rather than blocks. As a result, a transaction can be processed significantly faster than using Bitcoin. A quantum digital signature, which has qualities similar to the peer-to-peer cash system first presented in Bitcoin was utilized (Ikeda, 2018).

Because user privacy is not properly protected in current SIoT systems, which are centralized, Yi created a privacy protection solution for users to overcome these difficulties. They suggested a post-quantum ring signature as the preliminary step and then proposed a blockchain architecture based on ring signatures as the second step. Unlike standard SIoTs, the system is centered on post-quantum approaches, making it resistant to both classical and quantum computers (Yi, 2021).

The premier post-quantum investigation of the junction of blockchain law and security was conducted by Haney. His study was one of the first legal investigations of the intricate relationships between the federal reserve, congress and blockchain technology in the creation of money. As a result, the report calls into question long-held assumptions about blockchain technology's ability to decentralize economic influence. Building on scholarship from informatics, law, and economics, his work adopts an interdisciplinary approach to demonstrate that blockchain does not offer a secure means of constructing a payment system that is peer-to-peer (Haney, 2020).

Blockchain systems that are lattice-based have been proposed as being safe against quantum-era assaults in recent times. Despite their theoretical importance, due to handling capacity, many systems are unfeasible in practice. To solve the crucial concern of throughput, Li & Wu proposed a post-quantum blockchain with segregation witness, which may significantly reduce the proportion of signatures in block size. They demonstrated that the proposed post-quantum blockchain with segregation witnesses' existential unforgeability against adaptive chosen-message attacks in the random oracle based on the hardness assumption of the Short Integer Solution. (SIS) (Li & Wu, 2021).

Holcomb et al. advocated that credential-management methods proposed by Fabric and accompanying specifications be redesigned to include digital signatures that are hybrid in nature, which defend against both classical and quantum assaults with a single classical and quantum-safe signature. Their approach offers complete crypto-agility with advancement to a hybrid quantum-safe blockchain and the choice to employ current OQS signature technique for each node (Holcomb et al, 2021).

Some blockchain schemes are susceptible to quantum attacks due to the outstanding growth of quantum technology. Yuan et al. suggested an artificial intelligence-based quantum-resistant lattice-based blockchain infrastructure to overcome the critical problem of throughput. Their architecture is based on a lattice-based aggregate signature, effectively reducing the number of signatures in a block while maintaining the block size, and is shown to be secure and effective. Additionally, this discovery might support upcoming research on post-quantum blockchains. (PQB) (Yuan et al, 2021).

Banafa expatiated on the rudiments and uses of blockchain. Some things that were expatiated include peer-to-peer networks, distributed ledger, and the trust model of Blockchain technology. They also addressed Blockchain basics as well as its operations, underlying algorithms, and trust fundamentals. Proof of Work, Smart Contracts, and Proof of Stack, as well as currencies and blockchain networks comparable to Bitcoin and Ethereum, were all introduced. Blockchain technology, the Internet of Things, Artificial Intelligence, Cybersecurity, Digital Transformation, and Quantum Computing were all discussed (Banafa, 2020).

Zhang et al. advocated keeping the public keys and hash values of the blockchain signatures and their whole content on an interstellar file system. As a result, the amount of storage utilized by each transaction is considerably reduced. They designed a bitcoin trade technique to assess the effectiveness of the presented quantum-resistant blockchain system. It was established that the simulation platform was operational and available (Zhang et al, 2021).

Quantum computers, which outperform traditional computers in terms of speed and data processing capacity, are slowly making their way from a theoretical perspective to reality. The immense computing capacity of quantum computers will fundamentally alter the way that information encryption works today. (Zhang et al, 2021) After discussing two important uses of quantum information technology, the dangers of quantum supremacy for current encryption and blockchain consensus systems were explored. Meanwhile, a blockchain system incorporating quantum technology has been proposed in light of the shortcomings of the current blockchain technology as a way to avoid the threat of quantum supremacy (Zhang et al, 2019).

Abulkasim et al. devised a quantum-based blockchain-based sealed-bid auction protocol, where the transactions were stored on the blockchain which supports quantum communication and computation to improve security. The suggested protocol makes use of blockchain technologies and quantum computing to ensure that critical features and requirements are met. To demonstrate the benefits of their protocol, they presented a security analysis, evaluation, and comparison (Abulkasim et al., 2021).

Hijfte described how they could combine several technologies to create a more comprehensive solution. Of course, this is only a partial list; you could choose any combination of possible applications and achieve a better result. You should keep in mind that this is not always the case, and slapping applications together could easily lead to disaster. Their work outlined the fact that when developing a new process or application, or working with a variety of emerging technologies, there should be awareness that there is a level of risk involved (Hijfte, 2020).

Vigliotti & Jones proposed a framework to understand and implement blockchain technologies. Their work covered the various roles that blockchain technology plays in a variety of industries and explained current blockchain technologies, real-world use-cases, and their impact on businesses in non-technical terms. It also demonstrated how to devise strategies for identifying and implementing blockchain, smart contracts, and digital currency technologies in their organizations (Vigliotti & Jones, 2020).

Kearney and Perez-Delgado looked at the key cryptocurrencies in use today, such as ZCash, Bitcoin, Ethereum, and Litecoin to see how vulnerable they are to quantum attacks. They concluded with a comparison of the researched cryptocurrencies and the blockchain technology that underpin them, as well as their levels of vulnerability to quantum attacks (Bard et al, 2021).

Chen suggested a technique in which each signal node in a targeted system negotiates a quantum key with all its nearby nodes, determines the XOR results of any two quantum keys from all of these quantum keys and then embodies these XOR results into a transaction. A server contained all current transactions into a block that might be used to provide real-time quantum key services (Chen, 2020).

Quantum blockchain techniques that are motivated by quantum computing techniques were investigated and suggested for design by Krishnaswamy. Using non-deterministic self-executing processing, the breakdown of quantum state variables is investigated. Multiple nodes on the network interact together via a communication network to form a quantum blockchain network. Numerous networking use-cases are investigated, such as choosing the best access node for a specific user or determining which user has network access at any particular moment (Krishnaswamy, 2020).

MAIN FOCUS OF THE CHAPTER

Method

This chapter's goal was to locate, evaluate, and review contemporary quantum blockchain literature, as well as their approaches and weaknesses. A thorough search for content that met the inclusion requirements from 2017 to 2021 was conducted in five databases, including Science Direct, Google Scholar, Springer, ACM Digital Library, and IEEE Xplore, in November 2021. The terms "Blockchain" and "Quantum blockchain" were among those used. With the help of the Boolean operators "AND," "OR," and "NOT," the keywords were combined to produce a high-quality search strategy. Peer-reviewed journals and papers were taken into consideration. After lengthy discussion among the authors, the inclusion and exclusion criteria were developed based on the objective of the study. Reading through the records' titles, abstracts, and keywords to locate those that met the criteria for the preliminary selection. Using the reference list of the accepted literature, further pertinent articles were discovered. Using the Preferred Reporting Items for Systematic Reviews and Meta-Analysis flow diagram, the article selection and screening were reported.

Inclusion and Exclusion Criteria

For the paper to be considered for the review, it must be about a quantum blockchain or related to a quantum blockchain. Literature written in languages other than English, as well as any work that did not fall under the aforementioned purview, was not included.

Data Collection and Organization

Author discussions and unbiased, in-depth reviews of the literature served as the foundation for the data collecting and category creation. The following categories were developed solely for evaluation, analysis, and assessment of the study:

Category of Blockchain: The categories were according to the criteria; *access restrictions*, *type*, and *application*.

For the access restrictions, the sub-categories include *permissionless* and *permissioned*.

For the type, the sub-categories include *public*, *private* or *managed*, *consortium* and *hybrid*.

For the application, the sub-categories include *supply chain*, *accounting*, *tokenization*, *identity management*, *trade finance* and *others*.

Electronic Database: *Science Direct*, *Google Scholar*, *Springer*, *ACM Digital Library*, and *IEEE Xplo*re are the electronic databases or sources utilized.
Year of Publication: This category details the article's publication year (s).

The categorizations above do not take into account the literature on future directions.

Literature Evaluation and Analysis

The carefully picked papers were analyzed, studied, and scored based on the aforementioned categories. Each of the categories was analyzed to gauge the effectiveness of the quantum blockchain (category of blockchain - access restrictions, type and application, electronic database, and year of publication). The numerical statistics of the attributes of the categories were computed using the sum of counts for each type of attribute. The total number of articles given in the study was less than the number of counts for these categories since some articles were used in the "future directions and unanswered questions" section.

SOLUTIONS AND RECOMMENDATIONS

Results

After searching through several online databases, a total of 117 records were discovered after adhering to the inclusion and exclusion criteria in the reading of titles, abstracts, and keywords. After skimming the objective, method, and conclusion sections in the second evaluation of these publications, 47 of them did not satisfy the predetermined inclusion criteria were eliminated. 70 articles were read in their full and appraised after duplicates were removed. Following full-text reading, as depicted in Figure 2 below, a total of 53 publications were included in the study and analysis (mainly based on a survey of quantum blockchain). Figures 3 and 4 depict the topic of great interest known as "quantum blockchain."

Evaluation and Analysis

The publications were evaluated and analyzed as mentioned above, and the key findings are reported below.

Figure 2. Systematic review process flowchart

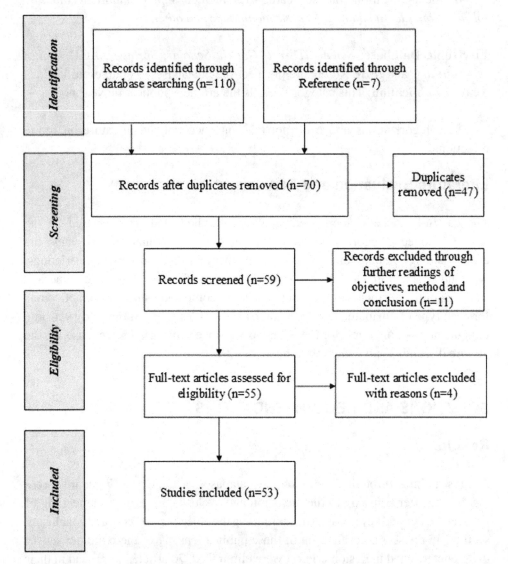

Articles in the Study

Fifty three (53) articles were taken into consideration when displaying the articles and their associated categorizations below.

Analysis of the year of publications: Table 1 and Figure 3

Table 1. Yearly distribution of articles

Year of publication	Frequency
2021	18
2020	16
2019	10
2018	7
2017	2

Figure 3. Yearly distribution of articles

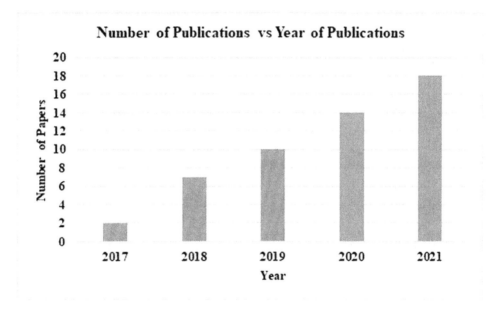

Analysis of the Data Sources: Table 2 and Figure 4

Table 2. Literature sources of articles

Data source	No. of articles
Science Direct	9
Google Scholar	9
Springer	19
ACM Digital Library	3
IEEE Xplore	13

Figure 4. Literature sources of articles

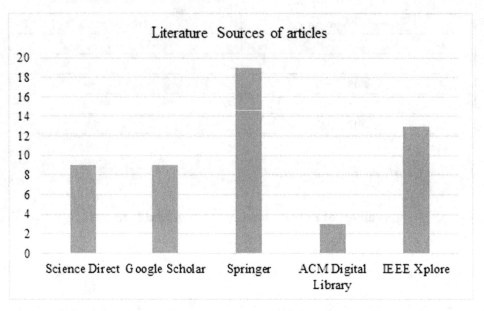

Analysis of Blockchain Access Restrictions: Table 3 and Figure 5

Table 3. Blockchain access restrictions

Blockchain Access Restrictions	No. of articles
Permissionless	24
Permissioned	29

Analysis of Blockchain Type: Table 4 and Figure 6

Table 4. Blockchain type

Blockchain Type	No. of articles
Public	23
Private (or Managed)	15
Consortium	7
Hybrid	7

Figure 5. Blockchain access restrictions

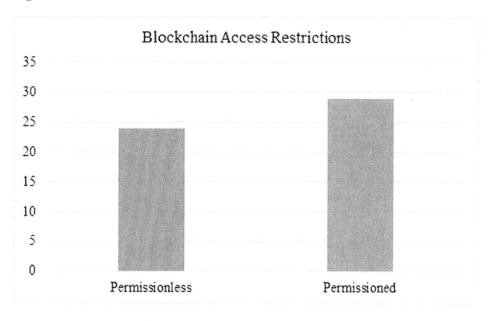

Figure 6. Blockchain type

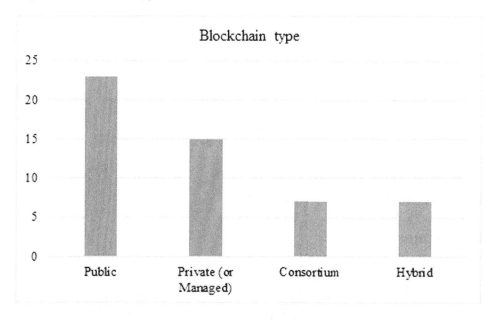

Analysis of Blockchain Application: Table 5 and Figure 7

Table 5. Blockchain application

Blockchain Application	No. of articles
Supply chain	6
Accounting	2
Tokenization	4
Identity Management	20
Trade and Finance	17
Others	4

Figure 7. Blockchain application

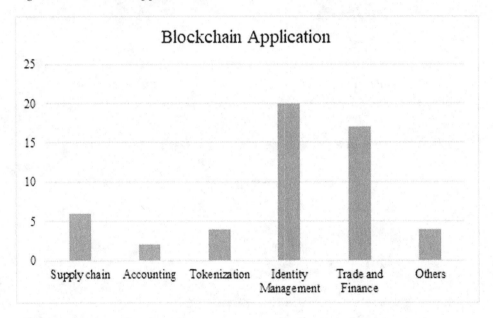

FUTURE RESEARCH DIRECTIONS

Healthcare

Towards the future direction of quantum blockchain and blockchain in general, investigators should concentrate on examining the following research areas; improvement of blockchain's interoperability with existing infrastructures, promotion of blockchain adoption, and addressing blockchain storage locations (Durneva et al, 2020). Accountable and secure distribution of medical records using blockchain based on smart cards is another future direction of blockchain technology that is very pivotal to the health sector as this will ensure a great deal of privacy and security (Lal & Marijan, 2020; Durneva et al, 2020).

Robotics

Swarm robotics requires an amalgamation of AI, blockchain, and blockchain for the Internet of Robotics Things (IoRT), as this helps to incorporate robotics into IoT scenarios (Strobel et al, 2020; Aditya et al, 2021).

Big Data

Adaptive blockchain architecture, cloud-based big data, and software-defined networking-based big data are all examples of the future of classical and quantum blockchain in big data. The application of blockchain in these areas will help to ensure security, privacy, scalability, transparency, and trust (Deepa et al, 2021).

Supply Chain

In the future, the construction supply chain may see the formation of soft cooperatives amongst businesses of various sizes executing their transactions on blockchain to provide project solutions, products, components, services, or to procure construction projects. Other areas of supply chain research for blockchain include tracing asset information whilst maintaining a record of ownership for each asset throughout its lifecycle, business models, procurement, smart contracts, data protection for managing data, and real-time tracking of materials and services (Tezel et al, 2020).

Internet of Things

Because IoT devices lack sufficient storage capacity to store a whole copy of the blockchain, it is necessary to integrate resource-controlled IoT devices with blockchain. This integration procedure is a potential future area for study that could help to advance blockchain and IoT research and development (Latif et al, 2021). In addition to networking and computing constraints, IoT devices struggle with a lack of authorisation and authentication, restricted compatibility, and other issues. Blockchains have the versatility to integrate with IoT devices since they can be used to store both structured and unstructured data over a network (Latif et al, 2021). The extension of blockchain to the IoT edge could be another future study direction. Blockchain's high performance and networking overhead prevent it from being used on resource-constrained IoT devices. Lightweight clients can be used with IoT gateways to push transactions into the blockchain network in order to solve this problem (Latif et al, 2021). Other potential prospects include IoT blockchain-based applications, IoT blockchain-based security, IoT data quality using blockchain, IoT blockchain data governance, IoT blockchain-based trust management, IoT blockchain-based automation, and IoT blockchain identity and identification management (Lunesu et al, 2021).

Cryptocurrency

The inability of cryptocurrencies to scale, the 1MB cap on bitcoin block sizes, and the 10 minute increase in block sizes are all problems. Due to its 7 transaction limit per second, Bitcoin is not appropriate for high-frequency trading. As a result, the larger the block, the more storage space is required, resulting in slower network diffusion. As a result, decentralization in the blockchain is required (Kaur et al, 2020). This is a fascinating subject for future research since understanding the origins of these coins and how they are reflected in their long-term performance of value is crucial for teaching and educating businesses about various ideas (Klarin. 2020).

Digital Processes, Payments, and Systems

Blockchain has the potential to provide significant added value by enabling the implementation of legally sound digital processes and systems, making it an excellent research topic. It has the potential to greatly benefit IoT's inherently dispersed and decentralized nature. Additionally, all building blocks that come with blockchain integration, such as smart contracts for automation and cryptocurrencies for service payments, may be added to the IoT Infrastructure (Lunesu et al, 2021).

Trust Management in Cloud Computing

Future directions in cloud computing when it comes to trust management include; trust framework, evaluation, delivery and authorization, robustness, and trust-aided decision (Li et al, 2021).

Tokenization

Ring Confidential Transactions (Durneva et al., 2020), which hide the payment amounts but can still be verified for accuracy by all blockchain participants, were proposed by Monero. Pedersen commitments and cryptographic range proofs, which stop the creation of new tokens without authorization, are used to make this possible. The ability to make transactions private and verifiable comes at the expense of storage space because the representation of a transaction now involves many cryptographic elements, such as signatures and proofs, that must be recorded on the ledger. Soon, the Monero community plans to replace one of the verbose facets in transactions, range proofs, with bulletproofs (Bünz et al, 2018; Kolb et al, 2020).

Vehicular Networks

Future directions for research into using blockchain in 5G vehicular networks are critical, however, some concerns and challenges must be addressed before integration and deployment can take place. These difficulties can be used as research topics (Bendechache et al, 2020).

Banking and Financial Markets

Future blockchain directions could include pragmatic governance frameworks and central bank growth into retail and wholesale Central Bank Digital Currencies (Schlapkohl, 2020). Furthermore, financial institutions are investigating blockchain applications for security trading (Makridakis et al, 2018).

Value Chain Management

Due to the fact that the current agri-food industry ecosystem is moving away from centralized systems and toward shared and distributed systems, research or future direction on the use of blockchain to achieve greater manufacturer cooperation in information and service sharing (Zhao et al, 2019).

Quantum Dimensions

Currently, quantum blockchain is relatively young with a lot of research ongoing in quantum computing and its applicability in diverse areas or sectors. The emergence of quantum computers and their related components will eventually lead to the development of quantum equivalents of classical methods, techniques, approaches, and the applicability of blockchain technology. This could offer potential speedups, security, and privacy compared to classical ones, hence could spur further research and developments.

Method and Shortfall of Some of the Quantum Blockchain Literature

The method and shortfall of some quantum blockchain literature are shown in Table 6 below.

Table 6. Method and shortfall of quantum blockchain literature

S/n	Citation	Method	Shortfall
1	(Fernandez-Carames & Fraga-Lamas, 2020)	Application of post-quantum cryptosystems to mitigate such attacks and impacts.	Future quantum algorithms will almost certainly leave the theoretical domain to play a larger role in real-world applications.
2	(Karbasi & Shahpasand, 2020)	IPFS and Ethereum smart contracts are being used to generate secure end-to-end encryption in messaging DApps in order to reduce the risk of MITM/interception attacks.	The DApps were not created on the Ethereum mainnet, and neither were the PAKE protocols and smart contracts put on the real IPFS.
3	(Xie et al, 2021)	A lattice signature scheme was suggested to fend off quantum computing, including a cuckoo filter to lessen the computational burden of the user verification stage.	Tighter coupling of blockchain and integrity verification scheme should be examined in future work, and the scheme's more complete characteristics should be met.
4	(Choi et al, 2020)	A private blockchain was created as part of the NPP ecosystem.	Did not conduct their research using a real power plant system, which is necessary to determine whether it has an effect on the performance of the safety system.
5	(Gao et al, 2018)	Proposed a PQB-based safe cryptocurrency mechanism that can withstand quantum computing attacks.	Even though their work will aid in the protection of blockchain security, it is not more realistic under the current technical conditions.
6	(Iovane, 2021)	Proposed a new data transmission protocol based on the BB84 protocol's quantum encryption potential as well as the possibilities given by distributed ledgers and blockchain.	Taking into account the complete decentralization of critical manufacturing, communication lines may theoretically be unsecured as well.
7	(Nieto-Chaupis, 2019)	A formalism that was presented allowed for simulation of blockchain dynamics for an e-commerce transaction and was solely based on quantum mechanics mathematics.	They were unable to fully utilize the properties of Quantum Mechanics in order to represent the complete dynamics of bitcoin movement in vast economies.
8	(Dolev & Wang, 2020)	A formalism that was presented allowed for the simulation of blockchain dynamics for an e-commerce transaction and was solely based on quantum mechanics mathematics.	Further research into the effects of the examined problems on blockchain in the SodsBC could be conducted.
9	(Sun et al, 2020)	A quantum blockchain system for lotteries and an auction protocol.	There hasn't been any formal tool development for the quantum blockchain's smart contract verification and definition.
10	(Iovane, 2021)	In a blockchain architecture, the validity and the assignment of a new block are fixed by an inventive negotiating process.	Despite their best efforts, they were unable to create a detailed study that would analyze how key generations affected a significant number of requests and users.

continues on following page

Table 6. Continued

S/n	Citation	Method	Shortfall
11	(Banerjee et al., 2020)	A technique that makes use of multiparty quantum weighted hypergraph entanglement.	The findings given here can be used to create brand-new entanglement quantum protocols as well as to improve already-existing ones.
12	(Rajan & Visser, 2019)	Encoding the blockchain into a temporary Greenberger, Horne, and Zeilinger (GHZ) state of non-coexisting photons.	Per the development of traditional blockchains and the viability of creating a global quantum network, their study could not be utilized to establish a novel research avenue in quantum information science.
13	(An & Kim, 2018)	QChain – a quantum-resistant decentralized PKI system using blockchain.	No implementation of QChain using C– language as an open-source project.
14	(Vignesh et al., 2021)	Using Hyperledger Sawtooth a quantum-built approach to handle and harness security for a democratic application was proposed	The study didn't address how quantum blockchain could make many applications simpler and more secure from machines that launch quantum theory-based attacks.
15	(Sun et al., 2019)	Added the multi-candidate situation to the straightforward voting system based on quantum blockchain.	Their work failed to improve the protocol such that it could have various advantages in both security and democracy.
16	(Sun, 2019)	The adoption of a vote-based consensus algorithm and a quantum key distribution (QKD)-based digital signature method.	Their efforts did not result in a methodical construction of the logic-based programming language for smart contracts on LC.
17	(Zhu et al., 2020)	Using blockchain as an IoV network, two brand-new, lightweight quantum-reflection protocols were suggested.	They failed in their attempts to design N-party semi-quantum-reflection methods for IoV key agreement and distribution.
18	(Chen, 2020)	Quantum relay blockchain, which realized the security separation between QKS and QKD network	A new scheme, quantum relay blockchain still needs to be modified to satisfy different business networks
19	(Krishnaswamy, 2020)	Extending Grover's algorithm-based techniques for amplitude magnification and modification, such as Oracle and Reflection Transforms	The main impediment to achieving a speedup is that the quadratic speedup achieved is insufficient to offset the substantial overhead of near-term quantum computers.
20	(Aditya et al., 2021)	Grover's and Shor's quantum algorithms	Their work did not provide post-quantum cryptography that can persist in the race against quantum algorithms, and whether quantum cryptography can be applied on a global scale and made more accessible to the masses remain

CONCLUSION

Discussion

According to Quarmby, JPMorgan Chase has published research on a quantum key distribution (QKD) blockchain network that is immune to quantum computing attacks. QKD is the only solution that has been mathematically demonstrated to be able to ward off a future quantum computing-based attack (Quarmby, 2022). Using post-quantum keys, Allende López et al. introduced a second signature in transactions, examined quantum-resistance principles in respect to blockchain networks, and developed a system to secure information transmission between blockchain nodes over the internet (Allende López, 2021).

The Quantum Resistant Ledger (QRL), a brand-new blockchain system that is post-quantum secure and employs post-quantum computing technologies in its design for absolute security, as audited by red4sec and x41 D-sec, presents important information about the future of post-quantum resistant blockchains (QRL, 2022). Zhang et al. presented a blockchain system based on a quantum-resistant digital signature (Zhang et al, 2021). Quantum resistance is the next blockchain frontier, with a system called QANplatform widely regarded as the first truly quantum-resistant blockchain.

Decentralized programs (DApps) are permitted on QAN, unlike some other purportedly quantum-resistant blockchains, and developers can quickly build quantum-resistant DApps utilizing the platform's free developer tools. As an alternative to QAN, the creators of many well-known blockchains are already thinking about implementing their own quantum-resistance techniques, such as the recently created commit-delay-reveal scheme, which may be used to convert Bitcoin to a quantum-resistant state. However, none of the top ten blockchains in terms of user numbers has yet to commit to a quantum-resistant signature technique, leaving the future of post-quantum encryption in limbo (Thompson, 2021).

With a quantum-resistant platform, the scalability and bandwidth issues with the blockchain are resolved. Blockchains must be protected against this unavoidable reality by using cryptographic keys that can withstand attacks from the most powerful computers on the planet. As a result, third-generation blockchain solutions are already being developed by platforms like Cellframe that have publicly shared their work. The Cellframe solution starts with quantum-resistant signatures, some of which are already integrated into the Cellframe architecture and some of which are finalist signatures from the NIST PQC contest, with many more integrations planned in line with the team's mission to build a secure and decentralized environment to maintain the freedom of the internet. The study of quantum-resistant blockchain techniques or schemes, as well as their standardization and implementation, may provide a path for future research (Jansen, 2021).

From Table 1 and Figure 3, most of the quantum blockchain literature reviewed in this paper was in 2021 followed by 2020, 2019, 2018, and 2017 respectively. This seems to indicate a trend of increasing research and interest in the area of quantum blockchain starting from 2017 to 2021. From Table 2 and Figure 4, Nineteen (19) articles were gotten from Springer, Thirteen (13) from IEEE Xplore, Nine (9) from ScienceDirect, Nine (9) from Google Scholar, and Three (3) from ACM Digital Library. This indicates that most of the quantum blockchain literature used in the analysis was from the Springer data source. From Table 3 and Figure 5, out of the Fifty Three (53) quantum blockchain literature used in the numerical analysis and graphical representations, Twenty Four (24) of the literature highlighted permissionless quantum blockchain and Twenty Nine (29) talked about permissioned quantum blockchain. From Table 4 and Figure 6, Twenty Three (23) of the articles talked about public quantum blockchains, Fifteen (15) on private (or managed) quantum blockchains, Seven (7) on consortium quantum blockchains, and Seven (7) on hybrid quantum blockchains. From Table 5 and Figure 7, Six (6) of the articles were related to supply chain, Two (2) on accounting, Four (4) on tokenization, Twenty (20) on identity management, Seventeen (17) on Trade and Finance, and Four (4) on others. To further have an insight on the differences between classical and quantum blockchains, a comparative analysis is shown in Table 6 below.

Comparison of Classical Blockchain and Quantum Blockchain

The comparison of classical blockchain and quantum blockchain is shown in Table 7 below.

Future work will be to develop and implement a low-level framework of the blockchain for land management and administration to make the whole process of land identification, verification, and acquisition transparent for the parties involved, in this case, the landowners and those purchasing the lands. This will resolve a major problem in Ghana and Africa. A quantum dimension of this blockchain for land management and administration will be looked at and explored even as quantum computing continues to be of great interest amongst researchers.

ACKNOWLEDGMENT

Special thanks go to all individuals who contributed towards the paper write up. No specific grant was given to this research by any funding organization in the public, private, or nonprofit sectors.

Table 7. Comparison of classical blockchain and quantum blockchain

	Classical Blockchain	Quantum Blockchain
1	Decentralized, distributed, public digital ledger comprising records	Encrypted, distributed, and decentralized database based on quantum mechanics (Chuntang et al, 2019)
2	Because asymmetric cryptography is used, quantum assaults present a threat to the sustainability of blockchain technology.	The viability of blockchain technology is not expected to be threatened because of the use of quantum-safe, quantum-resistant, and quantum cryptography (Kearney & Perez-Delgado, 2021)
3	It is operational and in use predominantly as the backbone of cryptocurrencies and crypto-wallets.	Although no quantum blockchain is currently functioning, some researchers are investigating the technology's possibilities (Orchid, 2021).
4	No blockchain functions like a time machine, hence the security of cryptocurrencies for decades cannot be guaranteed despite it being safe.	Victoria University researchers presented an idea, which would use blockchain that functions as a time machine to guarantee cryptocurrency futures for decades (Rajan, D., & Visser, M, 2019)
5	Many cryptocurrencies, such as Solana, Cardano, XRP, Bitcoin, Litecoin, Tether, BNB, USD Coin, Terra, Polkadot, Dogecoin, Ethereum, Avalanche, Polygon, and others, are already operational and use consensus algorithms.	The "quantum coin," a new sort of cryptocurrency, was created. Proposal to combine quantum entanglement and Distributed Proof-of-Stake (DPoS) to develop a new type of consensus mechanism that is faster and more efficient than current blockchain consensus methods (Orchid, 2021).
6	Improves trust in a network of actors, enables novel methods of arranging economic activity, and reduces the costs and time of intermediaries (Weking, 2020)	Quantum blockchain serves as a Quantum-aid to Classical Blockchain by offering Unprecedented Growth in Computing(Dey et al, 2021).
7	Classical blockchain technology is revolutionizing fintech and is creating a whole new digital sector of finance by preventing fraud, eliminating middlemen from transactions, and democratizing financial management (Kefford, 2021)	Quantum blockchain technology is an added advantage to Blockchain scalability. Supercharged data analysis, increased calculation speed, decreased false-positives in the detection of fraud, and effective Monte-Carlo simulation are four examples of fintech applications where an invasion can be used to provide a computing edge (Dey et al, 2021).
8	The majority of the major classical blockchains' signature systems are susceptible to quantum assaults (Bard et al, 2021).	There are no known attacks for quantum blockchains as the field is relatively young and more research is being conducted.
9	Blockchain systems are particularly sensitive to quantum assaults because the protected asset (the ledger) is inextricably linked to the encryption technologies utilized (Bard et al, 2021).	Due to the time machine element of the blockchain proposed by the researchers at Victoria University, financial transactions and cryptocurrencies might be safe for decades all things being equal.
10	A blockchain's cryptographic protocols are simple since they use conventional cryptography.	It is much more challenging to replace "post-quantum" cryptographic protocols used in blockchains than it is to replace more traditional cryptographic functions (Bard et al, 2021)

REFERENCES

Ablayev, F. M., Bulychkov, D. A., Sapaev, D. A., Vasiliev, A. V., & Ziatdinov, M. T. (2018). Quantum-Assisted Blockchain. *Lobachevskii Journal of Mathematics*, *39*(7), 957–960. doi:10.1134/S1995080218070028

Abulkasim, Mashatan, & Ghose. (2021). *Quantum-based privacy-preserving sealed-bid auction on the blockchain*. . doi:10.1016/j.ijleo.2021.167039

Aditya, U. S. P. S., Singh, R., Singh, P. K., & Kalla, A. (2021). A Survey on Blockchain in Robotics: Issues, Opportunities, Challenges, and Future Directions. *Journal of Network and Computer Applications, 196*. doi:10.1016/j.jnca.2021.103245

Allende Lopez, M., Lopez Leon, D., Ceron, S., Leal Batista, A., Pareja, A., Da Silva, M., Pardo, A., Jones, D., Worrall, D., Merriman, B., Gilmore, J., Kitchener, N., Venegas-Andraca, S.E. (2021). *Quantum-Resistance in Blockchain Networks.* doi:10.18235/0003313

An, H., & Kim, K. (2018). QChain: Quantum-resistant and Decentralized PKI using Blockchain. *2018 Symposium on Cryptography and Information Security.*

Azhar, M. T., Khan, M. B., & Khan, A. U. R. (2019). Blockchain based secure crypto-currency system with quantum key distribution protocol. *8th International Conference on Information and Communication Technologies, ICICT 2019*, 31–35. 10.1109/ICICT47744.2019.9001979

Banafa, A. (2020). *12 Quantum Computing and Blockchain: Facts and Myths. In Blockchain Technology and Applications*. River Publishers.

Banerjee, S., Mukherjee, A., & Panigrahi, P. K. (2020). Quantum blockchain using weighted hypergraph states. *Physical Review Research*, *2*(1), 1–7. doi:10.1103/PhysRevResearch.2.013322

BardD. A.KearneyJ. J.Perez-DelgadoC. A. (2021). Quantum Advantage on Proof of Work. doi:10.2139/ssrn.3979439

Bendechache, M., Saber, T., Muntean, G.-M., & Tal, I. (2021). *Application of blockchain technology to 5G-enabled vehicular networks: survey and future directions.* In *18th International Symposium on High Performance Mobile Computing & Wireless Networks for HPC (MCWN 2020)*, Barcelona, Spain.

Bennet, A. J., & Daryanoosh, S. (2019). Energy-Efficient Mining on a Quantum-Enabled Blockchain Using Light. *Ledger*, *4*. Advance online publication. doi:10.5195/ledger.2019.143

Bünz, B., Bootle, J., Boneh, D., Poelstra, A., Wuille, P., & Maxwell, G. 2018. Bulletproofs: Short proofs for confidential transactions and more. In *Proceedings of the IEEE Symposium on Security and Privacy (SP'18)*. IEEE. 10.1109/SP.2018.00020

Chen, H. (2020). Quantum relay blockchain and its applications in key service. *ACM International Conference Proceeding Series*, 95–99. 10.1145/3377644.3377657

Choi, M. K., Yeun, C. Y., & Seong, P. H. (2020). A Novel Monitoring System for the Data Integrity of Reactor Protection System Using Blockchain Technology. *IEEE Access: Practical Innovations, Open Solutions*, 8, 118732–118740. doi:10.1109/ACCESS.2020.3005134

Deepa, Pham, Nguyen, Bhattacharya, Prabadevi, Gadekallu, Maddikunta, Fang, & Pathirana. (2021). *A Survey on Blockchain for Big Data: Approaches, Opportunities, and Future Directions*. https://arxiv.org/pdf/2009.00858.pdf

Dolev, S., & Wang, Z. (2020). SodsBC: Stream of Distributed Secrets for Quantum-safe Blockchain. *Proceedings - 2020 IEEE International Conference on Blockchain, Blockchain 2020*, 247–256. 10.1109/Blockchain50366.2020.00038

Durneva, P., Cousins, K., & Chen, M. (2020). The Current State of Research, Challenges, and Future Research Directions of Blockchain Technology in Patient Care: Systematic Review. *Journal of Medical Internet Research*, 22(7), e18619. doi:10.2196/18619 PMID:32706668

Esgin, M. F., Zhao, R. K., Steinfeld, R., Liu, J. K., & Liu, D. (2019). Matrict: Efficient, scalable and post-quantum blockchain confidential transactions protocol. *Proceedings of the ACM Conference on Computer and Communications Security*, 567–584. 10.1145/3319535.3354200

Fernandez-Carames, T. M., & Fraga-Lamas, P. (2020). Towards Post-Quantum Blockchain: A Review on Blockchain Cryptography Resistant to Quantum Computing Attacks. *IEEE Access: Practical Innovations, Open Solutions*, 8, 21091–21116. doi:10.1109/ACCESS.2020.2968985

Gao, S., Zheng, D., Guo, R., Jing, C., & Hu, C. (2019). An anti-quantum e-voting protocol in blockchain with audit function. *IEEE Access: Practical Innovations, Open Solutions*, 7, 115304–115316. doi:10.1109/ACCESS.2019.2935895

Gao, Y. L., Chen, X. B., Chen, Y. L., Sun, Y., Niu, X. X., & Yang, Y. X. (2018). A Secure Cryptocurrency Scheme Based on Post-Quantum Blockchain. *IEEE Access,* 6(2), 27205–27213. doi:10.1109/ACCESS.2018.2827203

Gao, Y. L., Chen, X. B., Xu, G., Yuan, K. G., Liu, W., & Yang, Y. X. (2020). A novel quantum blockchain scheme base on quantum entanglement and DPoS. *Quantum Information Processing*, 19(12), 420. Advance online publication. doi:10.100711128-020-02915-y

Gregory, M. (2015). *Confidential Transactions*. Retrieved from: https://people.xiph. org/ greg/confidential_ values.txt

Haney Seamus Brain. (2020). *Blockchain: Post-quantum security & legal economics*. Author.

Holcomb, A., Pereira, G., Das, B., & Mosca, M. (2021). PQFabric: A Permissioned Blockchain Secure from Both Classical and Quantum Attacks. *2021 IEEE International Conference on Blockchain and Cryptocurrency (ICBC)*, 1-9. 10.1109/ICBC51069.2021.9461070

Ikeda, K. (2018). qBitcoin: A Peer-to-Peer Quantum Cash System. *Intelligent Computing*, 763–771. . doi:10.1007/978-3-030-01174-1_58

Iovane, G. (2021a). Computational quantum key distribution (CQKD) on decentralized ledger and blockchain. *Journal of Discrete Mathematical Sciences and Cryptography*, *24*(4), 1021–1042. doi:10.1080/09720529.2020.1820691

Iovane, G. (2021b). MuReQua Chain: Multiscale Relativistic Quantum Blockchain. *IEEE Access: Practical Innovations, Open Solutions*, *9*, 39827–39838. doi:10.1109/ACCESS.2021.3064297

Jansen, S. (2021). *Quantum-resistant platform solves scalability and bandwidth bottlenecks present on the blockchain*. https://cointelegraph.com/news/quantum-resistant-platform-solves-scalability-and-bandwidth-bottlenecks-present-on-the-blockchain

Jun, Z., Yong, Y., Xiao, W., & Fei-Yue, W. (2019). Quantum blockchain: can blockchain integrated with quantum information technology resist quantum supremacy? *Chinese Journal of Intelligent Science and Technology*, *1*(4), 409–414.

Karbasi, A. H., & Shahpasand, S. (2020). A post-quantum end-to-end encryption over smart contract-based blockchain for defeating man-in-the-middle and interception attacks. *Peer-to-Peer Networking and Applications*, *13*(5), 1423–1441. doi:10.100712083-020-00901-w

Kaur, A., Nayyar, A., & Singh, P. (2020). BlockChain. *Cryptocurrencies and Blockchain Technology Applications*, 25–42. doi:10.1002/9781119621201.ch2

Kefford, M. (2021). *4 Ways Blockchain Is Revolutionizing FinTech*. https://www.businessbecause.com/news/insights/7534/blockchain-fintech?sponsored

Khalid, Z. M., & Askar, S. (2021). Resistant Blockchain Cryptography to Quantum Computing Attacks. *International Journal of Science and Business*, *5*(3), 116–125. doi:10.5281/zenodo.4497732

Kiktenko, E. O., Pozhar, N. O., Anufriev, M. N., Trushechkin, A. S., Yunusov, R. R., Kurochkin, Y. V., Lvovsky, A. I., & Fedorov, A. K. (2018a). Quantum-secured blockchain. *Quantum Science and Technology*, *3*(3), 1–6. doi:10.1088/2058-9565/aabc6b

Kiktenko, E. O., Pozhar, N. O., Anufriev, M. N., Trushechkin, A. S., Yunusov, R. R., Kurochkin, Y. V., Lvovsky, A. I., & Fedorov, A. K. (2018b). Quantum-secured blockchain. *Quantum Science and Technology*, *3*(3), 035004. doi:10.1088/2058-9565/aabc6b

Klarin, A. (2020). The decade-long cryptocurrencies and the blockchain rollercoaster: Mapping the intellectual structure and charting future directions. *Research in International Business and Finance*, *51*, 101067. doi:10.1016/j.ribaf.2019.101067

Kolb, J., AbdelBaky, M., Katz, R. H., & Culler, D. E. (2020). Core Concepts, Challenges, and Future Directions in Blockchain. *ACM Computing Surveys*, *53*(1), 1–39. doi:10.1145/3366370

Krishnaswamy, D. (2020). Quantum blockchain networks. *Proceedings of the International Symposium on Mobile Ad Hoc Networking and Computing (MobiHoc)*, *2*, 327–332. 10.1145/3397166.3412802

Küfner, P., Nestmann, U., Rickmann, C., Küfner, P., Nestmann, U., Rickmann, C., & Verification, F. (2017). Formal Verification of Distributed Algorithms. *7th International Conference on Theoretical Computer Science (TCS)*, 209–224.

Lal, C., & Marijan, D. (2020). *Blockchain for Healthcare: Opportunities, Challenges, and Future Directions*. Simula Research Laboratory. https://www.simula.no/publications/blockchain-healthcare-opportunities-challenges-and-future-directions

Latif, S., Idrees, Z., Huma, Z., & Ahmad, J. (2021). Blockchain technology for the industrial Internet of Things: A comprehensive survey on security challenges, architectures, applications, and future research directions. *Transactions on Emerging Telecommunications Technologies*, *32*(11). Advance online publication. doi:10.1002/ett.4337

Li, B., & Wu, F. (2021). Post Quantum Blockchain with Segregation Witness. *2021 IEEE 6th International Conference on Computer and Communication Systems (ICCCS)*, 522-527. 10.1109/ICCCS52626.2021.9449309

Li, C., Tian, Y., Chen, X., & Li, J. (2021). An efficient anti-quantum lattice-based blind signature for blockchain-enabled systems. *Information Sciences*, *546*, 253–264. doi:10.1016/j.ins.2020.08.032

Li, C. Y., Chen, X. B., Chen, Y. L., Hou, Y. Y., & Li, J. (2019). A New Lattice-Based Signature Scheme in Post-Quantum Blockchain Network. *IEEE Access: Practical Innovations, Open Solutions, 7*, 2026–2033. doi:10.1109/ACCESS.2018.2886554

Li, W., Wu, J., Cao, J., Chen, N., Zhang, Q., & Buyya, R. (2021). Blockchain-based trust management in cloud computing systems: A taxonomy, review and future directions. *Journal of Cloud Computing, 10*(1), 35. Advance online publication. doi:10.118613677-021-00247-5

Lunesu, M. I., Tonelli, R., & Ioini, N. E. (2022). *Blockchain solutions for IoT.* https://www.frontiersin.org/research-topics/25758/blockchain-solutions-for-iot#overview

Makridakis, S., Polemitis, A., Giaglis, G., & Louca, S. (2018). *Blockchain: The Next Breakthrough in the Rapid Progress of AI.* Artificial Intelligence - Emerging Trends and Applications. doi:10.5772/intechopen.75668

Mesnager, S., Sınak, A., & Yayla, O. (2020). Threshold-based post-quantum secure verifiable multi-secret sharing for distributed storage blockchain. *Mathematics, 8*(12), 1–15. doi:10.3390/math8122218

Nieto-Chaupis, H. (2019). Description of Processes of Blockchain and Cryptocurrency with Quantum Mechanics Theory. *IEEE CHILEAN Conference on Electrical, Electronics Engineering, Information and Communication Technologies, CHILECON 2019, 7*, 31–34. 10.1109/CHILECON47746.2019.8988006

Noether, S., Mackenzie, A., & Research Lab, T. M. (2016). Ring Confidential Transactions. *Ledger, 1*, 1–18. doi:10.5195/ledger.2016.34

QRL. (2022). *Quantum Resistant Ledger. The Future of Post-Quantum Resistant Blockchain.* https://www.theqrl.org/the-future-of-post-quantum-resistant-blockchains/

Quarmby, B. (2022). *JPMorgan unveils research on quantum resistant blockchain network.* https://cointelegraph.com/news/jpmorgan-unveils-research-on-quantum-resistant-blockchain-network

Rajan, D., & Visser, M. (2019). Quantum blockchain using entanglement in time. *Quantum Reports, 1*(1), 1–9. doi:10.3390/quantum1010002

SchlapkohlK. (2020). The future of blockchain. https://www.ibm.com/blogs/blockchain/2020/04/the-future-of-blockchain/

Sharma, P., Bhatia, V., & Prakash, S. (2021). Securing Optical Networks using Quantum-secured Blockchain: An Overview. *IEEE Journal of Quantum Electronics*, 1–7. https://arxiv.org/abs/2105.10663

Sun, X., Kulicki, P., & Sopek, M. (2020). Lottery and auction on quantum blockchain. *Entropy (Basel, Switzerland), 22*(12), 1–9. doi:10.3390/e22121377 PMID:33279922

Sun, X., Sopek, M., Wang, Q., & Kulicki, P. (2019). Towards quantum-secured permissioned blockchain: Signature, consensus, and logic. *Entropy (Basel, Switzerland), 21*(9), 1–15. doi:10.3390/e21090887

Sun, X., Wang, Q., Kulicki, P., & Sopek, M. (2019). A Simple Voting Protocol on Quantum Blockchain. *International Journal of Theoretical Physics, 58*(1), 275–281. doi:10.100710773-018-3929-6

Sun, X., Wang, Q., Kulicki, P., & Zhao, X. (2018). Quantum-enhanced Logic-based Blockchain I: Quantum Honest-success Byzantine Agreement and Qulogicoin. https://arxiv.org/abs/1805.06768

Tezel, A., Papadonikolaki, E., Yitmen, I., & Hilletofth, P. (2020). Preparing construction supply chains for blockchain technology: An investigation of its potential and future directions. *Frontiers of Engineering Management, 7*(4), 547–563. doi:10.100742524-020-0110-8

Thompson, D. (2021). *Why Quantum Resistance Is the Next Blockchain Frontier.* https://www.techtimes.com/articles/264625/20210826/why-quantum-resistance-is-the-next-blockchain-frontier.htm

Van Hijfte, S. (2020). Blockchain and Other Emerging Technologies. In *Decoding Blockchain for Business.* Apress. doi:10.1007/978-1-4842-6137-8_2

Vigliotti, M. G., & Jones, H. (2020). The Future of the Blockchain. In *The Executive Guide to Blockchain.* Palgrave Macmillan. doi:10.1007/978-3-030-21107-3_10

Vignesh, V., Gopalan, S. H., Mohan, M., Ramya, R. S., & Ananthakumar, R. (2021). A Quantum-Based Blockchain Approach to Voting Protocol Using Hyperledger Sawtooth. *Journal of Physics: Conference Series, 1916*(1), 012088. Advance online publication. doi:10.1088/1742-6596/1916/1/012088

Weking, J., Mandalenakis, M., Hein, A., Hermes, S., Böhm, M., & Krcmar, H. (2020). The impact of blockchain technology on business models – a taxonomy and archetypal patterns. *Electronic Markets, 30*(2), 285–305. doi:10.100712525-019-00386-3

Wen, Chen, Fan, Yi, Jiang, & Fang. (2021). Quantum blockchain system. *Modern Physics Letters B, 35*(20). doi:10.1142/S0217984921503437

Wu, C., Ke, L., & Du, Y. (2021). Quantum resistant key-exposure free chameleon hash and applications in redactable blockchain. *Information Sciences*, *548*, 438–449. doi:10.1016/j.ins.2020.10.008

Xie, G., Liu, Y., Xin, G., & Yang, Q. (2021). Blockchain-Based Cloud Data Integrity Verification Scheme with High Efficiency. *Security and Communication Networks*, *2021*, 1–15. Advance online publication. doi:10.1155/2021/9921209

Yi, H. (2022, May 1). Secure Social Internet of Things Based on Post-Quantum Blockchain. *IEEE Transactions on Network Science and Engineering*, *9*(3), 950–957. Advance online publication. doi:10.1109/TNSE.2021.3095192

Yin, W., Wen, Q., Li, W., Zhang, H., & Jin, Z. (2017). An anti-quantum transaction authentication approach in blockchain. *IEEE Access: Practical Innovations, Open Solutions*, *6*, 5393–5401. doi:10.1109/ACCESS.2017.2788411

Yuan, B., Wu, F., Qiu, W., Wang, W., Zhu, H., & Zhou, D. (2021). Blockchain-Based Infrastructure for Artificial Intelligence with Quantum Resistant. *2021 4th International Conference on Artificial Intelligence and Big Data (ICAIBD)*, 627-631. 10.1109/ICAIBD51990.2021.9458982

Zhang, P., Wang, L., Wang, W., Fu, K., & Wang, J. (2021). A Blockchain System Based on Quantum-Resistant Digital Signature. *Security and Communication Networks, 2021*(2). doi:10.1155/2021/6671648

Zhao, G., Liu, S., Lopez, C., Lu, H., Elgueta, S., Chen, H., & Boshkoska, B. M. (2019). Blockchain technology in agri-food value chain management: A synthesis of applications, challenges and future research directions. *Computers in Industry*, *109*, 83–99. doi:10.1016/j.compind.2019.04.002

Zhu, H., Wang, X., Chen, C. M., & Kumari, S. (2020). Two novel semi-quantum-reflection protocols applied in connected vehicle systems with blockchain. *Computers & Electrical Engineering*, *86*, 106714. doi:10.1016/j.compeleceng.2020.106714

ADDITIONAL READING

Swan, M. (2020). *Quantum Blockchain*. Quantum Computing. doi:10.1142/9781786348210_0006

KEY TERMS AND DEFINITIONS

Asynchronous Blockchain: It is the blockchain network that can be designed whether to prioritize consistency or availability. If the network wants to prioritize availability, all transactions are added without any downtime. If the network wants to prioritize consistency, some transactions might not be processed or halted until all the previous transactions are confirmed.

Blockchain: Traditional Blockchain which uses pre-quantum cryptography and not secure from quantum attacks.

Cryptocurrency: Is a digital currency designed to work as a medium of exchange through a computer network that is not reliant on any central authority, such as a government or bank, to uphold or maintain it.

Cryptography: Is the technique of securing information and communications through use of codes so that only those people for whom the information is intended can understand it and process it. Thus, preventing unauthorized access to information.

Identity Management: Is the organizational process for ensuring individuals have the appropriate access to technology resources. This includes the identification, authentication and authorization of a person, or persons, to have access to applications, systems, or networks.

Lattice Cryptosystem: Is a generic term for construction of cryptographic primitives or scheme consisting of a set of algorithms that involve lattices, and is used to convert plaintext to ciphertext to encode or decode messages securely.

Permissioned Blockchain: Is a distributed ledger that is not publicly accessible. It can only be accessed by users with permissions. The users can only perform specific actions granted to them by the ledger administrators and are required to identify themselves through certificates or other digital means.

Permissionless Blockchain: Also known as trustless or public blockchains, are open networks available to everyone to participate in the consensus process that blockchains use to validate transactions and data. They are fully decentralized across unknown parties.

Quantum Blockchain: Blockchain systems running in Quantum Computers.

Quantum Key Distribution: Is a secure communication method which implements a cryptographic protocol involving components of quantum mechanics. It enables two parties to produce a shared random secret key known only to them, which can then be used to encrypt and decrypt messages.

Quantum-Resistant Blockchain: Blockchain systems with post-quantum cryptography i.e. post-quantum public-private key, hashing and related protocols.

Signature Scheme: Is a technique to assure an entity's acknowledgment of having seen a certain digital message.

Supply Chain: Is a network of individuals and companies who are involved in creating a product and delivering it to the consumer.

Tokenization: Is the process of exchanging sensitive data for nonsensitive data called "tokens" that can be used in a database or internal system without bringing it into scope.

Transparency: Transparency, as used in science, engineering, business, the humanities and in other social contexts, is operating in such a way that it is easy for others to see what actions are performed. Transparency implies openness, communication, and accountability.

Chapter 2
Introduction to Quantum–Resistant Blockchain

Omega John Unogwu
Universidad Azteca, Mexico

Ruchi Doshi
Universidad Azteca, Mexico

Kamal Kant Hiran
Sir Padampat Singhania University, India

Maad M. Mijwil
(iD) https://orcid.org/0000-0002-2884-2504
Baghdad College of Economic Sciences University, Iraq

ABSTRACT

Quantum-resistant blockchains refer to cryptographic processes that are resistant to attacks via quantum computers. Present public-key algorithms depend on the difficulty of deciphering the discrete log and factorization problem of large prime numbers. Shor's algorithm can be used to break the hash signatures by quantum computers. Therefore, it is necessary for the development of a post-quantum secure signature scheme or quantum-resistant blockchain for post-quantum blockchain security. This chapter will discuss the impact quantum computers are predicted to have on public key cryptography based on the following topics: quantum computers, public key cryptography, quantum threat to PKI, Shor's and Grover's algorithms, post-quantum cryptography, and quantum-resistant blockchain.

DOI: 10.4018/978-1-6684-5072-7.ch002

STRUCTURE

This chapter discusses the following topics:

- Blockchain – What it is
- Traditional Blockchain
    - Pre-quantum Cryptography
- Quantum Blockchain
- Blockchain systems running in Quantum Computers
- Quantum-resistant Blockchain
    - Quantum cryptography
    - Post-quantum Public and Private Keys
    - Hashing

OBJECTIVES

At the end of this chapter, the following should be well understood:

i.   The Blockchain Technology with its driving principles
ii.   Pre-quantum cryptography
iii. Quantum blockchain and the threat it poses
iv.   The implication of blockchain systems on quantum computers
v.   Quantum-resistant blockchain. The various attributes that enable it to be secure

INTRODUCTION

The novel computational data structure based on blockchain has several useful applications that operate a distributed, open, and unfettered record. However, each new cryptographic program should be conscious of the quickly developing technical advancements inside the lifespan of any potentially executed framework, the majority of which will be operational for a sizable amount of time. This chapter discusses the flaws in blockchain technology that have been made apparent by the development of quantum computers and offers general recommendations on the most effective way to make blockchain technology more resistant to such technological advancements. These recommendations include adopting novel developments in quantum blockchain, such as quantum-resistant blockchain, adopting novel developments in quantum blockchain, and adopting some post-quantum cryptography, such as post-quantum

Public and Private multiple crucial subroutines cryptography protocols are necessary for blockchain systems (Aggarwal, D, et al., 2018). A key aspect considered is the speed at which a quantum computer must operate to undermine a particular cryptocurrency.

BLOCKCHAIN: WHAT IT IS

Blockchain is a distributed open ledger that may effectively, permanently, and verifiably record transactions between two parties. It is an append-only database system that is transparent and includes the methods for obtaining consensus on data across a vast, decentralized network of agents with a low level of trust in one another.

It is a distributed database of records that is structured as a list of ordered blocks, where the committed blocks are absolute, the data is shared across a network of computers, and unlike a traditional database, which stores the data on a server, it does not provide a single point of vulnerability. It is distributed in the sense that the database is identical on each of its nodes (Allende, M., López, D.,et al., 2021). Data is stored in the form of transactions on a blockchain, which can represent everything from physical assets like houses and cash to intangible ones like patents, virtual transaction entities, or services.

Novel business models are created based on blockchain facilitations. Public blockchains have irreversible records and transactions are secure. Private keys need to be secured by blockchain users because it prevents unlawful intrusions from hackers who are bent on compromising their digital signatures. Blockchains have consensus algorithms to prevent malicious transactions. This enacts validation conditions for transactions. No transaction will be recorded in the ledger without validation because the consensus methods forbid changing any previous transaction.

How Blockchain Works

The blockchain depends on a twofold cryptographic primitive: hash functions, to authenticate the integrity of data, and public-key cryptography to validate data ownership. Hash functions take an input of any interval and generate a fixed-sized output thread. Public-key cryptography uses algorithms to generate a set of keys made up of a public key and a private key (Al-Housni, N., 2019). A participant uses his private key to sign transactions that he wants to publish on the network, and the receiver verifies the identity of the transaction's sender using the public key. Both primitives are assumed to be a one-way function, meaning that a hash function's input should be impossible to be derived from the output, or through the public key gain access to the private key.

Figure 1. The basic fields of blockchain applications

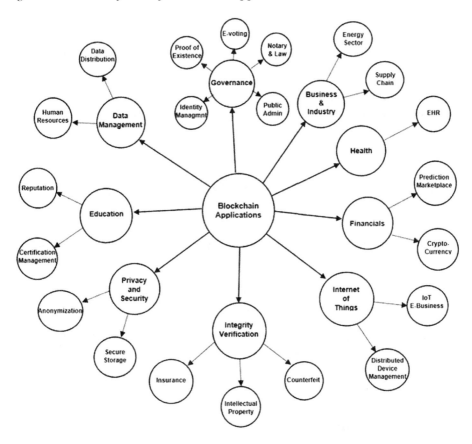

Five fundamental guideline principles underlying the technology

1. Decentralized Database

On a blockchain, every block has access to the whole database and its entire history. The information and data are not under the sole participant's control. Without an intermediary, each party can independently verify the records of its transaction partners (Bennett, C. H., et. al, 1997)

2. Transmission between peers

Peer-to-peer communication takes place without the use of a central node. Information is stored on each node and forwarded to every other node.

3.   Openness when Using a Pseudonym

Everyone with access to the system can see every transaction and the value it is associated with. On a blockchain, each node, or user, is uniquely identified by a 30-plus-character alphanumeric address. Users have the option of revealing their identities to others or remaining anonymous. In a blockchain, transactions happen between addresses (Jain, R.K., 2015)

4.   Records' Irreversibility

The records are connected to every transaction record that came before them, hence the word "chain," so that once a transaction is recorded into the database and the accounts are modified, they cannot be changed. To guarantee that the recording on the database is permanent, chronologically arranged, and accessible to everyone on the network, a variety of computational strategies and methods are used.

5.   Logic Computation

Blockchain transactions can be linked to computer logic and, in a sense, programmed because the ledger is digital. Users can then configure algorithms and rules that initiate transactions between nodes automatically (Lakhwani, K., et. al, 2020)

Pre-Quantum Cryptography

Pre-quantum cryptography converts human-readable data into secret code using a certain kind of cipher or algorithm. The difficulty of pre-quantum cryptography is to make encryption ciphers simple to understand but difficult to reverse engineer.

Cryptography Using Pre-Quantum, Quantum, and Post-Quantum Technologies

Pre-quantum cryptography transforms readable input into secret code using a specific kind of cipher known as an algorithm. Pre-quantum cryptography's goal is to create encoding ciphers that are simple to comprehend but difficult to decipher.

Information in quantum bits is processed by quantum computers using the principles of quantum physics (qubits). A quantum computer may process data exponentially quicker than a conventional, binary computer because each qubit can be a mixture of 0s and 1s (Patel, S. & Vyas, A. K., et. al 2022)

Contrarily, quantum cryptography makes use of geometric ciphers and the physical characteristics of atoms to convert understandable data into uncrackable secret code. Since quantum physics is still an emerging field of study and prototype quantum computers are exceedingly expensive to construct and run, this presents a significant challenge for post-quantum cryptography.

Table 1. Classical computing vs quantum computing vs post quantum cryptography

Classical Computing	Quantum Computing	Post-quantum Cryptography
Manipulates *0*s and *1*s to execute its operations	Uses quantum bits or Qubits to execute its operations	Uses asymmetric keys – Private and Public keys
Utilizes circuits with complementary metal semiconductors	Requires extreme cold environment to operate	Requires fiber-optics connections – Direct line of sight
Sends digital signals via bits	Sends data through particles or photons	Mainly limited to Quantum key distribution
Uses logic based on digital logic	Is based on quantum theory	The Private key must be kept confidential for security

QUANTUM BLOCKCHAIN: CONCEPT AND IMPLICATION

A decentralized, encrypted, and distributed database based on quantum information theory and quantum computation is known as a quantum blockchain. The data cannot be deliberately altered once it has been stored in the quantum blockchain.

Researchers have been concentrating more and more on the study of quantum blockchain in recent years due to the advancement of quantum computation and quantum information theory. This chapter summarizes the advances achieved in the sphere of quantum blockchain and briefly examines its benefits over traditional blockchain. In addition to the approach of applying quantum technology to a specific area of the general blockchain, the construction and framework of the quantum blockchain are introduced. The benefits of the quantum blockchain over the classical blockchain and its future possibilities are also briefly discussed.

The way that both quantum and "classical" computers process information differs significantly. Traditional computers store data in "bits" that can be either 0s or 1s, with each *0* or *1* denoting a high- or low-voltage electrical signal that the computer understands and produces. Instead of storing information in binary *0/1* or yes/no statements, quantum computers store information in "qubits" (quantum bits), floating point states that behave like a probability cloud.

Qubit is a medium in which quantum computers store information. These are physical structures that store information, like a classical computer bit, except that it utilizes the phenomena of superposition and entanglement. A qubit can exist in a superposition state, which can simultaneously be in a linear series of the *0* or *1* states, in contrast to a conventional bit, which can only ever be in one of the two states at any given moment.

Additionally, qubits can be entangled, which means that several qubits are linked together, such that altering the state of one will instantaneously alter the state of another qubit it is entangled with, regardless of those other qubits being physically distant from the original qubit. The basic purpose of a quantum algorithm is that it manipulates the qubits using an array of techniques, living the quantum state of the qubits shaped into the answer being sorted after with a very high probability. The qubit state will break down into the classical *0* or *1* state and will no longer exhibit superposition or entanglement when the product of a calculation is finally measured. Only the same number of classical bits in the result are obtained as the number of qubits used in the calculation. Quantum computers that utilize entanglement and superposition can summarily resolve problems from quantum chemistry and allied fields those conventional computers are unable to tackle, regardless of the amount of time, energy, or resources that are applied to them. But ahead of the quantum science realm, Shor's factoring algorithm postulates the model of a solution to a drawback in abstract number theory, one instance that underpins the internet security systems in everyday use currently.

Shor's Algorithm

The time needed to factor a set of numbers using quantum computers was reduced from years to hours by Peter Shor. The Public Key Infrastructure is built on asymmetric keys, which are susceptible to his method. Should this technique ever become feasible, any existing keys and data that are kept somewhere would need to be re-encrypted (Sharma, T. K., 2022).

The session keys generated by Shor's method would have an effect on the key exchange. When quantum computers are accessible, a spy can simply decipher the encrypted session they recorded. Data integrity and authentication loss can come from the spy duplicating the digital signatures that clients employ to verify the server certificate.

The Shor Algorithm

Pick any positive integer greater than zero. Using the Euclidean method (x, Y), find the largest common divisor *MNO*, where *Y* is the collection of natural integers *Y=1, 2,*

3, 4, 5, etc. The number obtained is a non-trivial divisor of *Y* if the maximal common factor *MNO* (*x, Y*)!= *1*. However, if *MNO* (*x, Y*) = *1*, the period must be established.

Finding the period *z* of the function f(*a*) = g*x* mod *Y* is required in this stage. That is, it is necessary to determine the least value of *z* such that *f*(*a*)=f(*x*+*z*). This phase can only be implemented using a quantum computer.

If *z* is an odd number, the process must start over; otherwise, the calculation moves on to the next stage

The operation must proceed to step 1 if $x^{z/2} + 1 = 0$ mod *Y*; else, the greatest common divisor of ($x^{z/2} - 1$, *Y*) must be calculated using the Euclidean algorithm. Finally, all of Y's non-trivial factors are discovered.

Here is an illustration of a summary of the aforementioned actions.

Step 1: Assume that *Y*, or 15 in this example, is the number to be factorized.

Step 2: Choose a number at random between 1 and *Y* (we'll call it *j*), or between 1 and 15; let's say *x*=4.

Step 3: Locate the MNO (*Y, x*). Euclid's division formula is used. If MNO is less than 1, MNO is a factor of *Y*. MNO (15,4) in this example equals 1, therefore move on to step 4.

Step 4: Now determine the smallest positive integer *z* such that *f*(*a*) = *f*(*a*+*z*) if *f*(*a*) = k^a mod *Y*. In the example that follows, this is possible.

If a variable is defined as *q*=1, proceed to

    Step 4.1: After that, *q**x mod *Y* can be determined. If the remaining is 1, proceed to the following step; if not, repeat the previous step until there is a 1 remainder. Do this by setting the value of *q* to the previous step's remainder as follows:

        1 * 4 mod 15 = 4
        4 * 4 mod 15 = 1

Since there were two transformations needed to obtain the remainder of 1, *z* = 2. Step 2 is required if *z* was an odd number; otherwise, move on to the following step.

Step 5: Determine the factors f1 and f2 using the formulas f1 = *MNO* (*p*+1, *Y*) and f2 = *MNO* (p-1, *Y*). To determine the value of p, we define p as being equal to the $(z/2)^{th}$ transformation's leftover. *p* = 4 in this instance. Specifically, the $(z/2)^{th}$ transformation.

Step 6: The components of *Y*, or 15, are given by f_1 = *MNO* (*p*+1, *Y*), or f_1 = *MNO* (5,15) = 5. f_2 = *MNO* (p-1, *Y*), which is f_1 = *MNO* (3,15) = 3.

Due to the tremendous level of complexity of the qubits, quantum computers have the ability to process data exponentially quicker than conventional computers.

They could theoretically resolve calculation issues that are thought to be beyond the capabilities of traditional computers.

Including the conventional blockchain, quantum blockchain has several characteristics like distribution and decentralization. The major features of quantum blockchain are security and effectiveness. Therefore, it needs to be protected. By implication, one of the most important ways to ensure communication security between nodes is to implement quantum key distribution (QKD) or quantum secure direct communication (QSDC). As a result, the principles of quantum physics ensure network authentication. Even the quantum blockchain may be protected from attacks by quantum computers in the future. The blockchain powered by quantum technology also has the ability to process transactions quickly. As a result, Proof of Work (POW) can speed up transaction times. The evolution of cryptocurrencies will be considerably aided by this composition.

Grover's Algorithm

Conversely, symmetric key encoding might be impacted by Grover's unstructured key search technique. The program searches for a particular item in a list using amplitude amplification. Grover's amplification approach only needs the $\ddot{O}N$ steps, but a traditional computer would need $N/_2$ or N steps. A quadratic acceleration reduces the amount of time needed to search through a large number of variables, but the method must run sequentially to fully utilize the quadratic acceleration.

Grover's approach can't be used since it requires serial processing, whereas quantum computers do in large quantities in parallel. If serial processing is taken into account, Grover's technique has less of an effect on symmetric key encryption and employing Advanced Encryption Standard (AES) 128 will still be secure. Grover's approach can be used to brute-force the symmetric key used in AES, which takes about 2^{64} iterations for a 128-bit key and about 2^{128} iterations for a 256-bit key. A symmetric key with twice length will therefore defend against upcoming quantum assaults (Zhang, P., 2021).

The effectiveness of mining operations can also be increased by applying the Grover algorithm to the blockchain as a whole. Anything is uncertain, in actuality. The parties who have access to them currently have an unfair edge in the mining awards until universal quantum computers are generally available. In general, the performance advantage of quantum blockchain over classical blockchain is mostly due to its efficiency and security. In conclusion, quantum blockchain will have a very broad range of applications in the future and will be the subject of numerous research directions because it has the advantages of faster processing speed and safer transactions based on quantum mechanics. One such application is the application of quantum blockchain. Quantum blockchain has promising development potential in the area of quantum digital currency. Despite the fact that several researchers have proposed concepts for quantum money, such as Quantum Bitcoin

How Blockchains Will Be Affected by the Development of Quantum Computing

Despite all the potential advantages that quantum computing may bring to the world, several aspects of the technology have raised questions in certain quarters of the international community. It has been argued that because blockchain technology uses asymmetric encryption, often known as public-key cryptography, it poses a threat to the viability of the system.

Figure 2. Blockchain-based transactions with public keys, private keys, and hash functions

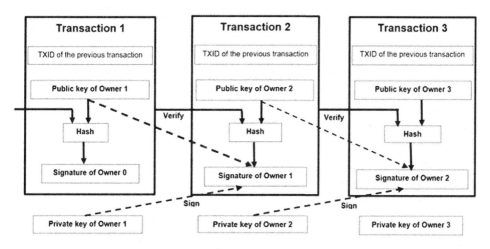

Asymmetric cryptography generates pairs of private and public keys. While the public key is made available to the general public, the private key is kept private. Asymmetric cryptography is based on the "one-way function," a mathematical concept that makes it easy to derive a public key from a private key but difficult to do the opposite.

Public keys are used as wallet addresses on a blockchain, whereas private keys are needed to access the money in a cryptocurrency wallet. A private wallet key cannot be generated from a public wallet address using traditional computing techniques, but vice versa.

On the other side, Quantum Key Distribution (QKD) is the secure transmission of symmetric keys during the operation of post-quantum cryptography (PQC) methods. For classical systems, it will be difficult in the upcoming quantum age to share the secret symmetric keys across an untrusted media. Its decipherment is attempted through quantum key distribution.

To process both quantum and classical ciphers in the PQC era, programs need be able to handle multiple cryptographic algorithms. The ability to protect new applications from quantum attacks while upholding conventional standards would be made possible by the use of hybrid key mechanisms. A new generation of encryption standards will eventually require that companies get ready.

Blockchain Systems Running in Quantum Computers

Blockchain systems do not need quantum computers; rather, quantum computing poses a serious danger to them by having the potential to one day provide the computational power necessary to crack the hitherto impenetrable encryption keys that underlie such systems.

Quantum-Resistant Blockchain

The study of prospective quantum computer assaults on (classical) cryptographic methods is a component of the topic of quantum resistant cryptography, also known as post-quantum cryptography.

For instance, the cryptocurrency known as the Quantum Resistant Ledger goes above and above to maintain the highest levels of functionality and security. It has a unique proof of stake mechanism and cryptographic algorithms that are resistant to quantum computing. Because it employs quantum-resistant hash-based digital signatures, the quantum-resistant ledger is impervious to assaults using both classical and quantum computing techniques.

Post-Quantum Cryptography

In order to defend against attacks from quantum computers, post-quantum cryptography, also known as quantum encoding, is being developed for conventional computers. Post-quantum cryptography aims to make it difficult for quantum computers to decrypt digital signatures in order to meet the difficulties presented by quantum algorithms. As it combines post-quantum cryptography with blockchain technology, post-quantum blockchain ensures high levels of security. From the study above, it is clear that post-quantum blockchain fits the following requirements, giving it the dual advantage of blockchain and the capacity to successfully fend off attacks by quantum computing:

- Post-quantum blockchain, which combines postquantum cryptography and blockchain technology, is resistant to known common attack techniques.
- Post-quantum blockchain has traceable signature scheme qualities and is resistant to known quantum algorithm assaults like Grover's and Shor's algorithms.
- Post-quantum cryptographic algorithms have traits like multivariate cryptography, hash function-based cryptography, lattice-based cryptography, code-based encryption, and others.
- These characteristics ensure the security of secret keys by preventing quantum computing attacks.

Post-Quantum Public Key

Current safe internet interactions are built on the Public Key Cryptography (PKC) system. PKC exhibits asymmetry. This implies that it uses two keys: a public key that is shared with all parties and a private key that the system uses to verify its identity. By creating the message's hash function and encrypting it with a public key, a message is delivered from the client to the recipient. The communication is encrypted by the server using its private key, which can only be decoded by the corresponding private key regardless of any unauthorized third-party attempts.

When post-quantum cryptography algorithms are running, symmetric keys are transferred safely through a process called quantum key distribution.

Post-Quantum Private Key

Unlike the public key, the private key is a secret key that is only known to its owner; nonetheless, both keys must be paired in order for the recipient to be able to read the original message using the key that must be used to decode the cipher text. The algorithms used to produce public keys are also used to produce private keys, resulting in strong, mathematically linked keys. Though the public key (the other key) can be made public without compromising the privacy of the private key

Hashing

The hash method maps a series of messages with a shorter fixed-length value, of any duration, and combines susceptibility, directionality, collision resistance, and high meaning. Hash is frequently employed to safeguard record reliability, or to ensure that no information is improperly changed. The hash value adjusts as the checked data is modified. Because the data is partial, it is important to respect the integrity of the data. SHA is the cryptographic hash function that adheres to the National Institute of Standards and Technology's general features (NIST). Hash functions can be used in blockchain to check the integrity of transactions and blocks. The header of a blockchain block contains the hash value of previous block data. The hash is compared by each user. An input value of any length can be converted by the hash algorithm into a binary value of a specific length. A hash value is a binary value that can be used to check the data's consistency. The hash algorithm is used in the well-known Proof-of-Work algorithm. The blockchain block contains the hash value of the data. Additionally, the signature frequently employed in blockchains is created by hashing the required data along with the private key.

CONCLUSION

From our research, it is clear that the threat that quantum computers pose to blockchain networks is mostly related to the insecure digital signatures of blockchain activities and the poor key-exchange protocols used for peer-to-peer communication over the network.

Applications should be able to handle several cryptographic algorithms in the PQC era in order to process both quantum and classical ciphers. New apps would be able to defend themselves against quantum threats while upholding the conventional standards by using hybrid key methods. Organizations will eventually need to get ready for new encryption standards.

The field of post-quantum cryptography is finally catching up, and four different types of cryptosystems—elliptic curves, lattices, isogenies, and hash-based signatures—are gaining popularity. The trustworthy cryptosystem is McEliece with Goppa codes. The security of blockchain is emphasized by quantum computer using the Shor's algorithm option. Quantum cryptographic ciphers can protect block chains and transactions. The security of blockchain is facilitated by post-quantum cryptography and quantum key distribution. Blockchain communities that aggressively search for new and effective ways to construct a Quantum-Resistant Blockchain are always developing innovative techniques to combat quantum computing processing power.

REFERENCES

Aggarwal, D., Brennen, G., Lee, T., Santha, M., & Tomamichel, M. (2018). Quantum Attacks on Bitcoin, and How to Protect Against Them. *Ledger*, *3*, 1–21. doi:10.5195/ledger.2018.127

Al-Housni, N. (2019). An Exploratory Study in Blockchain Technology. *PQDT - Global*, 89. https://www.proquest.com/dissertations-theses/exploratory-study-blockchain-technology/docview/2199337101/se-2?accountid=27931

Allende, M., López, D., Cerón, S., Leal, A., Pareja, A., Da, M., Pardo, S. A., Jones, D., Worrall, D., Merriman, B., Gilmore, J., Kitchener, N., & Venegas-Andraca, S. E. (2021). *Quantum-Resistance in Blockchain Networks*. ITE Department IDB Lab. http://www.iadb.org

Ansom, H. H. (1982). Strategic Intelligence. *Proceedings of the Academy of Political Science, 34*(4), 153. doi:10.2307/3700977

arXiv. (2019). How a quantum computer could break 2048-bit RSA encryption in 8 hours. *MIT Technology Review*. https://www.technologyreview.com/2019/05/30/65724/how-a-quantum-computer-could-break-2048-bit-rsa-encryption-in-8-hours/

Bard, D. A., Kearney, J. J., & Perez-Delgado, C. A. (2021). Quantum Advantage on Proof of Work. *SSRN Electronic Journal*. doi:10.2139/ssrn.3979439

Barker, W., & Polk, W. (2021). *Getting Ready for Post-Quantum Cryptography*. Academic Press.

Barua, T., Doshi, R., & Hiran, K. K. (2020). *Mobile Application Development*. De Gruyter.

Bennett, C. H., Bernstein, E., Brassard, G., & Vazirani, U. (1997). Strengths and weaknesses of quantum computing. *SIAM Journal on Computing*, *26*(5), 1510–1523. https://doi.org/10.1137/S0097539796300933

Bohr, N. (2020). *Global Future Council on Quantum Computing Frequently Asked Questions*. Academic Press.

Buchmann, J. A., Butin, D., Göpfert, F., & Petzoldt, A. (n.d.). *Post-Quantum Cryptography: State of the Art*. Academic Press.

Cheon, J. H., Han, K., Kim, J., Lee, C., & Son, Y. (2017). A practical post-quantum public-key cryptosystem based on spLWE. *Lecture Notes in Computer Science, 10157*, 51–74. doi:10.1007/978-3-319-53177-9_3

Choubisa, M., & Doshi, R. (2022). Crop Protection Using Cyber Physical Systems and Machine Learning for Smart Agriculture. In *Real-Time Application of Machine Learning in Cyber-Physical Systems* (pp. 134–147). IGI Global.

Daniels, A. (2019). *Information Security in an Internet of Things Network Based on Blockchains and User Participation*. Academic Press.

Fernandez-Carames, T. M., & Fraga-Lamas, P. (2020). Towards Post-Quantum Blockchain: A Review on Blockchain Cryptography Resistant to Quantum Computing Attacks. *IEEE Access: Practical Innovations, Open Solutions*, 8, 21091–21116. https://doi.org/10.1109/ACCESS.2020.2968985

Foley, C. P., Scientist, C., Gambetta, J., Rao, J. R., Dixon, W., & Head, G. (2021). *Is your cybersecurity ready to take the quantum leap?* https://www.weforum.org/agenda/2021/05/cybersecurity-quantum-computing-algorithms/

Grover, L. K. (1997). Quantum mechanics helps in searching for a needle in a haystack. *Physical Review Letters*, 79(2), 325–328. https://doi.org/10.1103/PhysRevLett.79.325

Hiran, K. K., Doshi, R., & Rathi, R. (2014). Security & Privacy issues of cloud & grid computing networks. *International Journal on Computertational Science & Applications*, 4(1), 83–91.

Hiran, K. K., Jain, R. K., Lakhwani, K., & Doshi, R. (2021). *Machine Learning: Master Supervised and Unsupervised Learning Algorithms with Real Examples (English Edition)*. BPB Publications.

Jain, R.K., Hiran, K., Raliwal, G. (2012) Quantum Cryptography: A new Generation of information security system. *Proceedings of Information Journal of Computers & Distributed Systems*.

Jakh-u, R. S. (2019). Independent Review of the Remote Sensing Space Systems Act. *SSRN Electronic Journal*. doi:10.2139/ssrn.3397158

Kappert, N., Karger, E., & Kureljusic, M. (2021). Quantum Computing – The Impending End for the Blockchain? *PACIS 2021 Proceedings*. https://aisel.aisnet.org/pacis2021/114

Kearney, J. J., & Perez-Delgado, C. A. (2021). Vulnerability of blockchain technologies to quantum attacks. *Array, 10*(November), 100065. doi:10.1016/j.array.2021.100065

Khalid, Z. M., & Askar, S. (2021). Resistant Blockchain Cryptography to Quantum Computing Attacks. *International Journal of Science and Business*, 5(3), 116–125. https://doi.org/10.5281/zenodo.4497732

Kiktenko, E. O., Pozhar, N. O., Anufriev, M. N., Trushechkin, A. S., Yunusov, R. R., Kurochkin, Y. V., Lvovsky, A. I., & Fedorov, A. K. (2018). Quantum-secured blockchain. *Quantum Science and Technology, 3*(3). doi:10.1088/2058-9565/aabc6b

Lakhwani, K., Gianey, H. K., Wireko, J., & Hiran, K. K. (2020). *Internet of Things (IoT): Principles, Paradigms and applications of IoT.* BPB Publications.

Lamarque, M., & Master. (2016). *The Blockchain Revolution: New Opportunities in Equity Markets.* https://dspace.mit.edu/handle/1721.1/104522

Li, C., Xu, Y., Tang, J., & Liu, W. (2019). Quantum Blockchain: A Decentralized, Encrypted and Distributed Database Based on Quantum Mechanics. *Journal of Quantum Computing, 1*(2), 49–63. https://doi.org/10.32604/jqc.2019.06715

Mahrishi, M., Hiran, K. K., Meena, G., & Sharma, P. (Eds.). (2020). Machine Learning and Deep Learning in Real-Time Applications. IGI Global.

Mosca, M. (2011). *Cybersecurity in an era with quantum computers: Will we be ready?* Academic Press.

Patel, S., Vyas, A. K., & Hiran, K. K. (2022). *Infrastructure Health Monitoring Using Signal Processing Based on an Industry 4.0 System, Cyber-physical Systems and Industry 4.0: Practical Applications and Security Management.* Academic Press.

Permenkes. (2018). Performance Analysis of Blockchain Platforms. *Master Thesis, 10*(2), 1–15.

Priyadarshi, N., Padmanaban, S., Hiran, K. K., Holm-Nielson, K. B., & Bansal, R. C. (Eds.). (2021). *Artificial Intelligence and Internet of Things for Renewable Energy Systems* (Vol. 12). Walter de Gruyter GmbH&Co KG.

Quantum Blockchain. (2020). doi:10.1142/9781786348210_0006

Quantum Cryptography vs Post-Quantum Cryptography. (n.d.). *FedTech Magazine.*

Rodenburg, B., & Pappas, S. P. (2017). *Blockchain and Quantum Computing.* Mitre Technical Report. https://www.mitre.org/sites/default/files/publications/17-4039-blockchain-and-quantum-computing.pdf

Sattath, O. (2020). On the insecurity of quantum Bitcoin mining. *International Journal of Information Security, 19*(3), 291–302. https://doi.org/10.1007/s10207-020-00493-9

Shahriar, M. A., Bappy, F. H., Hossain, A. K. M. F., Saikat, D. D., Ferdous, M. S., Chowdhury, M. J. M., & Bhuiyan, M. Z. A. (2020). Modelling attacks in blockchain systems using petri nets. *Proceedings - 2020 IEEE 19th International Conference on Trust, Security and Privacy in Computing and Communications, TrustCom 2020,* 1069–1078. doi:10.1109/TrustCom50675.2020.00142

Sharma, T. K. (2022). *Blockchain Operating System_ A Complete Overview.* Blockchain Counsil. https://www.blockchain-council.org/blockchain/blockchain-operating-system-a-complete-overview/

Shor, P. W. (1997). Polynomial-time algorithms for prime factorization and discrete logarithms on a quantum computer. *SIAM Journal on Computing, 26*(5), 1484–1509. https://doi.org/10.1137/S0097539795293172

Sigurdsson, G., Giaretta, A., & Dragoni, N. (2020). Vulnerabilities and Security Breaches in Cryptocurrencies. *Advances in Intelligent Systems and Computing, 925*(March), 288–299. doi:10.1007/978-3-030-14687-0_26

Tie-xiong, S. U., Shi-wen, Y., Zhi-qin, G., Xiao-lei, L. I., Bao-cheng, Z., & Yi, Z. (2001). Review on dynamic. Simulation model of complex structural joints. *Huabei Gongxueyuan Xuebao/Journal of North China Institute of Technology, 22*(3), 221–222.

Torino, P. (2019). *Introduction to Post-Quantum Cryptography.* Academic Press.

Van Trinh, T. (2020). *Quantum-safe Bitcoin How to protect blockchain systems from quantum-computer attacks.* University of Oslo.

We must address the security risks posed by quantum computers. (n.d.). *World Economic Forum.* https://www.weforum.org/agenda/2020/06/quantum-computers-security-challenges/

World Economic Forum. (2021). *Is your cybersecurity ready to take the quantum leap?* World Economic Forum. https://www.weforum.org/agenda/2021/05/cybersecurity-quantum-computing-algorithms/

Zhang, P., Wang, L., Wang, W., Fu, K., & Wang, J. (2021). A Blockchain System Based on Quantum-Resistant Digital Signature. *Security and Communication Networks, 2021*(2). doi:10.1155/2021/6671648

KEY TERMS AND DEFINITIONS

Advanced Encryption Standard (AES): The United States government selected the symmetric block cipher known as Advanced Encryption Standard (AES) to safeguard sensitive data.

Algorithm: Is a method for solving a problem that involves searching a database that is carried out step-by-step on a quantum computer.

Asymmetric Encryption: Also known as public-key cryptography is a method of encrypting and decrypting data.

Authentication: Is used by a client to verify that the server is what it purports to be.

Binary Computers: Are computers that express messages, computer processor commands, and other types of data using a two-symbol system based on numbers, "0s" and "1s."

Bits: Is a commonly used subdivision or unit of a single Bitcoin.

Blockchain: Is a distributed, duplicated digital ledger of all transactions that run via the network of computers on the blockchain.

Blockchain Systems: Is a method of storing data that makes it difficult or impossible to alter, tamper with, or trick the system.

Blockchain Technology: Is a shared, unchangeable ledger that simplifies the process of logging transactions and monitoring assets in a company network.

Classical Blockchain: Is a traditional blockchain, the most basic level, a digital log of transactions kept on numerous computers (referred to as nodes) connected by a network.

Cryptocurrency: Is a type of digital currency in which, as opposed to a centralized authority, a decentralized system uses encryption to verify transactions and keep records.

Cryptography: Is the method of securing information and communication based on mathematical principles. It is a technique for protecting crucial data from unauthorized access.

Data Integrity: Is established in blockchain because stored data is immutable and permanent and cannot be changed or erased.

Decentralized Database: Is a hybrid of a regular database and a distributed database, supported by many layers of blockchains and using a database interface or compute interface for data recording and transactions.

Euclid's Division Formula: Or lemma can be used to determine the HCF of two numbers. It says that if there are two integers a and b, then q and r must exist such that they satisfy the formula $a = bq + r$, where $O £ r < b$.

Goppa's Code: Is a general kind of linear code created by utilizing an algebraic curve X over a finite field, which is an algebraic geometric code.

Grover's Algorithm: Makes it possible to perform quantum searches, allowing users to swiftly identify values among many billions of unstructured data points.

Hacker: Is someone who utilizes computers to obtain data without authorization or one who steals from a vulnerable entity.

Hash: Is a function that takes an input string of any length and outputs an output of a defined length, satisfying the encrypted requirements necessary to complete a blockchain computation.

Intrusion: Is the occurrence of an unauthorized user obtaining data or access permission that they are prohibited from.

Logic Computations: Blockchain transactions can be linked to computational logic which is, in essence, programs due to the ledger's digital character, so users may create formulas and guidelines that initiate transactions between nodes automatically.

Malicious Transactions: Include any type of fraud, identity theft, or hacking done with the purpose of gaining an unfair advantage or benefiting from deceit.

McEliece Code: Robert McEliece first suggested the McEliece code as a code-based public key cryptosystem in 1978.

Node: Is one of the machines running the blockchain's software to verify and preserve the whole history of transactions on the network is referred to as a node.

Peer-to-Peer: Is the direct transfer of a resource, like digital money, between parties without the involvement of a centralized authority.

Private Key: Like a password, is a secret number that is used in cryptography. In cryptocurrencies, they are also employed to verify transactions and establish who owns a blockchain address.

Proof of Work (PoW): By making the process of mining, or recording transactions, challenging, Proof of Work is the mechanism that enables the Bitcoin network to remain stable. It is the blockchain network's initial consensus algorithm.

Post-Quantum Cryptography: Aims to create cryptographic systems that are resistant to both quantum and conventional computers and are compatible with current networking and communications protocols.

Public Keys: Make it possible for cryptocurrency transaction execution. It is paired with a private key and a cryptographic code and employed to transfer cryptocurrency to a wallet.

Quantum Key Distribution: QKD is a safe way to exchange encryption keys that are only known to shared parties, which may be used to encrypt and decrypt messages. Quantum physics is used to ensure communication security.

Quantum Secure Direct Communication (QSDC): Is a significant quantum communication protocol, that uses a direct conversation between communicating parties rather than the production of secret keys beforehand to send confidential information. Without the use of a private key, confidential information can be sent directly through a quantum channel.

Quantum-Resistant Blockchain: Is immune to attacks from quantum computers. It uses encryption and quantum mechanics to allow two parties to communicate safe data while also detecting and defending against outsiders.

Quantum-Resistant Ledger: Is a decentralized communication layer and post-quantum value storage that addresses the threat that quantum computing will bring to cryptocurrencies in the future.

Secure Hashing Algorithm (SHA): Is used for hashing data and certificates, designed to safeguard data.

Shor's Algorithm: Is a practical polynomial quantum technique for the factorization of integers that is tuned for finding prime factors in a hypothetical quantum computer.

Superposition: Is one of the characteristics that set a quantum computer apart from a conventional computer. Users can tokenize, trade, and profit from their potential future income using this decentralized fixed income protocol.

Chapter 3
Emerging Blockchain Technology vis–à–vis Limitations and Issues:
Emphasizing the Indian Context

Prantosh Kumar Paul
Raiganj University, India

ABSTRACT

Blockchain has now become blockchain technology, and this is the record of data that are encrypted, and here distributed database is required for the purpose of transaction, contract, and independent record. It is therefore a digital ledger and can be reachable in different platforms for different financial activities and services. It is supported by healthy digital currency systems like bitcoin transactions and does not depend on any third party systems. Blockchain supports the multiple numbers of shared copies, and it works in a same database. Very recently blockchain was considered as an important subfield of information technology. It is therefore treated as a tool, technique, as well as procedure for financial management. This chapter is based on existing literature on blockchain with basics and special focus on the issues and limitations. This chapter highlights the scenario of blockchain technology in India with opportunities, companies, and scenario of manpower availability and potentiality.

DOI: 10.4018/978-1-6684-5072-7.ch003

INTRODUCTION

Blockchain Technology is the encrypted and distributed database connected with the transaction, contract, and depends on different independent record. Blockchain is the digital ledger and a particular place is being used to store data. Blockchain is strengthening the financial segment and activities for proper digital currency like bitcoin transactions. Blockchain Technology is dedicated in tangible and intangible asset management, and here data can be tracked and recorded in a particular network and ledger (Chattu et.al., 2019). Blockchain technology supports registered members immediately, and that can be shared, and offer completely transparent information. Blockchain is needful in tracking the orders, payments, accounts, as well as production. Transaction details can be identified of the end users using blockchain therefore it is emerging in diverse areas viz. business and commerce, education and training, health and medical systems, government and administration, entertainment, banking and trade, etc. It is a type of fraud resistant system and gives transparent financial services than traditional business processes. Like other Information Technology components, blockchain technology also been increased and rising its applications in other areas and sector. Satoshi Nakamoto devised an immutable ledger of transactions that chains together blocks of data using digital cryptography to solve the double-spending problem associated with digital currencies. Blockchain Technology allows participants to do the business who may not known to each other but able in safe and secure business. The blockchain is responsible in identification of the participants including validates the transactions and also ensure that everyone follow the norms. Blockchain Technology and its basic advantages is depicted in Fig 1. The Blockchain Technology has several issues and challenges and in this regard country to country such issues are different. As far as India is concerned there are certain issues in regard to Blockchain Technology such as implementation and execution ranging from laws and regulations, norms and guidelines, financial aspects, and so on. Fig 1 depicted the basic advantages and benefits of Blockchain Technology at a glance (Chen, G., et.al., 2018).

There are number of places where blockchain may be applicable and among these important are important are Supply Chain Management, Voting Management System, Copyright and ownership protection affairs, personal and financial management, better retail management with royalty award, Healthcare, Transport and Tourism, etc. For example with proper supply chain management one can easily track the status of a product and that can more supportive to the existing GIS System.

Figure 1. Benefits of blockchain technology at a glance

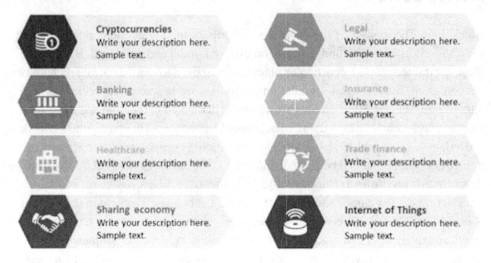

OBJECTIVE OF THE WORK

The chapter entitled 'Emerging Blockchain Technology Vis-à-Vis Limitations and Issues: Emphasizing Indian Context' is conceptual in nature and a theoretical work. This chapter is aimed with the following—

- To learn about the basic aspects of Blockchain including the features, as well as basic functions of the Blockchain Technology in brief manner.
- To learn regarding the Quantum Blockchain Technology in simple sense.
- To find out the limitations as well as disadvantages of the Blockchain technology in brief manner.
- To find out the issues and challenges of implementation of the Blockchain Technology in contemporary scenario.

METHODOLOGY ADOPTED

The present work is theoretical and collected from different secondary sources, and primary sources. Secondary sources are being used to collect aspects regarding Blockchain Technology such as features and functions. To gather latest technologies in the field of Blockchain, and for that website of different companies also studied to learn about the latest of the field. Furthermore, Governmental policies are studied on the topic Blockchain to reach the aim and objective of the work.

BLOCKCHAIN TECHNOLOGY: FUNDAMENTAL ASPECTS

Blockchain Technology is a kind of database and specially digital ledger. David Cham proposed the concept of Blockchain in the year 1982 and later Stuart Haber and W. Scott Stornetta in the year 1992 were also illustrated and mentioned some other aspects in their book on Blockchain (Gabison, 2016). The first implementation of Blockchain based Network completed by Satoshi Nakamoto and later the aspects of digital currency and Bitcoin become popular. Different tools, technologies were increased day by day in this Technology (Grover et.al., 2016). Different transactions of Blockchain are stored in a same network, and all these are broadly classified into three as mentioned here.

- Public Blockchain,
- Private Blockchain, and
- Hybrid Blockchain.

Public Blockchain is open in nature and works on decentralized of the computer networks, and such network is accessible to anyone for the transactions. In Public Blockchain system who validate the transaction normally receive rewards and for the same two models (Proof-of-work, Proof-of-stake) are being used. Bitcoin and Ethereum (ETH) are prime example of Public Blockchain and some of the featured characteristics in this regard are as follows—

- Higher amount of Security
- Open and flexible Environment
- Anonymous Nature
- No governance and regulations
- Full of Transparency and privacy
- Distributed in nature etc.

Private blockchains has some of the restrictions and such are not open like public blockchain. In addition to these here permission considered as important for the transaction. And regarding this, connection system administrators job is to be treated as worthy (Christ & Helliar, 2021. Private blockchain offers various kind of internal networking opportunities such as—

- Sophisticated privacy and secrecy.
- High level of efficiency.
- Faster and advanced transaction.
- Better and healthy scalability.

- Faster and speediness.

Hybrid Blockchains is important type of Blockchain which is combines from the public blockchain and private blockchain for the controlling and achieving higher goals including offering centralized and decentralized features. Hybrid Blockchains since a merged system therefore it comes with the feature of integrity, transparency, and security. Here maximum customization is also offered by the Hybrid Blockchains with robust confidentiality in the private network (Saini et. al. 2021). Different reasons are exits in popularization of the blockchain technologies such as—

- Blockchain Technology is being useful in Medical and health related data management.
- In the NFT market places, some of the technology are being used and among these blockchain considered as important.
- Royalties tracking for the music industry is done by the Blockchain Technology.
- For the Cross-border payments and similar transaction also Blockchain considered as important.
- For the Real-time and sophisticated IoT based systems also blockchain technology may be considered as effective, partially.
- Regarding personal identity security enhancement and development Blockchains are effective.
- Blockchains are being used for the purpose of Anti-money laundering tracking system
- Blockchains are useful in advanced and intelligent supply chain Systems and logistics monitoring systems designing and development.
- For the healthy and sophisticated logistics monitoring systems and development Blockchains are being used.
- Blockchains are being used for modern and advanced voting mechanism
- In Managing and advancing contemporary Advertising systems
- Advancing and enhancing Cryptocurrency exchange as well as management.
- In developing and advancing the real estate processing platform and systems.

Blockchain technology utilizations are rising gradually and applicable in diverse areas like Financial and Banking Services, Education and Research, Healthcare and Medical Systems, Government and Administration, Travel and Hospitality, and so on. And some of the areas are mentioned in Fig 2.

Figure 2. Emerging applications of Blockchain Technology

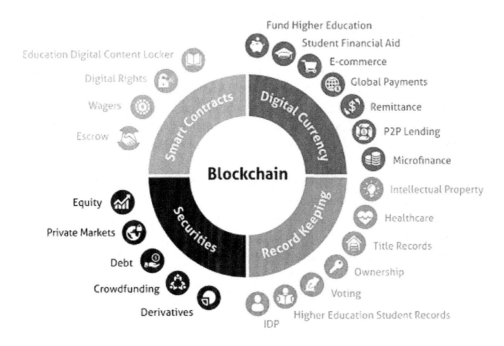

QUANTUM BLOCKCHAIN: THE FUNDAMENTALS

Quantum Technologies are improving and rising its applications in different places. Among the Quantum segment Quantum Mechanics, Quantum Computing, Quantum Informatics considered as worthy. Earlier within Quantum Informatics one of the important considered as Quantum Cryptography but in recent past Quantum blockchain also flourishing after the birth of blockchain systems (Jain, Hiran, & Paliwal, 2012). Quantum blockchain is an advanced version of the blockchain which is a decentralized and encryption based, and further it is distribution based and lies on quantum computation and quantum based information theory. The important fact is after storing and recording the data it is difficult to maliciously tampered with. Due to latest and emerging researches in the areas of Quantum Computing and Technologies recently the development of the Quantum blockchain is noticeable. According to the theory a 300 qbits enabled computer can perform more and more calculations instantly than there are atoms in the visible universe. The advanced and powerful quantum computer could successfully break down the conventional cryptography and even the sophisticated and protected blockchains.

Quantum blockchain is helps in proper security management using proper principles of quantum computers, the conventional blockchains is dedicated in collecting records and the same is connecting with the cryptography with the chronological order. As far as quantum blockchain is concerned here records of blocks basically encoded (here records are encoded into a series) with photons which are entangled with each other. Therefore here blocks are basically kept in chronological order and the same is entanglement within time. Furthermore in quantum blockchain transaction are transferred within a network of quantum computers. All the basic features of blockchain (such as following) also supports Quantum Blockchain systems—

- Blockchain is an advanced immutable and unalterable network and here users are unable to edit or modification.
- Blockchain systems normally having own distributed systems and every nodes follows own system transaction delivery.
- Since blockchain uses encryption therefore within the system any kind of transaction become easy and safe.
- Faster settlement become possible with the blockchain technologies and such system are more advanced and faster than existing systems.

Therefore all these traditional blockchain systems also able to gearup using quantum blockchain and technologies.

LIMITATION AND DRAWBACKS OF BLOCKCHAIN TECHNOLOGY

Blockchain technology concerned with different potential applications, and here various decentralized applications are also considered as worthy in financial aspects but there are certain issues and limitation of the technology and some of them are reported here as follows (also refer Fig 3).

Lack of Awareness—Lack of awareness regarding the Blockchain technology considered as one of the important limitation and drawbacks, and this is need to overcome by different methods and initiatives (Christ & Helliar, 2021).

Limited Skilled Human Resources—Ample opportunities available in the areas of Blockchain technology but there are important concern regarding shortage in skilled manpower in Blockchain technology including allied fields such as cryptography, botcoins etc. Ministries, industries and initiative of the association considered as worthy in this regard.

Figure 3. Some of the basic limitations of Blockchain Technology at a glance

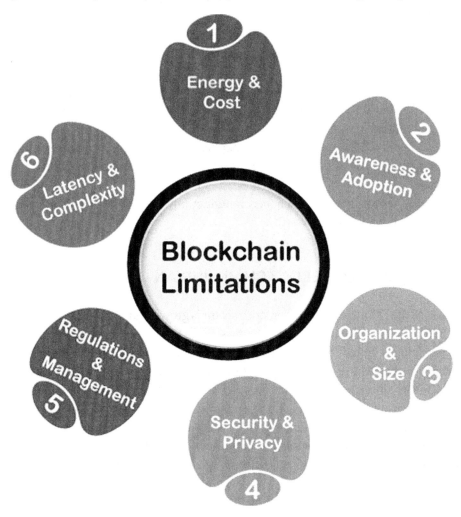

Immutable— Blockchain systems comes with various benefit and among these privacy is important one. Since in Blockchain technology modifying records are not allowed therefore here users faces problem in general revision and editing (Macrinici et. al., 2018).

Regarding Key Management— Blockchain technology uses different kind of keys and focused keys are public keys and private keys therefore the risk exists in such systems.

Scalability—Matters regarding scalability also considered as important in blockchain technology as here each participating node have to verify basic and required transaction. Bitcoin is not able in solving large scale matters and volume, and here issues of scalability treated as vital.

Consensus Mechanism—In every 10 minutes in a Blockchain technology block can be created and here every transaction need to reach a common consensus (Gereffi et.al., 2008).

Cost of Implementation—Blockchain technology gives us different opportunities and benefits, but at the same time implementation and execution of this technology is difficult due to cost of the projects.

Inefficiency—There are certain inefficiency can be noted in Blockchain technology and among these issues of the network, skill manpower considered as worthy and important.

Storage—The nature of blockchain is continuing always and therefore here storage is considered important and worthy.

MAJOR ISSUES OF BLOCKCHAIN: INDIAN CONTEXT

Almost all the IT and Informatics practice sector is growing in India (Paul, P.K., et.al. 2016). Blockchain technology is in growing stage in India with wide range of benefits and advantages. In India more than thirty thousand innovators and practitioners are working in the field of Blockchain and the field is getting recognized across the world for its advanced transparency as well as accountability in public & private sector (Jirgensons & Kapenieks, 2018). However the challenges and issues in regard to Blockchain is noticeable including the issues of scalability and interoperability. As far as Security and privacy is concerned certain challenges and issues treated as worthy. The bellow mentioned different issues and challenges, however listed in Fig: 4.

The law and regulation governing Information Technology Act is important and according to the Indian IT Act here data protection related clause and aspects considered as worthy and important (Khezr et.al., 2019). Blockchain technology is dedicated in storing data on the chain and the same is recorded on the network with every node and therefore it conflicts with the Section 43A of IT Act (Lin et.al., 2020). Data protection laws is required to protect the privacy of the users, and in the private blockchain also there are concerns regarding the control the level of privacy in different elements of the data recorded (Pane et. al., 2020).

Blockchain Technology is fallen the issues of data security and privacy due to the draft personal data protection bill, 2019 for the case/ clause of 'Right to be Forgotten' and this is not satisfied inherent core functionalities of blockchain (Omar et.al, 2021). As privacy is concerned with the data ownership therefore in this regard Blockchain can be designed in different context viz. public, private and hybrid.

Within blockchain the issues are exits regarding managing on-chain and off-chain data management for avoiding sensitive data. Blockchain Technology also comes with the concern of the banking related aspects and here non-repudiation via in-person verification considered as valuable, additionally cryptocurrency also being an important issue and conflicts with banking regulations (Milovanova et.al., 2020).

There are issues on transaction and allied aspects especially on Digital Signature as per the schedule I of the Information Technology Act., 2000. Here the concern of using Certificate Authority is treated as important particularly data privacy related aspects since in Blockchain all the nodes are having private keys, public keys and that is functional with its level. The aspect of Decentralized finance (DeFi) considered as worthy in the context of Blockchain Technology.

Figure 4. Major challenges and issues of Blockchain Technology

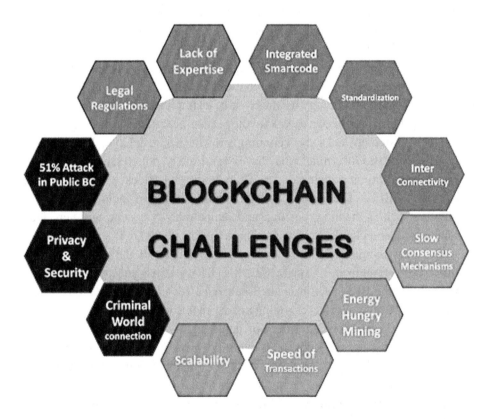

Modern age has witness in different kind of technological advancement especially in the field of Information Technology and within the emerging areas Blockchain Technology considered as prime one (Radanović & Likić, 2018). Some of the allied technologies such as machine learning, deep learning, cloud computing, big data are important in supporting overall development of Blockchain Technology. The advent of this technology leads good and affordable transparency and immutability. Recent applications of blockchain is increasing in diverse field such as registry of land title, managing vehicle life cycle, farm and insurance management, digital healthcare record management and so on. It is worthy to note that Blockchain is aimed being imbibed into the social, economic fabric of the country with support from Government and Private sectors involvement. Different companies are engaged with blockchain implementation for improved, effective operations. According to a study it has noted that, 56% of Indian business now planning to switch blockchain technology and in this regard initiative of Government of India is also noticeable through the Centre of Excellence (CoE) in Blockchain Technology which operates, and coordinating blockchain related projects. The initiative is worthy to rolling out before its realistic implementation (Gamage et.al., 2020).

Blockchain Technology needs a proper regulatory body, though there is a absence on any proper body but it is worthy to mention about the NITI AAYOG's stategy paper on Blockchain Technology for the cases of its implementation, suggestions. It is important to have a localized network for the peer-to-peer transactions for complete blockchain environment and socio-economic growth (Kursh & Gold, 2016). And in this regard each State Government may have own strategy, policies, initiative. There are certain organizations which are engaged in developing Blockchain Systems and among these SEBI i.e. The Securities and Exchange Board of India involved with the initiative such as creating, hosting, and maintaining a system, and here DLT (Distributed ledger technology) play an important role. Such DLT is also important in recoding and monitoring the securities the covenants of the non-convertible securities. With effect from 1st April, 2022 this DLT system is enacted for complete development of the BFSI sector using Blockchain Technology. Since banking as well as healthcare regulations is changing rapidly therefore a suitable and affordable regulations is expected for betterment of deploying systems. Recently *(In Dec., 2021)* National Strategy on Blockchain being released by Ministry of Electronics and Information Technology (MeitY) and this is a policy framework in seeking of planning and adopting suitable technology particularly for the e-governance and allied activities. The Government of India should looking after the Blockchain as a Service. In addition to in-general Blockchain strategy state-wise and specific Blockchain also considered as important and worthy. Blockchain supports in India encountered by the MeitY it order to offer robust security, trust and offering tamperevident transaction. The roadmap of the MeitY is include the assessment of the value of future plans, existing plans, deployments, adopting current plans (Kumar & Mallick, 2018). Ministry of Electronics and Information Technology (MeitY), Government of India is planned to focused on the following weak areas in order to develop the Blockchain Technology systems—

- Scalability,
- Security,
- Interoperability,
- Data localization, and
- Disposal of records.

Blockchain initiative also importantly noted with the initiative of the several private players and organizations and according to the report of Cross Tower the Blockchain industry will value USD 5 billion in 2021 to USD 262 billion with a projected 11 year term and this is resulting USD 1.1 trillion contributions in India. Therefore as per projected plan the growth of the GDP can be noticeable by the impact of Blockchain. The technology is to be wonderful impact for the implementation of digitalization and at the same time real Digital India initiative. There are huge human resources are required in order to implement Blockchain properly, with the support of Blockchain the functionality can grow in the areas of

- B2B (Business to Business)
- G2C (Government to Citizen)
- G2G (Government to Government)
- B2G (Business to Government)

The applications and implementation of the Blockchain can be possible in the diverse areas of healthcare, government and administration, cyber security and management, travel and tourism industry, education and training, etc. Blockchain therefore supports transparency and accountability and provide frictionless transactions with the citizens. According to some suspect the implementation of Blockchain is going to wear away the legacy systems, however it is to be mention that it may revamp the existing system and procedure effectively. The ecosystems of Blockchain supports and encourage transparency, immutability as well as decentralized approaches.

There are issues and challenges in involving fancy webs as well as futuristic illustrations, even it offer lot of flexibility to form and pass large set of data and information digitally. While distributing the information digitally into small pieces in different platform the data passes by the encryption by the technique of cryptography. Though using some strategy the deletion or editing of the data can be possible and blockchain can check and do the needful to the each datasets to its owner or proprietor only. The decentralization nature of Blockchain is responsible in creating greater trust within the users and this is become possible using quantum services and process. It is important to note that there are certain issues in crypto currency in India and the same need to solve accordingly. Availability of middleman is an important issue in India and they need to eliminate. It is worthy to note that among such professionals key are auditors, low end tech professionals, etc. The issue of trusting in an important issue in the banking sector and it has been started since 2008 during the financial crisis and to manage the fraudulent activities employing Blockchain treated as worthy. In reduction in identity theft with maximum transparency of the data is the valuable feature of Blockchain (Viriyasitavat et.al., 2019).

India as a developing country having some of the issues and problem such as food and waste systems, supply chain management etc. and all these case Blockchain can be effectively used for storing information including distribution of the food. Blockchain is adoptable due to economic benefits of food marketing also. Consumer-business relationship can be managed with the Blockchain Technology. According to the expert, lack of knowledge regarding the Blockchain considered as important drawback, here lack of knowledge from the industries, organizations, human resources considered as valuable (Siyal, 2019). In addition to these, poor and unavailable regulations and framework treated as valuable. According to NASSCOM the scenario and development stage of Blockchain Technology in India is running with several challenges, a report called 'NASSCOM Avasant India Blockchain Report 2019' highlighted that big and even midsized service providers are having less than five percentage of blockchain projects in India, and this is very low than that of North American nations and most of the European countries. It is worthy to note that, India accounted only 2 per cent of blockchain related start-ups, throughout the world.

SOME OF THE REPUTED ORGANIZATION FOR BLOCKCHAIN: INDIAN CONTEXT

Blockchain Technology in India is growing rapidly even though there are issues, and challenges in several aspects. The technology is being used for the recoding of bitcoin transaction with international network of the systems and computers. Here both private and public companies are using Blockchain Technology, and according to a study it has noted that 56% organizations are moving for their business growth using blockchain (Williams, 2019). In Health Informatics practice Indian Government is driving more and involved with several initiative and in this regard Blockchain Technology is applicable. For the low income family massive investment can be noted by the Government and here Blockchain implementation can be a worthy move.

As India is home to many reputed IT Company therefore the growth of Blockchain Technology is noticeable (Sun, Yan, & Zhang, 2016). Different survey and reviews displayed that there are different companies working deeply on this technology and specially from the Bangaluru, Hyderabad, Pune, Jaipur, Ahmedabad, Kolkata, Delhi. The details of some of the companies are depicted in Table 1.

Table 1. Some of the challenges of Blockchain Technology

Sl. No.	Companies	Description
1	Hyperlink InfoSystem	Hyperlink InfoSystem is a company working in India, USA, UAE, Canada and UK. They offered multiple blockchain services for almost all types of organizations. The company engaged with blockchain services along with other services viz. Web development, Big Data Analytics, IoT, CRM Solutions and so on.
2	Accenture	Accenture is a Fortune Global company offers services in Blockchain and allied services from its 492K employees operating from 200 cities and from 120 countries globally. Accenture Blockchain and Multiparty Systems specializes in the areas of supply chain, digital identity and financial services.
3	Fueled	Fueled is an emerging IT solution company and got several awards for its services focused on Blockchain Technology for the mobile app, CRM, POS, CMS, ERP, CDP and so on.
4	InfoSys	Infosys Limited is the second-largest Indian IT Company with 82 marketing division with 123 technology development centre and each places. The company strongly engaged in blockchain based services and for the same the organizations believes in identification and correlations with distribution of proper ecosystems, scale adoption etc.
5	Capgemini	Capgemini is a consulting, technology company with 270K employees engaged in Cloud Services with Blockchain solutions, and they do the same from 50 countries.
6	Tata Consultancy Services	TCS is well-known IT brand not only in India but also worldwide for its emerging service including Enterprise Apps, Blockchain, and the same is operated from 149 cities belongs to 46 countries.
7	Zensar Technologies	Zensar Technologies was established in the year 1991 and at present it has 10,000 employees operating from 20 countries globally offers Cloud Infrastructure, and advanced technological solutions with Blockchain Services.
8	Willow Tree Apps	WillowTree is an app development company offers blockchain services including app development, software development etc. Company uses latest technologies to render its services. Apart from India it has operating divisions in other countries.
9	Tech Mahindra	Tech Mahindra is a part of the company named Mahindra Group offers IT solutions in all industries. It operates by 1,25,000 staffs operated from 90 counties with huge support from blockchain based services.
10	HData Systems	HData Systems is offers Blockchain based technologies to increase the productivity, and for the same it uses some other allied technologies and platform such as big data analytics, data science, AI, machine learning, automation, etc.
11	SoluLab	SoluLab is one of the important company engaged in blockchain development having 50M+ active users and according to a study it has revealed that it has 97% customer success score. It is operated with Fortune 500 enterprises for offering its services.
12	Eleks	ELEKS is one of the top 100 Global Outsourcing IT company with focus on SMEs uses innovative technologies. It is operated with 2,000+ experts. ELEKS offer the services by the software development, product design with a strong emphasis on Blockchain based services.
13	Quytech	Quytech is a Blockchain and Game development IT Company engaged in blockchain services for the financial sector, healthcare sectors and startups.

continues on following page

Table 1. Continued

Sl. No.	Companies	Description
14	OpenXcell	OpenXcell is a software solutions development company offers development of innovative solutions which are futuristic and user-friendly, and finally support blockchain systems.
15	BrancoSoft	BrancoSoft is a dedicated software development IT outsourcing solutions established in the year 2011 as Thoughtwaver It has 50+ highly skilled IT experts offers blockchain solutions to the SMEs.
16	Sofocle Technologies	Sofocle is an Enterprise Blockchain company offers emerging technologies for enterprises, startups and governments across the sectors. The company has a strong partnerships with large ecosystem.
17	Sate Development	Sate offers Enterprise solutions having strength of Blockchain technology and it helps in distributed blockchain to power remarkable range of applications.
18	KrypC	KrypC is engaged in niche developments in the areas of Blockchain. KrypC offers considerable technology and expertise in diverse areas of cryptography and security.
19	Auxesis	Auxesis group is working with the Financial Technology emphasized Blockchain Technology with wide range of solutions for different organizations and economic sustainability for the start-ups.
20	Osiz Technologies	Osiz Technologies is a IT and Software Development Company offers solutions for the Entrepreneurs, Businesses and Industries with their expertise in blockchain technology.

BLOCKCHAIN TECHNOLOGY VIS-À-VIS HUMAN RESOURCE CONTEXT

Blockchain Technology is gaining its role in almost all the sector and therefore there are huge requirement in skilled and well knowledgeable professionals in the field of Blockchain and allied technologies (Sakhipov & Baygozhanova, 2020). And as a result in many countries Governments are taken initiative on introducing academic programs in the field of Blockchain which are emerging, skill based. Such academic programs not only training based but also come with full fledged degree. According to the study it has revealed that only a few universities offers degrees including Bachelors, and Masters in the areas of Blockchain Technology, and there are potentialities in introducing more programs in the field like MTech by Research, MS by Research, Ph.D. Program, Post Doctoral Training Program and so on (Paul et.al., 2017). It is worthy to note that, Blockchain Technology is offered not only as Blockchain Technology but also as a merger with other technology and some of the available nomenclature are listed herewith—

- Blockchain
- Blockchain Technology
- Blockchain & Financial Technology
- Blockchain Management
- Blockchain and Distributed Technology

- Blockchain and Distributed Ledger Technology
- Cryptography & Blockchain Technology
- IoT, Cyber Security with Blockchain Technology (Yang et.al., 2017).

Furthermore as per the study it has noted that Master of Science (both MS & MSc) are available. And popular Master of Business Administration is also offered with Blockchain Specialization. In India only Amity University offers Master of Computer Applications with Blockchain Specialization. Master in Blockchain Technologies is also noted in some of the universities as depicted in the following figure. Here Fig 5 shows the available programs in the field of Blockchain at Masters level as per study.

Figure 5. Some of the academic program on Blockchain Technology at Masters level as per methodology adopted

Sl. No.	Degrees offered	Universities
1	MS Information Systems (Blockchain Technology)	Northeastern University
2	MSc Blockchain Application & Financial Technologies	University of East London
3	MSc Blockchain	Dublin City University
4	MSc Blockchain & Distributed Ledger Technologies (Business & Finance)	The University of Malta
5	Master of Blockchain Enabled Business	RMIT University
7	Master in Global Business with Blockchain	The University of the Cumberlands
8	Masters in Blockchain Technologies	The Polytechnic University of Catalonia
9	Master in Blockchain Technologies	Global Institute of Leadership & Technology (The University of Barcelona)
10	MBA Blockchain Management	European University Business School

In India apart from traditional Higher Education emerging and technological education is growing (Kapur & Mehta, 2004). As far as India is concerned, Blockchain technology is offered in different institutions and universities with B.Sc., and B.Tech. nomenclature and with the subjects such as Computer Science, Computer Science and Engineering, Information Technology, and so on. Importantly the programs are offered with merged nomenclature such as Cryptography, Distributed Computing, Internet of Things (IoT), Cyber Security, etc. The details of some potential available program are depicted in Fig 6.

Figure 6. Blockchain Technology at Bachelors level in Indian Context

Sl. No.	Degrees offered	Universities
1	BSc IT (Blockchain Technology)	Techno India University
2	BSc IT (Blockchain Technology)	Parul University
3	BSc IT (Blockchain Technology)	Maulana Abul Kalam Azad University of Technology
4	BSc CS (Cryptography &Blockchain)	Karnavati University
5	BTech CSE (Cyber Security & Blockchain Technology)	SASTRA Deemed University
7	BTech CSE (Cyber Security & Blockchain Technology)	Ajeenkya DY Patil University
8	BTech CSE (Blockchain & Distributed Computing)	Vivekananda Global University
9	B.Engg. CSE (Blockchain Technology)	Chitkara University
10	B.Tech. CSE (Blockchain Technology)	University of Petroleum and Energy Studies
11	B.Tech. CS (Blockchain Technology)	Sharda University
12	B.Tech. CSE (Blockchain Technology)	SRM Deemed University
13	B.Tech- Blockchain Technology	Swarnim Startup & Innovation University
14	B.Tech-CSE (Blockchain Technology)	RIMT University
15	B.Tech-CSE (IoT,Cyber Security with Blockchain Technology)	Manakula Vinayagar Institute of Technology
16	B.Tech-CSE (IoT,Cyber Security with Blockchain Technology)	PSCMR College of Engineering & Technology
17	B.Tech-CSE (Blockchain Technology)	The Northcap University
18	BTech CS (Blockchain & Distributed Computing)	Srinivas University
19	B.Tech-CSE (Blockchain Technology)	Chandigarh University
20	B.Tech-CSE (IoT,Cyber Security with Blockchain Technology)	Vasireddy Venkatadri Institute of Technology
21	B.Tech-CSE (IoT,Cyber Security with Blockchain Technology)	Dronacharya Institute of Technology
22	B.Tech-CSE (IoT,Cyber Security with Blockchain Technology)	Gulzar Institute of Technology
23	B.Tech-CSE (Blockchain Technology)	Adamas University
24	B.Tech-CSE (Blockchain Technology)	Poornima University
25	B.Tech-CSE (IoT,Cyber Security with Blockchain Technology)	Sri Ramchandra Institute of Higher Education & Research Deemed University

According to the study it has revealed that, Blockchain Technology is mostly offered with B.Tech. (Bachelor of Technology) degree. However Chitkara University offers a degree called B.Engg. (Bachelor of Engineering) instead of Bachelor of Technology. Furthermore the study shows that most of such degrees available with 4 Years duration and basic eligibility is 10+2 with Pure Science. However Mangalore based Srinivas University offers Bachelor of Technology (B.Tech.) program to any 10+2 qualified. Different allied technologies play a vital role in strengthening IT Systems and among these important are Cloud Computing, Big Data and Analytics, Internet of Things, Crypto currency etc (Hiran & Henten, 2020). Blockchain is useful in government and business sectors. Manpower development is important in order to produce skilled manpower in the areas of banking and finance, agriculture and horticulture, healthcare and medicine, manufacturing and automotive. And there are different job titles available in the areas of Blockchain and among these important are listed in Fig 7.

Figure 7. Blockchain Technology at Bachelors level in Indian Context

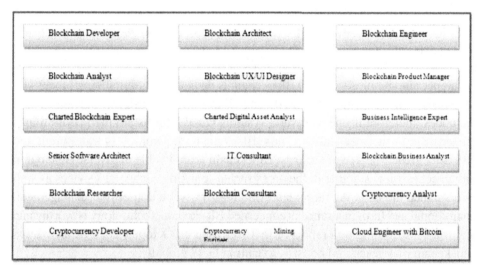

Blockchain Developer is most popular in within all the occupations and therefore having a blockchain degree is not only solving the carrier issues but also unlocking career opportunities as you go. Blockchain skilled professionals are doing following tasks—

- Developing programming code including crypto assets, abilities in blockchain data mining
- Creating as well as implementing cryptocurrencies with the features of hyper ledgers as well as in decentralized applications
- Analyzing importance and role of the business analytics in the areas of business, society and industries.
- To perform the specific needs and challenges of the Blockchain Technology and allied technologies as per current trend.
- To be able in solving management and allied problems in the organizations and institutions (Yang, 2019).

Thus Blockchain educated with Bachelors, Masters and Doctoral qualification should be considered as important in solving the manpower issues. Therefore proper designing and development of the curriculum considered as important. Although training program on the areas of Blockchain should be provided with prime importance.

KEY CHALLENGES IN INDIAN SCENARIO: THE SUMMARY

As far as implementation of Blockchain Technology is concerned lack of knowledge and finding primary challenge considered as important challenge in Indian context. Misconception about the Blockchain is that it may replace the existing systems but real fact is Blockchain Technology helps in integrating existing and new systems for higher amount of efficiency. Blockchain is dedicated in digitalizing blocks and connected with each and every node and all the records basically received by all the nodes, therefore if one or several systems failed in a system then entire things remain kept in the mechanism. Thus, Blockchain Technology is transparent and also offer greater degree of security. Blockchain is applicable in diverse field but in Indian context it is suitable in the areas such as banking, financial services as well as insurance industry. As far as land title registry, vehicle lifecycle management, institutional and farm insurance is concerned Blockchain Technology is worthy and important. According to a report of PwC released on October, 2021 expected that Blockchain may reach and boost 1.76 trillion GDP globally.

The report also expressed that, Blockchain Technology will able in offering provenance as well as traceability which is ultimately worthy in better supply chain management and that may impact about USD 41 billion in India in the year 2030. In addition to the concerned, Blockchain Technology is also suitable in securitization and payment with a worth value at 13.2 billion USD. The careful observation of the above content and study reveals that, Blockchain Technology has following key challenges in Indian context.

- Blockchain Technology has ample opportunities and benefits in diverse sector and at the same time it has very limited awareness regarding its potential utilizations and for the reasons it is not yet moved what the field is expected.
- Unregulated policies and business with reference to the cryptocurrency market considered as important challenge according to the experts, and furthermore there are certain issues in technology, its impact and its usage considered as worthy and important.
- Blockchain Technology is comes with several opportunities and benefits and having complete solutions but a common misconception is that Blockchain is

responsible in destroying existing systems and procedure. Here existing and latest approaches can be integrated together.

- Blockchain Technology is based on different technologies and systems and this is suitable for the financial services and in this regard different Indian banks are adopting Blockchain mechanism and ecosystems but still the concern of the regulations and framework considered as worthy.

- Integration of parallel technology and systems with the blockchain and allied technology such as cloud computing, big data and AI also considered as important and worthy.

- Cryptocurrency in India as illegal therefore the challenges in growth and development in the Blockchain Technology Systems also important to note and it is affects in Indian blockchain market. In India therefore startups are getting their funds from the Initial Coins Offering (ICO) than that of traditional funding process.

Blockchain Technological development in India also suffers from the issue of the manpower and human resources and the same may be developed by adopting suitable strategy and policy.

CONCLUDING REMARKS WITH SUGGESTION

Blockchain technology has significant impact in financial segment and in this regard not only private organization but also Government bodies, establishments and ministries playing leading role for the improvement of the Blockchain technology infrastructure. The study says that, Foreign Direct Investment in India has increased in India in the areas of Computing and IT industry was 26.14 billion USD in the areas of 2020-2021 though in the year 2019-20 it was just 7.67 billion US Dollar. Thus India is to be one of the important technological hubs for the change of the society. Here in addition to the Blockchain few more such as Cloud Computing, Big Data and Analytics, Internet of Things, Crypto currency may be considered as important part for overall and complete development of ICT infrastructure.

REFERENCES

Chattu, V. K., Nanda, A., Chattu, S. K., Kadri, S. M., & Knight, A. W. (2019). The emerging role of blockchain technology applications in routine disease surveillance systems to strengthen global health security. *Big Data and Cognitive Computing*, *3*(2), 25–35. doi:10.3390/bdcc3020025

Chen, G., Xu, B., Lu, M., & Chen, N. S. (2018). Exploring blockchain technology and its potential applications for education. *Smart Learning Environments*, *5*(1), 1–10. doi:10.118640561-017-0050-x

Christ, K. L., & Helliar, C. V. (2021). Blockchain technology and modern slavery: Reducing deceptive recruitment in migrant worker populations. *Journal of Business Research*, *131*, 112–120. doi:10.1016/j.jbusres.2021.03.065

Gabison, G. (2016). Policy considerations for the blockchain technology public and private applications. *SMU Sci. & Tech. L. Rev.*, *19*(1), 327–334.

Gamage, H. T. M., Weerasinghe, H. D., & Dias, N. G. J. (2020). A survey on blockchain technology concepts, applications, and issues. *SN Computer Science*, *1*(2), 1–15. doi:10.100742979-020-00123-0

Gereffi, G., Wadhwa, V., Rissing, B., & Ong, R. (2008). Getting the numbers right: International engineering education in the United States, China, and India. *Journal of Engineering Education*, *97*(1), 13–25. doi:10.1002/j.2168-9830.2008.tb00950.x

Grover, M., Reinicke, B., & Cummings, J. (2016). How secure is education in Information Technology? A method for evaluating security education in IT. *Information Systems Education Journal*, *14*(3), 29–37.

Hiran, K. K., & Henten, A. (2020). An integrated TOE–DoI framework for cloud computing adoption in the higher education sector: Case study of Sub-Saharan Africa, Ethiopia. *International Journal of System Assurance Engineering and Management*, *11*(2), 441–449. doi:10.100713198-019-00872-z

Jain, R. K., Hiran, K., & Paliwal, G. (2012). Quantum Cryptography: A New Generation Of Information Security System. *Proceedings of International Journal of Computers and Distributed Systems*, *2*(1), 42–45.

Jirgensons, M., & Kapenieks, J. (2018). Blockchain and the future of digital learning credential assessment and management. *Journal of Teacher Education for Sustainability*, *20*(1), 145-156.

Kapur, D., & Mehta, P. B. (2004). Indian higher education reform: From half-baked socialism to half-baked capitalism. *Center for International Development Working Paper*, *103*.

Khezr, S., Moniruzzaman, M., Yassine, A., & Benlamri, R. (2019). Blockchain technology in healthcare: A comprehensive review and directions for future research. *Applied Sciences (Basel, Switzerland)*, *9*(9), 1736–1745. doi:10.3390/app9091736

Kumar, N. M., & Mallick, P. K. (2018). Blockchain technology for security issues and challenges in IoT. *Procedia Computer Science*, *132*(1), 1815–1823. doi:10.1016/j.procs.2018.05.140

Kursh, S. R., & Gold, N. A. (2016). Adding fintech and blockchain to your curriculum. *Business Education Innovation Journal*, *8*(2), 6–12.

Lin, W., Huang, X., Fang, H., Wang, V., Hua, Y., Wang, J., Yin, H., Yi, D., & Yau, L. (2020). Blockchain technology in current agricultural systems: From techniques to applications. *IEEE Access: Practical Innovations, Open Solutions*, *8*, 143920–143937. doi:10.1109/ACCESS.2020.3014522

Macrinici, D., Cartofeanu, C., & Gao, S. (2018). Smart contract applications within blockchain technology: A systematic mapping study. *Telematics and Informatics*, *35*(8), 2337–2354. doi:10.1016/j.tele.2018.10.004

Milovanova, M. M., Markova, T. S., Mushrub, V., Ordynskaya, M. E., & Plaksa, J. V. (2020). Business education: Training in the use of blockchain technology for business development. *Revista Inclusiones*, 408-420.

Omar, I. A., Jayaraman, R., Salah, K., Yaqoob, I., & Ellahham, S. (2021). Applications of blockchain technology in clinical trials: Review and open challenges. *Arabian Journal for Science and Engineering*, *46*(4), 3001–3015. doi:10.100713369-020-04989-3

Pane, J., Verhamme, K. M., Shrum, L., Rebollo, I., & Sturkenboom, M. C. (2020). Blockchain technology applications to postmarket surveillance of medical devices. *Expert Review of Medical Devices*, *17*(10), 1123–1132. doi:10.1080/17434440.2020.1825073 PMID:32954855

Paul, P. K., Aithal, P. S., Bhuimali, A., & Kumar, K. (2017). Emerging Degrees and Collaboration: The Context of Engineering Sciences in Computing & IT—An Analysis for Enhanced Policy Formulation in India. *International Journal on Recent Researches In Science. Engineering & Technology*, *5*(12), 13–27.

Paul, P. K., Bhuimali, A., & Chatterjee, D. (2016). Retail Informatics: Basics and emerging scenario with special reference to Design and Development of Proposed MSc-Information Science (Retail Informatics) in Indian Scenario. *International Journal of Information Dissemination and Technology*, *6*(2), 140–144.

Radanović, I., & Likić, R. (2018). Opportunities for use of blockchain technology in medicine. *Applied Health Economics and Health Policy*, *16*(5), 583–590. doi:10.100740258-018-0412-8 PMID:30022440

Saini, H. K., Jain, K. L., Hiran, K. K., & Bhati, A. (2021). Paradigms to make smart city using blockchain. *Blockchain 3.0 for Sustainable Development, 10*, 21.

Sakhipov, A. A., & Baygozhanova, D. S. (2020). Blockchain Technology in Education. *Scientific Evolution*, (1), 36–39.

Siyal, A. A., Junejo, A. Z., Zawish, M., Ahmed, K., Khalil, A., & Soursou, G. (2019). Applications of blockchain technology in medicine and healthcare: Challenges and future perspectives. *Cryptography, 3*(1), 3. doi:10.3390/cryptography3010003

Sun, J., Yan, J., & Zhang, K. Z. (2016). Blockchain-based sharing services: What blockchain technology can contribute to smart cities. *Financial Innovation, 2*(1), 1–9. doi:10.118640854-016-0040-y

Viriyasitavat, W., Da Xu, L., Bi, Z., & Hoonsopon, D. (2019). Blockchain technology for applications in internet of things—Mapping from system design perspective. *IEEE Internet of Things Journal, 6*(5), 8155–8168. doi:10.1109/JIOT.2019.2925825

Williams, P. (2019). Does competency-based education with blockchain signal a new mission for universities? *Journal of Higher Education Policy and Management, 41*(1), 104–117. doi:10.1080/1360080X.2018.1520491

Yang, C. S. (2019). Maritime shipping digitalization: Blockchain-based technology applications, future improvements, and intention to use. *Transportation Research Part E, Logistics and Transportation Review, 131*, 108–117. doi:10.1016/j.tre.2019.09.020

Yang, X. M., Li, X., Wu, H. Q., & Zhao, K. Y. (2017). The application model and challenges of blockchain technology in education. *Modern Distance Education Research, 2*, 34-45.

ADDITIONAL READING

Queiroz, M. M., & Wamba, S. F. (2019). Blockchain adoption challenges in supply chain: An empirical investigation of the main drivers in India and the USA. *International Journal of Information Management, 46*, 70–82. doi:10.1016/j.ijinfomgt.2018.11.021

KEY TERMS AND DEFINITIONS

Blockchain Applications: Blockchain technology utilizations are rising gradually and applicable in diverse areas like Financial and Banking Services, Education and Research, Healthcare and Medical Systems, Government and Administration, Travel and Hospitality, and so on.

Blockchain Technology: Blockchain technology is the encrypted and distributed database connected with the transaction, contract, and depends on different independent record. Blockchain is the digital ledger and a particular place is being used to store data. Blockchain is strengthening the financial segment and activities for proper digital currency like bitcoin transactions.

Cryptocurrency: Cryptocurrency is the encrypted data and which are denotes a unit of currency. Here peer-to-peer network play important role which is called blockchain. This is helpful in securing ledger based digital transactions for the things viz. buying, selling, and transferring.

Financial Engineering: Financial Engineering is a branch of Interdisciplinary Engineering concentrated on designing, development and management of the financial systems, applications, machines, and automation systems.

NFT: NFT is a cryptographic tokens and responsible in dedicated blockchain system development and promotion which are cannot be replicated. The realtime and real-world issues such as artwork and real estate things can be managed and significantly developed.

Quantum: Quantum is the smallest parcels into which are normally having many forms of energy, and which are subdivided. Therefore, quantum is the quantized physical magnitude like magnetic moment.

Quantum Blockchain: Quantum blockchain is helps in proper security management using proper principles of quantum computers, the conventional blockchains is dedicated in collecting records and the same is connecting with the cryptography with the chronological order. Here records of blocks basically encoded (here records are encoded into a series) with photons which are entangled with each other.

Quantum Technologies: Quantum technologies are improving and rising its applications in different places. Among the Quantum segment Quantum Mechanics, Quantum Computing, Quantum Informatics considered as worthy.

Chapter 4

Design of a Blockchain–Powered Biometric Template Security Framework Using Augmented Sharding

Sarika Khandelwal

(iD) https://orcid.org/0000-0003-3336-820X

G. H. Raisoni College of Engineering, Nagpur, India

Shaleen Bhatnagar
Presidency University, India

Nirmal Mungale
G. H. Raisoni College of Engineering, Nagpur, India

Ritesh Kumar Jain
Geetanjali Institute of Technical Studies, India

ABSTRACT

Biometric templates must be secured with traceability, immutability, and high-trust capabilities. A variety of system models are proposed by researchers, most of which either utilize blockchains or machine learning for improved security and quality of service (QoS). The augmented sharding model is designed using light weight incremental learning framework, which assists in shard formation and management. Performance evaluation of the proposed model indicates that it is able to achieve high accuracy attack mitigation, along with low block mining delay and high throughput. This performance is compared with various state-of-the-art methods and an improvement of 10% in terms of delay and 14% in terms of throughput is achieved. Further, an attack detection accuracy of 99.3% is obtained for sybil, masquerading, and man in the middle (MITM) attacks. This text further recommends improvement areas which can be further researched for enhancing security and QoS performance of the proposed model.

DOI: 10.4018/978-1-6684-5072-7.ch004

INTRODUCTION

Securing biometric signatures is a multidomain task, which involves cryptanalysis, privacy protection, traceability integration, signal processing, classification, etc. In order to design a high efficiency secure biometric signature processing system, a wide number of system capabilities are needed. These includes but are not limited to, data security, resilience against tampering, high speed traceability, low computational complexity, and reduced power requirements. An example of such a model is depicted in figure 1, wherein processes like template enrolment, identity claim, and exception handling can be observed. The model utilizes user input for capturing biometric information including, fingerprints, facial data, etc. and provides this information for quality assessment, and feature extraction. The extracted features are given to a template database for storage, which is connected to a system administrator for managerial purposes. The connection between system admin and template matching module is facilitated using an application programming interface (API) layer. This layer exposes the data to various 3rd parties, which might be prone to spying, spoofing, or tampering attacks. Thus, there is a need for a security layer to be integrated between the system and any incoming and outgoing connections from it. Thus, the user data capturing connection, system administrator connection, application connection, and any other connection(s) must be secured using a high-performance security layer, which provides high-speed data read/write capabilities.

In order to design such a security layer, various cryptographic, key-exchange, privacy preservation, and machine learning approaches are proposed by the researchers over the years. A survey of these approaches can be observed from the next section of this text, wherein various nuances, advantages, limitations, and future issues are discussed.

Based on this discussion, it was observed during blockchain mining, each block needs to be scanned for evaluating unique and rule-based hash values. This requires substantial delay with increasing chain length, which reduces scalability of the system. To improve scalability, machine learning models are used, which aims at reducing redundant calculations during storage and retrieval, thereby increasing storage and retrieval speeds. Some of these models have limited integration capabilities with blockchain, due to their internal build structure. Other interfaceable models do not provide a significant performance improvement because large length blockchains require mandatory hash verification and rule validations. Thus, problem statement of this text is to maintain high security with good scalability under different network conditions. To achieve a solution for this problem statement, section 3 discusses design of the proposed blockchain powered biometric template security framework using augmented sharding (BLTSAS), and its performance evaluation. This evaluation also includes comparison with various state-of-the-art methods, which assists in estimating any performance gaps in the proposed model. Finally, this text concludes with some interesting observations about the proposed work, and recommends methods to further improve its performance.

Figure 1. An identity verification model using biometrics

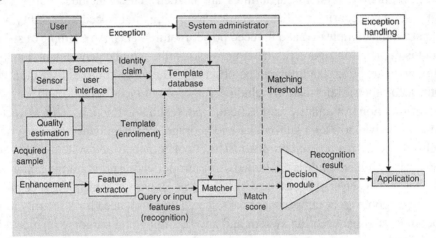

LITERATURE REVIEW

A wide variety of system models are developed for biometric signature security, these models utilize various encryption, hashing and data modification models in order to perform this task. For instance, the work in (Toutara et al., 2020; Sawant et.al., 2020; Goel et.al., 2020; Mohatar et.al., 2019) proposes use of blockchain, smart contracts, queue ordering, and Merkle trees, for biometric data validation and storage. These models propose an initial-level security framework for storing and validation of biometric data, thereby possessing moderate security and moderate QoS performance. The security performance can be improved using the work in (Dinesh et al.,2021; Baqari et al., 2020; Yazdinejad et al.,2020; Shankar et al., 2021; Jain et al., 2012) wherein effect of hash algorithms, blockchain access control, highly distributed blockchain model, and blockchain-based one-time-password (OTP) are proposed. These models work by improving authentication and storage performance of biometric systems via incorporation of highly secure encryption and hashing methods. But they lack in terms of QoS performance due to deployment of high complexity cryptosystems. Lower complexity models are proposed in (Waheed et al.,2020; Mastronardi et al.,2020; Goel et al.,2019; Ibrahim et al., 2021; Khazanchi et al., 2021) wherein smart contracts, radio frequency identification (RFID), low delay convolutional neural networks (CNNs), and centralized synchronization-based e-Voting systems are proposed. These systems utilize low complexity encryption and centralized processing models in order to provide security to biometric storage, which improves the QoS but introduces security vulnerabilities to the system.

Security performance of biometric systems can be improved via use of blockchain-based fuzzy signatures (Naganuma et al.,2020; Hiran et al., 2021), blockchain based self-sovereign identity (Othman et al.,2018), proof-of-work (PoW) based blockchain (Sarkar et al., 2019), and prime number utilization for blockchain verification (Iovane et al., 2019) as proposed in literature. These models provide high security, along with good QoS performance due to scalable blockchain deployments. This security performance can further improved using authentication protocols mentioned in (Ali et al., 2019), splitting of Geometric Centre both horizontally and vertically(Jangid et al.,2020), proof-of-stake (PoS) based blockchain(Jaffer et al.,2019), proof-of-authority (PoA) (Morano et al.,2020), and hybrid fusion of public key cryptography (Iovane et al.,2020; Tyagi et al.,2021). These models assist in improving biometric storage security via attack pre-emption, and addition of classification models as a measure of improved pattern analysis during attacks. Similar models are proposed in (Alharthi et al., 2021; Xiang et al., 2020; Gulati et al., 2019; Liu et al., 2019) wherein privacy preservation blockchain biometrics, permissioned blockchain-based user authentication, identity based blockchains, and identity based smart contracts. These models assist in improving biometric storage security and QoS performance by reducing redundancies during block formation and modification. It is observed that hash size can be increased in order to reduce complexity of hash validation, and inherently increasing blockchain security. Application specific storage models are defined in (Hongqing et al.,2018; Bathen et al.,2020; Madine et al.,2021; Wireko et al.,2028), wherein industrial data storage, self-driving data storage, and cross application electronic medical record (EMR) storage systems are defined. The efficiency of these models are further extended using (Acquah et al.,2020; Mandal et al.,2020), wherein distributed storage, and certificateless signcryption for internet of things (IoT) are proposed. These models assist in improving QoS of biometric storage via selective encryption, and reducing complexity of certificate exchange during blockchain formation. Based on these models it is observed that blockchain based models have become de-facto for storing biometric data, and have a wide range of research enhancements. One such system model is described in the next section, wherein sharding is used for improving security and QoS of biometric data.

DESIGN OF A BLOCKCHAIN POWERED BIOMETRIC TEMPLATE SECURITY FRAMEWORK USING AUGMENTED SHARDING

The proposed blockchain-based method for providing biometric template security uses augmented sharding. It is implemented using modified version of league championship algorithm (LCA), that assists in shard creation and maintenance. The modified LCA method selects the best sharding strategy for providing high security, low delay and good throughput performance. The protocol is divided into 2 parts, which combine together to form the final system,

- Proof of Work (PoW) based blockchain design for secure storage of biometric scans.
- Shard creation by tracking changes in biometric scans.
- Utilizing changes in biometric scans for shard management and merging.

The shard management and merging model is dependent on shard creation model; thus, they must be implemented in tandem for design of a highly secure biometric storage system. A detailed description of these parts is defined in the following sub-sections.

Proof of Work (PoW) Based Blockchain Design for Secure Storage of Biometric Scans

Design of a secure biometric storage model must be able to provide immutability, traceability, high speed retrieval and distributed computing capabilities. In order to design such a system model, this section proposes a PoW consensus based blockchain storage model. Each biometric scan is stored on the blockchain using the block structure observed from table 1, wherein blockchain entities including hash of previous block, type of biometric data stored, actual biometric data, timestamp of storage, a hash checking nonce value, and hash of the current block are stored. The secure hashing algorithm in 256-bit mode (SHA256) is used in order to generate hash values from the block.

Table 1. Design of the biometric scan storage block

Prev. Hash	Biometric Type	Biometric Data
Timestamp	Nonce	Block Hash

In order to store a given biometric scan into the blockchain, following steps are used,

- The biometric scan is converted into a 1D array without quantization.
- Information including scan size, scan dimensions, and other metadata is prepended to this biometric scan data.
- Using this information, a new block is formed as per table 1.
- A random value of nonce is generated, and block hash is evaluated using equation 1 as follows,

$$B_{hash} = SHA256(P_{hash} | B_{type} | B_{data} | T_s | nonce) \tag{1}$$

Where, P_{hash}, B_{type}, B_{daa}, and T_s represents previous hash, biometric type, biometric data, and timestamp of block creation.

- If this hash is already present in the chain, then a new nonce value is generated, which results into a new hash value.
- Once a unique hash value is generated, then the block is added to the chain, and this process is repeated for every new biometric scan.

As the number of scans increase, the complexity of hash generation also increases. This results into an increase in delay needed to add a block to the chain, which reduces quality of service (QoS) of the blockchain storage model. To improve this QoS, smaller blockchains (shards) are created, and managed as per the process defined in following sections respectively.

Shard Creation by Tracking Changes in Biometric Scans

Shard creation is the process of dividing the underlying blockchain into smaller chains, wherein each chain is independently managed by the main storage processing unit. It uses a modified version of LCA, and can be elaborated using the following steps,

- Input Parameters,
    - Number of games (NG)
    - Number of leagues (NL)
    - LCA learning rate (L_r)
    - Current number of shards (N_{curr})
    - Mean delay for adding a block to the chain (D_{mean})
    - Minimum length of shard (L_{min})
    - Minimum length of shard (L_{max})

- Initialize all games as 'to be mutated' and follow the given process in order to obtain the best shard length for the currently deployed blockchain solution in the network,
  - For each game 1 to NG
  - For each league 1 to NL
  - If the current league is marked as 'not to be mutated', then go to the next league, else process this league.
  - Formulate a random shard length ($S_{l_{new}}$) using equation 2, and generate a new shard with the given length,

$$S_{l_{new}} = rand(L_{min}, L_{max})\tag{2}$$

  - Evaluate number of packets processed per unit time (PPU_t) using equation 3, which is an estimate of number of blocks added to the shard in a given time interval,

$$PPU_t = \int_0^t \frac{B_p(t)}{B_t(t)}.dt + \int_0^t \frac{B_d(t)}{B_t(t)}.dt\tag{3}$$

Where, $B_p(t)$, $B_d(t)$ and $B_t(t)$ are the number of biometric signatures passed per unit time, dropped per unit time and total biometric packets added per unit time respectively.

- Evaluate league fitness using equation 4,

$$f_L = \frac{\sum_{i=1}^{N_s} \dfrac{\dfrac{E_{ci}}{E_{max}} + \dfrac{B_{ci}}{B_{max}}}{\dfrac{D_{ci}}{D_{max}}}}{N_s}\tag{4}$$

Where, N_c is the sample number of blocks added to the chain, D_i, E_i, and B_i represents end-to-end delay, energy needed and number of blocks successfully added to the chain for the given iteration.

- Find fitness of each league, and then evaluate threshold league fitness using equation 5 as follows,

$$L_{th} = \frac{\sum_{i=1}^{NL} f_i}{NL} * L_r \qquad (5)$$

- Mark all solutions as 'to be mutated', which have league fitness less than L_{th}, mark other solutions as 'not to be mutated', and go to the next game playing iteration.

Once all solutions are evaluated, then find the sharding solution that has maximum fitness, which indicates maximum energy saving, maximum block forwarding, and minimum end-to-delay performance. Let the selected shard length be SL_{sel}, find the average sidechain length (SL_{avg}) for the system using equation 6,

$$SL_{avg} = \frac{\sum_{i=1}^{N_{curr}} L_i}{N_{curr}} \qquad (6)$$

Where, 'L' is length of the current shard. Accept this new sidechain only if it satisfies equation 7,

$$SL_{sel} \geq SL_{avg} * L_r \text{ and } SL_{sel} \leq S_{max} * L_r \qquad (7)$$

This will indicate that the current blockchain shard is growing incrementally, and optimum number of blockchain shards are created. Based on this process, new shards are created and biometric information is added to them. This process is evaluated every time a new biometric data is added to the system, and is used to evaluate if a new chain is needed and creates the shard if needed. Once these chains are created, then shard management module is activated, which is described in the next section.

Utilizing Changes in Biometric Scans for Shard Management and Merging

Each blockchain shard is stored on a group of closely placed nodes. As soon as there are changes in the biometric storage capacity, then the merging and management layer is activated. This layer is capable of automatically managing the shards and merge or split them as per storage requirements. This is needed so that optimum number of blockchain shards are created, and each shard consists of an optimum number of biometric entries. In order to perform this task of automatic management, the following steps are executed,

- Input
  - Number of nodes in each shard (N_{shard})
  - Current number of shards (N_{curr})
  - Index of the shard which is being checked (S_i)
- A dynamic shard clustering model is used in order to identify the shard index to which current shard's data can be offloaded. This model works using the following steps,
  - Let the average value of biometric data in the current shard 'S_i' be (x_1, x_2, x_3, ...,x_n)
  - Find the average distance of all shards from the shard, using the following equation,

$$d_s = \frac{\sqrt{\sum_{j=1}^{N_{curr}} \sum_{k=1}^{n} \left(x_{j_k} - x_{i_k} \right)^2}}{N_{curr}^2} \tag{8}$$

  - Virtually merge all shards for the 'S_i' indexed sidechain into the given sidechain if the value of $d_s \leq R$, where R is selected depending upon system performance.
- Evaluate the following equation 9, for all shards where the merging process has been done,

$$f_{opt_j} = \frac{d_{s_j}}{E_j * F_j} \tag{9}$$

Where, f_{opt_j} is the optimization factor for the jth shard, while 'E' and 'F' are the average energy values, and average blockchain data forwarding ratios for storage devices participating in the given shard.

- Select the shard for merging with minimum value of f_{opt_j}, such that this value is less than the following variance threshold formulated in equation 10. If none of the shards follow the given threshold, then the current shard is not merged with any other shard, and is managed individually.

$$V_{th} = \sqrt{\frac{\left(\sum_{i=1}^{N_{curr}} f_{opt_i} - \frac{\sum_{j=1}^{N_{curr}} f_{opt_j}}{N_{curr}}\right)^2}{N_{curr}} * \frac{\sum_{i=1}^{N_{curr}} f_{opt_i}}{N_{curr}}} \qquad (10)$$

Due to this process, effective merging and management of shards is performed. Once the shard management layer is activated, then optimum shards are automatically created and managed with minimum supervision. All these modules are connected together in order to perform effective biometric data storage with high security. The performance of this network can be observed in the next section, wherein metrics like delay, throughput, and attack detection accuracy are compared with state-of-the art algorithms.

DATA COLLECTION AND RESULT ANALYSIS

In order to evaluate QoS and security performance of the proposed BLTSAS, the sharding system was tested with a large number of biometric data inputs. The numbers of users whose data is being stored was varied from 10 to 150, and the following attacks were injected into the system,

- Sybil attack
- Man-in-the-middle (MITM) attack
- Masquerading attack

Because of multiple sharding check points, and the immutable nature of the underlying PoW blockchain, the storage network is able to detect all these attacks with 100% accuracy. Thus, making the system highly secure against these known attacks and most probably any unknown attacks as well. Each biometric signature stored in the sharded network is passed through multiple validation, and verification checks, due to which such a high security performance is achieved. Upon completing these security checks, QoS parameters like end-to-end delay, energy consumption, throughput, packet delivery ratio and jitter are compared by varying the number of stored signatures from 10 to 50 for 10 to 150 users. The following tables showcase the QoS results for the proposed sharding protocol compared with non-sharding, (Naganuma et al.,2020) and (Alharthi et al., 2021) based systems. These results were obtained by calculating average values of energy consumed and delay needed by the given network storage during multiple biometric data storage. Based on this, delay to add multiple blocks to the shards for 10 users is tabulated in table 2 as follows, the table also compares delay performance of different non-sharding models, which assists in evaluating superiority of the proposed sidechain solution.

Table 2. Delay for 10 users

Num. Blocks	Delay (Naganuma et al.,2020) (us)	Delay (Alharthi et al., 2021) (us)	Delay (Proposed) (us)
10	869.4	1304.1	660.6
20	1081.8	1622.7	821.7
35	1251.9	1877.4	951.3
45	1355.4	2033.1	1030.5
50	1490.4	2236.5	1134
55	1627.2	2441.7	1237.5
65	1701.9	2552.4	1293.3
90	1763.1	2645.1	1341
100	1907.1	2862	1450.8

The speed is improved by almost 18% when compared with other sharding systems, which is due to effective shard creation and merging process. Similar performance improvement is observed for 50 users, and can be observed from table 3,

Table 3. Delay for 50 users

Num. Blocks	Delay (Naganuma et al.,2020) (us)	Delay (Alharthi et al., 2021) (us)	Delay (Proposed) (us)
10	1044	1565.1	792.9
20	1298.7	1946.7	986.4
35	1503	2252.7	1141.2
45	1626.3	2439.9	1236.6
50	1789.2	2684.7	1359.9
55	1953	2930.4	1484.1
65	2041.2	3063.6	1552.5
90	2115.9	3174.3	1609.2
100	2087.1	3132	1587.6

The delay is reduced by almost 20% when compared with (Naganuma et al.,2020), and 26.8% when compared with (Alharthi et al., 2021), that describe other sidechaining systems, which is due to automatic sidechain management and merging. Similar performance improvement is observed for 100 users, and can be observed from table 4,

Table 4. Delay for 100 users

Num. Blocks	Delay (Naganuma et al.,2020) (us)	Delay (Alharthi et al., 2021) (us)	Delay (Proposed) (us)
10	1260.9	1890.9	958.5
20	1568.7	2352.6	1192.5
35	1815.3	2722.5	1379.7
45	1965.6	2948.4	1494
50	2162.7	3243.6	1644.3
55	2360.7	3539.7	1794.6
65	2467.8	3700.8	1875.6
90	2556.9	3835.8	1944
100	2312.1	3468.6	1757.7

Figure 2. Delay performance of different sidechain algorithms

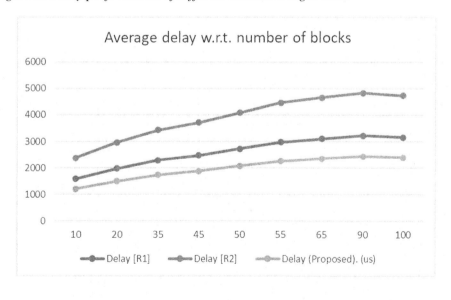

The speed is improved by almost 24% when compared with (Naganuma et al.,2020), and 31.5% when compared with (Alharthi et al., 2021), that describe other sidechaining systems, which is due to shard merging and automatic shard management. Thus, an average delay reduction of 20% is achieved, which can be observed from figure 2 wherein average delay is visualized against number of blocks.

Similar performance improvement is observed for energy consumption, and is tabulated in tables 5, 6 and 7.

Table 5. Energy for 10 users

Num. Blocks	Energy (Alharthi et al., 2021) (mJ)	Energy (Alharthi et al., 2021) (mJ)	Energy (Proposed) (mJ)
10	10.00	14.99	7.61
20	11.38	17.07	8.66
35	12.11	18.16	9.21
45	13.02	19.52	9.89
50	13.77	20.66	10.47
55	14.40	21.61	10.95
65	14.94	22.41	11.36
90	15.67	23.50	11.91
100	16.71	25.07	12.70

Table 6. Energy for 50 users

Num. Blocks	Energy (Naganuma et al.,2020) (mJ)	Energy (Alharthi et al., 2021) (mJ)	Energy (Proposed) (mJ)
10	13.00	19.49	9.88
20	14.80	22.19	11.25
35	15.74	23.61	11.97
45	16.93	25.38	12.87
50	17.90	26.85	13.62
55	18.73	28.09	14.24
65	19.42	29.12	14.76
90	20.37	30.55	15.48
100	21.84	31.42	16.35

Table 7. Energy for 100 users

Num. Blocks	Energy (Naganuma et al.,2020) (mJ)	Energy (Alharthi et al., 2021) (mJ)	Energy (Proposed) (mJ)
10	17.99	26.99	13.68
20	20.48	30.73	15.57
35	21.80	32.69	16.57
45	23.44	35.14	17.81
50	24.79	37.17	18.84
55	25.94	38.90	19.71
65	26.89	40.33	20.44
90	28.20	42.30	21.44
100	29.50	43.81	22.14

Energy consumption is reduced by 15% when compared with (Naganuma et al.,2020), and 23.6% when compared with (Alharthi et al., 2021), that describe other algorithms, which indicates an improvement in overall network lifetime. Comparison for 50 users can be observed from table 6.

As number of nodes increase, the energy efficiency is improved. For 50 users the energy consumption is reduced by over 20%, which is due to the fact that sidechain merging has larger effect as number of users are increased. This effect can be observed with 100 nodes in the following table 7.

From the results observed in the table 5, 6 and 7 it can be observed that the proposed sharding model has reduced the delay needed for communication by almost 20% when compared with other sidechain solutions. This indicates an increase in overall system speed, and implies that the proposed model can be used for real-time high speed biometric storage systems. This can also be observed from figure 2, wherein average delay performance of all communications is combined. Similarly, energy performance indicates that the proposed sharding solution is 18% more energy efficient than other sidechain systems. This can also be observed from figure 3, wherein energy performance of these algorithms is visually compared.

Similar comparison is done for other QoS parameters like throughput, jitter and packet delivery ratio. Results of this comparison can be observed from the following table 8, wherein it can be observed that the proposed sharding model outperforms other models for all the QoS parameters. Thereby making the system applicable for real-time use in high performance, high trustability, high transparency, and low energy, high security, biometric storage systems.

Figure 3. Energy performance of the proposed sharding architectures

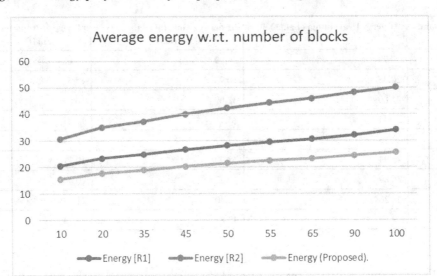

Table 8. Comparative performance of QoS parameters

Parameter	(Naganuma et al.,2020)	(Alharthi et al., 2021)	Proposed
Delay (us)	2100.60	3727.80	2029.50
Energy (mJ)	22.86	44.28	22.32
Throughput (kbps)	232.20	159.30	246.60
Jitter (us)	54.43	114.91	52.56
Packet delivery ratio (%)	89.08	75.72	89.55

An average performance improvement of over 20% is achieved in the overall QoS of the system, and can be observed from figure 4, wherein average performance improvement of different QoS parameters can be seen.

Due to this improvement, the underlying system can be used for real-time biometric storage, which require high security and high quality of service without compromising on either of the parameters. In terms of cost analysis, the model would be able to reduce deployment cost by 25% when compared with standard blockchain models. This cost analysis includes delay needed, energy consumed, throughput achieved, and packet delivery ratio of the proposed model w.r.t. existing blockchain models on different network deployments.

Figure 4. Average QoS improvement

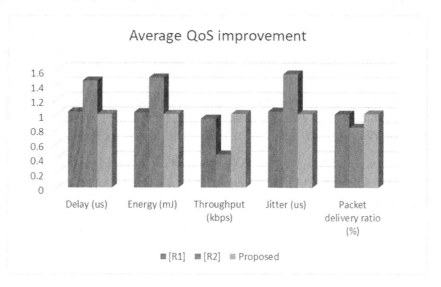

CONCLUSION AND FUTURE SCOPE

Sharding is used in order to reduce overall delay and energy consumption of biometric storage system via effective blockchain splitting. This splitting allows the blockchain to reduce number of computations needed in order to add, update, search and access internal blocks. Shards when combined can further improve upon the overall system performance by reducing delay and number of computations needed for hashing. Due to this combination, the proposed model is able to obtain over 20% reduction in communication delay, over 25% reduction in energy consumption, and over 20% improvement in overall storage throughput. Due to faster storage performance across fewer number of blocks, the probability of packet dropping is also reduced, this results in increasing the packet delivery ratio by 10% and reducing overall delay jitter by over 15% when compared with other sidechaining algorithms.

In future, researchers can further extend the performance of this algorithm by using better block truncation algorithms, and by utilizing improved machine learning models for shard creation. Moreover, the truncated data parts can be given moderate level of security in order to reduce chances of modification due to external and internal attacks, which will further strengthen network security.

REFERENCES

Acquah, M. A., Chen, N., Pan, J. S., Yang, H. M., & Yan, B. (2020). Securing Fingerprint Template Using Blockchain and Distributed Storage System. *Symmetry*, *12*(6), 951. doi:10.3390ym12060951

al Baqari, M., & Barka, E. (2020). *Biometric-Based Blockchain EHR System (BBEHR). In 2020 International Wireless Communications and Mobile Computing*. IWCMC. doi:10.1109/IWCMC48107.2020.9148357

Alharthi, A., Ni, Q., & Jiang, R. (2021). A Privacy-Preservation Framework Based on Biometrics Blockchain (BBC) to Prevent Attacks in VANET. *IEEE Access: Practical Innovations, Open Solutions, 9,* 87299–87309. doi:10.1109/ACCESS.2021.3086225

Ali, W. A., Sahib, N. M., & Waleed, J. (2019). Preservation Authentication and Authorization on Blockchain. *2019 2nd International Conference on Engineering Technology and Its Applications (IICETA)*. 10.1109/IICETA47481.2019.9012996

Bathen, L. A. D., Flores, G. H., & Jadav, D. (2020). RiderS: Towards a Privacy-Aware Decentralized Self-Driving Ride-Sharing Ecosystem. *2020 IEEE International Conference on Decentralized Applications and Infrastructures (DAPPS)*. 10.1109/DAPPS49028.2020.00004

Delgado-Mohatar, O., Fierrez, J., Tolosana, R., & Vera-Rodriguez, R. (2019). Biometric Template Storage With Blockchain: A First Look Into Cost and Performance Tradeoffs. *2019 IEEE/CVF Conference on Computer Vision and Pattern Recognition Workshops (CVPRW)*. 10.1109/CVPRW.2019.00342

Dinesh, A. D., Durga Prasad Reddy, C., Gopi, G. V., Jain, R., & Shankar, T. N. (2021). A Durable Biometric Authentication Scheme via Blockchain. *2021 International Conference on Advances in Electrical, Computing, Communication and Sustainable Technologies (ICAECT)*. 10.1109/ICAECT49130.2021.9392415

Goel, A., Agarwal, A., Vatsa, M., Singh, R., & Ratha, N. (2019). Securing CNN Model and Biometric Template using Blockchain. *2019 IEEE 10th International Conference on Biometrics Theory, Applications and Systems (BTAS)*. 10.1109/BTAS46853.2019.9185999

Goel, U., Sonanis, R., Rastogi, I., Lal, S., & De, A. (2020). Criticality Aware Orderer for Heterogeneous Transactions in Blockchain. *2020 IEEE International Conference on Blockchain and Cryptocurrency (ICBC)*. 10.1109/ICBC48266.2020.9169439

Gulati, H., & Huang, C. T. (2019). Self-Sovereign Dynamic Digital Identities based on lockchain Technology. *2019 SoutheastCon*. doi:10.1109/SoutheastCon42311.2019.9020518

Hiran, K. K., Khazanchi, D., Vyas, A. K., & Padmanaban, S. (2021). Machine learning for sustainable development. *Machine Learning for Sustainable Development*. doi:10.1515/9783110702514

Hongqing, G., Peiyong, S., Wenzhong, G., & Kun, G. (2018). Component-based Assembling Tool and Runtime Engine for the Machine Learning Process. *2018 International Conference on Cloud Computing, Big Data and Blockchain (ICCBB)*. 10.1109/ICCBB.2018.8756448

Ibrahim, M., Ravindran, K., Lee, H., Farooqui, O., & Mahmoud, Q. H. (2021). ElectionBlock: An Electronic Voting System using Blockchain and Fingerprint Authentication. *2021 IEEE 18th International Conference on Software Architecture Companion (ICSA-C)*. 10.1109/ICSA-C52384.2021.00033

Iovane, G., Bisogni, C., de Maio, L., & Nappi, M. (2020). An Encryption Approach Using Information Fusion Techniques Involving Prime Numbers and Face Biometrics. *IEEE Transactions on Sustainable Computing*, 5(2), 260–267. doi:10.1109/TSUSC.2018.2793466

Iovane, G., Nappi, M., Chinnici, M., Petrosino, A., Castiglione, A., & Barra, S. (2019). A Novel Blockchain Scheme Combining Prime Numbers and Iris for Encrypting Coding. *2019 IEEE Intl Conf on Dependable, Autonomic and Secure Computing, Intl Conf on Pervasive Intelligence and Computing, Intl Conf on Cloud and Big Data Computing, Intl Conf on Cyber Science and Technology Congress(DASC/PiCom/CBDCom/CyberSciTech)*. 10.1109/DASC/PiCom/CBDCom/CyberSciTech.2019.00117

Jaffer, S. A., Pandey, S., Mehta, R., & Bhavathankar, P. (2020). Blockchain Based Direct Benefit Transfer System For Subsidy Delivery. *2020 International Conference for Emerging Technology (INCET)*. 10.1109/INCET49848.2020.9154178

Jain, R. K., Hiran, K., & Paliwal, G. (2012). Quantum Cryptography: A New Generation Of Information Security System. *Proceedings of International Journal of Computers and Distributed Systems*.

Jangid, P. S., & Bharadi, V. A. (2020). Evolving Authentication Design Consideration and BaaS Architecture for Internet of Biometric things. *2020 International Conference on Convergence to Digital World - Quo Vadis (ICCDW)*. 10.1109/ICCDW45521.2020.9318664

Khazanchi, D., Vyas, A. K., Hiran, K. K., & Padmanaban, S. (Eds.). (2021). *Blockchain 3.0 for sustainable development* (Vol. 10). Walter de Gruyter GmbH & Co KG.

Liu, Y., Sun, G., & Schuckers, S. (2019). Enabling Secure and Privacy Preserving Identity Management via Smart Contract. *2019 IEEE Conference on Communications and Network Security (CNS)*. 10.1109/CNS.2019.8802771

Madine, M., Salah, K., Jayaraman, R., Al-Hammadi, Y., Arshad, J., & Yaqoob, I. (2021). appXchain: Application-Level Interoperability for Blockchain Networks. *IEEE Access: Practical Innovations, Open Solutions, 9*, 87777–87791. doi:10.1109/ACCESS.2021.3089603

Mandal, S., Bera, B., Sutrala, A. K., Das, A. K., Choo, K. K. R., & Park, Y. (2020). Certificateless-Signcryption-Based Three-Factor User Access Control Scheme for IoT Environment. *IEEE Internet of Things Journal, 7*(4), 3184–3197. doi:10.1109/JIOT.2020.2966242

Mastronardi, G., & Tato, S. I. (2020). HoSè: Hospital Security - How to make the surgical site safer using RFID blockchain and biometric techniques. *2020 IEEE International Symposium on Medical Measurements and Applications (MeMeA)*. 10.1109/MeMeA49120.2020.9137348

Morano, F., Ferretti, C., Leporati, A., Napoletano, P., & Schettini, R. (2019). A blockchain technology for protection and probative value preservation of vehicle driver data. *2019 IEEE 23rd International Symposium on Consumer Technologies (ISCT)*. 10.1109/ISCE.2019.8900982

Naganuma, K., Suzuki, T., Yoshino, M., Takahashi, K., Kaga, Y., & Kunihiro, N. (2020). New Secret Key Management Technology for Blockchains from Biometrics Fuzzy Signature. *2020 15th Asia Joint Conference on Information Security (AsiaJCIS)*. 10.1109/AsiaJCIS50894.2020.00020

Othman, A., & Callahan, J. (2018). The Horcrux Protocol: A Method for Decentralized Biometric-based Self-sovereign Identity. *2018 International Joint Conference on Neural Networks (IJCNN)*. 10.1109/IJCNN.2018.8489316

Sawant, G., & Bharadi, V. (2020). Permission Blockchain based Smart Contract Utilizing Biometric Authentication as a Service: A Future Trend. *2020 International Conference on Convergence to Digital World - Quo Vadis (ICCDW)*. 10.1109/ICCDW45521.2020.9318715

Shankar, T. N., Rakesh, P., Bhargawa Rao, T., Hari Bharadwaj, L., Rakesh, C., & Lakshmi Madhuri, M. (2021). Providing Security to Land Record with the computation of Iris, Blockchain, and One Time Password. *2021 International Conference on Computing, Communication, and Intelligent Systems (ICCCIS).* 10.1109/ICCCIS51004.2021.9397176

Toutara, F., & Spathoulas, G. (2020). A distributed biometric authentication scheme based on blockchain. *2020 IEEE International Conference on Blockchain (Blockchain).* 10.1109/Blockchain50366.2020.00068

Tyagi, S. K. S., Mukherjee, A., Pokhrel, S. R., & Hiran, K. (2020a). An Intelligent and Optimal Resource Allocation Approach in Sensor Networks for Smart Agri-IoT. *Smart Agri-IoT. IEEE Sensors Journal, 21*(16), 17439–17446. https://doi.org/10.1109/JSEN.2020.3020889

V., S., Sarkar, A., Paul, A., & Mishra, S. (2019). Block Chain Based Cloud Computing Model on EVM Transactions for Secure Voting. *2019 3rd International Conference on Computing Methodologies and Communication (ICCMC).* doi:10.1109/ICCMC.2019.8819649

Waheed, A., & Venkata Krishna, P. (2020). Comparing Biometric and Blockchain Security Mechanisms in Smart Parking System. *2020 International Conference on Inventive Computation Technologies (ICICT).* 10.1109/ICICT48043.2020.9112483

Wireko, J. K., Hiran, K. K., & Doshi, R. (2018). Culturally Based User Resistance to New Technologies in the Age of IoT In Developing Countries: Perspectives From Ethiopia. *International Journal of Emerging Technology and Advanced Engineering, 8*(4), 96–105.

Xiang, X., Wang, M., & Fan, W. (2020). A Permissioned Blockchain-Based Identity Management and User Authentication Scheme for E-Health Systems. *IEEE Access: Practical Innovations, Open Solutions, 8,* 171771–171783. doi:10.1109/ACCESS.2020.3022429

Yazdinejad, A., Srivastava, G., Parizi, R. M., Dehghantanha, A., Choo, K. K. R., & Aledhari, M. (2020). Decentralized Authentication of Distributed Patients in Hospital Networks Using Blockchain. *IEEE Journal of Biomedical and Health Informatics, 24*(8), 2146–2156. doi:10.1109/JBHI.2020.2969648 PMID:31995507

KEY TERMS AND DEFINITIONS

Application Programming Interface (API): It simplify software development and innovation by enabling applications to exchange data and functionality easily and securely.

Block: Block is a place in a blockchain where information is stored and encrypted.

Convolutional Neural Network (CNN): A convolutional neural network (CNN) is a type of artificial neural network used in image recognition and processing.

Hash: Hash is a function that meets the encrypted demands needed to solve for a blockchain computation.

Internet of Things (IoT): Describes physical objects (or groups of such objects) with sensors, processing ability, software, and other technologies that connect and exchange data with other devices and systems over the Internet or other communications networks.

Jitter: Is the variation in the time between packets arriving, caused by network congestion, timing drift, or route changes.

League Championship Algorithm (LCA): Is a population-based algorithm framework for global optimization over a continuous search space.

Man in the Middle (MITM) Attack: A man in the middle (MITM) attack is a general term for when a perpetrator positions himself in a conversation between a user and an application.

Proof of Authority (PoA): Is an algorithm used with blockchains that delivers comparatively fast transactions through a consensus mechanism based on identity as a stake.

Proof-of-Authority (PoA): Is an algorithm used with blockchains that delivers comparatively fast transactions through a consensus mechanism based on identity as a stake.

Proof-of-Stake (PoS): Is a cryptocurrency consensus mechanism for processing transactions and creating new blocks in a blockchain. A consensus mechanism is a method for validating entries into a distributed database and keeping the database secure.

Public Key Crytography (PKC): Public key cryptography involves a pair of keys known as a public key and a private key (a public key pair), which are associated with an entity that needs to authenticate its identity electronically or to sign or encrypt data.

Quality of Service (QoS): It is the use of mechanisms or technologies that work on a network to control traffic and ensure the performance of critical applications with limited network capacity.

Radio Frequency Identification (RFID): It is a type of passive wireless technology that allows for tracking or matching of an item or individual.

Secure Hashing Algorithm in 256-Bit Mode (SHA256): SHA-256 is a patented cryptographic hash function that outputs a value that is 256 bits long.

Threshold Cryptosystem: The basis for the field of threshold cryptography, is a cryptosystem that protects information by encrypting it and distributing it among a cluster of fault-tolerant computers.

Chapter 5

Green Currency Based on Blockchain Technology for Sustainable Development

Punit Sharma
https://orcid.org/0000-0001-5318-9124
Janardan Rai Nagar Rajasthan Vidyapeeth, India

Indu Sharma
Meera Girls College, India

Suman Pamecha
Janardan Rai Nagar Rajasthan Vidyapeeth, India

Kamal Kant Hiran
Sir Padampat Singhania University, India

ABSTRACT

English poet Samuel T. Coleridge wrote "O! lady, we receive but what we give? And nature alone lives in our lives." The Earth is one, but nations are not. New technology, especially blockchain paves the way toward a global village. This chapter analyses the ultimate solution to the global warming issue through the introduction of green currency based on blockchain technology to inculcate the concept of environmental protection in the next generation. We never value the free gifts of nature as the economies are driven by markets globally. Unless and until a monetary value is associated with environmental protection it's difficult to motivate the next generation to protect it. The introduction of green currency helps in creating a market. Development with the acceptance, protection, and maintenance of nature as it is is possible only through the use of advanced technologies. This chapter introduces a new concept of global green currency based on blockchain technology. This tool may ultimately present a platform as a solution to the global warming issue.

DOI: 10.4018/978-1-6684-5072-7.ch005

INTRODUCTION

Today, we are confronted with a truly global problem: global warming. It is truly global in the sense that it affects and also is accountable for not one or two countries, but the entire human race. According to the World Health Organization (WHO), climate change causes at least 150,000 fatalities every year, with that number anticipated to quadruple by 2030 (Paritosh Kasotia, n.d.). Global warming will have disastrous health implications. We've been working on it for a long time, but we haven't been able to come to an agreement since different countries have different objectives and instruments for dealing with the problem. Nobody is attempting to focus on a market-based solution to instill environmentally conscious habits in the next generation. We may redesign the economic system by introducing the concept of green currency, which naturally assigns value to the environment by re-establishing nature-human connectivity (Acheampong et al., 2018).

Comparison of Various Models Adopted to Solve Environment Issues

For the last fifty years, various steps are taken globally to limit global temperature to 1.5 to 2 degrees above the pre-industrial level. In the Kyoto agreement, carbon credit trading was made permissible between nations for sustainable development. This market failed due to various anomalies. After that, in the Paris agreement, all nations joined hands to fight this global issue(*The Paris Agreement*, n.d.)(Parry, 2019). Below we have tabularized the main features of various models adopted to solve Environment Issues and compared them with the proposed Green Currency Market approach. According to Berck and Helfand market based incentives (MBI) turns environment protection into just another market goods so this one is inferior to command and control (CAC) model. The superiority of one model over another depends upon the circumstances. (Berck & Helfand, 2005)

Table 1. Comparison between the proposed Green Currency Market approach and Environment Issues

GREEN TAX	GREEN SUBSIDY	Deposit/ Refund System	Pollution Permit Trading System	GREEN CURRENCY MARKET (New Proposed Approach)
Fee charged from the poluter	Financial assistance for pollution reduction	Imposes an upfront charge to pay for potential damage and refunds it for returning a product for recycling.	Establishes a market for rights to pollute by issuing tradeable pollution credits, allows emissions below a fixed level	Provides logic for pollution permits based on the potential of an area for development
Ex- Pigouvian tax, unit tax on the product equal to the MEC	1. abatement equipment subsidies- make abatement tech. affordable 2. Pollution reduction subsidies per unit but without entry, barriers its not effective in the long run	It is designed to force polluters to account for both the MPC and MEC	There is a provision for trading these permits	Links development potential with GA value, and logically determines saturation point for development
Not practically possible to calculate MEC, hence the level of tax		Targets potential polluters instead of the actual polluter		Permits trade for GA in VGC. A proper account is maintained through Blockchain technology
This model only allows output reduction, unrealistic as does not guarantee emission control				Transparent and fully technical system for trading VGC. Ensure economic as well as ecological balance in long run.

CONCEPT OF GREEN CURRENCY

At the moment, each country has its own monetary currency. In order to value the environment, we'll need an international virtual green currency based on green asset valuation. The environmental assets have total value but no marginal value is realized, that's why we never value environmental green assets. Because market prices are determined by marginal value rather than overall value, Marginal Value generation is a must in the case of environmental issues. Reservation of a reasonable price is a must for the environment if we are to handle the global warming issue adequately. First of all, the question arises-

Why do we undervalue the environment?
Why are nations abiding by treaties not interested to follow them strictly?
Why did the economic models fail to deal with the issue?
Why do we still not in a position to create a value system for Next-Gen regarding the environment?
Do the markets have a solution to this global problem?'

The answer in one world is the market. It is the culprit and the solution resides in the market itself(O'NEILL, 2001). If we focus on this issue absolutely and move in the right direction, we will definitely accomplish it. The current system of frictionless convertible currencies reduces the number of money-related control variables effectively to one. I argue that this one-dimensionality is the cause of the recurrent bubbles and crashes in the financial system for thousands of years. But now we can create new, complementary forms of money that enable better self-organization of our economy.(Dirk Helbing, 2014).

What are Green Assets?

Green assets cover all natural assets that facilitates our lives on this planet and protects us from ill of global warming due to rapid environmental degradation of forest and primitives (protectors of planet), there are lots of lessons to be learnt from them.(Pamecha & Sharma, 2022).

- Green Asset – This is an asset possessed by individuals, government, NGOs, industries, and institutions that has a positive environmental impact such as forests, open space, trees, water bodies, waste recycling plants, water treatment plants, grazing land, and farms, etc. It includes Natural Assets, Environmental Assets as well as Soft Assets.(*GREEN ASSETS*, n.d.)
- Natural Assets- Natural assets are not made or caused by humans for example biological assets, Land, Water Areas and their ecosystems, subsoil assets, and air.
- Environmental Assets- Environmental assets are natural but it includes human efforts to add more functionalities to them or to make them more valuable to society. For example, fertile land, transportation, beautiful landscape, discoveries of new species, and the ability of nature to recycle/

absorb society's waste, etc.(Regoniel, 2020)(BĂCESCU-CĂRBUNARU, 2018)

- Soft Assets- Soft assets of nature are non-infrastructure assets of nature or intangible assets of nature, for example, biodiversity, ecosystem services, etc.

Why Do We Need a Green Asset Market?

We do not value something for its goodness, we value it if it causes damage. This is why we undervalue green assets (GA). Technology can help us to save the planet. But more than anything, we must learn to value nature.(Marco Lambertini, 2018)

What is the value to the society of cleaner air and clean water bodies? What value does society place on segregating and recycling the waste in a city? The answer is zero. As Green assets are purely public goods without a market. As the preferences for GA are absent, we can't determine prices for GA. But Society drives utility from GA and put a value on it (Kolstad, 2011).

1. Use Value
2. Non-use Value (Existence Value)

We value the environment as we use it or it is necessary for our existence. The use might be current, expected, or possible (future use). We value it not because it is useful but because it might cause damage too. GA has a Non-use value also. We value GA not because we use it but because we wish for its existence. These are existence values, altruistic values, and bequest values. The issue here is we all value GA but are not ready to pay for it because of externalities. In the absence of well-defined property rights market does not exist (AdjeiFrempong & Kant Hiran, 2014; Wireko, J. K., Hiran, K. K., & Doshi, 2018).

Nobel laureate Ronald Coase argues that in the presence of externalities, assigning property rights allows bargaining to reach an efficient solution. But in the case of all existing GA, it's not feasible to assign property rights again and again. As the priorities change frequently and it only pacifies the damage for a while therefore does not permanently resolve the issue.

Economies always follow market rules and the assets without a market have eventually no real value unless and until a market is created giving measurable values to the asset. This calls for the calculation of green assets globally and assigning real value to them. In the age of advanced technologies, it is possible through establishing a virtual Green Currency Market based on blockchain technology.

What is Green Currency

A currency issued by a country's authority, and is generally accepted by all as a medium of exchange so that it can be traded for goods and services. But there are some major issues with the currencies, we use currently while creating a market for GA. Current monetary currencies have the following limitation-

1. Local in nature not Global
2. Intrinsic value not associated with real asset value
3. In physical form not virtual
4. Not generally accepted as issued by specific countries
5. Suffer from exchange rates issues
6. Undervalue GA due to non-revelation of preferences
7. Fails to provide the solution to public goods without market etc.

Above are some reasons why existing currencies in circulation can't resolve environmental issues. UN experts believe that currencies based on blockchain technology can play an important role in sustainable development, and improves our stewardship of the environment. One and only one quality is transparency. A transparent monitoring system could accurately track where and how the recovered waste is used, as well as identify who picked it, ensuring that the right people are rewarded for their efforts and the wrong could be identified(UN NEWS, 2021).

To solve global issues like global warming, pollution, and waste management we need a different currency that should be based on green assets valuation, virtual in nature, transparent in nature, governed and accepted by all, and traded globally and smoothly. The answer is Green Currency.

Procedure and Steps to Operationalize Green Currency

Collection of Data on Green Assets

Due to COVID-19 the current census has been postponed (Mijwil et al., 2022; Wireko et al., 2021). In the census, the authority collects data on assets held by each and every household, institution, enterprise, government, and non-government organization, etc. Surprisingly, we never collect data on green assets held by citizens. This means we do not value green assets. If we are really interested to establish a market for GA, first of all, we should introduce to calculate GA possessed by all stakeholders in the coming census. We all have green assets like – trees, green fields, water bodies, forests, rivers, etc. But we do not have proper data on it. Unless and until we have data on GA the market couldn't be established.

How to Assign Value to the Green Assets?

After the collection of data on GA, the question arises to evaluate or quantify the data? What is the Unit of GA? What is its value? What is the value of a tree, a water body, a forest area, green fields, or a river? The objective to calculate GA is to create a mechanism so that the development process continues/ sustains without harming the environment. To evaluate the value for GA, there might be a guiding principle of how much CO_2 or GHGs absorbed or how much O_2 is generated, by the asset? The unit of the GA might be Green Coin (GC) as an Environment Unit (EU). The valuation of GA is a cumbersome method as there is a need to assign value to each and every asset or activity scientifically, according to CO_2 absorption or O_2 generation at the global level. There must be a Modus Operandi or a protocol to assess the value of the. In the coming census, we can design a calculator also so that the enumerators can easily evaluate the GA possessed by an individual, an institution, an enterprise, or the government(Kailashi punit D., Kamal Hiran, 2021).

The absorption of CO2 by a tree depends upon various factors including age, and species (Teskey et al., 2008). It also varies with tree growth which again depends upon various factors. According to Eco Tree on an average 10 -40 kg of CO2 are absorbed per tree per year by a tree. A methodology based on Winrock International Forest Landscape Restoration (FLR), uses a carbon storage calculator to calculate this(onetreeplanted.org). On an average tree absorbs 10kg per year for the first 20 years. Forest Landscape Restoration (FLR) activities are being implemented around the world to improve the ecological and economic productivity of degraded lands(Berck & Helfand, 2005). Charl De Villers (de Villiers et al., 2014) goes further and calculates the carbon sequestration capacity of a tree according to its age. In a case study, he states that the tree volume increases slowly during the first 10 years and then increases dramatically during 10-40 years, and then stabilizes. He finds that the relationship between carbon sequestration and tree volume is the same as tree volume and tree age. Apart from this our oceans are a great source of O2 and Carbon sequestration. Great whales and phytoplankton play a major role (Roman et al., 2014). Each great whale sequesters 33 tons of CO2 on an average, a thousand times a tree. Phytoplankton captures about 40% of all CO2 produced by us and contributes to at least 50% of all oxygen in our atmosphere. While valuing we cannot ignore our oceans and various creatures on this planet. On the basis of the above studies, we can assign an Environment Unit value to a green area or forest area on the basis of its capacity to absorb CO2. Suppose government wishes to build a dam then the cost of construction will also include the cost of GA depleted, in EU assigned to the above calculations. Suppose this project needs to cut down 100 trees aging 40 years or more then this will cost about losing the opportunity of 4000 kg CO2 sequestration capacity forever. This is alarming as this can't be compensated instantly. If the authority plants the same number of trees somewhere then this will take the next 40 years to achieve this capacity level assuming a 100% survival rate. So, this needs to be compensated if and only if the government purchases the same capacity from stakeholders viz households, institutions, or other countries. By this logic, we can build an eco-system for Sustainable Development (Dadhich et al., 2021).

We can assign value to any green asset according to its CO2 sequestration capacity. For example, a tree at 10 years of age absorbs 10 kg CO2 per year is equivalent to suppose 10 EU. This might change with age and species. For every project, this must carefully be assessed and GA should be compensated with GA only, then only we can achieve the net-zero target.

Establishing Market for Green Currency

Once the data for GA have been collected and the valuation for EA is done. Then it provides us a clear-cut picture of a city, a village, a district, a state, a country, and the whole world for the potential for sustainable development. For example, for a locality, we have data on pollution and now also we have calculated the environmental assets of the locality. So, now we can assess the potential of the locality for sustainable development so that globally there will be no negative impact. If the area has potential, then only the development work is justifiable and it is permissible.

Now, if anyone wishes to do any development work which is supposed to distort the environment then the cost will not only be the monetary project cost (in local currency) but will also include environmental asset cost (in environmental units). One has to pay from his own EA or has to purchase VGC from the market. One has to pay this cost for the development work so that the global environment remains intact. Thus-

PROJECT COST = MONETARY PROJECT COST (in local currency) + ENVIRONMENT ASSET COST (in global virtual green currency)

For example, if the government wishes to broaden the national highway, then it purchases land from individuals or forest land. In this case, currently, we have no valuation for EA so government only pays the compensation in national currency and there is no surety that environmental loss will be covered in the future. Suppose the government plants trees then again, it's not justifiable as forests include not only covered tree area but also ecological and irreversible nature. So, if and only if one pays environment units (EU) then only, we can ensure ecological balance globally. This policy will surely balance the economy and environment. If this virtual green currency (VGC) market is created and no exchange is permissible between the country's local currency and VGC. Then for development, developed countries/

environment nonfriendly countries will be bound to purchase EA from the poor/ but environment-friendly countries, this will definitely balance economic development as well as ecological balance. And we will be in a new world, where all will be bound to value environmental assets. (Here we have hypothesized that developed countries are developed because they have overused global resources compared to developing or underdeveloped countries. So, it's justifiable to give this development opportunity to developing/ underdeveloped countries by introducing environmental asset costs of a project)

Figure 1. Potential for development

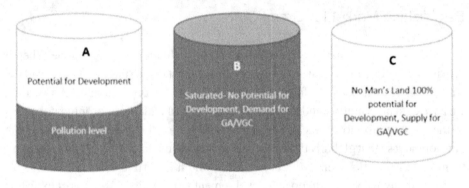

Figure 1 shows the potential for development in fig-A green asset valuation cannot fully absorb pollution, due to net positive pollution there is a limit to development which warns to focusing on green assets or the development process hinders. In Fig -B after some years country reaches a saturation point for development as there is a tradeoff between development and a green environment. So, in this stage, there is no possibility for development unless and until economic growth is decoupled with emission. Or the country has to purchase GA/ VGC from another one if it is mandatory to keep NET GREEN ASSET intact globally. Fig-C shows the no men's land on earth where there is no pollution and 100% GA this nation or state might be or the other those have net positive green assets are the suppliers of GA.

A country will demand GA or VGC for development. If the development process has saturated in a particular region this demand might be fulfilled by an individual, firm, household, or other state government who have the potential for development based on their GA valuation. The price for the virtual currency will depend on the forces of demand and supply of VGC. In long run, this will ensure economic equality as well as environmental parity. This will bound rich or developed countries to purchase EA/ VGC from underdeveloped countries or they have the option to invest in underdeveloped or developing countries after a saturation point.

Figure 2. Demand and supply for green currency

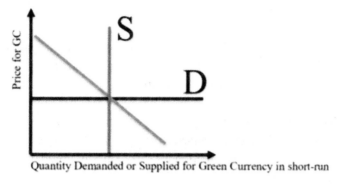

Figure 2 shows global demand and supply for green currency. As GC is a virtual currency its supply is based on global Green Asset valuation. Once the valuation is done in the coming census. Regions/ individuals with excess net GA will be the potential suppliers of GA. This will also depend on the threshold limits for emissions. This might hinder growth. In the short-run supply for GA will remain fixed. These GA will be convertible in VGC values globally. So, there will be a virtual value to GA and a motivation too. So, in long run as the demand for development increases, this will also raise the demand for green currency and will motivate countries to focus on green assets too. This way we have linked economic growth with the green assets through VGC, and created demand for GA / VGC globally. And sustainable green growth is possible. Note here it is assumed that GA is not convertible to any monetary assets currently used. This is shown in Figure 3

Figure 3. Emission-Growth decoupling through VGC

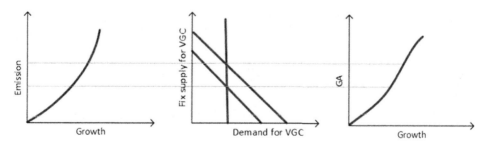

Role of Blockchain Technology in Establishing Green Currency Market

Blockchain Technology (Www.Ibm.Com, n.d.)- Blockchain is a shared, immutable ledger that facilitates the process of recording transactions and tracking assets tangible or non-tangible. Unique properties of BCT are-

Distributed ledger technology- all network participants have access
Immutable records- No one can change or tamper with the transaction record
Smart contracts- To speed up transactions, a set of rules is stored on the blockchain
    and executed automatically.

The Virtual Green Currency introduced here is centralized as the central agency at the world level will control it. This currency will not be backed with any intrinsic value but will be based on the Green Assets possessed by a country. This currency will not be interchangeable with monetary local currency so as to protect the environment.

As time goes on, sustainability will be one of the most important factors in determining the success of the blockchain sector. Cryptocurrencies built on the blockchain can only grow in popularity if we can develop a cryptographic mechanism that is both secure and fast. If you want to know how efficient a cryptocurrency is in terms of energy use, look at the way it creates and updates blocks of data—that is, how its users have agreed to record and validate the information contained in each block in the distributed database.

Figure 4. Green architecture

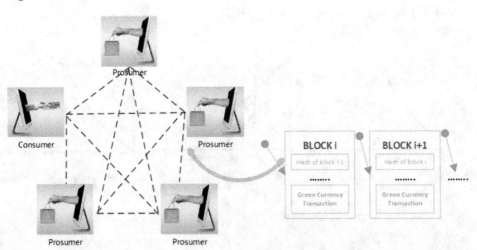

Bitcoin, the first cryptocurrency ever created in 2009, and the vast majority of other popular cryptocurrencies are all mined. As such, this is precisely the procedure that new green cryptocurrencies hope to rethink in order to lessen their excessive energy consumption. This wasteful energy consumption and its associated greenhouse gas emissions run counter to the original vision of digital currencies as a more democratic, egalitarian, and environmentally friendly alternative to fiat money issued by governments (Khazanchi et al., 2021; Saini et al., 2021).

Every cryptocurrency and digital currency are managed independently by its own distributed database, typically a blockchain, which acts as a public financial ledger. This database does not reside on a single machine, but rather on a network of interconnected computers (called "nodes") that constantly share and update data with one another.

Data mining is a complicated validation protocol that regulates the transactions included in each block and is managed by supercomputers. Because everyone in the network has access to the same information, consensus has been reached as to its veracity, making this validation process based on consensus. What we need is a system that allows information to be stored in discrete chunks, linked together so that it can be accessed and verified quickly and easily whenever needed.

Data mining is a collection of methods for gaining useful, non-obvious information from databases.

Mining cryptocurrencies relies on AI and data science as its foundation.

The 5 Biggest Benefits of a Green Currency System

A green currency system can offer a number of benefits to society. The first is that it will be easier for the world to achieve sustainability. Secondly, it will create a more equitable economic system. Thirdly, it will reduce the risk of inflation and economic crashes. Fourthly, it would allow people to take care of their own needs without relying on others. Fifth and finally, it would help create a more cooperative society.

The benefits of a green currency system are numerous and varied in scope. They range from providing financial stability for individuals to creating an equitable economy for all members of society

CONCLUSION

First and foremost, there is a need to establish value in the environmental assets that are utterly overlooked by society owing to ignorance. The new virtual green currency based on blockchain technology has the potential to play a key role in the development of a market for green currency based on environmental green assets.

This paper suggests one technology-based method to evaluate green assets and establish a market for green currencies. There are various other technologies also available to verify data captured and asset valuation. i.e. GPS. If this happens, it will certainly have a long-term impact on individual and societal behavior when it comes to the proper use of natural resources. In fact, by not assigning a monetary value to green assets, we are undervaluing the efforts of people who are devoted to preserving them for a long-ago, particularly the primitives.

REFERENCES

Acheampong, P., Zhiwen, L., Hiran, K. K., Serwaa, O. E., Boateng, F., & Bediako, I. A. (2018). Examining the Intervening Role of Age and Gender on mobile payment Acceptance in Ghana: UTAUT Model. *Canadian Journal of Applied Science and Technology*, 5(2).

AdjeiFrempong, M., & Kant Hiran, K. (2014). Awareness and Understanding of Computer Forensics in the Ghana Legal System. *International Journal of Computers and Applications*, 89(20), 54–59. Advance online publication. doi:10.5120/15752-4640

Băcescu-Cărbunaru, A. (2018). Global Demographic Pressures and Management of Natural Resources – Foresights about the Future of Mankind. *Review of International Comparative Management*, 19(1), 40–53. doi:10.24818/RMCI.2018.1.40

Berck, P., & Helfand, G. E. (2005). The case of markets versus standards for pollution policy. *Natural Resources Journal*, 45(2), 345–367.

Dadhich, S., Pathak, V., Mittal, R., & Doshi, R. (2021). Machine learning for weather forecasting. Machine Learning for Sustainable Development. doi:10.1515/9783110702514-010

de Villiers, C., Chen, S., jin, C., & Zhu, Y. (2014). Carbon sequestered in the trees on a university campus: A case study. *Sustainability Accounting. Management and Policy Journal*, 5(2), 149–171. doi:10.1108/SAMPJ-11-2013-0048

Green Assets. (n.d.). Local Govt and Municipal Knowledge Base Australia. http://lgam.wikidot.com/green-asset

Helbing. (2014). A better financial system for the future. *ETH Zurich - Swiss Federal Institute of Technology*, 1–14.

Kailashi Punit, D., & Kamal Hiran, I. S. (2021). *Essence of life Divide By Zero*. Notion Press.

Kasotia. (n.d.). The Health Effects Of Global Warming: Developing Countries Are The Most Vulnerable. *UN Chronicle*. https://www.un.org/en/chronicle/article/health-effects-global-warming-developing-countries-are-most-vulnerable

Khazanchi, D., Vyas, A. K., Hiran, K. K., & Padmanaban, S. (2021). Blockchain 3.0 for sustainable development. *Blockchain 3.0 for Sustainable Development.* doi:10.1515/9783110702507/EPUB

Kolstad, C. D. (2011). Intermediate Environmental Economics (2nd ed.). Oxford University Press.

Lambertini. (2018). *Technology can help us save the planet. But more than anything, we must learn to value nature.* World Economic Forum.

Mijwil, M. M., Aggarwal, K., Doshi, R., Kant Hiran, K., Sundaravadivazhagan, B., & Mussanah, A. (2022). Deep Learning Techniques for COVID-19 Detection Based on Chest X-ray and CT-scan Images: A Short Review and Future Perspective Solving Traveling Salesman Problem (TSP) View project Digital Image Processing View project Deep Learning Techniques for COVID-19 Detection Based on Chest X-ray and CT-scan Images: A Short Review and Future Perspective. *Asian Journal of Applied Sciences, 10*(3), 2321–0893. doi:10.24203/ajas.v10i3.6998

O'Neill, J. (2001). Markets and the environment: Domesday scenario. *Economic and Political Weekly, 411*(8954), 1865–1873.

Pamecha, S., & Sharma, P. (2022). Waste Management Under Swachh Bharat Mission With Reference to National Green Tribunal's Guidelines in Smart City Udaipur. *Sanshodhan, 11*(1), 12. doi:10.53957anshodhan/2022/v11i1/169814

Parry, I. (2019). Putting a price on pollution. *Finance & Development, 56*(4), 16–19.

Regoniel, P. (2020). *Environmental and Natural Resources: 3 Key Differences.* https://simplyeducate.me/2020/09/28/environmental-and-natural-resources/

Roman, J., Estes, J. A., Morissette, L., Smith, C., Costa, D., McCarthy, J., Nation, J. B., Nicol, S., Pershing, A., & Smetacek, V. (2014). Whales as marine ecosystem engineers. *Frontiers in Ecology and the Environment, 12*(7), 377–385. doi:10.1890/130220

Saini, H. K., Jain, K. L., Hiran, K. K., & Bhati, A. (2021). Paradigms to make smart city using blockchain. Blockchain 3.0 for Sustainable Development.

Teskey, R. O., Saveyn, A., Steppe, K., & McGuire, M. A. (2008). Origin, fate and significance of CO_2 in tree stems. *The New Phytologist, 177*(1), 17–32. doi:10.1111/j.1469-8137.2007.02286.x PMID:18028298

The Paris Agreement. (n.d.). https://unfccc.int/process-and-meetings/the-paris-agreement/the-paris-agreement

UN News. (2021). *Sustainability solution or climate calamity? The dangers and promise of cryptocurrency technology.* https://news.un.org/en/story/2021/06/1094362

Wireko, J. K., Brenya, B., & Doshi, R. (2021). Financial Impact of Internet Access Infrastructure of Online Learning Mode on Tertiary Students in Covid-19 Era in Ghana. *2021 International Conference on Computing, Communication and Green Engineering, CCGE 2021.* 10.1109/CCGE50943.2021.9776422

Wireko, J. K., Hiran, K. K., & Doshi, R. (2018). Culturally based User Resistance to New Technologies in the Age of IoT in Developing Countries: Perspectives from Ethiopia. *International Journal of Emerging Technology and Advanced Engineering.* https://vbn.aau.dk/en/publications/culturally-based-user-resistance-to-new-technologies-in-the-age-o

KEY TERMS AND DEFINITIONS

Blockchain Technology: Blockchain is a shared, immutable ledger that facilitates the process of recording transactions and tracking assets in a business network. An asset can be tangible (a house, car, cash, land) or intangible (intellectual property, patents, copyrights, branding).

Deposit and Refund System: A system that imposes an upfront charge to pay for potential pollution damages that are returned for positive action, such as returning a product for proper disposal or recycling.

Environmental/Ecological Parity: Green currency market generates demand for and supply of green assets globally. Nations and persons with rich green assets get rewarded and nations having low green assets have to check development or purchase GA. That's how the global green assets parity is maintained.

Externalities: A cost or benefit arising from any activity which does not accrual to the person or organization directly involved but extends to a third party outside the market. Externalities are positive or negative. Environment degradation creates negative externality as it generates costs to the third party. The environment is a public common good so those who are responsible for the damage need not pay for the damage as property rights are not well defined.

Green Assets: A green asset is an asset that generates more energy than it consumes. This creates a positive impact on the environment, as well as provides a net positive benefit to the economy. Green assets cover all-natural assets that facilitate our lives on this planet and protect us from the ills of global warming due to the rapid environmental degradation of the forest. These assets are particularly protected and possessed by primitives. An asset possessed by individuals, government, NGOs, industries, and institutions that has a positive environmental impact such as forests, open space, trees, water bodies, waste recycling plants, water treatment plants, grazing land, farms, etc. It includes Natural Assets, Environmental Assets as well as Soft Assets.

Green Assets Valuation: Green assets are becoming more popular and as a result, new valuation techniques have been developed to measure their value. These techniques take into account the environmental benefits of green assets, such as reduced air pollution and greenhouse gas emissions, and this can translate into higher returns. We can assign value to any green asset according to its CO_2 sequestration capacity or O_2 generation capacity.

Green Currency Based on GAV: On the basis of green asset valuation a value could be assigned to green assets and green currency could be launched based on or operated globally through blockchain technology. This GC will be not centrally controlled like the current money market and also global currency in the true sense and will control or check the development process considering the potential of the environment and pressure on it. Apart from this Green Currency has intrinsic value.

Green Currency Market: The market developed and is based on the global transaction of green currency through blockchain technology. This market will motivate all those who preserve the environment and also checks pressure on natural resources. GCM generates demand for and supply of green assets globally.

Green Subsidy: A payment or tax concession that provides financial assistance for pollution reductions or plans to abate in the future using environment-friendly techniques of production.

Green Tax/Pollution Charges: A fee charged to the polluter that varies with the number of pollutants released.

Individual and Social Behavior: Individual behavior can be defined as a mix of responses to external and internal stimuli. It is the way a person reacts in different situations and the way someone expresses different emotions like anger, happiness, love, etc. Social behavior is behavior among two or more organisms within the same species and encompasses any behavior in which one member affects the other. This is due to interaction among those members. In the case of humans, social behavior can be determined by both the individual characteristics of the person, and the situation they are in.

Pollution Permits Trading System: The establishment of a market for rights to pollute, using either credits or allowances.

Potential for Development: Nature can meet our needs but not greed. Nature nurtures naturally all living beings, but it has its own limitations. Unless and until it revies which takes too much time resources are limited. The introduction of green asset valuation and the green currency market presents a guiding principle to control unsustain growth. As the growth of a country depends upon the use of natural resources globally the current economic models have no checks on the growth and development process as all models never take into account the capacity or the potential of growth.

Property Rights: The rights of an owner over the property. As property rights of the environment, green assets, and public goods or common goods are not well defined it hinders economic efficiency. So, to enhance economic efficiency green assets possessed by individuals, firms, governments, or organizations must be calculated and an asset value must be assigned to the owner. Due to negative externality, too much of the good will be produced as the market price does not reflect external costs.

Sustainable Development: Sustainable development is an organizing principle for meeting human development goals while also sustaining the ability of natural systems to provide the natural resources and ecosystem services on which the economy and society depend.

Chapter 6
Blockchain in Gaming

Alok Singh Gahlot
MBM University, India

Ruchi Vyas
ⓘ https://orcid.org/0000-0003-0458-2880
MBM University, India

ABSTRACT

Blockchain is a leading-edge innovation that gives the possibility to streamline numerous enterprises like gaming. There have been many investigations done utilizing blockchain innovation in money, wellbeing, and different areas, yet gaming is a region yet to be conquered. This chapter will explain how blockchain innovation can be utilized in games. Blockchain is known to make exceptional computerized resources that can be copied and make decentralized environments. There are two parts of blockchain innovation that can change the gaming industry. Blockchain has generally affected our ways of life somewhat recently. A word that frequently emerges while discussing blockchain is bitcoin. Current answers for planning and building decentralized blockchain applications need interoperability. Thus, blockchains and existing advancements don't incorporate well in a brought together system. The authors propose a design expecting to effortlessly connect existing decentralized advances and blockchains. Blockchain gaming is an arising diversion worldview.

INTRODUCTION

The innovation of Blockchain was done in 1991 by Stuart Haber and W. Scott Stornetta, famous mathematicians who had desire to create a framework so that timestamps could be stored. BC is a special informational index which changes from

DOI: 10.4018/978-1-6684-5072-7.ch006

a simple informational collection, in a manner it stores data; BC store information in various blocks which are tied together through cryptography. Whenever new information arrives, that is placed in a new block. When blocks of data are stacked, they are bound to the block just before it. and the data is saved with it in subsequent queries (Khazanchi et. al, 2021). A wide variety of data could be stored in BC but the considered application was record transactions. Bitcoin uses BC in decentralized manner, so clients could be easily controlled but when used socially or personally it cannot be controlled. The distributed blockchain is constant, indicating that the data entered is irreversible. For Bitcoin, this means that transactions are always recorded and visible to everyone. The major objective of BC is to record and distribute electronic information, but not to change it at the same time. Therefore, BC is the base for permanent records or keeping track of transaction record which can't be adjusted, erased or erased. This explains why blockchain is commonly referred to as the evolution of outbound records. (Besançon et al., 2019; Deshpande et.al.,2017)

A blockchain stage permits clients and engineers to make novel purposes of a current blockchain framework. Ethereum is one of the models which has a local digital money known as ether but this model permits making shrewd agreements and tokens that could be programmed and utilized in beginning coin contributions, and non-fungible tokens. Development is done at Ethereum framework and hubs on the Ethereum organization. Usage of blockchain technology is done in varied industries such as companies where financial exchange is being done could also be used by government to secure data, it could also be used in real estate, securing certain personal information, Insurance industry could also use blockchain so that contracts are be visible to each and every customer, supply chain management is the best application of blockchain. (Besançon et al., 2021; Pillai et.al.,2020)

Background

Utilizing blockchain innovation in your product or application, you can believe its security as it deals with the decentralized syntax. It urges you to make instalments or available resources move every minute of every day. You don't have to stand by lengthy days as you do physically. No outsider can treat the framework as it is just a two-way exchange process. Besides, it saves time as there is no requirement for endorsement from any mediators. Blockchain innovation offers high precision as it gives different hubs check to affirm the blockchain transaction. The force of saving complex records is irrefutable. (Anjum et al., 2017; Hardjono et.al.,2018)

Blockchain gaming alludes to games based on blockchain systems or games coordinated with blockchain innovation to work with NFT creation, exchanging and proprietorship abilities. The impact of the two universes of blockchain and gaming has set out new open doors for the gaming business. Not at all like conventional, exceptionally brought together games, where the game engineers controlled all resources and money, blockchain games are decentralized. Blockchain games intend to scatter in-game resources for their players, and these resources have esteem past the games (Jin et al., 2018). In blockchain games, digital currencies and NFTs are utilized for buying in-game resources that can be traded for cryptographic forms of money and genuine cash. Thus, from the second a gamer procures a NFT reward, players gain full responsibility for resources, which can be exchanged and sold in and outside the games.

Table 1. Comparison between various methodologies

	Ethereum	Ripple	Quorum
Industry Usage	All Industries	Financial sector	All Industries
Permission	Permissionless	Permissioned	Permissioned
Cryptocurrency	ETH	XRP	None
Algorithm	PoW	Probability Voting	Majority Voting
Smart Contract	Yes	No	Yes

There are in total four protocols used by blockchain technology which are universally used it includes public blockchain, hybrid blockchain, private blockchain and consortium blockchain. These protocols are being used as per the requirement of project. (Gordon et al., 2018) There are certain parameters where each protocol is better than other. There are certain levels by which comparison could be done between them. Public is a protocol which doesn't require any permission it is open to all as anyone could be part of it whether developer or network member while private protocol require certain level of permission and could not be used by anyone it basically requires certain governance. (Xu et al., 2019; Tasatanattakool et.al.,2018) Transactions done in private blockchain could be accessed by network members only it. Whereas hybrid blockchain is combination of both type of other blockchains as it provides flexible atmosphere as at certain situation it provides features of private while at certain position it gives features of public.

The gaming business has made considerable progress since the underlying long stretches of arcades and quarter spaces when gamers paid to play. Then, after 10 years came console computer games with games turning out to be more modern and expensive simultaneously. Gamers stuck to their control centre went through hours playing with next to zero genuine communication with other gamers. Since games were facilitated on unified servers, gamers could play with those living in the different geological areas (Golosova et al., 2018 Min et.al.,2019) The gaming scene was profoundly brought together, firmly constrained by the game designers and distributers. Doubtlessly arousing a lot of shame for the gamers, in-game buys were made by government issued currency and had no worth past the domain of the game. Be that as it may, this was before the appearance of blockchain decentralization (Jain et al., 2012; Choubisa et.al.,2022).

Figure 1. Infrastructure of blocks in blockchain

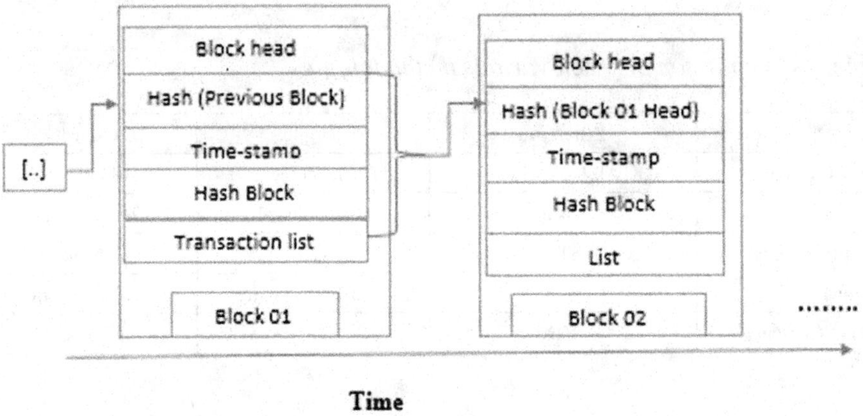

RELATED WORK

Blockchain Systems A blockchain framework comprises of blockchain information structure, agreement model and PP organization. The blockchain information structure, by definition, is a constantly developing chain of squares, everyone has cryptographic hash of the previous block, a time stamp, and its data. The blockchain information structure is intended to oppose alterations. With the assistance of PP framework and evidence of-work agreement model proposed in Bitcoin, the blockchain framework can be used to help decentralized information synchronization, which turns into the underpinning of decentralized records. To add more qualities to the blockchain environment, Ethereum was carried out to work with decentralized brilliant agreements, which are permanent and straightforward executable projects facilitated by the blockchain. These days, the blockchain-based decentralized applications (DApps) have been stretched out to different regions, including introductory coin contributions (ICO), informal organizations, arranged games, and IoT (Hiran et al., 2014; Hiran et.al.,2021).

General Consensus Models As examined, PoW requires taking an interest hubs to do futile numerical works for the honour of composing blocks, which brings the energy and time shortcoming issue to the blockchain frameworks. Hence, various novel agreement models have been proposed as options for universally useful blockchains. Confirmation of-Stake picks the maker of the new square in view of their stake on the organization. For instance, coin age is characterized as the hour of the coin left unspent, the higher the coin age of an individual, the almost certain the singular will mine another square. At the end of the day, the more extravagant an individual is, the more squares the singular will mine in the blockchain. Nonetheless, since holding tokens in various forks present no additional upward for the partners, PoS blockchains will bring forth an enormous number of forks that decrease the worth of the organization. This is known as the nothing in question issue. Confirmation of Excellence is a theoretical model referenced in the PoS whitepaper. That's what it expressed a competition is held occasionally to mint coins in light of the presentation of the competition members, emulating the awards of genuine competitions.

Basically, the hub for the blockchain to hold agreement with is picked by means of a game. Be that as it may, in this model, great players will be bound to dominate a match, this causes what is happening where great players will actually want to over and over compose blocks. Along these lines, the blockchain will turn into a somewhat incorporated stage constrained by world class players. Designated Proof of Stake (DPoS) agreement model tackles the PoW upward issue from another angle: network members delegate their freedoms of creating squares to a little gathering of super nodes, which compose blocks in turns for all clients in the blockchain network. High throughput and low inertness have been accomplished in such a model. Nonetheless, general society is as yet reprimanding that DPoS being a to some extent brought together stage since it is difficult to forestall the super nodes from conniving with one another. A comparable thought has been taken on by Proof of Vote (PoV), which is facilitated by the circulated hubs constrained by consortium accomplices who come to a decentralized assertion by casting a ballot. The key thought is to lay out various security character for network members so the accommodation and confirmation of the squares are chosen by the offices' democratic in the association without the relying upon an outsider middle person or wild open mindfulness (Patel et al., 2022, Barua, T., et, al., 2020).

Bitcoin creation is done, when, EOS utilizes Delegated Proof of Stake (DPoS) as a procedure for accomplishing game plan, which compromises decentralization to increment throughput. There is no unified norm between all BC plans, and this prompts the need for research concerning interoperability. Especially, proposes a layered arrangement to also cultivate correspondence between BC. Some examination works besides try to address interoperability issues inside a specific field. This is what's going on of, which dismantles how to use BC headway to moreover cultivate information parting among patients and clinical thought affiliations. Normalization endeavours have come from the IEEE Blockchain Initiative and the IEEE Standards

Association. For instance, a plan zeroed in on the Internet of Things. At the same time, the Enterprise Ethereum Alliance (EEA) plans subtleties for BC clients, worked for the Ethereum natural framework, that could have adventure usage. Unfortunately, these proposals will not be easily contacted various applications and applied to other BC. For example, the EEA means to show up at endeavours, so they don't think about decentralization in their subtleties. The plan proposed by IBM has tantamount cut off points: regardless of the way that they integrate a public association for clients, the BC is managed by an executive and its arrangement is achieved by trusted in members. Additionally, in the PC game industry, Hoard plans to additional promptly coordinate BC in game engines for engineers, as well as to separate complexities of the BC for players. In any case, they don't propose a nonexclusive design for DBA (Saini, H. K. et al., 2021)

Certain Research Shows and consistently elaborate connection points in the BC space have generally been standardized with a granular viewpoint. The ERC-proposes a unified spot of association arranged to control both fungible and non-fungible resources. At this point, these guidelines essentially cover the BC side of a resource, by concluding magnificent comprehension points of communication contraptions need to help with dealing with the resources. In any case, this approach is restricted as it doesn't ponder the environment overall. For instance, collectible resources, for example, Crypto Kitties are tended to by pictures. These photographs are bound together and obliged by the servers of the undertaking's affiliation. This plan decision could be had a go at expecting that any decentralized picture aggregating standard was associated with the ERC-standard. Undoubtedly, most decentralized applications can't utilize just BC advancement, as it right by and by has two or three endpoints. For instance, the expense of everlastingly dealing with a huge load of information (for example pictures) on the Ethereum BC is restrictive. As such, fashioners need to utilize BC just for the centre treatment of the application. Non-tremendous dealing with, storing up and other subordinate undertakings ought to be managed by different instruments, as dispersed record limit plans. Interoperability between a BC and these instruments is a test, and it ought to be better thought about while building rules. (Hou et al., 2022; Bodhke et.al.,2020)

One of the approaches used in research where a virtual universe is created and selling of land is done. The land owner can make model in three-dimensional video such that interaction could be done easily. Such researches have shown how games could be designed and be executed in virtual atmosphere. The specification is required by programmers so that they could create designs of game environment and how it is being executed so that create the virtual environment and how game will proceed further. The major thing is if a game is already being created then there must be proper new design so that it should look and feel attractive to attract more clients. The complete architecture must not be complicated and must be simple and could be easily understood by the database administrator. When we use blockchain technology in games there are certain tools which are required to be integrated.

PROPOSED LAYERED MODEL

Figure 2. Working of layered model

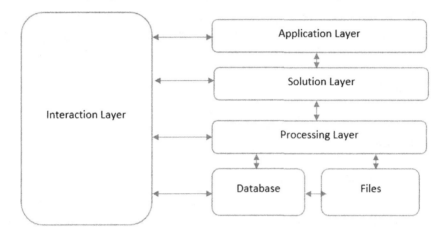

The Major motive of the layered plan showed in the above Figure is to give the blocks to help a database. There are four layers in the model which are interaction layer, application layer, solution layer, processing layer all the layers are responsible for smooth working as every layer interacts with each other while processing layer is the one which is doing majority task of interacting with the database and file stored while providing data to upper layers so that further processing can be done smoothly. The interaction layer provides smooth conduction and working of the model. It furthermore avoids unsuitable blocks. It is Inspired from the Open Systems Interconnection Model; where every layer has to interact with other layers on regular basis where in Blockchain technology interaction is not enough for enormous information storage.

Decentralizing could be used despite a block to execute on all application. Static limit could be coursed on Inter Planetary File System for anything that has a centre that can pick the substance they have. In any case, all things being equal, to lose the reports expected for a thing, they can have a centre which goes probably as an entry in the event that no one else is supported to have the archives. Various endeavour rather to give money related inspiration to store data. For model, File Coin is a Blockchain layer in view of top of Inter Planetary File System, likewise, pointing to gaining decentralizing limit the Ethereum climate. Major difficulties looked on record accumulating layer is to precisely check necessities of an application, to the extent that data openness, decentralizing the data setback contravention.

In certain situation, we cannot use directly the decentralized amassing devices referred to above, as they so to speak support static records. Anyway, a couple of exercises Orbit database, a layer on top of Inter Planetary File System, and Gun use battle freely copied datatypes. Thus, information collected uses datatypes which are appropriate for required situation, as it is possible % of an opportunity to decide confusion between peers, regardless, when they go detached reliably. According to Brewers theorem a database can have 2 of the 3 properties which could be stability, accessibility, resilience. After using above model, we could see difference in certain use cases. In processing layer validation of information integrity is done which manages the game.

CONCLUSION

Blockchain technology has made revolution in many areas including enabling procure trades with no prerequisite. In 2009, Bitcoin used BC advancements, there has been increase in number of BC development plans. The major applications were electronic cash systems with the appointment of an overall information containing all trades. These trades are using cryptographic hashes, and trades are stamped and checked using key matching. The trade history actually and securely keeps a chain of events with the end goal that any undertaking to adjust or change a past trade will be in a manner which require multiple calculation of all subsequent blocks of trades. The usage of BC technology is still in its starting stages, but it depends on comprehensively seen cryptographic norms and storing data. As of now, there is a huge load of advancement around the development, and many proposed algorithms uses it. Pushing ahead, in all likelihood, the advancement will disappear, and BC development will end up being essentially another instrument that can be used. Through this dispersion, a BC relies upon association already built, cryptographic, and recordkeeping advancements yet includes them in another manner. It will be important innovation that can look at the developments and both the advantages and damages of using them. Once a BC is done and by and large embraced, it could turn out to be difficult to change it. At the point when data is kept in a BC, that data is everlastingly, wherever there is a raise. BC development is still new and should deal with BC advancement accessible to them we use it simply in appropriate conditions.

REFERENCES

Anjum, A., Sporny, M., & Sill, A. (2017). Blockchain standards for compliance and trust. *IEEE Cloud Computing, 4*(4), 84–90. doi:10.1109/MCC.2017.3791019

Barua, T., Doshi, R., & Hiran, K. K. (2020). Mobile Applications Development. In *Mobile Applications Development*. De Gruyter.

Besançon, L., Da Silva, C. F., & Ghodous, P. (2019, May). Towards blockchain interoperability: Improving video games data exchange. In *2019 IEEE international conference on blockchain and cryptocurrency (ICBC)* (pp. 81-85). IEEE.

Besançon, L., Ghodous, P., Gelas, J. P., & Da Silva, C. F. (2021, March). Modelling of Decentralised Blockchain Applications Development. *The 2020 International Conference on High Performance Computing & Simulation (HPCS 2020).*

Blockchain for industry 4.0: A comprehensive review. (n.d.). *IEEE Access, 8,* 79764–79800. doi:10.1109/ACCESS

Choubisa, M., & Doshi, R. (2022). Crop Protection Using Cyber Physical Systems and Machine Learning for Smart Agriculture. In *Real-Time Applications of Machine Learning in Cyber-Physical Systems* (pp. 134–147). IGI Global.

Deshpande, A., Stewart, K., Lepetit, L., & Gunashekar, S. (2017). *Distributed Ledger Technologies/Blockchain: Challenges, opportunities and the prospects for standards. Overview report. The British Standards Institution.* BSI.

Golosova, J., & Romanovs, A. (2018, November). The advantages and disadvantages of the blockchain technology. In *2018 IEEE 6th workshop on advances in information, electronic and electrical engineering (AIEEE)* (pp. 1-6). IEEE.

Gordon, W. J., & Catalini, C. (2018). Blockchain technology for healthcare: Facilitating the transition to patient-driven interoperability. *Computational and Structural Biotechnology Journal, 16,* 224–230. doi:10.1016/j.csbj.2018.06.003 PMID:30069284

Hardjono, T., Lipton, A., & Pentland, A. (2018). *Towards a design philosophy for interoperable blockchain systems.* arXiv preprint arXiv:1805.05934.

Hiran, K. K., Doshi, R., & Rathi, R. (2014). Security & privacy issues of cloud & grid computing networks. *International Journal on Computational Sciences & Applications, 4*(1), 83–91. doi:10.5121/ijcsa.2014.4108

Hiran, K. K., Jain, R. K., Lakhwani, K., & Doshi, R. (2021). *Machine Learning: Master Supervised and Unsupervised Learning Algorithms with Real Examples (English Edition)*. BPB Publications.

Huo, R., Zeng, S., Wang, Z., Shang, J., Chen, W., Huang, T., Wang, S., Yu, F. R., & Liu, Y. (2022). A comprehensive survey on blockchain in industrial internet of things: Motivations, research progresses, and future challenges. *IEEE Communications Surveys and Tutorials*, 24(1), 88–122. doi:10.1109/COMST.2022.3141490

Jain, R. K., Hiran, K., & Paliwal, G. (2012). Quantum Cryptography: A New Generation of Information Security System. *Proceedings of International Journal of Computers and Distributed Systems*. doi:10.1109/ICOIN.2018.8343163

Jin, H., Dai, X., & Xiao, J. (2018, July). Towards a novel architecture for enabling interoperability amongst multiple blockchains. In *2018 IEEE 38th International Conference on Distributed Computing Systems (ICDCS)* (pp. 1203-1211). IEEE. 10.1109/ICDCS.2018.00120

Khazanchi, D., Vyas, K., & Ajay, K. H. (2021). *Kamal and Padmanaban, Sanjeevikumar. Blockchain 3.0 for Sustainable Development*. De Gruyter. doi:10.1515/9783110702507

Min, T., & Cai, W. (2019, June). A security case study for blockchain games. In *2019 IEEE Games, Entertainment, Media Conference (GEM)* (pp. 1-8). IEEE.

Patel, S., Vyas, A. K., & Hiran, K. K. (2022). Infrastructure Health Monitoring Using Signal Processing Based on an Industry 4.0 System. *Cyber-Physical Systems and Industry 4.0: Practical Applications and Security Management*, 249-260.

Pillai, B., Biswas, K., & Muthukkumarasamy, V. (2020). Cross-chain interoperability among blockchain-based systems using transactions. *The Knowledge Engineering Review*, 35, 35. doi:10.1017/S0269888920000314

Saini, H. K., Jain, K. L., Hiran, K. K., & Bhati, A. (2021). Paradigms to make smart city using blockchain. *Blockchain 3.0 for Sustainable Development, 10*, 21.

Tasatanattakool, P., & Techapanupreeda, C. (2018, January). Blockchain: Challenges and applications. In *2018 International Conference on Information Networking (ICOIN)* (pp. 473-475). IEEE.

Xu, X., Weber, I., & Staples, M. (2019). Blockchain in Software Architecture. In *Architecture for Blockchain Applications* (pp. 83–92). Springer. doi:10.1007/978-3-030-03035-3_5

KEY TERMS AND DEFINITIONS

Algorithm: An algorithm is a step-by-step procedure to solve any problem or a task which does not depend on a particular programming language, above chapter has used a layered architecture where computer games use blockchain safely.

Bitcoin: Bitcoin uses a particular technology which is not using any bank or government authority as maintaining and managing all transaction is done over a network which is completely safe. It is an open source no one owns or controls it as anyone can participate in it. It does not require any prior payments.

Blockchain: A blockchain is a distributed database or ledger that is shared among the nodes of a computer network. As a database, a blockchain stores information electronically in digital format. Blockchains are best known for their crucial role in cryptocurrency systems, such as Bitcoin, for maintaining a secure and decentralized record of transactions. The innovation with a blockchain is that it guarantees the fidelity and security of a record of data and generates trust without the need for a trusted third party.

Cryptocurrency: Cryptocurrency is a kind of currency made to exchange over internet or it could be as digital currency where government is not reliable to store just as normal currency in bank.

Data Integrity: Today's era is of big data, but it is equally important to maintain that data safely in reference to any currency data integrity must be managed properly.

Decentralized Application: A decentralized application (dApp) is a type of distributed open-source software application that runs on a peer-to-peer (P2P) blockchain network rather than on a single computer. DApps are visibly like other software applications that are supported on a website or mobile device but are P2P supported.

Ethereum: Ethereum is the community-run technology powering the cryptocurrency ether (ETH) and thousands of decentralized applications. Ethereum is used in all industries, and it uses smart contracts.

Hash: A cryptographic hash function is an algorithm that takes an arbitrary amount of data input credential and produces a fixed-size output of enciphered text called a hash value, or just hash. That enciphered text can then be stored instead of the password itself, and later used to verify the user.

Interoperability: Blockchain interoperability is not a set rule book. It refers to a broad range of techniques that allow different blockchains to listen to each other, transfer digital assets and data between one another and enable better collaboration.

NFT: Non-fungible token are tokens which cannot be replicated and are being used in blockchain. They could be anything representing a real-world entity just like real estate or an artwork. Selling or buying these tokens is called tokenizing which reduces the probability of fraud.

PoW: The Proof of Work consensus algorithm involves solving a computational challenging puzzle in order to create new blocks in the bitcoin blockchain.

Quantum Computing: It is a Technology that uses laws of quantum mechanics to solve difficult and classical problems.

Ripple: Ripple is the company that is behind XRP, the cryptocurrency where XRP is a technology that is mainly known for its digital payment network and protocol. Many major banks use the XRP payment system. Bitcoin transaction confirmations may take many minutes with high transaction costs, while XRP transactions are confirmed in seconds with little cost.

Smart Contract: Smart contract can be defined as set of instructions being stored on a blockchain system which gets executed over a particular condition which is already defined earlier in a proper manner. Smart contacts get executed automatically which helps in reducing time wastage and this done over an agreement.

Time Stamp: A time stamp is input of signing authority which is a piece of data or information at specific time it uses protocol which checks or certifies all timestamps using X.509 certificates and public key infrastructure.

Chapter 7
A Scrutiny Review of CPS 4.0–Based Blockchain With Quantum Resistance

Chandani Joshi
Sir Padampat Singhania University, India

Chitra Bhole
Sir Padampat Singhania University, Udaipur, India & K. J. Somaiya Institute of Engineering and Information Technology, Mumbai, India

Naveen Vaswani
Sir Padampat Singhania University, Udaipur, India & Thadomal Shahani Engineering College, Mumbai, India

ABSTRACT

Data collection mechanisms have become effectively advanced by leveraging the internet of things and cyber physical systems. The sensors are heavily developed with intricate details to capture data in varied forms which can be stored and used as an information base for knowledge extraction using analytics and statistical prognostication in artificial intelligence sub-branches. Storing this data with a different approach that ensures stringent security measures is done using blockchain. The loopholes that compromise the security of blockchain are quantum computing for which quantum resistant blockchain ideas are discussed. This chapter finally sheds some light on the effective approach to implement the CPS 4.0-based blockchain mechanism with detailed scrutiny.

DOI: 10.4018/978-1-6684-5072-7.ch007

INTRODUCTION

The world works with a lot of data collected on daily basis. The collection mechanisms of the data over the period of time have also became advance. The collection mechanisms are not only confined to numerical based data but also to multimedia data that is non-structured and documented type. The data collection is done using various modern-day sensors and attachments. This data requires lot feature engineering and a lot of expression can be given to it if utilized in a proper manner. Internet of Things (IoT) (Kumar S, 2019; Madakam S, 2015; Rehman H.u et al., 2017) and Cyber Physical System (CPS) (Aguida, 2020; Jazdi, 2014; Rawung et al.,2014) can be used for collection of the data in varied ways. IoT (Lakhwani et.al., 2020) systems are embedded and have many sensors that are connected through a micro-controller or micro-processor system that leverage the internet and cloud platform for connectivity. CPS also has many unit level sensors that work on physical level for collecting the data. This data is just collected form of information base from which knowledge can be extracted. The data collected from CPS/IoT can be used to perform many analytics and prognostication techniques for improving the state of the system. But this is not where the limitations are attained, another technology related to storing and management of data for better security and varied reasons is Blockchain (Nakamoto, 2009; Vujicic et.al.,2018). The intricate details will be explained in the further section of the article but in easy terminology the blockchain is a data storing mechanism that ensures transparency and decentralized system. Blockchain are heavily encrypted and give the security their top most priority. All the blocks are heavily encrypted with real-time hashes and connected with a strong link that use redundancy to ensure all the blocks are at the same operating state throughout the transactions and operations. This however will be tackled with the use of quantum computing (Bhatt et al,2019; Ladd et al,2010; Jazaeri et al,2019). The basis of current state-of-the-art systems fall less to break the blockchain because of the hash keys. These hash keys are not a challenge for quantum computer as it operates on quantum bits (qubits) which process many possibilities of one problem simultaneously. This is still a far-fetched problem as the number of qubits required to break the current state-of-the-art blockchain system is difficult but won't be a problem in span of 10 years down the line. The quantum computers will easily be able to calculate the private key based on the public key in fraction of time which seems an impossible problem currently. Many suspicions are raised even before this has taken place that the quantum computers will replicate the hash performed and forge the transaction before the record is written on the block by replacing the hash. This process will be seamlessly easy yet many infractions are involved, but suspicion tingles the curiosity and it definitely has by forcing researchers to work with quantum resistant blockchain (Allende et al,2021; Ferna'ndez et al,2020; Zhang et al.,2021) that discusses some ideas to make current blockchain more secure and unbreakable. Although many aspects are involved that the cryptographical algorithms required will have to be rewritten for a quantum computer in such fashion which will for sure differ from traditional systems. The integration of blockchain into CPS 4.0 (Patel et al.,2022) industrial standard is another aspect for which this article discusses the idea in the further sections.

METHODOLOGY

Cyber Physical System

Any technology has many physical level components involved in it. Smart interaction between these is essential at many levels. The cyber physical systems (Aguida, 2020; Jazdi, 2014; Rawung et al.,2014) can be defined as interaction using network of physical and computational components engineered together. It can be also termed as a combination of varied technologies, viz. Artificial Intelligence, Machine Learning (Alpaydin, 2020; Sarker,2021; Shinde, et al. 2018), Deep Learning (Goodfellow et al., 2016; LeCun,2015), Internet of Things (Kumar S, 2019;Madakam S, 2015;Rehman H.u et al.,2017), Big Data Analytics (Elgendy et al,2014) and Robotics. The main confusion that instills the mind of the people is difference between internet of things and cyber physical systems. The simple answer to this is internet of things is associated with objects that are connected with internet and eventually coupled together whereas cyber physical system is computation integration with network for physical process. The cyber physical systems allow recording of the data in a direct manner using the sensors of the system. The physical processes are affected using actuators. The thin line between the physical and digital world can be evaluated and saved easily using the cyber physical system. Creating a connection with each other on global scale is possible easily. It provides multi-modal human-machine interfaces for easier interaction. Generating information directly from the device is possible. Self-monitoring is possible as personal level IP-address is assigned. The cyber physical system 4.0 (CPS 4.0) is industrial exposure of the traditional cyber physical system. It does empower the manufacturing sector with its latest advancement. The intent of connecting the existing physical systems with CPS 4.0 standard is current goal. If we breakdown the varied technologies involved, it is a clear indication of CPS implementation as data is the main required component of it and in this modern world, data is allocated on a very large level which can certainly leverage these technological areas. Starting with internet of things also abbreviated as IoT is connecting the sensor based micro-controllers and micro-processors with the internet for creating smart applications. The primary aspects of IoT are networking, communication, security, volume of the data used for solving a business problem and social impacts. The interconnected devices give an expression to IoT that transmit and receive data in massive volumes. Integrated circuits such as System on a Chip (SoC) (Martin et al.,2001) and Field Programmable Gate Array (FPGA) (Zheng et al.,2001) can be used to collect the data in proper manner. The main powerful point of the IoT based system is using the network for cloud integration (Hiran K, et al., 2021). The cloud computing (Mathew et al. 2017) gives an expression to serving and using application programming interface (APIs). Real-time streaming and integration of various network based systems is easily possible using IoT based systems currently. The cloud also leverages the massive storage capacities of the data so that the devices need not be dependent on the on-chip storage system. A lot of analytics can be performed using this data and this is where the areas of data science will be used, which will be explained in this section in some time. The main task is managing the heterogeneous data and putting it to use. Time sensitive data can be used for generating latency and non-useful attributes can be discarded. The main considerable point for such system is internet which does open paths to various developments. The analytics can be performed on different levels. Artificial Intelligence is a very broad term and can be derived in many segments. It can be considered as an applied branch of statistics. Prognostication based models are the main constituent when related to IoT or CPS. The analytics is study of the collected data for providing the best business solution but Artificial Intelligence (AI) can be leveraged for creating the prognostication aspect for taking some sensor based decisions. The prognostication based learning can be linked with inferential statistics branch for which Machine Learning is the applied (Mahrishi et al., 2020) branch. Machine Learning in broader sense is associated with learning the patterns and parameters of the data to yield a prediction. This prediction is probabilistic so a lot of metric analysis is necessary to clear the infractions. The machine learning has many learning methods (Hiran K et al., 2021) and divisions that can be understood in detail. The learning methods broadly considered can be supervised learning (Kotsiantis, 2007) and unsupervised learning (La"ngkvist et al.,2014). The supervised learning is associated when the labels for the particular feature parameters of the data are given whereas for unsupervised learning the labels are not present and it is purely related to learning the pattern from the data. Both the learning procedures can be used when extracting the data from the IoT based system. Supervised learning has 2 main divisions, viz. Classification (Cormack, R.M., 1971) and Regression (Maulud et al., 2020). The simple understanding of the classification is recognizing the object or entity from the set of given labels. Regression is prediction of the continuous values. Classification is discrete. Classification has types such as binary and multi-class. The binary classification (Kumari et al.,2017; Gupta et al.,2022) is where only 2 labels are given, for instance true/false, yes/no etcetera. Most basic algorithm for binary classification is logistic regression (Peng et al., 2002) that uses the logit function for separating the 2 distinct classes from each other. Considering the CPS, this can be used when there is need to turn on/off something based on some set of parameters. For classes more than 2 there are many other set of algorithms. These models are available in parametric and non-parametric methods where decision tree (Quinlan J.R, 1986), random forest (Breiman L,2001; Kanvinde et al.,2022), support vector machines (Hearst et al., 1998) and k-nearest neighbors (Cunningham et al., 2021) fall under non-parametric learning methods that are commonly used. Considering parametric learning methods, logistic regression for binary and discriminant analysis (Huberty,1975; Gupta et al.,2022; Ramayah et al.,2010) is an example of parametric multi-class learning algorithm. Random Forest falls under non-parametric ensemble learning method. Ensemble learning is a process of learning where a set of weak learners are combined to form a strong learner. These are much more generalized in nature as compared to the basic learners. The ensemble learning is divided into bagging (Breiman L, 1996) and boosting (Gupta et al.,2021, Opitz et al.1999) style algorithms. Bagging is also known as bootstrap aggregation and random forest is its type, boosting is another ensemble learning that works on improving the performance of the weak learners on every step. The types of boosting ensemble learning methods are AdaBoost (Freund et al.,1999; Schapire,1999), Gradient Boosting (Natekin et al., 2013), XGBoost (Chen T. et al., 2016) and CatBoost (Prokhorenkova et al., 2018). More generalized learners can be found with stacked generalization (Wolpret, 1992) method that provides learning procedure by combining various learners stacked with each other for best possible results. The data if allocated in a bigger amount can then be used with Deep Learning (Goodfellow et al., 2016; LeCun,2015). It is an extended branch of machine learning that works with non-parametric system. The parameters learned about the prediction flow is very different from traditional learning algorithms and gives effective predictions even on very massive dataset. The deep learning system uses artificial neural network inspired by biological neurons in humans. These networks are very vast and learns the parameters using activation layers and hidden neurons. Even single neuron is declared arbitrarily and is assigned a certain weight and bias that is modulated with data using the activation function. These activation functions are mathematical functions used for smoothening the information gained by the network. Rectified Linear Unit (Agarap, 2018) and Tangent Hyperbolic (De Ryck et al., 2021) are some types of commonly used activation functions. These layers arranged in certain proportion learn the patterns from data sequentially in the forward propagation. Later this data is validated and loss of information is computed with loss functions. Binary cross-entropy and categorical cross-entropy are type of some loss functions. The loss is then optimized till the start of network using loss optimizers. These loss optimizers calculate the gradient of the weights, biases and learnt features to reduce the loss as much as possible. This entire process is known as backward propagation (LeCun et al., 1998). Adam (Gupta et al.,2022, Kingma et al.,2014), AdaGrad (Duchi J et al., 2011) and Stochastic Gradient Descent (Ruder S,2016) are some common types of loss optimizers.

The forward and backward propagation together constitute one learning epoch and there can be many epochs in a network. This procedure is not only confined to the numerical data. The sensors are getting smarter and data collection procedures are also improving. The data collected can be image, videos, text and audio. The image and videos fall under the computer vision problems that can be solved using deep learning. The classification performed in computer vision using deep learning is done using a specific type of neural network known as convolutional neural network suggested by (Albawi et al.,2017; LeCun et al.; Musale et al.,2021; Yamashita et al.,2018) in which they had that used set of filters also known as kernels for extracting features from image. These filters perform various image processing methods to extract information from the images including the error level analysis (Gupta, A et al.,2022) The data can be used for transfer learning with some popular convolutional neural networks trained on Image-Net (Russakovsky, O et al.,2015) dataset, which is a dataset of over 1000 classes. Some commonly used convolutional neural networks are AlexN (Russakovsky, O et al.,2015), VGG-16 (Simonyan, K et al.,2014), ResNet (Gupta A et al.,2022; He K. et al.,2016), Inception Net (Szegedy, C et al.,2015). These are very parameter rich and can be used to advantage if the data collected from sensors is in form of images. If the data is pertaining to the detection of certain objects, object detection algorithms like Yolo used by (Bochkovskiy, A et al.,2020; Redmon, J et al. 2016), R-CNN (Girshick, R et al.,2015), Fast RCNN (Girshick, R et al.,2015), Faster RCNN (Ren, S et al.,2015) can be used. If data should be used to highlight the certain portion from the data, image segmentation can be used with algorithms like U-Net(Ronneberger, O et al.,2015), Bottleneck Supervised Network(Li, S et al.,2018) and Yolact(Bolya, D et al.,2019;Bolya D et al.,2020, Joshi, R.M et al.,2022). If the data is in text format, this falls under the natural language processing category. The system of NLP with machine learning uses basic text management for learning word representations using bag of words (Zhang, Y et al.,2010) and TF-IDF (Tambe, S et al.,2022). If deep leaning needs to be used, one can work with Recurrent Neural Network(Cho, K et al.,2014). This can run into vanishing gradient problem in backward propagation for which LSTM(Joshi R et al.,2022; Staudemeyer R, et al.,2019) can be used. Learning procedure to improve the working with LSTM, Bidirectional LSTM(Cui, Z et al.,2018) is used that takes the input of the sequence from future that helps discard the information that is not useful. Modern systems for speed in learning and training with better accuracy have considered working with transformer (Vaswani A. et al.,2017; Joshi R. et al.,2022) architectures that take the input of entire sequence and work with encoders and decoders. The machine translation was one of the primary tasks that were considered. Later tasks like Named Entity Recognition (Li, J., Sun et al.,2020) were given importance. The most common set of transformer is BERT (Devlin, J et al.,2018) which literally means bidirectional encoder representations from transformer. Many more advancements were brought after BERT and still very high end research is under process. Considering audio input the neural network like WaveNet(Oord, A.v.d et al.,2016) can be used to understand the audio and make audio translations.

Blockchain

The data in the distributed manner when is monitored by a centralized system has many loopholes. It is specifically controlled by one single-body and monitoring of the system has a moderator. This compromises security on different dimensions of operation. This was practically a need for a decentralized solution, one which has no moderator and is not adjourned by any entity whatsoever. This ensures a very secure operation and provides transparency as tampering with the data is practically impossible. This is where the discovery of Blockchain(Nakamoto, 2009; Vujicic,et.al.,2018) proved to be ultimate solution. The blockchain is an extremely compact and secure database system that ensures many aspects of security as its top priority. The key-point that should be taken into consideration is, it is distributed yet provides a very top tier security. The most considerable point of the blockchain was its decentralized nature. From a very top view it looks and operates like a typical database but inside operation is far more different. The structuring of the data is different as it stores the information in blocks as its name implies. Then a chain of these blocks is made that is linked with the previous block. This is redundant and changing one block is impossible. A change to one block requires all the blocks to grant access, which also is adjourned by the rules of a smart contract. So practically this makes it heavily decentralized in working and impossible to break. The chain is tightly linked and requires to reflect change in all the blocks which is great for any application that is for preserving the integrity and avoiding tampering of the data.

Figure 1. Blockchain diagram

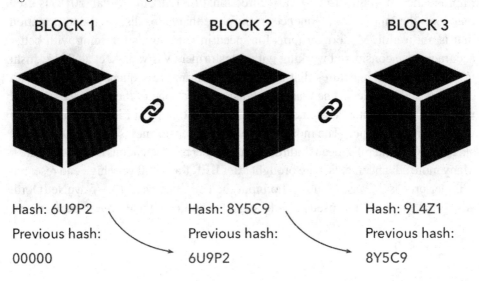

These blocks operate on a real-time mechanism, so this makes it harder to make changes. This application heavily influenced the cryptocurrency(Farell, R,2015; Jose, K.A,2018) area as the real time of the transaction was necessary. This uses transparency and real time changes for security reasons (Hiran, K et al). Bitcoin is a very famous cryptocurrency that is traded on daily basis and operates on blockchain. The currency is peer to peer and required all the properties listed by the blockchain. The records stored in traditional databases are with typical non-redundant process, where as blockchain does with blocks and the data stored is known as ledger. The concept of decentralization is implemented in blockchain, making the ledgers decentralized and calling the process as decentralized ledger transfer for any transaction process. The benefit of the blockchain application was massive cost reduction that eliminates the need of third party verification.

Quantum Computing

A lot of things will be consecutively explained in this article along the way pertaining to quantum blockchain, but first understanding the quantum computer as a bigger picture is necessary. The term was coined in 1981 itself when creating exponentially growing simulations in physics were the need. This problem persisted without a definite solution until the area of quantum mechanics (Bhatt et al,2019; Ladd et al,2010; Jazaeri et al,2019) was discovered. The NP problems in computer science are no different from complex problems in physics or chemistry which grow exponentially.

Figure 2. Quantum computing

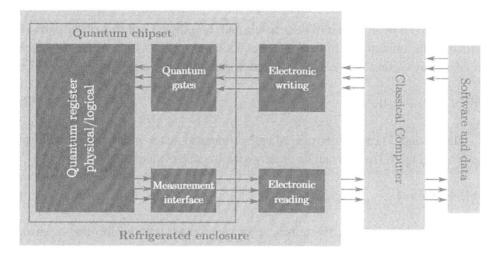

Traditional solution was paralleling the pipelines in which process of the data takes place, which does work but many problems are left hanging as parallelization solves the problem in linear time and fails to cover for exponentially growing time. The expression to work with quantum computers can be given through quantum mechanics itself as it using quantum bits instead of normal bits. The context of superposition (Li, T., Yin et al.,2016) is the most important concept in quantum mechanics as it gives the intuition of how things work. It has a very different understanding as it states the world operates in a simulation and the possibility of the two events happening are evident but the event happens where the native experiences the dynamics of it happening. This is a very deep explanation and can be broken down in very subtle explanation as measurements collapse the superposition to observed state of the native. This is the root idea of the quantum mechanics. The quantum computing holds all the possible dynamics from the quantum mechanics and it is not a replacement for the traditional computers available currently as all the operations taking place on it are working in different system. Some research gives an estimation that problems from Bounded-Error Quantum Polynomial-Time can be brought to polynomial time using the quantum computing, although it is just an estimation. For understanding the mathematical intuition of the quantum computing, one needs to focus on superposition intuition from quantum mechanics as it directly is associated with qubits (quantum bits) which are the bits of the quantum computers. The basic intuition can be developed with the spinning particle in the state of superposition using dirac notation, which is an equation of linear dimension of particle imposing position in upward and downward direction.

$$\alpha_0 |0\rangle + \alpha_1 |1\rangle \tag{1}$$

where the $|0\rangle$ is upward spin of the particle and $|1\rangle$ is downward spin of the particle with α as the amplitude. This makes the equation of superposition where the states are the basis vectors. These can be linked to quantum state equation.

$$|\Psi\rangle = \alpha_0 |0\rangle + \alpha_0 |1\rangle. \tag{2}$$

The $|0\rangle$ and $|1\rangle$ can be considered as 2 orthogonal states and their probabilities need to add up to 1 which can be presented with simple equation as

$$|\alpha_0|2 + |\alpha_1|2 = 1 \tag{3}$$

The deeper insights of the qubit can be represented with by forming a tensor product of the composite system in quantum states.

$$|v\rangle \otimes |\omega\rangle$$

where

$$|a\rangle|b\rangle = |a\rangle \otimes |b\rangle = [xu, xv...yu, yv...] \tag{4}$$

The information of 2 bits consisting of 0 and 1 in 2-qubit computation is given by

$$|\Psi_0\rangle |\Psi_1\rangle = \alpha_0\beta_0 |00\rangle + \alpha_0\beta_1 |01\rangle + \alpha_1\beta_0 |10\rangle + \alpha_1\beta_1 |11\rangle \tag{5}$$

The equation 5 is the representation of 2-qubits and this does increase exponentially overtime causing a very high computation. 3-qubits won't even fit easily here and 64-qubits has 20 digits of bits. Quantum gates are something that certainly separates the traditional bits and qubits equation where superposition is manipulated with a linear unit with $|\phi\rangle \rightarrow U|\phi\rangle$. This unitary operation can be given as

$$UU^\dagger = U^\dagger U = I \tag{6}$$

where U has a complex conjugate which when transposed is given as $U^\dagger$. These are efficient for preserving the norm and maintains the total probability after the state of transformation to 1 for maintaining the superposition on the surface of observational units giving equation as

$$|||\phi\rangle = ||U|\phi\rangle|| \tag{7}$$

This certainly gives an edge for collapsing the superposition to linear unit of the complex algorithms. Assuming the Shor's (Shor P.W., 1999) algorithm for cracking RSA (Rivest, R.L et al.,1978) can be computed to polynomial time with equation

$$|\Psi\rangle = \frac{1}{\sqrt{2^q}} \sum |x\rangle a^x \bmod 15\rangle \tag{8}$$

In a similar fashion the classical computing falls short for solving such exponential time problems. The quantum computers compute the complex Discrete Fourier Transform in a very simple manner and can be given as

$$X_k = \sum x_n . e^{-\frac{2\pi i}{N}km} \tag{9}$$

This makes the use of quantum computing as an aid for traditional systems and not a replacement as the technology is just evolving itself.

Quantum Blockchain

This term is specifically coined for the advent threat to the blockchain systems using quantum computing technologies. The strongest point of a blockchain is its security which is very strong and almost unbreakable. The amount of the entire chain that needs to be broken needs the person to acquire atleast 51% of the entire chain. This is currently impossible with the state-of-the-art systems, but can be done with quantum computing in the near future. The only reason of the quantum computers able to calculate different bits in parallel fashion, the superposition is an important concept. The entanglement is the prime factor that can break the blockchain in upcoming years. In quantum mechanics it is linked with the perfect entanglement of the particle interaction with each other. The changes in one particle affect the other particles in same dimension space. So considering the superposition and entanglement, the tasks will be performed in a sequential manner and parallelization will merely become a complex problem in high performance computing. Superposition uses qubits which exponentially grow, as 2-qubits result in 4 different outcomes taking place simultaneously whereas 4 qubits will work with 16 different outcomes and so on. Current state-of-the-art qubits are less likely to break a blockchain. The blockchain is a distributed decentralized ledger and is tightly coupled protected by cryptography algorithms. A powerful system with high number of qubits can perform alteration before the data goes into the ledger. This task will be seamlessly become possible with the quantum computers. Since the data performs hashing before being added to the ledger and one tampered document will create an infraction in the integrity, the alteration will be done before the write operation. If one-way mathematical functions are used the alteration can be performed. Every blockchain intended for certain operation has a smart contract. This has digital signatures. These can be broken using one-way mathematical functions. One example of it is a trapdoor function. This is used to compute the solution in a reverse manner. Basically there is a single way in which the operation will take place and if a reverse solution is used the deliberated information is leaked. It does require additional information though, so in the case of blockchain this will be a difficult task. The trapdoor functions have been there since the ages of asymmetric and public-key encryption techniques were discovered. The RSA (Rivest, R.L et al.,1978) and Rabin (Yaqin, A et al.,2019) were cryptographical functions that did survive the trapdoor function. Considering the prime factorization involved where there exponential modulo of the composite number, the trapdoor functions faced limitations. This is where quantum computers can break that chain as it works efficiently with the exponential functions. Another one-way mathematical function is one-way hash function. One-way hash function is a compression mathematical function that takes variable length of input and hashes it into fixed length binary sequence. It is very difficult to compute the inverse function with a traditional computer, but this task will be not daunting for a quantum computer. Quantum computing the reverse calculations will become very commonplace. Manipulation in the transaction history will become very easy. Changing the hash of blockchain is not possible because it spoils the chain and it will inform the entire peer-to-peer network. That is the reason the breakage can be caused without spoiling the hash. The record needs to be changed, then the result is supposed to be encrypted and hash should be checked if it is same as earlier otherwise entire system is failed. Calculating a private key from a public key will be also possible using the quantum computer. RSA is one of the algorithms that work with public and private key systems. The RSA can be cracked using the Shor's (Shor P.W., 1999) Algorithm. For breaking a public key, 2 prime number combinations are required. Quantum computers factor very large numbers in fraction of seconds. So breaking modern day RSA will not be a daunting task for quantum computers in upcoming years. If we currently consider the time complexity of the prime factorization given in equation below

$$O\left(\exp\left(\sqrt{\frac{64}{9}n}\left(\log n\right)^2\right)\right) \tag{10}$$

where it operates in Big-Oh complexity and n is number of bits to represent the product of prime numbers which Shor's algorithm can perform. The time complexity for it can be simplified easily by

$$O(n^3 \log n)$$

with number of gates as

$$O(n^2 \log n \log \log n) \tag{11}$$

The prime factorization works with favorable odds. The Shor's (Shor P.W., 1999) algorithm is from a class of models that are known as Bounded-Error Probabilistic Polynomial Time (BPP). This function for quantum computing can be denoted as

$$f_x(a) = x^a \bmod N \tag{12}$$

This is used for computing the greatest common divisor (GCD) effectively. The considerable time complexity is $O(n)$ and computing polynomial time is common practice but usually worst case scenario is considered as exponential.

Quantum Resistant Blockchain

The quantum resistant blockchain remains essential after understanding the threats of the quantum computers for blockchain as they can tamper the information before writing the record on blocks without breaking the hash. Before understanding the resistant system of it, the problems could be understood in more depth. Many advance problems can be focused. Hashcash proof-of-work was represented for Bitcoin (Aggarwal, D et al.,2017) where using a Grover search algorithm(Grover, L K et al.,1996), the quantum computers can easily perform fewer hashes in quadratic time that beats the traditional computer. The gate speeds can range upto 100 Ghz allowing quantum computers to solve the problem about 100 times faster. The private key derived from the public key will be main issue of concern. Traditional modern day computers are inefficient for performing that, but this task won't be daunting for quantum computers. The entanglement and superposition will be used for cracking the cryptography. The system will use (Roetteler, M et al.,2017) quantum resource estimation for computing the discrete logarithms for elliptic curve. Majority of blockchain uses the Elliptic Curve Digital Signature Algorithm (ECSDA) (Al-Zubaidie et al., 2019; Bi W. et al.,2018; Sonnino et al.,2016) for cryptographical hashes. Considering quantum computer, Shor's algorithm can be used to break Elliptic Curve Digital Signature Algorithm (Proos, J et al.,2003) where private key can be derived from public key that can create a transaction for handling wallet. Since ECSDA can be broken, RSA (Rivest, R.L et al.,1978) is not a challenge. Quantum factoring with shor's algorithm was demonstrated over silicon photonic chip (Politi, A et al.,2009) that gave a small insight on the breakdown of experiment.

Figure 3. Quantum resistant blockchain

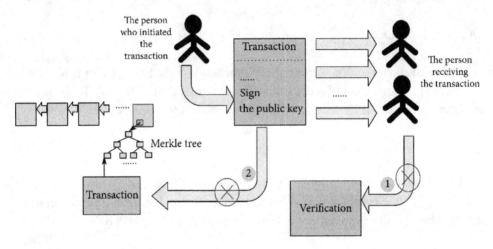

Greater developments were brought with Variational Quantum Factoring (Anschuetz et al.,2018) which is more stable and error-less than traditional shor's algorithm. The algorithm is still under development but will work efficiently with Noisy Intermediate Scale Quantum (NISQ) (Bharti, K et al.,2022) computers. The concept of post-quantum cryptography (Bavdekar, et al.,2022; Jain R et al.) can make some changes and this will definitely become the basis for quantum resistant blockchain. Bringing the change in schemes of signature will be the primary task of quantum resistant blockchain which won't be a easy task for sure. This will be bringing change in every single cryptocurrency wallet. The need for consensus will be next challenge where it is supposed to be implemented through a fork. Reaching the apex with consensus for a decentralized system like blockchain is not an easy task certainly. It is like scaling the entire bitcoin in a longer run. The most important task among all will be post-quantum cryptography as it is like writing an entire scheme of security-based algorithms. Considering the stateful signatures using the XMSS (Buchmann, J et al.,2011) is first aspect. For making it user friendly the use of

WOTS+ (Hu¨lsing, A et al.,2017) is an aspect. Handling the 41kB signatures using the SPHINCS (Bernstein et al., 2014) is one more aspect. Handling the side channel attacks using BLISS (Espitau et al.,2017) is one more aspect. IOTA signatures are very common solution for shifting at the moment. The quantum resistant ledger (Stewart, I et al.,2018) uses XMSS and better functioning. The safe solution for transferring of the funds is by committing to quantum resistance suggested by Stewart, which can be termed as defense for bitcoin against a fast quantum computing attack. This is a quantum resistant signature scheme that has been implemented. The hash of the public key and quantum resistant public key is made. This creates a strong system as tampering of private key through the public key is avoided as there is quantum resistant public key. The quantum capable adversaries will be a challenge in upcoming period for which delay phase will work much more effectively. Not reusing any addresses is terminology that makes the Bitcoin quantum resistant. An eclipse attack (Heilman, E et al.,2015) is a network level attack performed on peer to-peer systems. This can cut slack for extra time required to work with the public keys for making the respective private keys. The simple solution for this is using First In First Out (FIFO) system because it will ensure the transactions are in order as they come and forged transactions can be avoided. Since the transactions are taking place, the man-in-the-middle attack is very common but fortunately RSA and ECDSA can be used which cannot be broken. The attack if smartly handled applied before the original transaction reaches the network can cause damage. Speaking of multicast, it is also not much effective. The signature schemes once designed will secure blockchain from quantum-based attacks and quantum resistant blockchain will be able to avoid them to certain extent.

CPS Blockchain

The cyber physical system has a hierarchical structure where system levels are complementary. The level of the CPS that interacts with the physical level and is known as unit level. It is the smallest unit and do not impose threat to entire integrity of the system.

The CPS 4.0 industry standard, works with the automatic flow of the range interactions. There are many system level CPS that are considered as System-Of System. The merging of blockchain in this hierarchy is one of the ideas that needs to be implemented. The higher hierarchy units of CPS can be implemented with the blockchain. The data storing mechanism in such a system will ensure a very definitive approach of safeguarding the data with transparency and decentralized system.

Figure 4. CPS blockchain

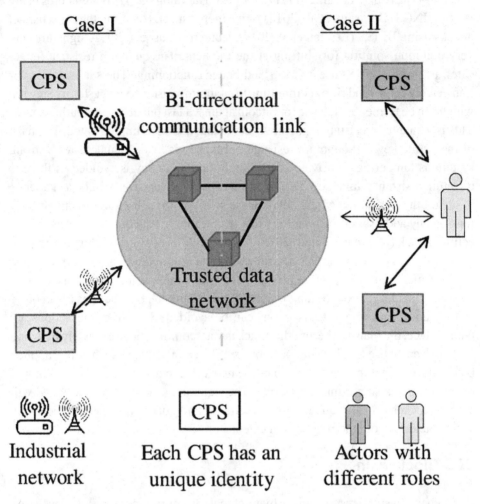

CPS Blockchain Applications

The wide variety of applications for cyber physical systems are already discussed by many researchers, but in this section, we will discuss the subtle ways with which one can incorporate the best use of blockchain in current state-of-the-art systems.

Transportation- The transportation uses the cyber physical systems for well-balanced management of the road network. The transportation network requires a lot of sensors and this can help retain a lot of information for better understanding of the network. The interactions of different vehicles on the road does make a difference and this information is supposed to be secure. Disruptions in it can cause damages on different plane, for which blockchain can prove to be efficient.

Agriculture- The impact of environment disrupts the harvesting of the crops so many sensors are trying to make agriculture smart. This can create a difference in the amount of irrigation and mapping the quality of crops. The collection of the crops also accounts in record of collected harvest and number of crops that were available. This is where the need of transparency and security arises. Blockchain in this situation can make a difference as the transparency of the harvested crop will be notified and seen by the all levels of management. So, the loss or stealing can be kept with notified on record of premise.

Smart Grids- Clean energy is one of the prominent tasks that is associated with smart grids and smart management in it is essential. Wastage of water is done on a very high level for which employing some sensors can play great role. The use of CPS with Blockchain in such area can prove to be an efficient cause. Managing the use of energy used on daily basis and smartly inducing the resources can be done effectively.

Smart Buildings- Current state-of-the-art CPS used in buildings can monitor the temperature and humidity. The use of CPS can be extended further to make buildings more earthquake resistant. Detailed analysis of every apartment can later be induced for any architectural faults. Since information about every apartment is very sensitive, using blockchain can prove to be effective.

Future Scope

The standards that are established in pristine order at this very moment from this article focus on the broad perspective that can be subjected to very wide variety of changes. The improvements in the base CPS 4.0 system itself can prove to be improvements in entire CPS ecosystem itself. The changes that can be brought, would be development of the hardware systems that we currently look at in a significant manner. These include the state-of-the-art systems that closely work with sensor-based system. Now these can change significantly when there is a major adhering to the standard protocols itself. Using RISC based systems as such where entire base serialization changes in the assembling of the system will to development in the entire implementations. Another small subtle change can be observed at the application level where the machine learning algorithms themselves become more welcoming and conducive to work with the sensor-based data. These day by day are showing improvements in the respective areas and can be extended for the better good of the CPS.

CONCLUSION

This article depicts a very vivid review of the CPS based Blockchain. Certainly, the concept is just an idea and the required approach with the CPS 4.0. The article sheds light on basics of blockchain, quantum computing and quantum effects on blockchain and quantum resistant blockchain. The ideas are linked with one another sequentially in this article. This article does open many new problems about the implementation of the ideas by giving them an expression. This article can be referenced as a material for understanding all the prerequisites required to implement the systems.

REFERENCES

Agarap, A. (2018). *Deep learning using rectified linear units (relu)*. arXiv preprint arXiv:1803.08375.

Aggarwal, D., Brennen, G., Lee, T., Santha, M., & Tomamichel, M. (2017). *Quantum attacks on Bitcoin, and how to protect against them*. arXiv preprint arXiv:1710.10377.

Aguida, M., Ouchani, S., & Benmalek, M. (2020). A Review on Cyber-Physical Systems: Models and Architectures. In *2020 IEEE 29th International Conference on Enabling Technologies: Infrastructure for Collaborative Enterprises (WETICE)* (pp. 275-278). IEEE.

Al-Zubaidie, M., Zhang, Z., & Zhang, J. (2019). *Efficient and secure ECDSA algorithm and its applications: a survey*. arXiv preprint arXiv:1902.10313.

Albawi, S., Mohammed, T., & Al-Zawi, S. (2017). Understanding of a convolutional neural network. In *2017 International Conference on Engineering and Technology (ICET)* (pp. 1-6). Academic Press.

Allende, M., Leon, D., Ceron, S., Leal, A., Pareja, A., Da Silva, M., Pardo, A., Jones, D., Worrall, D., & Merriman, B. (2021). *Quantum-resistance in blockchain networks*. arXiv preprint arXiv:2106.06640.

Alpaydin, E. (2020). *Introduction to machine learning*. MIT Press.

Anschuetz, E., Olson, J., Aspuru-Guzik, A., & Cao, Y. (2018). *Variational quantum factoring*. arXiv preprint arXiv:1808.08927.

Bavdekar, R., Chopde, E., Bhatia, A., Tiwari, K., & Daniel, S. (2022). *Post Quantum Cryptography: Techniques, Challenges, Standardization, and Directions for Future Research*. arXiv preprint arXiv:2202.02826.

Bernstein, Hopwood, Hulsing, Lange, Niederhagen, Papachristodoulou, Schwabe, & Wilcox-O'Hearn (2014). SPHINCS: Practical Stateless Hash-Based Signatures. *IACR Cryptol. ePrint Arch., 2014*, 795.

Bharti, K., Cervera-Lierta, A., Kyaw, T., Haug, T., Alperin-Lea, S., Anand, A., Degroote, M., Heimonen, H., Kottmann, J., Menke, T., Mok, W.-K., Sim, S., Kwek, L.-C., & Aspuru-Guzik, A. (2022). Noisy intermediate-scale quantum algorithms. *Reviews of Modern Physics*, *94*(1), 015004. doi:10.1103/RevModPhys.94.015004

Bhatt, H., & Gautam, S. (2019). Quantum Computing: A New Era of Computer Science. In *2019 6th International Conference on Computing for Sustainable Global Development (INDIACom)* (pp. 558-561). Academic Press.

Bi, W., Jia, X., & Zheng, M. (2018). *A secure multiple elliptic curves digital signature algorithm for blockchain*. arXiv preprint arXiv:1808.02988.

Bochkovskiy, A., Wang, C. Y., & Liao, H. Y. (2020). *Yolov4: Optimal speed and accuracy of object detection*. arXiv preprint arXiv:2004.10934.

Bolya, D., Zhou, C., Xiao, F., & Lee, Y. (2019). Yolact: Real-time instance segmentation. In *Proceedings of the IEEE/CVF international conference on computer vision* (pp. 9157–9166). IEEE.

Bolya, D., Zhou, C., Xiao, F., & Lee, Y. (2020). Yolact++: Better real-time instance segmentation. *IEEE Transactions on Pattern Analysis and Machine Intelligence*. PMID:32755851

Breiman, L. (1996). Bagging predictors. *Machine Learning*, *24*(2), 123–140. doi:10.1007/BF00058655

Breiman, L. (2001). Random forests. *Machine Learning*, *45*(1), 5–32. doi:10.1023/A:1010933404324

Buchmann, J., Dahmen, E., & Hülsing, A. (2011). XMSS – A practical forward secure signature scheme based on minimal security assumptions. In Proceedings of the 4th International Conference on Post-Quantum Cryptography, PQCRYPTO'11 (pp. 117–129). Springer. doi:10.1007/978-3-642-25405-5_8

Chen, T., & Guestrin, C. (2016). Xgboost: A scalable tree boosting system. In *Proceedings of the 22nd acm sigkdd international conference on knowledge discovery and data mining* (pp. 785–794). 10.1145/2939672.2939785

Cho, K., Van Merrienboer, B., Gulcehre, C., Bahdanau, D., Bougares, F., Schwenk, H., & Bengio, Y. (2014). *Learning phrase representations using RNN encoder-decoder for statistical machine translation*. arXiv preprint arXiv:1406.1078.

Cormack, R. M. (1971). A Review of Classification. *Journal of the Royal Statistical Society. Series A (General)*, *134*(3), 321–367. doi:10.2307/2344237

Cui, Z., Ke, R., Pu, Z., & Wang, Y. (2018). *Deep bidirectional and unidirectional LSTM recurrent neural network for network-wide traffic speed prediction*. arXiv preprint arXiv:1801.02143.

Cunningham, P., & Delany, S. (2021). k-Nearest neighbour classifiers-A Tutorial. *ACM Computing Surveys*, *54*(6), 1–25. doi:10.1145/3459665

De Ryck, T., Lanthaler, S., & Mishra, S. (2021). On the approximation of functions by tanh neural networks. *Neural Networks*, *143*, 732–750. doi:10.1016/j.neunet.2021.08.015 PMID:34482172

Devlin, J., Chang, M. W., Lee, K., & Toutanova, K. (2018). *Bert: Pre-training of deep bidirectional transformers for language understanding*. arXiv preprint arXiv:1810.04805.

Duchi, J., Hazan, E., & Singer, Y. (2011). Adaptive Subgradient Methods for Online Learning and Stochastic Optimization. *Journal of Machine Learning Research*, *12*(61), 2121–2159.

Elgendy, N., & Elragal, A. (2014). Big data analytics: a literature review paper. In Industrial conference on data mining (pp. 214–227). doi:10.1007/978-3-319-08976-8_16

Espitau, T., Fouque, P.-A., Gérard, B., & Tibouchi, M. (2017). Side-Channel Attacks on BLISS Lattice-Based Signatures: Exploiting Branch Tracing against strongSwan and Electromagnetic Emanations in Microcontrollers. *Proceedings of the 2017 ACM SIGSAC Conference on Computer and Communications Security*. 10.1145/3133956.3134028

Farell, R. (2015). *An Analysis of the Cryptocurrency Industry*. Academic Press.

Fernández-Caramès, T., & Fraga-Lamas, P. (2020). Towards Post-Quantum Blockchain: A Review on Blockchain Cryptography Resistant to Quantum Computing Attacks. *IEEE Access: Practical Innovations, Open Solutions*, *8*, 21091–21116. doi:10.1109/ACCESS.2020.2968985

Freund, Y., & Schapire, R. E. (1999). A Short Introduction to Boosting. Academic Press.

Girshick, R., Donahue, J., Darrell, T., & Malik, J. (2014). Rich feature hierarchies for accurate object detection and semantic segmentation. In *Proceedings of the IEEE conference on computer vision and pattern recognition* (pp. 580–587). 10.1109/CVPR.2014.81

Girshick, R. (2015). Fast r-cnn. In *Proceedings of the IEEE international conference on computer vision* (pp. 1440–1448). IEEE.

Goodfellow, I., Bengio, Y., & Courville, A. (2016). *Deep learning*. MIT Press.

Grover, L. (1996). A fast quantum mechanical algorithm for database search. In *Proceedings of the twenty-eighth annual ACM symposium on Theory of computing* (pp. 212–219). 10.1145/237814.237866

Gupta, A., Joshi, R., & Laban, R. (2022). *Detection of Tool based Edited Images from Error Level Analysis and Convolutional Neural Network. arXiv preprint arXiv:2204.09075.*

Gupta, A., Joshi, R., Tambe, S., Laban, R., Tandlekar, G., & Chitre, V. (2022). Optimization Effects for Word Representations with L2-Regularized Non-Parametric Model for Contrasting Epochs. In *2022 3rd International Conference for Emerging Technology (INCET)* (pp. 1–6). 10.1109/INCET54531.2022.9824562

Gupta, A., Nair, S., Joshi, R., & Chitre, V. (2022). Residual-Concatenate Neural Network with Deep Regularization Layers for Binary Classification. In *2022 6th International Conference on Intelligent Computing and Control Systems (ICICCS)* (pp. 1018–1022). 10.1109/ICICCS53718.2022.9788437

Gupta, A., Shetty, S., Joshi, R., & Laban, R. (2021). Succinct differentiation of disparate boosting ensemble learning methods for prognostication of polycystic ovary syndrome diagnosis. In *2021 International Conference on Advances in Computing, Communication, and Control (ICAC3)* (pp. 1–5). 10.1109/ICAC353642.2021.9697163

Gupta, A., Soni, H., Joshi, R., & Laban, R. (2022). *Discriminant Analysis in Contrasting Dimensions for Polycystic Ovary Syndrome Prognostication.* arXiv preprint arXiv:2201.03029.

Gupta, A., Thustu, S., Thakor, R., Patil, S., Joshi, R., & Laban, R. (2022). *Prediction of Maneuvering Status for Aerial Vehicles using Supervised Learning Methods.* arXiv preprint arXiv:2206.10303.

He, K., Zhang, X., Ren, S., & Sun, J. (2016). Deep residual learning for image recognition. In *Proceedings of the IEEE conference on computer vision and pattern recognition* (pp. 770–778). IEEE.

Hearst, M., Dumais, S., Osuna, E., Platt, J., & Scholkopf, B. (1998). Support vector machines. *IEEE Intelligent Systems & their Applications, 13*(4), 18–28. doi:10.1109/5254.708428

Heilman, E., Kendler, A., Zohar, A., & Goldberg, S. (2015). Eclipse Attacks on Bitcoin's Peer-to-Peer Network. *USENIX Security Symposium*.

Hiran, K. (2021). Investigating Factors Influencing the Adoption of IT Cloud Computing Platforms in Higher Education: Case of Sub-Saharan Africa With IT Professionals. *International Journal of Human Capital and Information Technology Professionals, 12*(3), 21–36. doi:10.4018/IJHCITP.2021070102

Hiran, K., Jain, R., Lakhwani, K., & Doshi, R. (2021). *Machine Learning: Master Supervised and Unsupervised Learning Algorithms with Real Examples (English Edition)*. BPB Publications.

Huberty, C. J. (1975). Discriminant Analysis. *Review of Educational Research, 45*(4), 543–598. doi:10.3102/00346543045004543

Hülsing. (2017). *WOTS+ – Shorter Signatures for Hash-Based Signature Schemes*. Academic Press.

Jazaeri, F., Beckers, A., Tajalli, A., & Sallese, J. M. (2019). A review on quantum computing: From qubits to front-end electronics and cryogenic MOSFET physics. In *2019 MIXDES-26th International Conference "Mixed Design of Integrated Circuits and Systems"* (pp. 15–25). Academic Press.

Jazdi, N. (2014). Cyber physical systems in the context of Industry 4.0. *2014 IEEE International Conference on Automation, Quality and Testing, Robotics*, 1-4. 10.1109/AQTR.2014.6857843

Joshi, R., & Gupta, A. (2022). *Performance Comparison of Simple Transformer and Res-CNN-BiLSTM for Cyberbullying Classification*. arXiv preprint arXiv:2206.02206.

Joshi, R., Gupta, A., & Kanvinde, N. (2022). *Res-CNN-BiLSTM Network for overcoming Mental Health Disturbances caused due to Cyberbullying through Social Media*. arXiv preprint arXiv:2204.09738.

Kanvinde, N., Gupta, A., & Joshi, R. (2022). *Binary Classification for High Dimensional Data using Supervised Non-Parametric Ensemble Method*. arXiv preprint arXiv:2202.07779.

Kingma, D., & Ba, J. (2014). *Adam: A method for stochastic optimization*. arXiv preprint arXiv:1412.6980.

Kotsiantis, S. (2007). Supervised Machine Learning: A Review of Classification Techniques. In *Proceedings of the 2007 Conference on Emerging Artificial Intelligence Applications in Computer Engineering: Real Word AI Systems with Applications in EHealth, HCI, Information Retrieval and Pervasive Technologies* (pp. 3–24). IOS Press.

Krizhevsky, A., Sutskever, I., & Hinton, G. (2012). Imagenet classification with deep convolutional neural networks. *Advances in Neural Information Processing Systems*, 25.

Kumar, S., Tiwari, P., & Zymbler, M. (2019). Internet of Things is a revolutionary approach for future technology enhancement: A review. *Journal of Big Data*, 6(1), 1–21. doi:10.118640537-019-0268-2

Kumari, R., & Kr, S. (2017). Machine Learning: A Review on Binary Classification. *International Journal of Computers and Applications*, 160(7), 11–15. doi:10.5120/ijca2017913083

Ladd, T., Jelezko, F., Laflamme, R., Nakamura, Y., Monroe, C., & O'Brien, J. (2010). Quantum computers. *Nature, 464*(7285), 45–53.

Lakhwani, K., Gianey, H., Wireko, J., & Hiran, K. (2020). *Internet of Things (IoT): Principles, paradigms and applications of IoT*. BPB Publications.

Längkvist, M., Karlsson, L., & Loutfi, A. (2014). A review of unsupervised feature learning and deep learning for time-series modeling. *Pattern Recognition Letters*, 42, 11–24. doi:10.1016/j.patrec.2014.01.008

LeCun, Y., Bengio, Y., & Hinton, G. (2015). Deep learning. *Nature, 521*(7553), 436–444.

LeCun, Y., Bottou, L., Bengio, Y., & Haffner, P. (1998). Gradient-based learning applied to document recognition. *Proceedings of the IEEE, 86*(11), 2278–2324. doi:10.1109/5.726791

Li, J., Sun, A., Han, J., & Li, C. (2020). A survey on deep learning for named entity recognition. *IEEE Transactions on Knowledge and Data Engineering, 34*(1), 50–70. doi:10.1109/TKDE.2020.2981314

Li, S., & Tso, G. (2018). *Bottleneck supervised u-net for pixel-wise liver and tumor segmentation*. arXiv preprint arXiv:1810.10331.

Li, T., & Yin, Z. Q. (2016). Quantum superposition, entanglement, and state teleportation of a microorganism on an electromechanical oscillator. *Science Bulletin, 61*(2), 163–171. doi:10.100711434-015-0990-x

Madakam, S., Lake, V., Lake, V., Lake, V., & ... (2015). Internet of Things (IoT): A literature review. *Journal of Computer and Communications*, *3*(05), 164–173. doi:10.4236/jcc.2015.35021

Mahrishi, M., Hiran, K., Meena, G., & Sharma, P. (2020). *Machine Learning and Deep Learning in Real-Time Applications*. IGI Global. doi:10.4018/978-1-7998-3095-5

Martin, G., & Chang, H. (2001). System-on-Chip design. In *ASICON 2001. 2001 4th International Conference on ASIC Proceedings* (Cat. No.01TH8549) (pp. 12-17). 10.1109/ICASIC.2001.982487

Mathew, S., Gulia, S., Singh, V. P., & Sachin Dev, V. (2017). A Review Paper on Cloud Computing and Its Security Concerns. RICE. doi:10.15439/2017R70

Maulud, D., & Abdulazeez, A. (2020). A Review on Linear Regression Comprehensive in Machine Learning. *Journal of Applied Science and Technology Trends*, *1*(4), 140–147. doi:10.38094/jastt1457

Musale, M., & Joshi, R. (2021). Compendious Comparison of Capsule Network and Convolutional Neural Network through end-to-end Digit Classification Application. In *International Journal of Intelligent Communication*. Computing and Networks.

Nair, S., Gupta, A., Joshi, R., & Chitre, V. (2022). *Combining Varied Learners for Binary Classification using Stacked Generalization*. arXiv preprint arXiv:2202.08910.

Nakamoto, S. (2009). Bitcoin: A Peer-to-Peer Electronic Cash System. Academic Press.

Natekin, A., & Knoll, A. (2013). Gradient boosting machines, a tutorial. *Frontiers in Neurorobotics*, *7*. PMID:24409142

Oord, A., Dieleman, S., Zen, H., Simonyan, K., Vinyals, O., Graves, A., Kalchbrenner, N., Senior, A., & Kavukcuoglu, K. (2016). *Wavenet: A generative model for raw audio*. arXiv preprint arXiv:1609.03499.

Opitz, D., & Maclin, R. (1999). Popular ensemble methods: An empirical study. *Journal of Artificial Intelligence Research*, *11*, 169–198. doi:10.1613/jair.614

Patel, S., Vyas, A., & Hiran, K. (2022). Infrastructure Health Monitoring Using Signal Processing Based on an Industry 4.0 System. *Cyber-Physical Systems and Industry 4.0: Practical Applications and Security Management*, 249–260.

Peng, C.-Y. J., Lee, K. L., & Ingersoll, G. M. (2002). An Introduction to Logistic Regression Analysis and Reporting. *The Journal of Educational Research*, *96*(1), 3–14. doi:10.1080/00220670209598786

Politi, A., Matthews, J., & O'brien, J. (2009). Shor's quantum factoring algorithm on a photonic chip. *Science, 325*(5945), 1221–1221. doi:10.1126cience.1173731 PMID:19729649

Prokhorenkova, L., Gusev, G., Vorobev, A., Dorogush, A., & Gulin, A. (2018). CatBoost: Unbiased boosting with categorical features. *Advances in Neural Information Processing Systems*, 31.

Proos, J., & Zalka, C. (2003). *Shor's discrete logarithm quantum algorithm for elliptic curves*. arXiv preprint quant-ph/0301141.

Quinlan, J. (1986). Induction of Decision Trees. *Machine Learning, 1*(1), 81–106. doi:10.1007/BF00116251

Ramayah, T., Ahmad, N. H., Halim, H. A., Siti, R. M. Z., & Lo, M.-C. (2010). Discriminant analysis: An illustrated example. *African Journal of Business Management, 4*, 1654–1667.

Rawung, R., & Putrada, A. (2014). Cyber physical system: Paper survey. In *2014 International Conference on ICT For Smart Society (ICISS)* (pp. 273-278). Academic Press.

Redmon, J., Divvala, S., Girshick, R., & Farhadi, A. (2016). You only look once: Unified, real-time object detection. In *Proceedings of the IEEE conference on computer vision and pattern recognition* (pp. 779–788). 10.1109/CVPR.2016.91

Rehman, H., Asif, M., & Ahmad, M. (2017). Future applications and research challenges of IOT. In *2017 International Conference on Information and Communication Technologies (ICICT)* (pp. 68-74). 10.1109/ICICT.2017.8320166

Ren, S., He, K., Girshick, R., & Sun, J. (2015). Faster r-cnn: Towards real-time object detection with region proposal networks. *Advances in Neural Information Processing Systems*, 28.

Rivest, R., Shamir, A., & Adleman, L. (1978). A Method for Obtaining Digital Signatures and Public-Key Cryptosystems. *Communications of the ACM, 21*(2), 120–126. doi:10.1145/359340.359342

Roetteler, M., Naehrig, M., Svore, K., & Lauter, K. (2017). Quantum resource estimates for computing elliptic curve discrete logarithms. In *International Conference on the Theory and Application of Cryptology and Information Security* (pp. 241–270). 10.1007/978-3-319-70697-9_9

Ronneberger, O., Fischer, P., & Brox, T. (2015). U-net: Convolutional networks for biomedical image segmentation. In *International Conference on Medical image computing and computer-assisted intervention* (pp. 234–241). 10.1007/978-3-319-24574-4_28

Ruder, S. (2016). *An overview of gradient descent optimization algorithms.* arXiv preprint arXiv:1609.04747.

Russakovsky, O., Deng, J., Su, H., Krause, J., Satheesh, S., Ma, S., Huang, Z., Karpathy, A., Khosla, A., Bernstein, M., Berg, A. C., & Fei-Fei, L. (2015). Imagenet large scale visual recognition challenge. *International Journal of Computer Vision*, *115*(3), 211–252. doi:10.100711263-015-0816-y

Sarker, I. (2021). Machine learning: Algorithms, real-world applications and research directions. *SN Computer Science*, *2*(3), 1–21. doi:10.100742979-021-00592-x PMID:33778771

Schapire, R. (1999). A Brief Introduction to Boosting. In *Proceedings of the 16th International Joint Conference on Artificial Intelligence* - Volume 2 (pp. 1401–1406). Morgan Kaufmann Publishers Inc.

Shinde, P., & Shah, S. (2018). A Review of Machine Learning and Deep Learning Applications. In *2018 Fourth International Conference on Computing Communication Control and Automation (ICCUBEA)* (pp. 1-6). 10.1109/ICCUBEA.2018.8697857

Shor, P. (1999). Polynomial-time algorithms for prime factorization and discrete logarithms on a quantum computer. *SIAM Review*, *41*(2), 303–332. doi:10.1137/S0036144598347011

Simonyan, K., & Zisserman, A. (2014). *Very deep convolutional networks for large-scale image recognition.* arXiv preprint arXiv:1409.1556.

Sonnino, A., & Sonnino, G. (2016). *Elliptic-Curves Cryptography on High-Dimensional Surfaces.* arXiv preprint arXiv:1610.01518.

Staudemeyer, R., & Morris, E. (2019). *Understanding LSTM–a tutorial into long short-term memory recurrent neural networks.* arXiv preprint arXiv:1909.09586.

Stewart, I., Ilie, D. I., Zamyatin, A., Werner, S. M., Torshizi, M. F., & Knottenbelt, W. J. (2018). Committing to quantum resistance: A slow defence for Bitcoin against a fast quantum computing attack. *Royal Society Open Science*, *5*(6), 5. doi:10.1098/rsos.180410 PMID:30110420

Szegedy, C., Liu, W., Jia, Y., Sermanet, P., Reed, S., Anguelov, D., Erhan, D., Vanhoucke, V., & Rabinovich, A. (2015). Going deeper with convolutions. In *Proceedings of the IEEE conference on computer vision and pattern recognition* (pp. 1–9). IEEE.

Tambe, S., Joshi, R., Gupta, A., Kanvinde, N., & Chitre, V. (2022). *Effects of Parametric and Non-Parametric Methods on High Dimensional Sparse Matrix Representations*. arXiv preprint arXiv:2202.02894.

Vaswani, A., Shazeer, N., Parmar, N., Uszkoreit, J., Jones, L., Gomez, A. K., & Polosukhin, I. (2017). Attention is all you need. Advances in neural information processing systems, 30.

Vujicic, D., Jagodic, D., & Randic, S. (2018). Blockchain technology, bitcoin, and Ethereum: A brief overview. *2018 17th International Symposium INFOTEH-JAHORINA (INFOTEH)*, 1-6.

Wolpert, D. H. (1992). Stacked generalization. *Neural Networks*, 5(2), 241–259. doi:10.1016/S0893-6080(05)80023-1

Yamashita, R., Nishio, M., Do, R., & Togashi, K. (2018). Convolutional neural networks: An overview and application in radiology. *Insights Into Imaging*, 9(4), 611–629. doi:10.100713244-018-0639-9 PMID:29934920

Yaqin, A., Dahlan, A., & Hermawan, R. (2019). Implementation of Algorithm Rabin-Karp for Thematic Determination of Thesis. In *2019 4th International Conference on Information Technology, Information Systems and Electrical Engineering (ICITISEE)* (pp. 395-400). Academic Press.

Zhang, P., Wang, L., Wang, W., Fu, K., Wang, J., & He, D. (2021). A Blockchain System Based on Quantum-Resistant Digital Signature. *Sec. and Commun. Netw., 2021*.

Zhang, Y., Jin, R., & Zhou, Z. H. (2010). Understanding bag-of-words model: A statistical framework. *International Journal of Machine Learning and Cybernetics*, 1(1), 43–52. doi:10.100713042-010-0001-0

Zheng, W., & Ren, Z. (2010). Field Programmable Gate Array Design and Implementation for Fast Fourior Transform Processor. In *2010 International Conference on E-Business and E-Government* (pp. 4039-4042). 10.1109/ICEE.2010.1014

Chapter 8
Quantum and Blockchain for Computing Paradigms Vision and Advancements

Neha Gupta
Symbiosis University of Applied Sciences, Indore, India

ABSTRACT

Blockchain and quantum technology breakthroughs are currently being debated publicly across a variety of forums. There are numerous applications and capabilities that can provide transparent, redundant, secure, accountable environments thanks to these technologies. To ensure resource-dependent high security requirements, certain cryptographic primitives and protocols can be used effectively. Quantum proofs, safe quantum solutions, and anti-quantum systems will assess any system for quantum attacks and create a secure quantum computing system. Therefore, this work intends to encourage experts from different fields to provide technology-integrated solutions that combine cost-effective and quality service, quickly, securely, and meet requirements. Researchers will be encouraged to provide helpful overviews and guidance in dealing with real-time applications from post-quantum technologies.

INTRODUCTION

The blockchain quantum is more concerned with security. For example, the fragility of Shor's method makes RSA public key encryption an important transitional technology for applications (LaPierre, 2021). For readers and practitioners who want to learn how to build, test, operate, deploy and maintain a next-generation system with interfaces, this book is an excellent resource. Secure cryptography

DOI: 10.4018/978-1-6684-5072-7.ch008

expertise and innovation. Ultimately, this chapter might serve as a useful guide for IT professionals to assist them comprehend the importance of technological transition and quantum computing activities during this transition(Grover, 1996). Future applications could benefit greatly from emerging technologies like quantum computing, configuration, design, and communication interfaces. There are enough safe bits in the computing world to protect networks from quantum attacks if these environments are used (Hilal et al., 2022; Sarmah, 2019). Using protocols like semi-DIQIP, it is possible to strengthen the security of a secure network by automatically identifying sections of the system and creating a trust network. It's not just software that quantum computing and quantum research come in handy, though. As a way to exhibit quantum technology, businesses can utilise devices such as quantum memory and quantum repeaters to show off their capabilities. When it comes to long-distance quantum communication, for example, a single quantum repeater could help reduce costs and improve security. One of the most current and most popular technologies is quantum computing. It has been almost a century since any practical application of quantum mechanics has been developed, yet now is the perfect time for virtually any organisation to begin working on it. A number of researchers in 1979 pointed to the theoretical underpinning of quantum computers in the late 1970s and early 1980s, according to the research. It was suggested that quantum computers could be built (Arulprakash & Jebakumar, 2022; L. Wang & Wang, 2022).

The Quantum Gate Model is being offered as a first answer by many businesses claiming to be working on quantum computers, including IBM. Google, Microsoft, and a slew of other companies are investigating devices of this type. It is extremely risky to use quantum computers to address all utility problems. There will be both classical and quantum computers in the universal infrastructure, with the quantum computer having substantial performance limitations. It is possible to solve some problems substantially more quickly with quantum algorithms like Grover's or Shor's (Berman et al., 2005; Fluhrer, 2017). Previously unsolved issues will now be dealt with promptly. A number of researchers, both academic and industry, have expressed an interest in quantum computing as a result of recent developments. Because of the development of quantum computers, which were unable to provide the same level of security as blockchain technology before it, the technology began to advance. Smart contracts can be hacked, and eventually, all technology will stop working altogether.

Even simple computers can solve the most difficult mathematical problems that are used to secure the blockchain. Cryptocurrencies are protected by public-key cryptography. Quantum computers could pose a threat to the crypto business, where some funds have lost billions of dollars due to public key encryption breaches. The rightful owner of a digital object can be impersonated if the encryption is compromised. If quantum computing becomes powerful enough, any security promises will be null and void. Quantum computers would need thousands of qubits to decrypt data, compared to just a few hundred qubits in contemporary computers (Xu et al., 2022; S. Zhang & Lee, 2020). Continuous qubits can be used for this purpose, allowing for longer stats than are now accessible. It is hoped that quantum computers will be able to attain similar speeds on a far broader scale. It's obvious that this has an impact on a wide range of fields in computer and information science, where systems depend on the difficulty of calculations to perform properly. System failures can occur if there is a considerable increase in acceleration. To be more specific, this is true for cryptosystems that use asymmetry in the computational cost required to compare two functions. Large primes can be multiplied quickly, but merging large composite numbers into two primes is extremely difficult, making RSA encryption sluggish. Having a hash function is significant because it's simple to compute yet hard to reverse. In order to establish a nearly unique fingerprint, they pick a specified hash value and look for a pre-selected image that matches that hash value. (Barua et al., 2020; Khazanchi et al., 2021).

Figure 1. Model of how the cryptosystem works

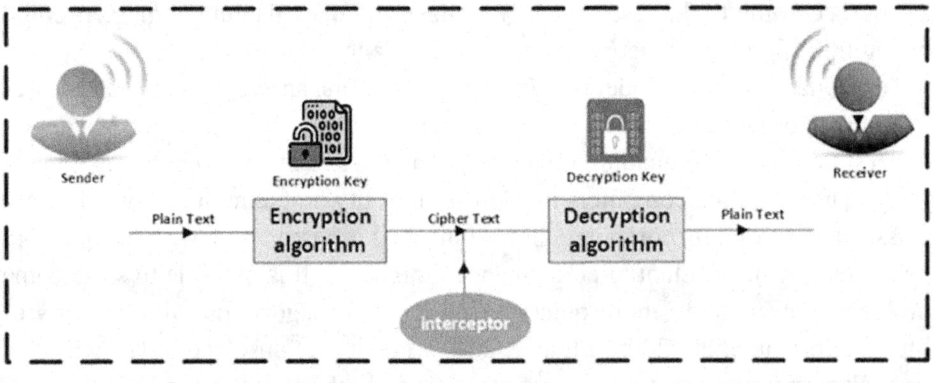

BACKGROUD OF BLOCKCHAIN AND ALGORTHAM

Blockchain-related data structures and algorithms are of interest to the author. The primary goal of creating the blockchain was to address the issue of double-spending in relation to the digital currency Bitcoin. An open, decentralised digital ledger that is secure against change and verifiable by anybody is implemented via the core components. Faster than canonical sources to prevent mass rewrites of entire sequences of blocks from some point in the past, denial of service, or chain growth attacks. For this reason, a working requirement has been added to prohibit rewrites of long chains (Saini et al., 2021).

1) There is a record of every transaction ever made on the blockchain. It's stored on public servers, so anyone can access it.
2) There are four basic elements in each block:
   a) a hash value,
   b) a data block,
   c) a nonce. The nonce is only used once to construct a new block.
   d) The block's hash.

When the previous block's hash code is included in a later block, it ensures the previous block's integrity. Modifying the earliest blocks in the chain would introduce inconsistency into the hash, and a hash that contains data cannot be changed without interrupting the entire block sequence, and vice versa. To generate a new block, adding a nonce to the hash needs a lot of effort. It is impossible to recreate a long chain of blocks with new data using this implementation of the work requirement (Lakhwani et al. 2020).

ALGORITHMS FOR QUANTUM COMPUTATION

Understanding two basic algorithms is essential for understanding how blockchains work in the context of quantum computers and quantum-enhanced assaults. Two algorithms: Shor's algo and Grover's algo. Finding a single input to the black box function is much faster with algorithmic search than with brute force search as a first step. Integer factoring through the general number field sieve (the most well-known way of factorization procedure) is made exponentially faster using the following method, which can also be used to situations involving hidden subgroups and discrete logarithms (Hiran, 2021; Vyas et al., 2021). Some of the known asymmetric cyphers, such as public key cryptography (PKC) and digital signatures, are vulnerable to these difficulties. This duo of quantum algorithms poses a serious threat to blockchain implementations.

The Algorithm of Grover

The block chain relies on cryptographic hashes to protect itself from previous blocks being modified. The dispersed nature of the chain and the computational work necessary to recompute a chain of blocks make it resistant to long-term revisions. The reversal of the hash function (Grover, 1996).

Algorithm of Shor

Generalized number field sieving (the most efficient algorithm for computing numbers) has a complexity that is super polynomial compared to Shor's approach, but less than exponential (longer is shorter than exponential at input length). It's almost impossible to break an 096-bit RSA key using classical calculation, but it is possible to break it using quantum computation. Consequently, quantum computing attacks will be possible on any part of a blockchain implementation based on RSA or comparable techniques. For Shor's algorithm, factoring complex arithmetic numbers, which are the product of two large primes, is the first step in accomplishing this aim. Factorization, on the other hand, is a subset of the larger unknown. For Shor's algorithm, factoring huge composite integers, which are the product of two large primes, is the first step in accomplishing this aim (Grover, 1996; Monz et al., 2016). All of these issues can be resolved by modifying Shor's algorithm, which is a special example of the more general hidden subgroup problem. As a result, cryptographic techniques such as ElGamal encryption, authentication systems based on the use of digital signatures, Diffie-Helman key exchange, and elliptic curve cyphers are no longer feasible due to the discrete logarithm problem. Economic certainty. In addition to establishing a hash collision or inverting a function using Grover's technique, the Shor algorithm shows that a quantum computer is vulnerable to other attacks (Berman et al., 2005; Budd et al., 2020; Shor, 1999).

Full Collision: Algorithm Attack via Grover

Complete collisions of hash values are achievable if tiny data can be added to block content and a given hash to match the block's content. In general, it is tough to solve this problem. In general, it is believed that the source material will be searched by brute force until a match for an already known hash is found, which may include enough extra bits to exhaust the hash space. This demands a time investment proportional to the size of the hash space for optimal hashing (Almohammadi et al., 2017; Mehul Mahrishi et al., 2020). However, this time can be reduced by exploiting known flaws in the hash mechanism. In the case of this standard attack, we can assume an execution time of $O(n)$. A speedup of $O(n)$ can be expected over the standard collision-search algorithm thanks to Grover's $O(n)$ time technique. As a result, the blockchain's integrity can be preserved even if a modified block is inserted into the chain. That's about half the time it would take to find a hash collision using brute force. This assault is only relatively quick, therefore raising the hash length might be an option. However, the processing work to compute zeros with longer hash functions tends to restrict chain ability and may render the blockchain inoperable (see below). Asymmetric attacks, where the attacker has quantum computing while the defender has only classical processing, are considered the worst-case scenario by the security community. Since the trade-off in time for generating hash functions and reversing them should remain the same when both sides have the same computer capability, this is a slightly better scenario. The corollary of this is that whoever develops quantum computing capability first will have an advantage, but only until the defenders themselves obtain that ability. At this stage, we expect the system to either be operational again or to be unrepairable and should be discarded (Fluhrer, 2017; Grover, 1996).

Mining Time: Grover's Algorithm Attack

Another issue comes to light when we examine the blockchain's mining process. Nonce calculations are what we're doing here. There is a pre-image to partially specified hash in this calculation, which increases the computing effort required for writing the chain. Replay attack: Grover's approach accelerates nonce generation, significantly speeds up reconstructing the chain from modified blocks, and significantly reduces computational effort required by extension. In the generation of further blocks in the chain, quantum computer-based parties can soon surpass opponents with merely traditional computing power. As a result, the mining process in cryptocurrency applications is more faster, allowing users to mine more coins faster. The quickest miners dominate the development of new blocks in consensus blockchains and other ledger applications, giving you power over the contents of the blockchain. There is nothing stopping a complete reconstruction of the blockchain in a trivial period of time if nonce creation is even faster. If that history is replaced by faster growth than any other history, then a real chain can grow. Fast-growing chains dominate the blockchain and effectively rewrite history since the longest chain has traditionally been recognised as the acknowledged truth (Chen et al., 2021; López-Incera et al., 2020).

Quantum-Resistant Cryptography

The development of quantum computing will have a profound effect on our understanding of cryptography methods. The NSA's Information Assurance Agency (IAD) estimates that it will take 20 years for the algorithms in the national security system to reach full functionality and that they will be built to last at least 30 years. Exactly when large-scale quantum computers will be developed is still a mystery, but many experts believe that they will be completed within the timeframes listed above (Hiran, Doshi, et al., 2014; Tyagi et al., 2020; Wireko, J. K., Hiran, K. K., & Doshi, 2018). So the development of "quantum-resistant" encryption methods has been designated a top priority by the government. In the theoretical framework of (classical) cryptographic methods, there exists the possibility of quantum computer attacks against quantum-resistant encryption, also known as post-quantum cryptography (Mohamed, 2020; L. J. Wang et al., 2021). However, as previously said, the field is still relatively new and therefore rife with uncertainty and lacks widely agreed standards. After the "US Innovation and Competitiveness Law" was passed by Congress, NIST was tasked with conducting an investigation into the state of encryption standards and policies in the United States. In addition, it is stated or demanded that the future be developed in the manner required. This procedure has already begun at NIST, and an update on its progress will be made available to the public. Regarding this process, IAD said: "NSA believes that within a few years, the external crypto community will be able to develop quantum-tolerant algorithms and reach broad agreements on standardization".

Cryptography Based on Quantum Mechanics for Blockchain Protocols

Functions that use a Hash Table To be sure, we'll make a few well-known remarks about what aspects might be critical when constructing structures that incorporate blockchain technologies completely, even though needs are still being advanced for quantum - resistant cryptography. The hashing feature is the first factor to consider. Grover's set of criteria offers a quadratic speedup over classical methods for comparing hash capabilities, as described in the preceding sections. For secure applications, the preferred computational complexity can be recovered by simply increasing the number of bits utilised in the calculation, rather than by using an exponential speedup like Shor's set of rules. Due to the set of rules' quadratic speedup, the maximum number of bits that can be used is two. As previously stated, hashing is used to protect a blockchain in two ways. An inverted hash or the location of a collision is computationally challenging, which is why the number one strategy relies on this fact to work. It becomes more difficult to find a unique data block with the same hash over time. Rather of using classical algorithms, Grover uses a set of principles for calculating the size of a hash region. A quantum-resistant preference would require two times the hash time of a comparable requirement that considers the most effective classical algorithms if a positive stage of issue is required for protection (Lily Chen, Stephen Jordan, Yi-Kai Liu, Dustin Moody, 2016; Shor, 1999).

Signing a block is a second way in which hash functions can be used for security in the blockchain. One way to do this is to find a nonce with all of the block's main bits set to zero. This is computationally challenging because when calculating a partial collision of the hash feature, it is the same thing. In other words, this problem is exactly the "proof of paintings" that a signature is supposed to demand. To ensure a minimum level of 'proof of work', the hashing time can be increased, just like the signing time can be increased to ensure a minimum level of security against a quantum attack (Fernandez-Carames & Fraga-Lamas, 2020; Grover, 1996). As a result, using the traditional devices that can signal a statistics block, the required artwork becomes computationally two times more difficult or takes twice as long with each additional bit. Thus, any blockchain system using hash-based signatures and defending against a spoofing attack from a quantum device may be incompatible with the device requirements for enforcement. (Hiran, Frempong, et al., 2014).

Post-Quantum Cryptography for Mechanisms Beyond the Hash Function of a Block Chain

There will likely be significant concerns with quantum threats to various factors outside of the blockchain itself in addition to the hash aspects of blockchain-based technology, as described above. Encryption techniques may be required if the blockchain ledger is to be spread. There may even need to be a variety of protocols in place defining which entities are permitted to grow the blockchain, for example, wherever identification verifications or virtual signatures may be used. Modern widely used encryption techniques are frequently insufficient to protect against the possibility of quantum computing in many of these scenarios. The safety of many modern cryptographic algorithms is predicated on the problem of a mathematical difficulty, as stated before (Easwaran et al., 2022; Hiran et al., 2012). When it comes to digital signatures, the Digital Signature Algorithm (DSA) is the standard choice because it relies on discrete logarithms, while the *Elliptic Curve Digital Signature Algorithm* (ECDSA) is a promising DSA variant and an example of elliptic curve cryptography. All three algorithms are based on the difficulty of computing discrete logarithms (ECC). A sufficiently powerful quantum computer can easily solve Shor's set of rules for factorization, discrete logarithms, and ECC problems. NIST hasn't yet defined quantum-resistant cryptographic standards, although there are some potential ideas for cryptographic systems that can withstand both classical and quantum attacks (H. Zhang et al., 2019; S. Zhang & Lee, 2020).

The following are a few of the most promising regions:

- The use of encryption that relies solely on hashes. Merkle's hash-tree public-key signature system (1979) is the classic example, which builds on Lamport and Diffie's one-message-signature notion.
- There are code-based cryptography: McEliece's public-key encryption scheme with buried Goppa-code is a classic example (1978).
- In cryptography, lattices are used as the basis. The Hoffstein–Pipher–Silverman "NTRU" public-key encryption system has garnered the most

attention, despite the fact that it is no longer historically the principal instance (1998).

- Cryptography based on multivariate quadratic equations. Hidden Field Equations (without variation) (1996) public-key-signature system by Patarin and Matsumoto and Imai are one of many intriguing instances (Trichni et al., 2022; Xu et al., 2022).

Figure 2. A cryptographic hash function was used to build Blockchain
Source: Bitcoin Whitepaper

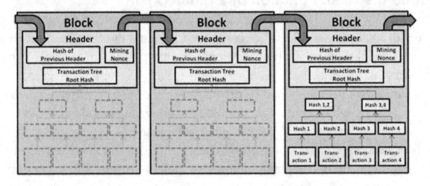

Cryptography Based on Quantum Theory

Future crypto-structures can also take advantage of quantum functions, which are already being used in a new era. For quantum attacks, quantum cryptography is superior to post-quantum cryptography, which depends entirely on conventional techniques and existing technology. To put it another way, quantum cryptography is a part of quantum data technology, which suggests that quantum outcomes can develop basically novel approaches to cryptography in the process of creating them. Quantum key distribution (QKD) is the most advanced and fully-fledged quantum cryptography age yet to emerge. It is possible to generate a random bitstream among events using the QKD protocol (P. Wang et al., 2022; P. Zhang, 2022). An OTP or Vernam-cipher is used to encrypt the mystery message once the random message is connected. We don't need complex mathematical procedures to secure this way of distributing a secret shared key; quantum physics serves as our sole foundation. As a result of Heisenberg's uncertainty precept, the Quantum No-cloning theorem, which asserts that a sign product of human quantum garbage cannot be cloned without introducing detectable flaws, any eavesdropper will be prevented from getting away with it (Niemi, 2021; Wireko et al., 2021). Once a random key is associated among occurrences using a QKD protocol, the encrypted message is regarded cryptographically or unconditionally secure.

Figure 3. Post-quantum cryptography

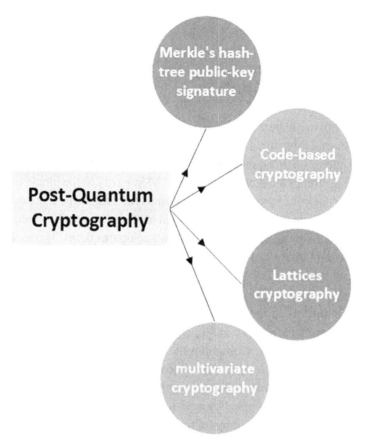

Quantum information technology has reached its peak in the QKD field. Such arrangements have been used in the private and public sectors to promote transmitters and receivers through commercial corporations. Personal networks (e.g. dark fibres), which cannot be repeated or routed, are currently the only viable option in the current period. The current limitations to QKD's widest possible application place severe restrictions on its usefulness, but the age is progressing at a rapid pace and will therefore become significantly larger in the near future. QKD is one of many concepts being studied right now that has the potential to have a substantial influence on blockchain-based systems. A quantum stream can encode and transmit data at the same time, for example (instead of merely distributing a key over a quantum channel). As an alternative, there is the "Quantum Bitcoin," which employs quantum cryptography to mine and confirm blocks on a traditional blockchain. Protocols exist to encode and store data that are protected against tampering by a quantum ledger. As an alternative to virtual signature systems, there are also quantum bit dedication protocols. It's encouraging to see some of these ideas come to fruition, but the reality is that most of these technologies are as difficult to implement as quantum computing itself (Berman et al., 2005; Mosteanu & Faccia, 2021).

THREAT TO BLOCK CHAIN

We are faced with two features of blockchain's promises being invalidated in the setting of quantum computing. It is first believed that hash inversion is a computationally challenging operation. If a quantum computer dramatically simplifies the process of verifying the upstream blockchain's validity, the integrity of the blockchain's entries is compromised. Grover's approach, which finds the pre-image to a function value, may do it far more quickly than the traditional brute force search, which isolates the generating input by producing each output and compares them. The blockchain can be attacked using Grover's algorithm in two different methods. First and foremost, Hash collision detection is possible with this algorithm. It can be used to replace existing blocks while still preserving the integrity of the blockchain (English et al., 2016; Fingerhuth et al., 2018). Secondly, it can speed up the generation of nonces, maybe to the point where entire record chains could be quickly reconstructed with consistent modified hashes, weakening the integrity of the chain. To discover the pre-image of a given value under a difficult-to-invert function, the approach is employed in both scenarios. Information transmission between participants and digital signatures could be compromised by a quantum computer for an implementation of public or private key cryptography on the blockchain.

METHODS OF QUANTUM BLOCKCHAIN

Networks Based on Quantum Computing

In each node, the blockchain is stored. Similar to the traditional blockchain, this phase's goal is to decentralized add valid blocks. The issue with building a quantum blockchain network is that it might have dishonest nodes and that the blocks generated could have unreliable origins. The newly generated blocks are spatial bell states, therefore transferring this to the associated temporal case requires more research. The -protocol can be used in the quantum network to validate the block generated from the untrusted source. More significantly, this is accomplished via other network nodes, some of which may be dishonest, in a decentralized fashion. First, a quantum random number generator. Generator of numbers to select a verifier node at random. Then the unreliable source divulges an n-qubit state that might be a legitimate block. Each qubit is given to each node, j, by the unreliable source for verification. Now that j: j is a multiple, the validating node creates random angles of 0 and j. The verifier is one of the nodes to which the angles are distributed. Then each measure their qubit in the basis (Arulprakash & Jebakumar, 2022).

Overview of Quantum-Enhanced Logic-Based Blockchain

In actuality, quantum-secured blockchain (QB) is improved and applied in QLB. By switching from the conventional Byzantine agreement protocol to the quantum honest-success Byzantine agreement protocol and embedding quantum protection and quantum certificates into the syntax of transactions, the quantum-secured blockchain is improved. Qulogicoin is the cryptocurrency that was developed and sent using this blockchain. In a way, the blockchain that Kiktenko et al. QB constructed is safer and can survive quantum computer attacks. To increase the effectiveness of the blockchain, a new quantum Byzantine agreement (QBA) protocol was created to replace the traditional Byzantine agreement. Quantum security and quantum certifications will be incorporated into the QLB transaction syntax to increase the blockchain's strength(Sarmah, 2019; L. Wang & Wang, 2022).

KEY FEATURES OF BLOCKCHAIN

- A decentralized consensus mechanism is used to validate transactions and assure the authenticity of information.
- Data are represented as blocks in a sequence, making new information (e.g. new transactions) irrevocable.
- Each information factor delivered is a brand new block that references its predecessor. An extrude is, therefore, not possible as all blocks are connected.
- Data are saved in a sequence of blocks in numerous locations. As lengthy as every block has get entry to its predecessor, all different information may be saved in special locations, i.e. in a decentralized manner.
- Stronger accept as true with and protection via decentralized garage and not unusual place reputation with the aid of using all
- Participants of the safety of saved information. This helps fighting fraud, proving the high-satisfactory and starting place of goods, and tracing defective substances in deliver chains

- Verified facts, which incorporates the opportunity to verify the authenticity of a report degree or different facts saved with the aid of using blockchain enterprises.
- Reduced complexity and expanded reliability, as the usage of decentralized garage decreases the opportunity that a server shutdown will make information inaccessible(Trichni et al., 2022; S. Zhang & Lee, 2020).

Blockchain Domain and Sector

Blockchain has an extensive variety of use instances with inside the monetary offerings sector. The maximum not unusual place capabilities are:

- Payments and remittance: Cross-border bills are normally intermediated with the aid of using clearing firms, and hence normally situation to intermediation expenses in a couple of layers that result in operational complexity and counterparty dangers. By contrast, blockchain permits for direct peer-to-peer transactions that restrict the want for intermediaries
- Credit and lending: The use of clever contracts affords capacity advantages that would make lending secure and save you crises. Blockchain technology also are used to elevate capital via crowd investment and different way and may doubtlessly effect on traditional and new monetary intermediaries. Examples encompass blockchain-primarily based totally tokens and preliminary coin offerings (Sarmah, 2019).
- Trading and settlement: The use of blockchain technology can cause near-real-time clearing and settlement, decreasing dangers associated with duplicated facts and related time lags.
- Compliance: Blockchain technology may be carried out to especially cope with monetary reporting and compliance issues. Blockchain should make it viable to document gamers and moves in a transparent, streamlined style and in keeping with regulatory requirements.
- Asset management: There are a couple of use instances on this area, which includes tasks targeted at the fund distribution price chain and the improvement of clever switch agents. Beyond finance, blockchain represents a probable step forward for an extensive variety of commercial sectors, way to new technological notions which includes disintermediation and performance profits that would be key to those industries. Seventy four having started as the idea of cryptocurrencies which includes Bitcoin (S. Nakamoto, 2016).

POSSIBLE APPLICATIO OF QUANTUM COMUTING IN FUTURE

- Optimization: Many optimization troubles are trying to find a worldwide minimum factor solution. By the use of quantum annealing, the optimization troubles can be solved in advance than the use of supercomputers.
- Machine Learning / Big statistics: ML and deep gaining knowledge of researchers are in search of for green approaches to educate and take a look at fashions the use of huge statistics set. In order to speed up the process of education and testing, quantum computing can be utilised.
- Simulation: Simulation is a useful tool for anticipating potential errors and taking countermeasures. Complex systems can be simulated using quantum computing.
- Material Science: The calculations of the complex interactions of atomic structures constrain chemistry and textile technology. There are new quantum replies that promise to speed up the process of re-creating these interactions (English et al., 2016).

CONCLUSION

In summary, authors described the blockchain strategies along side the quantum strategies. How Blockchain is getting applied withinside the distinct sectors with the improvements. A blockchain protocol with information-theoretically steady authentication primarily based totally on a community wherein every pair of nodes is attached with the aid of using a QKD link. We have experimentally examined our protocol through a three-birthday birthday celebration city fiber community QKD. In addition to the usage of QKD for authentication, it's far redefined the protocol of including new blocks and a manner this is dramatically distinct from present day cryptocurrencies. Rather than concentrating the improvement of recent blocks withinside the arms of person miners, we appoint the information-theoretically steady broadcast protocol wherein all of the nodes attain a settlement approximately a brand new block on identical terms. A important benefit of our blockchain protocol is its capacity to keep transparency and integrity of transactions in opposition to assaults with quantum algorithms. Our consequences consequently open up opportunities for understanding scalable quantum-secure blockchain structures. If realized, any such blockchain platform can restriction financial and social dangers from approaching breakthroughs in quantum computation technology. Typical key technology fees of presently to be had QKD technology are enough for working a largescale blockchain structures primarily based totally on our protocol. Moreover, wonderful development in idea and exercise of quantum communications, such as current experiments on ground-to-satellite tv for pc QKD and quantum repeaters, may want to open the door to growing a public international QKD community ("the quantum Internet" and increasing quantum-secure blockchain structures to the worldwide scale. The improvement of the "quantum Internet" will permit our protocol to keep anonymity of every community member. A member might be capable of get entry to the worldwide QKD community from any station, authenticate themselves to different events the usage of their non-public seed keys (see Methods) and enact a favored transaction. Quantum and Blockchain paradigm will deliver improvements in such a lot of fields.

REFERENCES

Almohammadi, K., Hagras, H., Alghazzawi, D., & Aldabbagh, G. (2017). *A survey of artificial intelligence techniques employed for adaptive educational systems within e-learning platforms.* doi:10.1515/jaiscr-2017-0004

Arulprakash, M., & Jebakumar, R. (2022). *Towards developing a Block Chain based Advanced Data Security-Reward Model (DSecCS) in mobile crowd sensing networks. Egyptian Informatics Journal.* doi:10.1016/j.eij.2022.03.002

Barua, T., Doshi, R., & Hiran, K. K. (2020). *Mobile Applications Development.* Mobile Applications Development. doi:10.1515/9783110689488

Berman, G. P., Kamenev, D. I., & Tsifrinovich, V. I. (2005). Collective decoherence of the superpositional entangled states in the quantum Shor algorithm. *Physical Review A, 71*(3), 032346. Advance online publication. doi:10.1103/PhysRevA.71.032346

Budd, J., Miller, B. S., Manning, E. M., Lampos, V., Zhuang, M., Edelstein, M., Rees, G., Emery, V. C., Stevens, M. M., Keegan, N., Short, M. J., Pillay, D., Manley, E., Cox, I. J., Heymann, D., Johnson, A. M., & McKendry, R. A. (2020). Digital technologies in the public-health response to COVID-19. In Nature Medicine (Vol. 26, Issue 8). doi:10.103841591-020-1011-4

Chen, Jordan, Liu, & Moody. (2016). Report on Post-Quantum Cryptography. *Huabei Gongxueyuan Xuebao/Journal of North China Institute of Technology, 22*(3).

Chen, J., Gan, W., Hu, M., & Chen, C. M. (2021). On the construction of a post-quantum blockchain for smart city. *Journal of Information Security and Applications, 58*, 102780. Advance online publication. doi:10.1016/j.jisa.2021.102780

Easwaran, B., Hiran, K. K., Krishnan, S., & Doshi, R. (Eds.). (2022). *Real-Time Applications of Machine Learning in Cyber-Physical Systems.* doi:10.4018/978-1-7998-9308-0

English, M., Auer, S., & Domingue, J. (2016). *Block Chain Technologies & The Semantic Web : A Framework for Symbiotic Development.* Computer Science Conference for University of Bonn Students.

Fernandez-Carames, T. M., & Fraga-Lamas, P. (2020). Towards Post-Quantum Blockchain: A Review on Blockchain Cryptography Resistant to Quantum Computing Attacks. *IEEE Access: Practical Innovations, Open Solutions, 8,* 21091–21116. Advance online publication. doi:10.1109/ACCESS.2020.2968985

Fingerhuth, M., Babej, T., & Wittek, P. (2018). Open source software in quantum computing. In PLoS ONE (Vol. 13, Issue 12). doi:10.1371/journal.pone.0208561

Fluhrer, S. R. (2017). Reassessing Grover's Algorithm. *IACR Cryptology EPrint Archive, 2017.*

Grover, L. K. (1996). A fast quantum mechanical algorithm for database search. *Proceedings of the Annual ACM Symposium on Theory of Computing, Part F129452.* 10.1145/237814.237866

Hilal, A. M., Hassine, S. B. H., Larabi-Marie-Sainte, S., Nemri, N., Nour, M. K., Motwakel, A., Zamani, A. S., & al Duhayyim, M. (2022). Malware Detection Using Decision Tree Based SVM Classifier for IoT. *Computers. Materials and Continua, 72*(1). Advance online publication. doi:10.32604/cmc.2022.024501

Hiran, K. K. (2021). Impact of Driving Factors on Cloud Computing Adoption in the Higher Education. *IOP Conference Series. Materials Science and Engineering, 1131*(1), 012016. Advance online publication. doi:10.1088/1757-899X/1131/1/012016

Hiran, K. K., Doshi, R., Kant Hiran, K., & Rathi, R. (2014). Role of Internet Access Infrastructure on Traveler Behaviour in Intelligent Transportations Systems within the Smart City. *International Journal on Computational Science & Applications, 4*(1). Advance online publication. doi:10.5121/ijcsa.2014.4108

Hiran, K. K., Frempong, M. A., Kant, K., & Head, H. (2014). Awareness and Understanding of Computer Forensics in the Ghana Legal System Article in International Journal of Computer Applications · February. *International Journal of Computers and Applications, 89*(20), 975–8887. doi:10.5120/15752-4640

Hiran, K. K., Jain, R. K., Hiran, K., & Paliwal, G. (2012). Quantum cryptography: A new generation of information security system. *International Journal of Computers and Distributed Systems,* Error! Hyperlink reference not valid.2. https://www.researchgate.net/publication/320404164

Khazanchi, D., Vyas, A. K., Hiran, K. K., & Padmanaban, S. (2021). Blockchain 3.0 for sustainable development. *Blockchain 3.0 for Sustainable Development.* doi:10.1515/9783110702507/EPUB

Lakhwani, K., Gianey, H. K., Wireko, J. K., & Hiran, K. K. (2020). *Internet of Things (IoT): Principles, Paradigms and Applications of IoT (English Edition).* https://www.amazon.in/Internet-Things-IoT-Principles-Applications-ebook/dp/B085DQ919Z

LaPierre, R. (2021). *Shor Algorithm.* doi:10.1007/978-3-030-69318-3_13

López-Incera, A., Hartmann, A., & Dür, W. (2020). Encrypt me! A game-based approach to Bell inequalities and quantum cryptography. *European Journal of Physics, 41*(6), 065702. Advance online publication. doi:10.1088/1361-6404/ab9a67

Mahrishi, M., Hiran, K. K., Meena, G., & Sharma, P. (2020). *Machine Learning and Deep Learning in Real-Time Applications.* IGI Global. https://www.igi-global.com/book/machine-learning-deep-learning-real/240152

Mohamed, K. S. (2020). Cryptography Concepts: Integrity, Authentication, Availability, Access Control, and Non-repudiation. New Frontiers in Cryptography. doi:10.1007/978-3-030-58996-7_3

Monz, T., Nigg, D., Martinez, E. A., Brandl, M. F., Schindler, P., Rines, R., Wang, S. X., Chuang, I. L., & Blatt, R. (2016). Realization of a scalable Shor algorithm. *Science, 351*(6277), 1068–1070. Advance online publication. doi:10.1126cience.aad9480 PMID:26941315

Mosteanu, N. R., & Faccia, A. (2021). Fintech frontiers in quantum computing, fractals, and blockchain distributed ledger: Paradigm shifts and open innovation. *Journal of Open Innovation, 7*(1), 19. Advance online publication. doi:10.3390/joitmc7010019

Nakamoto, S. (2016). *Bitcoin: A Peer-to-Peer Electronic Cash System.* Available: https://bitcoin.org/bitcoin.pdf

Niemi, H. (2021). AI in learning: Preparing grounds for future learning. *Journal of Pacific Rim Psychology, 15.* Advance online publication. doi:10.1177/18344909211038105

Saini, H. K., Jain, K. L., Hiran, K. K., & Bhati, A. (2021). Paradigms to make smart city using blockchain. Blockchain 3.0 for Sustainable Development.

Sarmah, S. S. (2019). Application of block chain in cloud computing. *International Journal of Innovative Technology and Exploring Engineering, 8*(12), 4698–4704. Advance online publication. doi:10.35940/ijitee.L3585.1081219

Shor, P. W. (1999). Polynomial-time algorithms for prime factorization and discrete logarithms on a quantum computer. *SIAM Review, 41*(2), 303–332. Advance online publication. doi:10.1137/S0036144598347011

Trichni, S., Omary, F., & Bougrine, M. (2022). New Blockchain Protocol for Partial Confidentiality and Transparency (PPCT). *International Journal of Advanced Computer Science and Applications, 13*(2). Advance online publication. doi:10.14569/IJACSA.2022.0130273

Tyagi, S. K. S., Mukherjee, A., Pokhrel, S. R., & Hiran, K. (2020). An Intelligent and Optimal Resource Allocation Approach in Sensor Networks for Smart Agri-IoT. *Smart Agri-IoT. IEEE Sensors Journal, 21*(16), 17439–17446. doi:10.1109/JSEN.2020.3020889

Vyas, A. K., Dhiman, H., & Hiran, K. K. (2021). Modelling of symmetrical quadrature optical ring resonator with four different topologies and performance analysis using machine learning approach. *Journal of Optical Communications.* doi:10.1515/joc-2020-0270

Wang, L., & Wang, Y. (2022). Supply chain financial service management system based on block chain IoT data sharing and edge computing. *Alexandria Engineering Journal, 61*(1), 147–158. Advance online publication. doi:10.1016/j.aej.2021.04.079

Wang, L. J., Zhang, K. Y., Wang, J. Y., Cheng, J., Yang, Y. H., Tang, S. B., Yan, D., Tang, Y. L., Liu, Z., Yu, Y., Zhang, Q., & Pan, J. W. (2021). Experimental authentication of quantum key distribution with post-quantum cryptography. *NPJ Quantum Information, 7*(1), 67. Advance online publication. doi:10.103841534-021-00400-7

Wang, P., Chen, X., & Jiang, G. (2022). Quantum Demiric-Selcuk Meet-in-the-Middle Attacks on Reduced-Round AES. *International Journal of Theoretical Physics, 61*(1), 5. Advance online publication. doi:10.100710773-022-05003-2

Wireko, J. K., Brenya, B., & Doshi, R. (2021). Financial Impact of Internet Access Infrastructure of Online Learning Mode on Tertiary Students in Covid-19 Era in Ghana. *2021 International Conference on Computing, Communication and Green Engineering, CCGE 2021.* 10.1109/CCGE50943.2021.9776422

Wireko, J. K., Hiran, K. K., & Doshi, R. (2018). Culturally based User Resistance to New Technologies in the Age of IoT in Developing Countries: Perspectives from Ethiopia. *International Journal of Emerging Technology and Advanced Engineering.* https://vbn.aau.dk/en/publications/culturally-based-user-resistance-to-new-technologies-in-the-age-o

Xu, M., Zhao, F., Zou, Y., Liu, C., Cheng, X., & Dressler, F. (2022). BLOWN: A Blockchain Protocol for Single-Hop Wireless Networks under Adversarial SINR. *IEEE Transactions on Mobile Computing*, 1. Advance online publication. doi:10.1109/TMC.2022.3162117

Zhang, H., Ji, Z., Wang, H., & Wu, W. (2019). Survey on quantum information security. *China Communications*, *16*(10), 1–36. Advance online publication. doi:10.23919/JCC.2019.10.001

Zhang, P. (2022). Quantum Attacks on Sum of Even–Mansour Construction with Linear Key Schedules. *Entropy (Basel, Switzerland)*, *24*(2), 153. Advance online publication. doi:10.3390/e24020153 PMID:35205449

Zhang, S., & Lee, J. H. (2020). Analysis of the main consensus protocols of blockchain. *ICT Express*, *6*(2), 93–97. Advance online publication. doi:10.1016/j.icte.2019.08.001

ADDITIONAL READING

Gill, S. S. (2021). Quantum and blockchain based Serverless edge computing: A vision, model, new trends and future directions. *Internet Technology Letters*, e275.

Kiktenko, E. O., Pozhar, N. O., Anufriev, M. N., Trushechkin, A. S., Yunusov, R. R., Kurochkin, Y. V., Lvovsky, A. I., & Fedorov, A. K. (2018). Quantum-secured blockchain. *Quantum Science and Technology*, *3*(3), 035004. doi:10.1088/2058-9565/aabc6b

Koh, L., Dolgui, A., & Sarkis, J. (2020). Blockchain in transport and logistics–paradigms and transitions. *International Journal of Production Research*, *58*(7), 2054–2062. doi:10.1080/00207543.2020.1736428

Mosteanu, N. R., & Faccia, A. (2021). Fintech frontiers in quantum computing, fractals, and blockchain distributed ledger: Paradigm shifts and open innovation. *Journal of Open Innovation*, *7*(1), 19. doi:10.3390/joitmc7010019

Passarelli, M., Cariola, A., & Bongiorno, G. (2022). Trends in Blockchain Technologies: A Bibliometric Analysis. In Blockchain Technology Applications in Businesses and Organizations (pp. 208-238). IGI Global. doi:10.4018/978-1-7998-8014-1.ch010

Singh, P., & Singh, N. (2020). Blockchain with IoT and AI: A review of agriculture and healthcare. *International Journal of Applied Evolutionary Computation*, *11*(4), 13–27. doi:10.4018/IJAEC.2020100102

KEY TERMS AND DEFINITIONS

Cryptocurrencies: Cryptocurrencies are digital tokens. They are a type of digital currency that allows people to make payments directly to each other through an online system. Cryptocurrencies have no legislated or intrinsic value; they are simply worth what people are willing to pay for them in the market.

Grover's Algorithm: In quantum computing, Grover's algorithm, also known as the quantum search algorithm, refers to a quantum algorithm for unstructured search that finds with high probability the unique input to a black box function that produces a particular output value, using just $O\sqrt{N}$ evaluations of the function, where N is the size of the function's domain. It was devised by Lov Grover in 1996.

Post-Quantum Cryptography: Post-quantum cryptography refers to cryptographic algorithms (usually public-key algorithms) that are thought to be secure against an attack by a quantum computer. These complex mathematical equations take traditional computers months or even years to break. However, quantum computers running Shor's algorithm will be able to break math-based systems in moments.

Protocols: Protocols are crucial components of Blockchain technologies that enable information to be shared automatically across cryptocurrency networks securely and reliably. In the field of computing, protocols are essentially rules that define how data is allowed to be transferred between different computer systems.

Quantum Bitcoin: Quantum computers will eventually break much of today's encryption, and that includes the signing algorithm of Bitcoin and other cryptocurrencies.

Quantum Cryptography: Quantum cryptography is a method of encryption that uses the naturally occurring properties of quantum mechanics to secure and transmit data in a way that cannot be hacked. Cryptography is the process of encrypting and protecting data so that only the person who has the right secret key can decrypt it.

Shor's Algorithm: It is a quantum computer algorithm for finding the prime factors of an integer. It was developed in 1994 by the American mathematician.

Chapter 9

Quantum Blockchain for Smart Society:
Applications, Challenges, and Opportunities

Manish Dadhich
Sir Padampat Singhania University, India

Harish Tiwari
Sir Padampat Singhania University, India

ABSTRACT

Smart cities are a futuristic urban development concept that uses ICT to enable citizens, governments, and organizations to collect and share real-time data. Q-BoC technology can provide a new level of convenience and security for communication and transactions among all of a smart city's many stakeholders. Information technology, including quantum blockchain, has been integrated to govern physical, social, and business infrastructures in today's rapidly developing smart cities. Innovative technologies and concepts such as the IoT, 5G, artificial intelligence, and quantum blockchain have become necessary for an intelligent and advanced society. In recent years, both academics and industry have demonstrated a strong interest in the revolution of smart cities. Smart cities can deliver a variety of smart functions, such as intelligent transportation, Industry 5.0, governance, Healthcare 5.0, and smart banking, to improve people's quality of life. The chapter explores the application, challenges, and opportunities for making a smart society.

DOI: 10.4018/978-1-6684-5072-7.ch009

1. INTRODUCTION

Blockchain is a novel computer expertise application method that includes distributed data storage, point-to-point transmission, consensus mechanics, and an encryption technique (Aggarwal et al., 2019). In Blockchain, every node has its own allocated ledger for keeping transaction history. All the nodes are joints that validate all the blockchain rules. These nodes organize transactions into blocks and determine which genuine transactions should be included in the Blockchain. Communication and trust between nodes in a blockchain network are riled on digital signature technology, which primarily enables information identification, authenticity, and integrity verification (Alam, 2021). According to (Bhavin et al., 2021), Blockchain is a modern technology system in which the sequence of cryptographic blocks is linked together to form a decentralized peer-to-peer (P2P) net. Blockchain can accomplish validation, authorization, answerability, safety, integrity, privacy, and non-repudiation for real-time applications that a centralized system may not provide effectively in a smart community position. Similarly, (Kappert et al., 2021) discussed several blockchain-based consensus techniques and their efficiency and viability in various submissions. (Sun et al., 2016) investigated edge-centric IoT and cloud-centrical IoT structures, highlighting several safety measures for such decentralized methods. They also investigated the security issues that come with using Blockchain.

(Khan et al., 2021) investigated the numerous security and privacy challenges that arise in an IoT setting. (Shalendra Singh Rao, n.d.; Solaiman et al., 2021) investigated numerous safety threats to blockchain and damage consequences and proposed several strategies for improving security in an allocated system. (Ahl et al., 2020) examined the function of distributed ledger in the regional energy marketplace and smart grids' transactive energy controlling structure. Augmented reality, AI-ML-IoT system, robotics, and fog computing are increasingly driving factors behind global new-age city programs. Similarly, Fog computing has significant transportation applications, including, smart traffic management control and vechicle management systems also monitoring independent automobiles and self-spacing (Gill et al., 2019). Additionally, it is a more viable solution because of its low energy consumption and small footprint. Governments can employ these apps to improve citizen security and environmental stewardship. Moreover, it may be employed as in alternative services such as fire and natural disasters by providing early warning of critical circumstances to make sound decisions. Because of the ubiquity of Blockchain, several published literature studies, such as those shown in Table 1 (P. Sharma et al., 2022). For Examples, Smart cities (Costa & Peixoto, 2020), IoT (Sun et al., 2016), cloud (Selvaraj & Sundaravaradhan, 2020), healthcare systems (Ben et al., 2021), data centre networking (Forson & Vuopala, 2019), finance (M. Dadhich, M. S. Pahwa, 2021), digital currency (C. Li et al., 2019), smart grid (Sengupta et al., 2020), infrastructure (Haji, 2021), smart agriculture (Gill et al., 2019), automated vehicle (Srinivas Aditya et al., 2021), biometrics (Ioannou et al., 2020), Arial communications (R. L. Kumar et al., 2021).

Table 1. Execution measures and sources Q-BoC

Sources & Year	1	2	3	4	5	6	7	8	9	10	11	12
(Costa & Peixoto, 2020)	i	i	-	-	i	-	i	i	i	-	-	-
(Sun et al., 2016)	-	i	-	-	i	-	-	-	-	i	-	i
(Alam, 2021)	i	-	i	-	i	-	-	i	-	i	-	-
(Ben et al., 2021)	i	-	-	i	-	-	i	-	i	-	i	-
(Forson & Vuopala, 2019)	-	i	-	-	i	-	i	i	-	i	-	i
(Garcia, 2018)	-	-	-	-	-	i	-	-	-	i	-	-
(C. Li et al., 2019)	i	-	i	i	-	i	i	-	i	-	i	i
(Sengupta et al., 2020)	-	i	-	-	-	-	-	i	-	-	-	-
(Haji, 2021)	-	-	i	-	i	i	-	-	-	-	i	-
(Kappert et al., 2021)	i	-	i	-	i	-	-	-	i	i	-	-
(Srinivas Aditya et al., 2021)	-	i	-	-	-	i	-	-	-	-	-	-
(Ioannou et al., 2020)	i	i	-	-	-	-	i	-	i	-	-	i
(R. L. Kumar et al., 2021)	i	-	i	-	i	-	-	i	i	-	-	i

1: Smart cities; 2: IoT; 3: Cloud; 4: Healthcare System; 5: Data Center Networking; 6: Finance; 7: Digital Currency; 8: Smart Grid; 9: Infrastructure; 9: Smart Agriculture; 10: Automated vehicle 11: Biometrics; 12: Arial communications.

Implementing Q-BoC in wider smart communities regarding functions and procedure models appears to be understudied. Furthermore, despite its potential, current studies have not focused on the role of Q-BoC in implementing security and secrecy aspects in smart societies. As a result, we evaluate Q-BoC's utility, applications, challenges, and opportunities in various smart communities in this study. Smart governance, cloud, e-voting, SCM, infrastructure, telecom, smart home, IoT, finance, healthcare, biometric, industry 4.0, digital currency, surveillance, energy, and smart cities are predominantly explored by the study.

Figure 1. Applications of 5G quantum blockchain (Q-BoC)

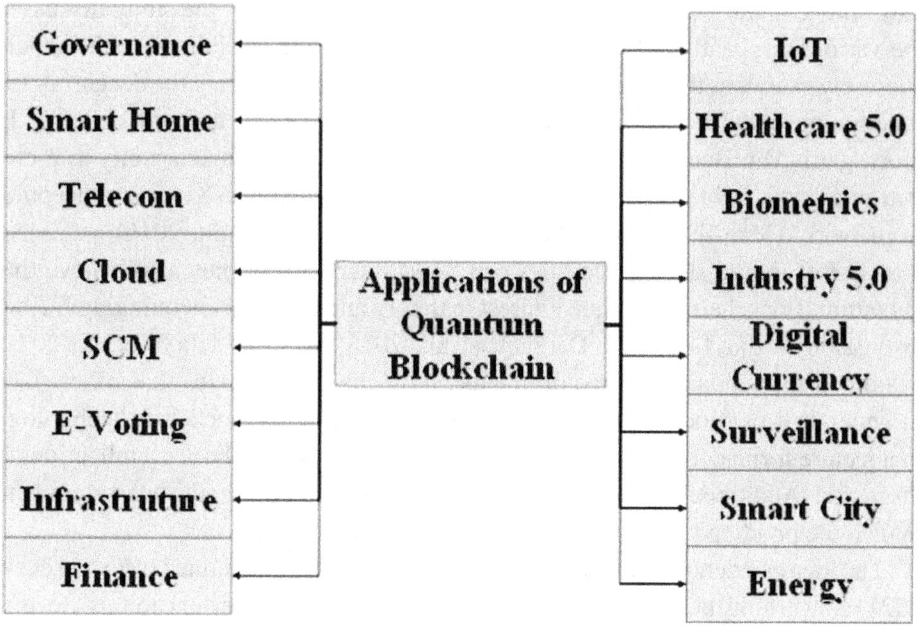

2. REVIEW OF LITERATURE

(Birda, 2019) studied that a smart city's varied character makes it vulnerable to attacks, particularly at the level of resource-constrained devices when high-level security protocols cannot be implemented. Furthermore, the smart city's centralized structure encourages illegal data retention and manipulation by specific persons or groups; these groups might even prevent the passage of signals from one participant to another. (Fernandez-Carames & Fraga-Lamas, 2020) applied Blockchain to construct Block-VN, a vehicle network planning in a smart town. The proposed architecture proved secure and ran in a distributed manner to construct a new distributed transport management system. Several additional studies (Gill et al., 2019; Hebert & Di Cerbo, 2019; Kappert et al., 2021) have successfully combined Blockchain with smart cities. (Manish Dadhich et al., 2019; Srinivas Aditya et al., 2021) introduced a novel authentication and encryption protocol inspired by quantum walks (QIQW). The suggested protocol provides a blockchain agenda for securely exchanging data between IoT devices. Rather than employing traditional cryptographic hash functions to link the chain's blocks and quantum botch purposes. The framework's primary benefits include enabling IoT nodes to communicate data with other nodes successfully while maintaining complete control over their records.

(Yapa et al., 2021) studied the potential for Q-BoC in Smart Grid 3.0, that may enable a unified decentralization progression. Moreover, the study discussed the various applications for upcoming smart grid action. Additionally, the article concisely examines the blockchain integration problems, ensuring the decentralized functioning of future autonomous electrical networks is secure and scalable. In this regard (Van Den Bosch, 2020) proposed the concept of a smart city as a city that integrates technology into its human-centric agenda. Based on a conceptual framework, (Manish Dadhich, Purohit, et al., 2021; Sun et al., 2016) examined how Q-BoC based sharing facilities can build smart cities. They also believe that Quantum Blockchain will pique interest in theory and practice, encouraging further discussion in this field. (M. Dadhich et al., 2018; Srinivas Aditya et al., 2021) examined the fundamental requirements and technical obstacles that robots face in general. It provides a comprehensive understanding of blockchain technology in a lecture format. Then, the part of Blockchain in various robotics applications is discussed. Additionally, numerous technological hurdles that must be overcome to realize the budding of Blockchain for robots are emphasized.

The idea and denotative of innovative smarter cities are explained by (Shan et al., 2021) concerning the expansion status of China's advanced smarter capitals. Several progress patterns in the construction of smarter towns are analyzed and judged, and the shortcomings and deficiencies in the building of innovative smarter cities are examined. They also discussed the policy recommendations to promote development (Q-BoC) in smart cities. It serves as a valuable reference for comprehending China's innovation's development concept and overall development state. The most significant Blockchain-based solutions developed in recent years address the issues highlighted by traditional cloud-based apps (Manish Dadhich, 2017; Sengupta et al., 2020).

3. BLOCKCHAIN-ENABLED SMART CITY FRAMEWORK

To realize the whole goal of smartness in modern cities, structure, conveyance, services, and various other amenities must be enhanced or reinvented (Casino et al., 2019; Manish Dadhich et al., 2022). It is vital to note that the expansion of smart cities includes the development of high-tech structures and the participation of residents in the conveyance and development of amenities. This may be accomplished by collecting and distributing data to end-users and choice-makers to accomplish the smart city system. This objective may be reached by adopting synchronized procedures in digital systems. Developing machinery, viz. data science, AI, cloud and IoT, enables participation and collaborative evolution. Several studies (Alam, 2021; Bhavin et al., 2021; Brotsis et al., 2021; Casino et al., 2019; Fernandez-Carames & Fraga-Lamas, 2020) and reports have said that the evolution to smart cities would be undertaken progressively to confirm accomplishment and sustainability, tackling the most unrelenting challenges that influence people's lives. Utilities (such as water, food and electricity) are among the most sensitive components of smart cities since they provide essential services to all people.

ICT is often regarded as a critical factor in creating smart cities. Quantum Blockchain (Q-BoC) technology is a relatively new technical breakthrough that encompasses a variety of underlying technologies and protocols. (Q-BoC) has the potential to be a major driver and asset in smart cities and development (see figure 2). Smart cities are a futuristic urban development concept that combines ICT to allow residents, governments, and organizations to collect and exchange real-time data. Q-BoC technology can bring a new level of convenience and security for communication and transactions amongst all the various stakeholders of a Smart city. With the rapid development of smart cities today, information technology, including quantum Blockchain, has been combined to manage physical, social, and business infrastructures.

Figure 2. Role of Q-BoC in smart city projects
(Seon, 2021)

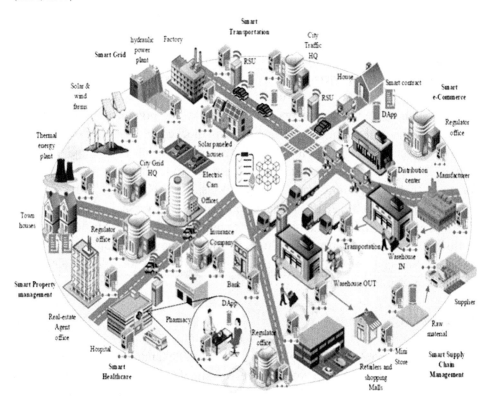

4. APPLICATIONS OF BLOCKCHAIN

4.1 Smart Cities

Cities are the epicentre of human settlement, economic building blocks, and the foundation for global innovation. Cities support information interchange, capacity structure, and the supply of knowledge-rigorous business facilities through their fundamental infrastructure. This necessitates the construction of trustworthy frameworks using Q-BoC to better steer socio-economic development in metropolitan areas (Casino et al., 2019; R. Sharma et al., 2020; Tribis et al., 2018). Cities are attracting a growing percentage of the world's population. In 2014, metropolitan regions housed 56% of the world's population; statistics anticipated increasing to 67% by 2050. Cities are becoming more important in the economics and well-being of nations, with cities accounting for most of the economic activity (Pólvora et al., 2020). Cities simultaneously have administrative, organizational, logistical, social, and environmental issues. Improved administrative efficiency, new models for public participation, and a better understanding of the value of electronic information and the need to secure it transform the relationship between cities and their inhabitants.

4.2 Financial System

Blockchain technology is currently being employed in various financial industries, including corporate, services, financial, forecast marketplaces, and commercial contracts. It is predicted to play a crutial role in the world-wide economy's long-term sustainability, advancing customers, the present banking organization, and people. The global financial sector is looking into using blockchain-based applications for monetary assets like securities, insurance, and derivative deals. For example, Q-BoC promises a significant shift in capital markets and a more efficient way to conduct functions such as securities and derivatives transactions (Gill et al., 2019), digital outlays (Aggarwal et al., 2019), management policies, universal banking facilities, financial auditing (Manish Dadhich, 2016; Schulz & Feist, 2021). Furthermore, the Q-BoC mechanism has partnered with a consortium of the world's major institutions, including Barclays and Goldman Sachs, to develop a workable blockchain-based financial market framework.

4.3 E-Voting

E-voting has been regarded as a positive and inevitable landmark for several years, with the potential to speed up voting processes, simplify and cut election costs, and strengthen democracies. On the other hand, existing electronic voting arrangements rely on a single entity's proprietary and central plan, undermining voters' faith in the voting method (Agbesi, 2020). BitCongress and Liquid Democracy are two distributed voting structures that propose outlines for implementing distributed judgment-making. In general, Q-BoC provides an open-source, peer-to-peer, devolved, and separately verifiable system to acquire the trust of voters and voting controllers while remaining compliant with domestic regulations (Aggarwal et al., 2019).

4.4 IoT

Around 80% of the world's information today was created in the last two years. The growth rate will accelerate due to a) IoT devices and b) population expansion (Marsal-Llacuna, 2020). While the potential for Q-BoC and IoT technologies to expand is enormous, the symbiotic link between these two disciplines opens a universe of possibilities. For instance, despite their flaws, distributed wireless sensor networks are pillars of technical and human growth. (Schulz & Feist, 2021) studied how blockchain building might enhance IoT by minimizing its faults and boosting its potential. Q-BoC and its intrinsic capabilities are primarily driving the increased attention and investments in building decentralized IoT platforms. The central concept allows secure and auditable data sharing in heterogeneous context-aware setups with many networked smart devices. Furthermore, the network's great scalability and efficient administration are enabled by operating autonomously and decentralized (Pólvora et al., 2020).

4.5 Healthcare Administration

Q-BoC could play a critical role in community healthcare 4.0, longitudinal healthcare annals, automated health claims settlement, online patient admittance, patient data input, user-oriented medical research, drug faking, clinical experimental, and precision medication. (P. Sharma et al., 2022) suggested that dealing with patients' E-Healthcare Accounts (EHAs) is the area with the most growth possibility. As part of the medical record, an EHR includes a patient's brief medical past and statistics, predictions, and information relevant to the patient's ailments and clinical progress during treatment. (Srinivas Aditya et al., 2021) considered the Q-BoC system for healthcare 4.0 as a procedure via which handlers may access and preserve their health information while ensuring security and privacy. A series of studies (Krishnapriya & Sarath, 2020; Sengupta et al., 2020; Xiang & Zhao, 2022) confirmed no centralized owner or hub for a hacker to corrupt or breach the medical data. Records are stored in a distributed manner (they are public and easily verifiable across non-affiliated provider organizations). Data from several sources is brought together in a single and consistent data fount, updated and always available.

4.6 Energy industry

The potential uses of Q-BoC in the energy segment are many, and they might have a huge impact on both procedures and platforms (Bowen et al., 2013). For example, Q-BoC can lower costs, permit new business frames and markets, manage intricacy, data safety, and possession. Grids could also engross prosumers in the energy marketplace, allowing for the formation of energy societies (Brotsis et al., 2021; Casino et al., 2019; Garcia, 2018). Q-BoC can improve the energy market system's transparency and confidence while ensuring accountability while respecting privacy rules and increasing its efficiency. According to (Bhavin et al., 2021), blockchain technology might also be used to create peer-to-peer energy transactions and energy managing schemes for electric vehicles. It's also worth noting that Q-BoC facilitates the energy sector's decarbonization, allowing it to move toward more decentralized energy sources.

4.7 Education

In the case of ubiquitous learning environments, Blockchain can solve susceptibility, security, and privacy and can be utilized to store educational data associated with reputational rewards. (Yapa et al., 2021) proposed a distributed blockchain-based academic record and reputation system that non-experts can handle. According to (D. Li et al., 2021a), teachers upload blocks to the Blockchain that store students' learning successes. Educational certificate administration can also benefit from Blockchain, which improves data security and trust in digital infrastructures and credit management. Furthermore, Q-BoC based approaches have the potential to improve personal and academic learning's digital accreditation. Educational information centres using Blockchain technology might be set up to collect, report, and analyze data about school systems to improve decision-making. Finally, in scholarly publishing, Q-BoC can be utilized for document verification or better handling manuscript submissions and promptly completing relevant reviews (Yapa et al., 2021).

4.8 Governance

Q-BoC enabled applications may alter municipal and state governments' work by removing intermediaries from transactions and record-keeping (Van Den Bosch, 2020). Q-BoC's accountability, computerization, and security for processing community records can prevent corruption and enhance essential e-government services. In the word of (Sang & Li, 2019), Q-BoC could be used as a secure communication stand for connecting corporal, social, and business structures in intelligent cities. Blockchain governance aims to render similar essential services as the state and its related public entities, regionalized and efficient while preserving the same validity. Registration of official documentation, attestation, identity, marriage contracts, taxes, and voting are examples of such services (Agbesi, 2020).

4.9 Citizenship and essential services

Integrating digital technologies into routine life necessitates machinery that can accurately identify and certify users' basic attributes such as term, discourse, credit score, age, address and other personal characteristics (Asri et al., 2021). As a result, digital identification has emerged as a critical security measure. (Costa & Peixoto, 2020) examined the pros and cons of various decentralized identity management approaches. Furthermore, according to (Alasbali et al., 2022), one-sixth of the world's population has no written evidence of their existence. Migrants and expatriates are affected by this circumstance because their nations may refuse to hand over documentation if they, for example, belong to the opposition. As a result, Q-BoC has become a tool for enhancing global citizen equality and possibilities.

4.10 Miscellaneous functions

This section covers research on blockchain-based functions that aren't covered by the other sections. For example, Q-BoC is being used by crowd-funding platforms (M. Dadhich, M. S. Pahwa, 2021). Blockchain applications in the humanitarian and philanthropic sectors (Sun et al., 2016). It can also be utilized in smart city contexts to develop smart, reliable, distributed, and autonomous transportation systems and securely operate case tickets (D. Li et al., 2021a). According to (R. Sharma et al., 2020), Q-BoC is projected to play a key role in environmental management. For example, inside emission trading schemes, pollution control and sustainable corporate development. Blockchain might be employed as a novel emission link method adopted by the corporates. Intriguing applications are social media, digital marketing, sentiment analysis, sale projection, and customer retention. User-centric Q-BoC might allow handlers to control, locate, and claim possession of any content they communicate. Some IT-related blockchain applications, such as edge computing and the creation of computational source distribution methods (Manish Dadhich et al., 2022; TK et al., 2021), grid computing (Motlagh et al., 2020), cloud computing (Manish Dadhich, Rao, et al., 2021; Kathuria et al., 2018), and the usage of Q-BoC as a software connective and dynamics of social sharing.

5. CHALLENGES AND OPPORTUNITIES FOR SMART SOCIETY

New hazards accompany the recompense of smart cities. For example, IoT devices that are heavily used as vital structures (e.g., water systems, which might influence residents' health and safety) are vulnerable to cyber-assaults (Sengupta et al., 2020). As a result, it is critical to continually monitor and regulate service networks to reduce the risk of assaults on information and functioning technologies, resulting in cities being wiser and more useful places to live. The term 'smart water system' denotes technological and societal advancements that enable the improved delivery, usage, administration, and optimization of water utility services. Investment in interacting and communication structures, data gathering and assessment, social and crowdsourcing tools, rules and information safety are required to implement effective smart utilities on both the technical and social fronts (Bhavin et al., 2021; M. dadhich & N. Kumar, 2015). Conventional data administration of smart utilities is typically managed on centralized systems in today's information technology architecture. These centralized systems are vulnerable in terms of safety and confidentiality. Using Q-BoC to increase reliable transmission among smart utility equipment is a viable answer to security breaches. Blockchain is a potential method for a decentralized and secure data management system that offers tamper-proof immutability and traceability. Thus, this section outlines many critical open research challenges that impede the use of Q-BoC in smart cities. As seen in table 2, opportunities have also been discussed based on an extensive literature review.

6. IMPLICATIONS

The study's results advance the literature on smart society's applications, challenges, and opportunities. It fosters awareness among various segments of users. In summary, the study aims to provide a systematic, in-depth, and consistent understanding of smart society, which may be helpful for researchers, administrators, and academicians while developing urban and rural frameworks to deal with complex technological changes. The research is equally important from a practical standpoint. First, the findings indicate a shortage of Q-BoC implementation for making a smart society. Furthermore, the findings may motivate blockchain providers to develop more effective techniques and solve the primary impediment that hampers the growth of a smart society. The study also renders a cumulative overview of a smart society. Thus, developing economies can make necessary plans to cope with Q-BoC changes and take a step ahead to develop society.

Table 2. Summary of challenges and opportunities

Sources	Challenges	Causes	Opportunities
(Costa & Peixoto, 2020; Marsal-Llacuna, 2020; Sun et al., 2016)	Sustainability	• Smart city devices deplete energy resources. • Consensus techniques consume more energy. • High implementing cost and maintenance.	• Utilization of renewable energy assets. • Utilization of energy reaping. • Utilization of energy-capable unanimity algorithms.
(Aggarwal et al., 2019; Alam, 2021; N. Kumar & Dadhich, 2014)	Algorithm of Adaptive Consensus	• Smart city applications have a wide range of requirements • The fact that many blockchain consensus methods are designed objective dependent	• An adaptive consensus mechanism based on game-theoretic principles. • An algorithm based on artificial intelligence for reaching a consensus.
(Brotsis et al., 2021; P. Sharma et al., 2022)	Scalability	• Record number of Smart IoT devices. • Traditional consensus algorithms require all blockchain nodes to store all records.	• Scalability on a horizontal plane is the best technique. • A PoW system based on parallel mining is used.
(Costa & Peixoto, 2020; M. dadhich & N. Kumar, 2015; Seon, 2021)	Potential	• Authentication of virtual transactions. • Splitting effect due to propagation suspension. • Emphasis on-chain based encryption and user data privacy.	• Propagation based on Nearest Neighbors Selecting (CNS). • Avoid forking with an acknowledgement-based approach.
(Alasbali et al., 2022; D. Li et al., 2021b)	High Processing Memories	• Scalability restrictions. • Huge data repository. • Centralized off-chain space is sometimes inaccurate. • Distributed off-chain storage is publicly reachable.	• High computing remembrances located within the node itself. • High storage capacity for off-node computation. • Off-chain space such as IPFS should be used. • Encrypt data before storing it in off-chain storage that a single party does not control.
(Krishnapriya & Sarath, 2020; Marsal-Llacuna, 2020)	Protected Economical Models	• Public blockchain directs and transaction links could reveal user identity. • Why Unified digital identity management is not safe. • They are dependent on humans. • Everyone has access to user data in the public Blockchain.	• For each transaction, use a new id and beaters for cryptocurrencies. This gives the user complete control over their identity and data. • SSI and DID safe, decentralized recovery procedures, distributed consent for data sharing. • Double-blind zero-knowledge proofs-based data are shared for anonymity.
(Pólvora et al., 2020; Sengupta et al., 2020)	Immutability and chain finitude	• Smart contracts, once employed, are immutable. • Using a new deal has an issue of trust and disparity. • Smart contracts may not initiate deterministic external applications.	• Desire data and rationality. • Proxy-contract to sense contract delegate call. • Event-triggered Oracle data support for deterministic outward data.

7. LIMITATIONS AND FUTURE SCOPE

This work offers a holistic perspective that could be further explored in various ways to produce useful research or practical results. Blockchain technologies have ushered in a true revolution in which quantum blockchain refers to a decentralized, encrypted, and distributed database. Once registered on the quantum blockchain, the data will not be interfered with maliciously. The advancement of quantum computers and quantum info theory has drawn many researchers to study quantum blockchain soon. Further, every node in a blockchain must execute a similar process for each transaction's authentication at the same time, incurring a hefty compute cost. As a result, creating a lightweight blockchain model is necessary and ideal for applications with specific requirements constraints. Q-BoC innovations and their use in smart cities to improve quality of life are blistering topics in today's research circles. However, numerous obstacles and need limits remain studied and handled before blockchain may be used in sustainable metropolitan advancement programs. This study can aid academics in identifying and addressing the difficulties of building and developing Q-BoC based solutions for IoT-built smart towns. The research would serve as a springboard for further research and discussion on the applications, challenges, opportunities, design, and implementation of Q-BoC based smart city sharing services.

8. CONCLUSION

Blockchain-based smart cities are a pivotal step that must be protected from future quantum assaults since they include sensitive information and data about users and their various components. This article provides a broad overview of the potential future risks of a Blockchain-based smart society. The study examined the quantum Blockchain-based smart cities' facts, challenges, and opportunities and presented some of the most interesting post-Quantum solutions. Consumer, civilian, military and government activities can benefit from Blockchain. However, this is a very fast-paced and flexible environment. As a result, keeping up with and understanding the most recent breakthroughs in the expansion and implementation of Blockchain, which is the subject of this thorough analysis, is critical. The present research revealed several prospective research challenges, and possibilities as part of the survey addressed below. The study performed technical due diligence on future blockchain applications as part of the discussion. The work conducted a rigorous literature analysis on blockchain applications in notable intelligent city applications and attempted real-world case studies of how blockchain technology was successfully used to provide dependable and secure services in smart metropolises. The study also examined the open research problems impeding Blockchain's adoption as a critical technology for creating smart cities.

REFERENCES

Agbesi, S. (2020). Institutional Drivers of Internet Voting Adoption in Ghana : A Qualitative Exploratory Studies. *Centre for Communication, Media & Information Technology, 1*, 53–76. doi:10.13052/nbjict1902-097X.2020.003

Aggarwal, S., Chaudhary, R., Aujla, G. S., Kumar, N., Choo, K. K. R., & Zomaya, A. Y. (2019). Blockchain for smart communities: Applications, challenges and opportunities. *Journal of Network and Computer Applications, 144*, 13–48. doi:10.1016/j.jnca.2019.06.018

Agrawal, T. K., Kumar, V., Pal, R., Wang, L., & Chen, Y.TK. (2021). Blockchain-based framework for supply chain traceability: A case example of textile and clothing industry. *Computers & Industrial Engineering, 154*, 107130. doi:10.1016/j.cie.2021.107130

Ahl, A., Yarime, M., Goto, M., Chopra, S. S., Kumar, N. M., Tanaka, K., & Sagawa, D. (2020). Exploring blockchain for the energy transition: Opportunities and challenges based on a case study in Japan. *Renewable and Sustainable Energy Reviews, 117*(September), 109488. doi:10.1016/j.rser.2019.109488

Alam, T. (2021). Blockchain cities: The futuristic cities driven by Blockchain, big data and internet of things. *GeoJournal, 1*, 1–10. doi:10.100710708-021-10508-0

Alasbali, N., Azzuhri, S. R., Salleh, R. B., Kiah, M. L. M., Shariffuddin, A. A. A. S. A., Kamel, N. M. I. N. M., & Ismail, L. (2022). Rules of Smart IoT Networks within Smart Cities towards Blockchain Standardization. *Mobile Information Systems, 2022*, 1–11. Advance online publication. doi:10.1155/2022/9109300

Asri, A., Le Masson, V., Montalescot, V., Lim, P. E., Nor, A. M., Hussin, H., & Shaxson, L. (2021). The role of migrants in the Malaysian seaweed value-chain. *Marine Policy, 134*, 104812. Advance online publication. doi:10.1016/j.marpol.2021.104812

Ben, W., Ben, I., Kondrateva, G., & Hikkerova, L. (2021). The role of trust in intention to use the IoT in eHealth : Application of the modified UTAUT in a consumer context. *Technological Forecasting and Social Change, 167*(February), 120688. doi:10.1016/j.techfore.2021.120688

Bhavin, M., Tanwar, S., Sharma, N., Tyagi, S., & Kumar, N. (2021). Blockchain and quantum blind signature-based hybrid scheme for healthcare 5.0 applications. *Journal of Information Security and Applications, 56*, 1–15. doi:10.1016/j.jisa.2020.102673

Birda, R. K. (2019). Study of ICT and E-Governance Facilities in Tribal District of Rajasthan. *Kamal, 9*(7), 39–49.

Bowen, W. M., Park, S., & Elvery, J. A. (2013). Empirical Estimates of the Influence of Renewable Energy Portfolio Standards on the Green Economies of States. *Economic Development Quarterly, 27*(4), 338–351. doi:10.1177/0891242413491316

Brotsis, S., Limniotis, K., Bendiab, G., Kolokotronis, N., & Shiaeles, S. (2021). On the suitability of blockchain platforms for IoT applications: Architectures, security, privacy, and performance. *Computer Networks, 191*, 1–29. doi:10.1016/j.comnet.2021.108005

Casino, F., Dasaklis, T. K., & Patsakis, C. (2019). A systematic literature review of blockchain-based applications: Current status, classification and open issues. *Telematics and Informatics, 36*, 55–81. doi:10.1016/j.tele.2018.11.006

Costa, D. G., & Peixoto, J. P. J. (2020). COVID-19 pandemic: A review of smart cities initiatives to face new outbreaks. *IET Smart Cities, 2*(2), 64–73. doi:10.1049/iet-smc.2020.0044

Dadhich & Pahwa. (2021). Analytical Study of Financial Wellbeing of Selected Public and Private Sector Banks: A CAMEL Approach. *IEEE Explore, Emerging Trends in Industry 4.0 (ETI 4.0)*, 1–6. . doi:10.1109/ETI4.051663.2021.9619424

Dadhich, M. (2016). A Comparative Study of Investment Portfolio of Life fund of LIC of India and ICICI Prudential Life Insurers. *International Journal of Research in Economics and Social Sciences, 6*(10), 229–238.

Dadhich, M. (2017). Impact of Demonetization on Indian Economy. *International Journal of Research in Social Sciences, 7*(8), 208–215.

Dadhich, M. (2019). Stochastic pattern of major indices of Bombay stock exchange. *International Journal of Recent Technology and Engineering, 8*(3), 6774–6779. doi:10.35940/ijrte.C6068.098319

Dadhich, M., Rao, S. S., Sethy, S., & Sharma, R. (2021). Determining the Factors Influencing Cloud Computing Implementation in Library Management System (LMS): A High Order PLS-ANN Approach. *Library Philosophy and Practice*, 6281.

Dadhich, M., Hiran, K. K., Rao, S. S., & Sharma, R. (2022). Impact of Covid-19 on Teaching-Learning Perception of Faculties and Students of Higher Education in Indian Purview. *Journal of Mobile Multimedia, 18*(4), 957–980. doi:10.13052/jmm1550-4646.1841

Dadhich, M., Pahwa, M. S., & Rao, S. S. (2018). Factor Influencing to Users Acceptance of Digital Payment System. *International Journal on Computer Science and Engineering, 06*(09), 46–50. doi:10.26438/ijcse/v6si9.4650

Dadhich, M., Purohit, H., & Bhasker, A. A. (2021). Determinants of green initiatives and operational performance for manufacturing SMEs. *Materials Today: Proceedings, 46*(20), 10870–10874. doi:10.1016/j.matpr.2021.01.889

Fernandez-Carames, T. M., & Fraga-Lamas, P. (2020). Towards Post-Quantum Blockchain: A Review on Blockchain Cryptography Resistant to Quantum Computing Attacks. *IEEE Access: Practical Innovations, Open Solutions, 8*, 1–27. doi:10.1109/ACCESS.2020.2968985

Forson, I. K., & Vuopala, E. (2019). Online learning readiness: Perspective of students enrolled in distance education in Ghana. *The Online Journal of Distance Education and E-Learning, 7*(4), 277–294.

Garcia, P. (2018). Biometrics on the blockchain. *Biometric Technology Today, 1*(5), 5–7. doi:10.1016/S0969-4765(18)30067-5

Gill, S. S., Tuli, S., Xu, M., Singh, I., Singh, K. V., Lindsay, D., Tuli, S., Smirnova, D., Singh, M., Jain, U., Pervaiz, H., Sehgal, B., Kaila, S. S., Misra, S., Aslanpour, M. S., Mehta, H., Stankovski, V., & Garraghan, P. (2019). Transformative effects of IoT, Blockchain and Artificial Intelligence on cloud computing: Evolution, vision, trends and open challenges. *Internet of Things (Netherlands), 8*, 1–26. doi:10.1016/j.iot.2019.100118

Haji, K. (2021). E-commerce development in rural and remote areas of BRICS countries. *Journal of Integrative Agriculture, 20*(4), 979–997. doi:10.1016/S2095-3119(20)63451-7

Hebert, C., & Di Cerbo, F. (2019). Secure blockchain in the enterprise: A methodology. *Pervasive and Mobile Computing, 59*, 1–14. doi:10.1016/j.pmcj.2019.101038

Ioannou, A., Tussyadiah, I., & Lu, Y. (2020). Privacy concerns and disclosure of biometric and behavioral data for travel. *International Journal of Information Management, 54*(January), 102122. doi:10.1016/j.ijinfomgt.2020.102122

Kappert, N., Karger, E., & Kureljusic, M. (2021). Quantum Computing – The Impending End for the Blockchain? *PACIS 2021 Proceedings,* 1–14.

Kathuria, A., Mann, A., Khuntia, J., Saldanha, T. J. V., Kauffman, J., Kathuria, A., Mann, A., Khuntia, J., & Saldanha, T. J. V. (2018). A Strategic Value Appropriation Path for Cloud Computing A Strategic Value Appropriation Path for Cloud Computing. *Journal of Management Information Systems, 35*(3), 740–775. doi:10.1080/07421 222.2018.1481635

Khan, S. N., Loukil, F., Ghedira-Guegan, C., Benkhelifa, E., & Bani-Hani, A. (2021). Blockchain smart contracts: Applications, challenges, and future trends. *Peer-to-Peer Networking and Applications, 14*(5), 2901–2925. doi:10.100712083-021-01127-0 PMID:33897937

Krishnapriya, S., & Sarath, G. (2020). Securing Land Registration using Blockchain. *Procedia Computer Science, 171*(2019), 1708–1715. doi:10.1016/j.procs.2020.04.183

Kumar, M., & Dadhich, N. (2015). An Analysis of Factors Affecting to Entrepreneur Development in Rajasthan. *International Journal of Management, IT and Engineering, 5*(12), 41–48.

Kumar, N., & Dadhich, M. (2014). Risk Management for Investors in Stock Market. *EXCEL International Journal of Multidisciplinary Management Studies, 4*(3), 103–108.

Kumar, R. L., Pham, Q. V., Khan, F., Piran, M. J., & Dev, K. (2021). Blockchain for securing aerial communications: Potentials, solutions, and research directions. *Physical Communication, 47,* 1–19. doi:10.1016/j.phycom.2021.101390

Li, C., Xu, Y., Tang, J., & Liu, W. (2019). Quantum Blockchain: A Decentralized, Encrypted and Distributed Database Based on Quantum Mechanics. *Journal of Quantum Computing, 1*(2), 49–63. doi:10.32604/jqc.2019.06715

Li, D., Luo, Z., & Cao, B. (2021a). Blockchain-based federated learning methodologies in smart environments. *Cluster Computing.* Advance online publication. doi:10.100710586-021-03424-y PMID:34744493

Li, D., Luo, Z., & Cao, B. (2021b). Blockchain-based federated learning methodologies in smart environments. *Cluster Computing, 1,* 1–15. doi:10.100710586-021-03424-y PMID:34744493

Marsal-Llacuna, M. L. (2020). The people's smart city dashboard (PSCD): Delivering on community-led governance with blockchain. *Technological Forecasting and Social Change, 158,* 1–11. doi:10.1016/j.techfore.2020.120150

Motlagh, N. H., Mohammadrezaei, M., Hunt, J., & Zakeri, B. (2020). Internet of things (IoT) and the energy sector. *Energies*, *13*(2), 1–27. doi:10.3390/en13020494

Pólvora, A., Nascimento, S., Lourenço, J. S., & Scapolo, F. (2020). Blockchain for industrial transformations: A forward-looking approach with multi-stakeholder engagement for policy advice. *Technological Forecasting and Social Change*, *157*, 1–18. doi:10.1016/j.techfore.2020.120091

Sang, Z., & Li, K. (2019). ITU-T standardization activities on smart sustainable cities. *IET Smart Cities*, *1*(1), 3–9. doi:10.1049/iet-smc.2019.0023

Schulz, K., & Feist, M. (2021). Leveraging blockchain technology for innovative climate finance under the Green Climate Fund. *Earth System Governance*, *7*, 1–10. doi:10.1016/j.esg.2020.100084

Selvaraj, S., & Sundaravaradhan, S. (2020). Challenges and opportunities in IoT healthcare systems : A systematic review. *SN Applied Sciences*, *2*(1), 1–8. doi:10.100742452-019-1925-y

Sengupta, J., Ruj, S., & Das Bit, S. (2020). A Comprehensive Survey on Attacks, Security Issues and Blockchain Solutions for IoT and IIoT. *Journal of Network and Computer Applications*, *149*, 1–20. doi:10.1016/j.jnca.2019.102481

Seon, C. (2021). Blockchain for IoT-based smart cities : Recent advances, requirements, and future challenges. *Journal of Network and Computer Applications*, *181*(February), 103007. doi:10.1016/j.jnca.2021.103007

Shalendra Singh Rao, M. D. (n.d.). Impact of Foreign Direct Investment in Indian Capital Market. *International Journal of Research in Economics and Social Sciences*, *7*(6), 172–178.

Shan, Z., Zhang, Y., Zhang, Y., Tang, S., & Wang, W. (2021). A review of recent progress and developments in China smart cities. *IET Smart Cities*, *3*(4), 189–200. doi:10.1049mc2.12020

Sharma, P., Jindal, R., & Borah, M. D. (2022). A review of smart contract-based platforms, applications, and challenges. *Cluster Computing*, *1*, 1–27. doi:10.100710586-021-03491-1

Sharma, R., Kamble, S. S., Gunasekaran, A., Kumar, V., & Kumar, A. (2020). A systematic literature review on machine learning applications for sustainable agriculture supply chain performance. *Computers & Operations Research*, *119*, 1–12. doi:10.1016/j.cor.2020.104926

Solaiman, E., Wike, T., & Sfyrakis, I. (2021). Implementation and evaluation of smart contracts using a hybrid on- and off-blockchain architecture. *Concurrency and Computation*, *33*(1), 1–17. doi:10.1002/cpe.5811

Srinivas Aditya, U. S. P., Singh, R., Singh, P. K., & Kalla, A. (2021). A Survey on Blockchain in Robotics: Issues, Opportunities, Challenges and Future Directions. *Journal of Network and Computer Applications*, *196*, 1–37. doi:10.1016/j.jnca.2021.103245

Sun, J., Yan, J., & Zhang, K. Z. K. (2016). Blockchain-based sharing services: What blockchain technology can contribute to smart cities. *Financial Innovation*, *2*(26), 1–9. doi:10.118640854-016-0040-y

Tribis, Y., El Bouchti, A., & Bouayad, H. (2018). Supply chain management based on blockchain: A systematic mapping study. *MATEC Web of Conferences, 200*. 10.1051/matecconf/201820000020

Van Den Bosch, H. (2020). Humane by choice, smart by default: 39 building blocks for cities of the future. *IET Smart Cities*, *2*(3), 111–121. doi:10.1049/iet-smc.2020.0030

Xiang, X., & Zhao, X. (2022). Blockchain-assisted searchable attribute-based encryption for e-health systems. *Journal of Systems Architecture*, *124*, 1–15. doi:10.1016/j.sysarc.2022.102417

Yapa, C., de Alwis, C., Liyanage, M., & Ekanayake, J. (2021). Survey on blockchain for future smart grids: Technical aspects, applications, integration challenges and future research. *Energy Reports*, *7*, 6530–6564. doi:10.1016/j.egyr.2021.09.112

ADDITIONAL READING

Abd El-Latif, A. A., Abd-El-Atty, B., Mehmood, I., Muhammad, K., Venegas-Andraca, S. E., & Peng, J. (2021). Quantum-Inspired Blockchain-Based Cybersecurity: Securing Smart Edge Utilities in IoT-Based Smart Cities. *Information Processing and Management. Elsevier Ltd*, *58*(4), 1–12. doi:10.1016/j.ipm.2021.102549

Alasbali, N., Azzuhri, S. R. B., Salleh, R. B., Kiah, M. L. M., Shariffuddin, A. A. A. S. A., Kamel, N. M. I. N. M., & Ismail, L. (2022). Rules of Smart IoT Networks within Smart Cities towards Blockchain Standardization. *Mobile Information Systems*, *2022*, 1–11. Advance online publication. doi:10.1155/2022/9109300

Krishna, B., Rajkumar, P., & Velde, V. (2021). *'Integration of blockchain technology for security and privacy in internet of things', Materials Today: Proceedings.* Elsevier Ltd. doi:10.1016/j.matpr.2021.01.606

Sharma, R., Kamble, S. S., Gunasekaran, A., Kumar, V., & Kumar, A. (2020). A systematic literature review on machine learning applications for sustainable agriculture supply chain performance. *Computers and Operations Research. Elsevier Ltd, 119*, 1–12. doi:10.1016/j.cor.2020.104926

KEY TERMS AND DEFINITIONS

Asynchronous Blockchain: It is the blockchain network that can be designed whether to prioritize consistency or availability. If the network wants to prioritize availability, all transactions are added without any downtime. If the network wants to prioritize consistency, some transactions might not be processed or halted until all the previous transactions are confirmed.

Blockchain: Traditional blockchain which uses pre-quantum cryptography and not secure from quantum attacks.

Cryptocurrency: Is a digital currency designed to work as a medium of exchange through a computer network that is not reliant on any central authority, such as a government or bank, to uphold or maintain it.

Cryptography: Is the technique of securing information and communications through use of codes so that only those persons for whom the information is intended can understand it and process it, thus preventing unauthorized access to information.

Identity Management: Is the organizational process for ensuring individuals have the appropriate access to technology resources. This includes the identification, authentication and authorization of a person, or persons, to have access to applications, systems, or networks.

Lattice Cryptosystem: Is a generic term for construction of cryptographic primitives or scheme consisting of a set of algorithms that involve lattices and is used to convert plaintext to ciphertext to encode or decode messages securely.

Permissioned Blockchain: Is a distributed ledger that is not publicly accessible. It can only be accessed by users with permissions. The users can only perform specific actions granted to them by the ledger administrators and are required to identify themselves through certificates or other digital means.

Permissionless Blockchain: Also known as trustless or public blockchains, are open networks available to everyone to participate in the consensus process that blockchains use to validate transactions and data. They are fully decentralized across unknown parties.

Quantum Blockchain: Blockchain systems running in quantum computers.

Quantum Key Distribution: Is a secure communication method which implements a cryptographic protocol involving components of quantum mechanics. It enables two parties to produce a shared random secret key known only to them, which can then be used to encrypt and decrypt messages.

Quantum-Resistant Blockchain: Blockchain systems with post-quantum cryptography, i.e., post-quantum public-private key, hashing, and related protocols.

Signature Scheme: Is a technique to assure an entity's acknowledgment of having seen a certain digital message.

Supply Chain: Is a network of individuals and companies who are involved in creating a product and delivering it to the consumer.

Tokenization: Is the process of exchanging sensitive data for nonsensitive data called "tokens" that can be used in a database or internal system without bringing it into scope.

Transparency: Transparency, as used in science, engineering, business, the humanities and in other social contexts, is operating in such a way that it is easy for others to see what actions are performed. Transparency implies openness, communication, and accountability.

Chapter 10

Advancements in Blockchain Technology With the Use of Quantum Blockchain and Non–Fungible Tokens

Farhan Khan
Geetanjali Institute of Technical Studies, India

Rakshit Kothari
ⓘ https://orcid.org/0000-0003-2893-1504
Geetanjali Institute of Technical Studies, India

Mayank Patel
ⓘ https://orcid.org/0000-0002-8580-4184
Geetanjali Institute of Technical Studies, India

ABSTRACT

Blockchain is a new but quickly growing technology in the world, which was developed by a pseudonymous Satoshi Nakamoto in 2009 as the cryptocurrency Bitcoin. Blockchain was un-hackable but now, due to use of quantum computers, it is possible to tamper with blockchain. As a counter to this, the researchers have come up with quantum blockchain using the principles of quantum cryptography. Today we see that the technology has given birth to many new technologies as well. One of its examples is non-fungible tokens (NFTs). These are a new sort of blockchain-based token that is unique and indivisible. They were first created in 2014. These are blockchain-based virtual assets. Since early 2021, the phenomena and its marketplaces have increased dramatically.

DOI: 10.4018/978-1-6684-5072-7.ch010

INTRODUCTION

The Blockchain technology first introduced in 2009 by a pseudonym creator named as Satoshi Nakamoto is one of the most popular technology in the world today. It was first introduced as a medium of currency named as Bitcoin which has revolutionized the method of money holdings and transfer. Being referred as un-hackable this technology is reason for many changes in the currently existing system. It is basically a chunk of data that has been linked together (Antonucci et. al., 2019). Being a peer-to-peer technology the blockchain becomes more secure as all the transactions are updated in the public ledger and its copy is maintained by each user active on the network it is impossible to tamper data (Frauenthaler et. al., 2020).

The Blockchain is taught to be un-hackable but now a days this is also becoming a false promise as with the rise of quantum computing it is now possible to manipulate the blockchain network as the quantum computer are million times more powerful than the currently existing classical computer. But as the answer of the question lies within the question only the researcher has come up with a solution we call Quantum-Resistant Blockchain.

As it is seen that the technology has given birth to a number of new technologies one of the most significant and rapidly evolving technology is Non-Fungible Token (Salman, Jain & Gupta, 2019). The term "near-field technology" (NFT) denotes a considerable development above earlier technologies. Proponents of blockchain technology and technologists have been criticized for their unduly optimistic and technologically deterministic outlooks. The current craze for NFTs has gripped the globe and is causing controversy. One thing is clear, however: These tokens are going to have a crucial role in constructing virtual lands termed as "METAVERSE". The NFTs in broad terms open gates for fresh opportunities in the field of internet, gaming, real estate and also for the venture capitalists (Khalid & Askar, 2021). NFTs have a huge potential to make a lot of money for art creators and institutions simply by putting on sale an art with a digital signature. To construct a worldwide commercial environment an individual and the companies are dependent on each other to develop, transmit and preserve the crucial data, while NFTs offer an independent space for this.

History of Evolution

The history of evolution that is from where we have started and where we are now. An equal exchange system known as "Barter's System" was used in the beginning stages of evolution (Abou & Saade, 2019). For example, if one person has a lot of apples but no mangos, and the other has a lot of mangos but no apple, they can trade the apples and mangos by means of exchange in order to meet their requirement (Gupta & Patel, 2021).

Following this, the Era of Coins began where now the man-made coins were used. They came with huge variations like rectangular or cubic, big or small (Kothari, Choudhary & Jain, 2021). The major disadvantage for this was that the coins may vary from territory to territory as different territories had different regimes and value of a coin might be nothing in other territory, as at that time there was no Standard Regulation for money (Kuperberg, 2020).

Then, in the 7th CE came the Era of Paper notes originating form a Chinese Empire, which continues to control the globe today (Sheikh, Patel & Sinhal, 2020). All because today the world is undertaking the United-States Dollar as a perfect currency exchange medium.

Finally, the Digital Era came in 2009, introducing us with a new form of currency know as cryptocurrency a blockchain based secured, decentralised currency for trade and transfer of money having the feature of anonymity means of money trade and transfer that is posing a threat to the present centralised system (Latifi, Zhang & Cheng, 2019). Bitcoin is the first ever successful electronic currency created by a pseudonymous creator Satoshi Nakamoto.

Lastly, on May 3 2014, Kevin McCoy coined the first NFT, named Quantum, as a technological advancement (Malik, Dedeoglu, Kanhere & Jurdak, 2019). In 2015, the makers of the Spells of Genesis game used Counterparty to become the foremost for releasing the blockchain base game assest (Kothari, Patel & Sharma, 2021).

BLOCKCHAIN

General Definition

- A blockchain is nothing more than a database that links together encrypted data blocks to create a continuous single source of truth for the data.
- Digital assets are dispersed, creating a permanent record of the asset, as opposed to being copied or relocated.
- The asset is decentralized, allowing for transparency and real-time public access.
- A visual record of alterations protects the document's legitimacy and increases confidence in the assets.

Blockchain is a perfect option for almost every business due to its built-in security features and public ledger.

Key Elements of Blockchain

Distributed Ledger Technology (DLT)

All the network participants (nodes) are able to access the distributed-ledger and its immutable transaction record (Salman, Jain & Gupta, 2019). This shared ledger eliminates the needless duplication that is typical in conventional business networks by simply recording transactions once.

Permanent Records

No participant is permitted to alter or change a transaction after it has been added to the shared ledger. If an error is discovered in a transaction record, a fresh transaction should be created to fix it, and both the transactions them must be available (Somy et. al., 2019).

Smart Contract

The blockchain stores a set of instructions known as smart contracts, which are automatically carried out to expedite transactions (Tasatanattakool & Techapanupreeda, 2018). A smart contract might establish the conditions for transferring corporate bonds, the terms of payment for travel insurance, and many other things (Menaria, Nagar & Patel, 2020).

How Blockchain Works

The working procedure of the blockchain is very simple and easy to understand. The most important thing in this whole procedure that both the users (Thuraisingham, 2020), the transaction originator as well as the transaction receiver, must have a blockchain wallet to store the data. A software known as a blockchain wallet enables user to spend their cryptocurrencies like BTC, ETH, and others (Putz & Pernul, 2020). Such wallets are secured using cryptographic techniques (private and public keys), enabling users to monitor and manage their transactions.

At beginning when the user initiates the transaction on network, a new block is generated to represent that transaction (Wan, Eyers & Zhang 2019). After the block creation the transaction is being broadcasted via the peer-to-peer network of computers known as nodes, who eventually confirm the transaction.

After the transaction has been confirmed, it is being merged with another blocks in order to form a new data block for the ledger. It worth's noting that all the fresh transaction creates a secured block, that is encrypted and linked to others using cryptographic principles. Whenever a fresh block is formed, it is included into currently existing Blockchain network, confirming its security and immutability.

Cryptocurrencies, smart contract, documents, or any other important data may all be a part of a validated transaction.

Advantages

Secure

Being an open-source ledger, all the transactions are made public which helps in the eliminations of fraud and double dealing. In order to maintain the integrity of transaction these are supervised by the miners and is validated only it 51% of the network agrees (Wang, Li, Wang & Chen, 2021).

Zero Third Party Interference

Blockchain is an independent technology which is not under the control of any national of state province, hence no one have a legal right to alter these digital currencies.

Secure Transaction

All transactions are recorded on the blockchain, which cannot be altered or amended. Both the parties involved in the transaction as well as the general public are free to see the data at any time (Yin, Wen, Li, Zhang & Jin, 2018). The overall security of these online transactions is enhanced by this.

Quick Transaction

Blockchain technology allows transactions to be completed in a couple of minutes. Whereas the bank transactions might take at least of two week for the monetary (referring to bank to bank transfer of money). At this stage, a person doing virtual transactions using crypto can finish a number of transactions.

Decentralised and Anonymity

There is no need of any central authority to maintain the network or validate the transaction. Also, it provides the user the power of anonymity making user independent.

Disadvantages

Difficulties while Updating

The application is to be updated on each node of Peer to Peer network, else if in case any node of that network refuses to accept the changes, the programme is forked.

Difficulty in Development

To achieve consensus and enable scalability, it is important to begin with very complex protocols (Yu, Lv, Shao, Guo, Zou & Zhang, 2018). It is impossible to swiftly implement an idea in the aim of afterwards adding new features and growing the application without forking or redeploying the network (Saini, H. K., 2021).

Crime

Blockchain technologies are also responsible for increasing the crime rates as it decentralized making it free from any control of central authority as well as it allows anonymous transaction which makes the user untraceable (Choubisa, M., et al. 2022)

High Energy Consumptions

The core drawback of Blockchain technology is the high energy consumption. As maintaining the real-time ledger necessitates the utilization of energy. In addition, mining farms use a lot of energy since miners try to find a unique solution in order to validate transactions, which take a lot of computer power as the solution is to be selected from trillions of combinations.

Applications of Blockchain

International Payments

The most important application of this technology is the it facilitates the user with the international payments without high fee charges and can be completed in fractions of seconds; hence therefore it can also be termed as Borderless Transfer.

Securing IOT Networks

Although the IOT(Internet-of-Things) make our life easier, it also makes it possible for dishonest actors to access our data and seize control of vital infrastructure.

Greater security can be achieved by storing passwords and another important data on a distributed network as opposed to a centralised server. Additionally, a blockchain offers security against data alteration because it is essentially immutable (Hiran, K. K., & Doshi, R. 2013).

Storage of Data

When used with data storage systems, blockchain technology may increase security and integrity. Data can be kept decentralised, making it more harder to hack into and erase all the data available on the network whereas a centralised data storage provider can have a few redundancy locations (Yin, Wen, Li, Zhang & Jin, 2018). Additionally, it suggests that data is easier to get because access isn't restricted to a single company's operations. In certain cases, blockchain data storage could be less expensive.

Non-Fungible Tokens

NFTs, or Non Fungible tokens, are frequently thought of as a way to obtain the rights to digital art. Placing the NFT on blockchain assures that there is only single copy of a piece of digital art since the blockchain forbids data duplication. This may give you the impression that you are purchasing physical art without the headaches of storage and maintenance.

Record and Identity Management

The federal, state, and local governments keep track of personal information such as dates of birth and death, marriage status, and property transactions. Although some of these papers are only on paper, organising this data might be difficult. Furthermore, it's time-consuming, ineffective, and inconvenient for citizens to physically visit the local government offices to make the modifications. The use of blockchain technology might simplify recordkeeping and increase data security.

Healthcare

Fundamental details like gender, age, height and weight are some basic examples of healthcare data that are highly suited for blockchain, as are potentially basic medical records like immunisation history or vital signs (Hiran, K. K., & Doshi, R. 2013). All of this information cannot be used to individually identify a patient, thus it may be kept on a public blockchain that is seen by lots of people without compromising privacy.

Supply Chain Management

The uniqueness of the blockchain ledger makes it perfect for tasks like live product tracking as they move through the supply chain and change hands. The use of a blockchain opens up a lot of opportunities for businesses exporting these goods. A supply chain's procedures might be organised using records on the blockchain, such as allocating goods to different shipping containers after they reach at a port. A novel and adaptable method of organising and using monitoring data is provided by blockchain.

Blockchain Security Issues

Security Flaws

The most of blockchain transfers have far less secure destinations, despite the fact that blockchain has been dubbed "un-hackable". For instance, as a result of bitcoin-trading or investments, a sizeable amount of bitcoin may be transferred into a form of wallet known as "hot wallet," or a virtual saving account. These wallets couldn't possibly be as safe as the actual blocks of the blockchain.

A number of third-party service providers could be used to support blockchain transactions. A few examples are payment processor, smart contract, and blockchain based payment system. These third party blockchain service providers typically have weak security on their own websites and applications, which leaves them open to attack (Jain, R. K., 2012).

Issues with Extensibility

Today blockchains are one of the largest ever constructed technology, it will continue to grow only in size. This makes the experts concerned, as these large-scale blockchain have not been thoroughly examined. Some basic worries revolve around the possibility that as fast ecosystem matures, more vulnerabilities might be recognised and exploited, or the technological foundation which enables these blockchains will be becoming more prone to common threats.

Regulation-Related Problems

The absence of clear legislative standards presents another challenge to blockchain security. The blockchain sector has no homogeneity, making it challenging for developers to learn from previous mistakes.

Inadequate Testing

Blockchain is being used in many other industries, despite the fact that it has historically been connected to bitcoin transactions. The issue is that the code of non-cryptocurrency apps is frequently experimental and untested, which leaves room for vulnerability discovery and exploitation by hackers.

QUANTUM BLOCKCHAIN

As it is in the nature that the answer lies in the question the only thing is that we have to reframe the question and inspect from the end.

Similarly, the answer to the quantum-related threat to blockchain can be overcome by employing quantum. As the quantum computers are a million times faster than traditional computers and can break complicated encryption in fractions of a second, cryptography is now unable to compete with quantum computing. As a result, we will be moving towards Quantum Cryptography as a solution.

In quantum cryptography the Data is encrypted using the principles of quantum physics instead of general mathematical encryption technique, which is fundamentally un-hackable . In detail we can say that, Cryptography in general terms is a method for the encryption of data or scrambling of plain text using the mathematical formulas so that only intended parties with appropriate "key" can read it. By definition, quantum cryptography employs the laws of quantum physics to encrypt data and transfer it in an impenetrable manner (Doshi, R. 2018).

Difference Between Mathematical and Quantum Cryptography

Table 1 shows a comparison between the Mathematical and the Quantum cryptography.

Working of Quantum Cryptography

Quantum physics uncertainty principle provides the earliest basis for quantum cryptography. Quantum cryptography becomes the projected answer as future quantum computers are expected to handle the discrete logarithmic problems and widely used encryption methods such as AES, RSA, and DES are expected to fail. As an illustration, consider that it is employed to generate a shared, confidential, and randomized stream of bits that enables two systems, named as John and Smith, to interact. Quantum Key Distribution is the term for this. Following the exchange of this key between John and Smith, extra information can be exchanged using well-known cryptographic procedures these are (Yu, Lv, Shao, Guo, Zou & Zhang, 2018).

Table 1.

The Mathematical Cryptography	The Quantum Cryptography
It is generally a technique based on mathematical calculations.	It is generally a technique based on quantum laws.
It marks the presence of digital signatures.	In it the digital signatures are not present.
The bit-rate is completely dependent on the computational power.	The average bit-rate is one(1) MbPS.
The bit storage is of 2n, n-bit strings.	The bit storage is of 1 n-bit string.
It have a independent communication medium.	It have a dependent communication medium.
It is widely used.	It is sophisticated.
The total expense is very less.	The total expense is high.

Depending on the Heisenberg Principle of Uncertainty: BB84 and its Variants

A polarizer is used to pass a single-photon pulse. John may polarise a single-photon pulse with a certain polarizer and encode binary value bits to the polarizer's output (vertical, horizontal, circular, etc.). Smith may match the situations with John and ascertain the validity of his estimates by receiving the photon beam and guessing the polarizer. If Harold had been attempting to decode, the polarisation by his polarizer would have generated inconsistencies in Smith and John's match instances, alerting them to eavesdropping. In such a setup, if Harold tries to listen in on a conversation, John and Smith will be alerted.

- In contrast to the original BB84's four polarisation states, the B92 protocol only has two.
- Similar protocol SSP, used by the BB84, encrypts bits using 6 states.
- Another technique that employs attenuated lasers is SARG04, which outperforms BB84 in multi-photon systems.

According to the Quantum Entanglement: E91 and Variants

Each particle is received by John and Smith from a single source that emits a pair of entangled photons. For each photon sent, John and Smith would exchange encoded bits and match cases, similar to the BB84 technique. However, because of the Entanglement principle, the results of John and Smith's match instances will be the polar opposite in this scenario. Complement bits in bit strings will be interpreted by any of them. Then one of them can reverse bits to come up with a key. This test can demonstrate the lack of eavesdroppers because Bell's Inequality should not hold for entangled particles. Because a third photon is in entanglement with energy levels adequate for non-detect ability is virtually impossible, this system is completely safe.

- The Entangled Particles Theory may be applied to the SARG04 and SSP protocol models.

Quantum Cryptography Failure point:

Photon Number Splitting (PNS) Attack

Because sending a single photon is impossible, a pulse is sent instead. Harold can collect some of the photons from a pulse, and when John and Smith have matched their bits, Harold may be using a similar polarizer as Smith to obtain the keys being undiscovered (Gupta & Patel, 2021; Khazanchi, D. et al 2021).

Faked-State Attack

Harold makes a copy of Smith's photon detector and therefore collects and passes the photons meant for Smith. Despite the fact that Harold is aware of these encoded bits, Smith believes the he has received it from John.

NON-FUNGIBLE TOKEN

Non-Fungible Token Usability

Like blockchain, NFTs offer a wide range of applications, but the major area of use will be

Gaming

Non-fungible tokens are steadily transforming the gaming industry by providing play-to-earn gaming model and allowing players to access their unique digital assets quickly and easily.

As of today, online game operates on the centralized servers due to which the sharing of in-game assets with someone is little bit complex (Wan, Eyers & Zhang 2019). Whereas with upcoming decentralized games such as *Axie Infinity* it will be easier to share in-game assets allowing the user to play freely.

NFT gaming allows people to earn while playing as for example *CryptoKitties,* it opened the way for the crypto-collectibles sector to flourish allowing players to trade their kitties as NFT and one of the most expensive kitty sold was Founder Cat #40 ($1.04 million).

Game collectible items such as weapons, skins, maps and accessories are referred as Game-relevant NFTs

Metaverse

Deriving from a science fiction novel *Snow Crash* in 1992, the metaverse can be broken into two parts: "meta" meaning beyond and "verse" meaning universe, thus combinedly referring to something which is beyond the universe.

Proving the meaning today metaverse is a world with limitlessness, it is a 3d virtual world combination of "Virtual and Augmented Reality" extending it to "Mixed Reality".

NFTs act as a gateway to the metaverse, facilitating in the construction of identity, community, and social experiences inside it (Gupta & Patel, 2021).. These will help in maintaining interoperability outside the virtual world by using augmented reality, engagement and location-based features.

Virtual Lands can also be traded in the metaverse, as Decentraland has done by enabling anyone to purchase land in the metaverse.

NFTs will help in proving ownership over art in the metaverse. Take, for example, Leonardo Da Vinci's painting Monalisa, anyone throughout the globe could have a replica, but the real will only be possessed by an individual or organization, and the replicas will not be valued as high as that of the real. Also the NFTs can be referred as the Monalisa of Metaverse unique, priceless and irreplaceable.

Other Areas of Use

- Intellectual property and patents: Traditional IP rights procedures like trademark and copyright did not make the user capable of proving ownership over the whole art however the non-fungible tokes will.
- Logistics Operations: NFTs may also assist businesses in tracking their products from production to transportation and delivery. Customers can see what it is they are paying for and also the mechanism of supply-chain is transparent as well.
- Estate Industry: The real estate industry is among the most NFT-ready industries. NFTs may also be utilized in the Estate domain for simplifying and speeding up the deals by simply enabling a smart contract for property deals (allowing automated payment mechanism), and can also establish

decentralized renting. The NFT with timestamp now could be utilized for the transfer of property related paper, facilitating with confirmation of ownership, and tracking the changes in the land value over the period of time.

- Ensuring the genuineness of the product: In the near future, actual items will be able to be evaluated for authenticity and validity since the blockchain can permanently record product information. The non-fungible tokens can also be utilized to take a look on data from the manufacturing process, assuring that everything has been done equitably.

- Identification of Artwork: It can help determine the legitimacy of an object and reduce or eliminate the distribution of counterfeit artwork. This also ensures that the object is authentic, especially if it was acquired at an auction house.

- Voting in Elections: Many nations require voters to provide a picture ID as well as proof of citizenship to the voting booth during elections. Many on the other hand, cannot vote as they might not have any Identification Document or any other specified proof of residency. The NFT can be a useful solution for this problem as it can be used as a mark of digital ID for people without requiring any physical document. Because NFTs stand like an official record for who voted as well as where they voted, it will also help to prevent fraudulent voting and cheating.

Similarities and Distinctions Between Cryptocurrency and Non-Fungible Tokens

Similarities

- Both are empowered by blockchain mechanism.
- Both are needed to be mined/minted for transfer.
- Both are open to all hence no one is restricted from buying/selling cryptocurrency or NFT's.
- Both provide anonymity to the user.
- Both uses public ledger for record keeping.
- Both require the digital wallet to be stored.

The question of what distinguishes NFT from other cryptos arises as a blockchain-based technology. The difference may be negligible for some, but it is enormous for others.

Differences

As a reference to the preceding table, NFT can be anything, unexpectedly, even a tweet. The first ever tweet by Twitter's founder Jack Dorsey was auctioned at a platform named as Valuables and the highest bid to it was of nearly $2.89 Million in March 2021. Hence it can be seen as that these tokens can be anything you want it to be.

Table 2. Comparison between cryptocurrency and non-fungible token

Cryptocurrency	Non-Fungible Token
Crypto coins are fungible so two coins will always have same value.	As the name suggest these are non-fungible hence no two tokens are same.
These are divisible, for example a bitcoin can be divided into one hundred million Satoshi.	These are indivisible and exist as single entity.
For mining it uses "Proof of Work" (PoW) protocol.	For minting it uses "Proof of Stake" (PoS),
It represents currency.	It is essentially digital representation of distinct real-world entity.
Each cryptocurrency has its own blockchain and uses it for storing values and validating transactions	It is based on the blockchain of a coin, for example, many NFTs mint on the Ethereum blockchain.

Method of Creation and Auctioning

As of now we learned all about the NFTs now it is the time to get into it by learning the process of creation and auctioning (Wan, Eyers & Zhang 2019).. It would not be a complicated if you love to create unimaginable art.

Pick Unique Creation

The initial phase is of selecting a masterpiece as we know these can be anything as discussed above it may be a painting you painted, any song sung by you, your films, images, and literally anything. So, choose the most unique and an eye-catching art.

Get Some Crypto

Now as the artwork is selected, second step is to have plenty of cryptocurrency. As most of these tokens today are built on Ethereum it is more preferred to have Ethereum in wallet.

It is not mandatory to build it on Ethereum only as it can be done on any blockchain several other options are Solana, Polkadot, Bitgert or any. Ethereum is preferred as it is most widely used and is recognized by almost every NFT exchange.

Now a question arises in mind that I am here to sell my NFT then why I required to hold cryptocurrency.

The important point of consideration is that the trading platforms will charge the creator in order to mint the tokens, but what is the meaning of minting an NFT?

In simple words Minting NFT can be defined as the process of transforming the art from being a digital one to a NFT and permanently storing this content in on the Ethereum blockchain, and after that our art cannot be changed or erased.

Our NFT is now ready to be traded on the NFT trading platforms.

Pick a Marketplace:

Now that you have everything correct now it's the step of finding a suitable marketplace for minting and auctioning the NFT (it must be noted that the process may vary from platform to platform as all have different methods to follow). All that is required to create is the minting procedure, as described above.

Describe the artwork like what it is about, what makes it unique, why to buy it and so on.

Launch an Auction:

The final step is of selling an NFT it can be either put on sale directly or can be sold by the means of auctioning these can be described as:

- Open auction: It allows the public to bid as high as they can until you accept it.
- Timed Auction: A type of auction which lasts for a specified time period decided by us, such as a day, week, or longer.
- Fixed Price: Instead of auctioning you can also set a fix price for your NFT.

Profit and Fees

As the NFT is being trades through the platform, they will be charging some commission fee (depending on the platform) for the NFT sale, also some transaction fee for the transfer of crypto from the wallet of the one who bought to the one who sold, don't worry these are not huge amount.

Some famous marketplaces to trade NFTs are:

- OpenSea
- Axie Marketplace
- Larva Lab /CryptoPunks
- NBA Top Shot Marketplace
- Rarible
- SuperRare
- KnownOrigin

Figure 1. Comparison of volume traded at marketplaces

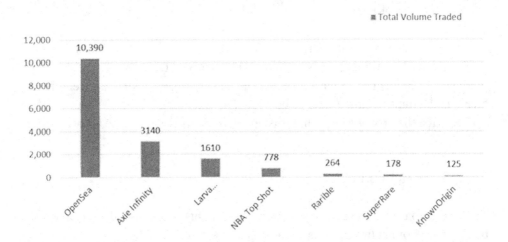

Procedure of Buying Non-Fungible Token

As the NFTs are different from the crypto these cannot be directly purchased in fiat currency like Dollar or Euro, today majority of these are traded with the Ethereum.

The procedure for buying an NFT is very simple and is comprises of following steps:

1. Create a digital crypto wallet to hold cryptocurrency such as Exodus, Metamask, or Trezor.
2. Now get the crypto from the coin exchange platform that you prefer.
3. Connect the wallet to the marketplace you want like OpenSea, Rarible and many more.
4. Finally select the NFT you want and mint it.

The popularity of the NFT determines its price, rarer and unique the NFT will be having more prices, some of these examples are the Ocean-Front ($6 million), Crossroad ($6.6 million), The First 5,000 Days ($69 million) are among the more costly sold NFTs on the market.

Increased Adoption

The NFTs by the year 2021-2022 have witnessed a lightening rise in the popularity and sales, the sales exceeded $2.5 Billion in the beginning of the year. As evident from google trends. Answer to this enormous rise can be by understanding the human behaviour of collecting things. Obviously, the statement is correct; let consider an example of childhood days: if we walked to the marketplace and saw a new thing, we yearned to possess it irrespective of whether it was helpful or not; we desired it because we loved it, and we had to overshow it the following day at school. Likewise, a fan of Robert Downy Jr. will surely want to have the jacket worn by Robert now and will be prepared to pay any amount to have it. The NFTs function similarly, and their appeal is due to human nature.

Figure 2. Rise in Popularity of NFT in the last year

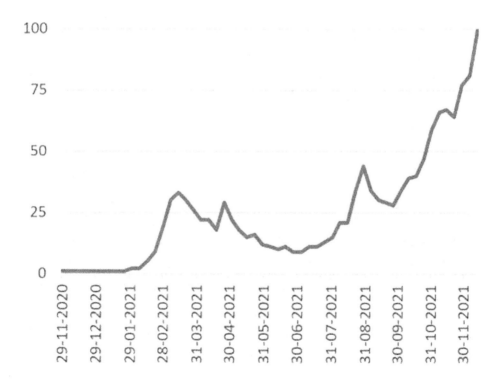

Advantages

Possession

The capability to prove possession is the key advantage of non-fungible tokens. Because they operate on a blockchain, NFTs can help to link ownership to a specific account. These tokens also cannot be distributed among the multiple users. Customers are also protected from getting counterfeit NFTs due to the ownership benefits of NFTs.

Authenticity

The integrity of the blockchain network on which NFTs are resides, ensures their authenticity by preventing them from being altered, removed, or replaced.

Opportunity for Economic Growth

Content providers are frequently concerned that platforms are robbing them of their earnings and earning potential by not giving them what they deserve. For example, under standard royalties, a normally published author make up to between 6–21% royalties on print books, which is very little if value is compared with the art[10]. As a solution to this, NFT makes the artist independent of this middleman model, allowing them to sell their art freely at a price they want.

The ownership proof of artwork is embedded in the metadata of the NFT. As a consequence, when the creators work is sold, the proceeds go directly to them. The developer might get royalties whenever the NFT is transferred to a new owner by putting smart contracts in place while building it, as the inventor's address is included in the NFT metadata (Wireko, J. et al., 2018)

Enhance Market Efficiency

The most evident advantage of NFTs is their ability to boost market efficiency. At the moment, a wonderful example is being played out in various areas of the art world. Artists may now interact directly with their fans, doing away with the necessity for expensive agents and drawn-out negotiations.

Open to All

This is feature enables everyone to create, sell and trade NFT irrespective of age, gender, race or anything.

Anonymity

There is no need of any document submission for creating a NFT, beneficiary for the people who choose to remain anonymous

Drawbacks

Illiquid and Ephemeral Assets

The NFT industry is illiquid due to their immaturity and volatility. NFTs are not well recognized, and there are not many people interested in buying or selling them. As a result, trading NFTs can be highly challenging, especially during periods of stress. It also indicates that NFT price is highly volatile, as the popular art you hold today by paying millions may become obsolete in the future.

Impossible to Digitalize Physical Art

Having a physical and digital art both are frequently different. Also, it is impossible to digitalize any existing physical art. Hence seeing an art by own eyes in real has an allure that these tokens lack

Non-Environmentally Friendly

A significant amount of computing power is necessary to build blockchain records, which needs a considerable amount of electricity. A little fraction of the total power is of renewable sources, while the major is obtained by the combustion of coal and different fossil fuels, which emits CO_2 and ultimately leading to pollution and global warming.

Subject to Theft

Blockchain being a hack-proof technology can be subjected to theft hence NFTs are also vulnerable to a number of security breaches and attacks since they are digital products. These hacks are not referring to data alteration rather it points to exposure of private key as it may lead to wallet manipulation and thievery. Furthermore, most of the NFT exchanges employ inadequate or outdated security standards, leaving them vulnerable to a number of threats.

Open to All

Being a advantage this feature is also a disadvantage as there is no content-filtering mechanism to check what type of content it is, it might be any post promoting terrorism or nudity

Anonymity

It is impossible to track someone as the real identity is not known by anyone, which can lead to increase in illegal activities.

Artificial Intelligence, Natural Art and the NFT

Artificial intelligence one of the most crucial and continuously evolving branch of computer science, overtaking humans at most of the sectors some these includes medical, driving, manufacturing, cooking and many more. Literature and art were the two fields at which artificial intelligence was not supposed to develop, as they cannot possess the human consciousness and imagination, however, these claims appear to be untrue in the near future due to recent developments. GPT3, and DALL-E are the greatest advancement in the AI industry developed by OpenAI.

GPT-3 named as Generative Pre-trained Transformer 3, is an advancement in the field of Natural Language Processing, capable of human-like language generation, answering questions, writing essay and much more. Basically, it is a deep learning-based auto-regressive language model operating on 175 Billion parameters and trained using a combination Common Crawl, WebText2, Books1, Books2, Wikipedia Corpus datasets, ready to challenge the human intelligence.

DALL-E is a text-to-image processing system capable of generating images based on the textual command given in the general language (English most preferably). This model operates on 12 billion auto-regressive transformer parameters (from GPT3) that were trained on 250 million pairings of pictures and text obtained over the internet. It generates output from a description using zero-shot learning, which requires no additional training.

As of now, we can see that AI is currently being used in a range of sectors, including chat-bots, surgical robots and much more. Similarly for the NFT it is also expected that the AI will be used for generating it. As, because today the artworks created by AI are becoming a key point of interest compared to the traditional art, as can be seen below figure-3, which is 12 month recorded data.

It is because the art can be easily created with the help of AI as we only have to give the command of art we want, some popularly used platforms are:

- Hotpot AI
- Artbits AI, and many more

Figure 3. Comparison between AI and natural art

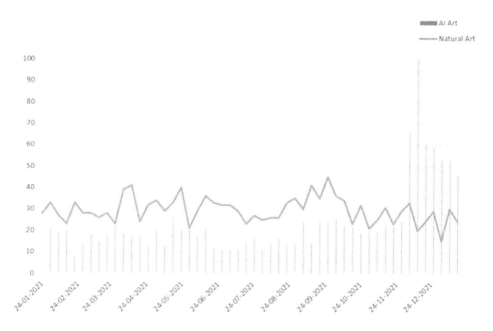

Fractional NFT

As because NFT's popularity is growing every day, everyone wants to hold the greatest NFT that he can get but due to the popularity the famous projects have grown to heights, considering Bored Ape Yacht Club and CryptoPunks as example, that it is not feasible for a middle-class person to buy due to high prices.

As a solution to this, the idea of Fractional NFT comes in play under this situation. A fractional NFT is simply a token that can be broken into tiny fractions, enabling multiple people to assert ownership over a similar NFT. The NFT is fractionalized via a smart contract, which creates a certain number of tokens linked to the unique original, facilitating each individual holder with a fixed percent of sovereignty over the whole NFT, also these now could be traded on markets.

A question might be alarming in your mind that it was said the NFT is indivisible and exist as whole then how it can be fractionalized. The answer to this is simple as in the whole process of fractionalization the original NFT is not cut into pieces and distributed, rather it have a well-defined standard procedure for this.

As we know, ERC-721 is the standard used to create NFT, likewise ERC-20 is used to create Fungible token, and a smart contract is used to generate fungible ERC-20 tokens linked with the indivisible ERC-721 with the total fraction defined by the owner. The price of these ERC-20 tokens is decided by their current market price and the number of tokens created. These tokens are now interchangeable; hence they will always have the same value and can be exchanged for one another and are even ready to be traded in the marketplace. At the time of decision-making related to the NFT, all the owners come together and vote for the change they want.

Some popular platforms to create/buy fractional NFTs are:

- Fractional.art
- Unic.ly
- Otis
- NIFTEX
- nft20
- NFTX

Figure 4. Transaction frequency V/S time

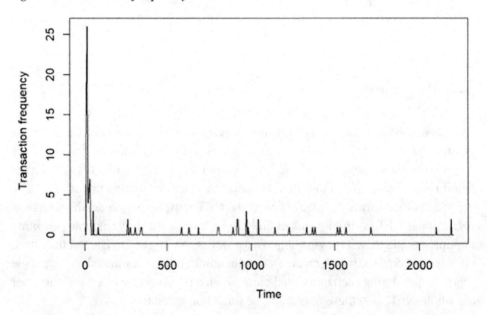

Final Words

It is obvious fact that the value of something varies from person to person. As for an artist it is a great way to display your work to the world while still earning money. Also the tech lover are embracing the Metaverse also some people started to buy lands in the imagined realm, so if you're a businessman, it's an excellent area to invest and earn money. It's fantastic for art lovers to be able to add more and more one-of-a-kind pieces to their collections. Allowing us to have a P2P data sharing. Also employing some techniques for discovering and recording the events, a distributed network which is permanent and resistant to mistakes and manipulation is required. The revolutions that have made this possible are blockchain and distributed ledger technology.

CONCLUSION

As a technology, the blockchain is growing and even have the potential to push all the limits but as with the great power comes greater responsibility, it is our first and foremost responsibility to maintain the blockchain, we cannot rely on the buggy system for our future hence we always have to overcome the faults with powerful solutions.

REFERENCES

Abou, J., & Saade, R. G. (2019). Blockchain applications–usage in different domains. *IEEE Access: Practical Innovations, Open Solutions, 7*, 45360–45381. doi:10.1109/ACCESS.2019.2902501

Antonucci, F., Figorilli, S., Costa, C., Pallottino, F., Raso, L., & Menesatti, P. (2019). A Review on blockchain applications in the agri. *Journal of the Science of Food and Agriculture, 99*(14), 6129–6138. doi:10.1002/jsfa.9912 PMID:31273793

Choubisa, M., Doshi, R., Khatri, N., & Hiran, K. K. (2022, May). A Simple and Robust Approach of Random Forest for Intrusion Detection System in Cyber Security. In *2022 International Conference on IoT and Blockchain Technology (ICIBT)* (pp. 1-5). IEEE. 10.1109/ICIBT52874.2022.9807766

Doshi, R. (2018, June). An Institutional Adoption Framework of the Cloud Computing in Higher Education: Case of Sub-Saharan Africa. *International Journal of Research in Engineering, IT and Social Sciences, 8*(6), 51–56.

Frauenthaler, P., Sigwart, M., Spanring, C., Sober, M., & Schulte, S. (2020, November). ETH relay: A cost-efficient relay for ethereum-based blockchains. In *2020 IEEE International Conference on Blockchain (Blockchain)* (pp. 204-213). IEEE. 10.1109/Blockchain50366.2020.00032

Gupta, H., & Patel, M. (2021, March). Method Of Text Summarization Using Lsa And Sentence Based Topic Modelling With Bert. In *2021 International Conference on Artificial Intelligence and Smart Systems (ICAIS)* (pp. 511-517). IEEE. 10.1109/ICAIS50930.2021.9395976

Hiran, K. K., & Doshi, R. (2013). Robust & secure digital image watermarking technique using concatenation process. *International Journal of ICT and Management*.

Hiran, K. K., & Doshi, R. (2013). An artificial neural network approach for brain tumor detection using digital image segmentation. *Brain*, 2(5), 227–231.

Jain, R. K., Hiran, K., & Paliwal, G. (2012). Quantum Cryptography: A New Generation Of Information Security System. *Proceedings of International Journal of Computers and Distributed Systems*.

Khalid, Z. M., & Askar, S. (2021). Resistant blockchain cryptography to quantum computing attacks. *International Journal of Science and Business*, 5(3), 116–125.

Khazanchi, D., Vyas, A. K., Hiran, K. K., & Padmanaban, S. (Eds.). (2021). *Blockchain 3.0 for sustainable development* (Vol. 10). Walter de Gruyter GmbH & Co KG. doi:10.1515/9783110702507

Kothari, D., Patel, M., & Sharma, A. K. (2021, January). Implementation of Grey Scale Normalization in Machine Learning & Artificial Intelligence for Bioinformatics using Convolutional Neural Networks. In *2021 6th International Conference on Inventive Computation Technologies (ICICT)* (pp. 10711074). IEEE. 10.1109/ICICT50816.2021.9358549

Kothari, R., Choudhary, N., & Jain, K. (2021). CP-ABE Scheme with Decryption Keys of Constant Size Using ECC with Expressive Threshold Access Structure. In *Emerging Trends in Data Driven Computing and Communications* (pp. 15–36). Springer. doi:10.1007/978-981-16-3915-9_2

Kuperberg, M. (2020, November). Towards enabling deletion in append-only blockchains to support data growth management and GDPR Compliance. In *2020 IEEE International Conference on Blockchain (Blockchain)* (pp. 393-400). IEEE. 10.1109/Blockchain50366.2020.00057

Latifi, S., Zhang, Y., & Cheng, L. C. (2019, July). Blockchain-based real estate market: One method for applying blockchain technology in commercial real estate market. In *2019 IEEE International Conference on Blockchain (Blockchain)* (pp. 528-535). IEEE. 10.1109/Blockchain.2019.00002

Malik, S., Dedeoglu, V., Kanhere, S. S., & Jurdak, R. (2019, July). Trustchain: Trust management in blockchain and iot supported supply chains. In *2019 IEEE International Conference on Blockchain (Blockchain)* (pp. 184-193). IEEE. 10.1109/Blockchain.2019.00032

Menaria, H. K., Nagar, P., & Patel, M. (2020). Tweet sentiment classification by semantic and frequency base features using hybrid classifier. In *First International Conference on Sustainable Technologies for Computational Intelligence* (pp. 107-123). Springer. 10.1007/978-981-15-0029-9_9

Putz, B., & Pernul, G. (2020, November). Detecting blockchain security threats. In *2020 IEEE International Conference on Blockchain (Blockchain)* (pp. 313-320). IEEE. 10.1109/Blockchain50366.2020.00046

Saini, H. K., Jain, K. L., Hiran, K. K., & Bhati, A. (2021). Paradigms to make smart city using blockchain. *Blockchain 3.0 for Sustainable Development, 10*, 21.

Salman, T., Jain, R., & Gupta, L. (2019, July). A reputation management framework for knowledge-based and probabilistic blockchains. In *2019 IEEE International Conference on Blockchain (Blockchain)* (pp. 520-527). IEEE. 10.1109/Blockchain.2019.00078

Sheikh, R., Patel, M., & Sinhal, A. (2020). Recognizing MNIST handwritten data set using PCA and LDA. In *International Conference on Artificial Intelligence: Advances and Applications 2019* (pp. 169177). Springer. 10.1007/978-981-15-1059-5_20

Somy, N. B., Kannan, K., Arya, V., Hans, S., Singh, A., Lohia, P., & Mehta, S. (2019, July). Ownership preserving AI market places using blockchain. In *2019 IEEE International Conference on Blockchain (Blockchain)* (pp. 156-165). IEEE. 10.1109/Blockchain.2019.00029

Tasatanattakool, P., & Techapanupreeda, C. (2018, January). Blockchain: Challenges and applications. In *2018 International Conference on Information Networking (ICOIN)* (pp. 473-475). IEEE. 10.1109/ICOIN.2018.8343163

Thuraisingham, B. (2020, October). Blockchain technologies and their applications in data science and cyber security. In *2020 3rd international conference on smart blockchain (SmartBlock)* (pp. 1-4). IEEE. 10.1109/SmartBlock52591.2020.00008

Wan, L., Eyers, D., & Zhang, H. (2019, July). Evaluating the impact of network latency on the safety of blockchain transactions. In *2019 IEEE International Conference on Blockchain (Blockchain)* (pp. 194-201). IEEE. 10.1109/Blockchain.2019.00033

Wang, Q., Li, R., Wang, Q., & Chen, S. (2021). *Non-fungible token (NFT): Overview, evaluation, opportunities and challenges.* arXiv preprint arXiv:2105.07447.

Wireko, J. K., Hiran, K. K., & Doshi, R. (2018). Culturally Based User Resistance to New Technologies in the Age of IoT In Developing Countries: Perspectives From Ethiopia. *International Journal of Emerging Technology and Advanced Engineering, 8*(4), 96–105.

Yin, W., Wen, Q., Li, W., Zhang, H., & Jin, Z. (2018). An anti-quantum transaction authentication approach in blockchain. *IEEE Access: Practical Innovations, Open Solutions, 6,* 5393–5401. doi:10.1109/ACCESS.2017.2788411

Yu, S., Lv, K., Shao, Z., Guo, Y., Zou, J., & Zhang, B. (2018, August). A high performance blockchain platform for intelligent devices. In *2018 1st IEEE international conference on hot information-centric networking (HotICN)* (pp. 260-261). IEEE. 10.1109/HOTICN.2018.8606017

ADDITIONAL READING

Zheng, Z., Xie, S., Dai, H. N., Chen, X., & Wang, H. (2018). Blockchain challenges and opportunities: A survey. *International Journal of Web and Grid Services, 14*(4), 352–375. doi:10.1504/IJWGS.2018.095647

KEY TERMS AND DEFINITIONS

Artificial Intelligence: Artificial intelligence is basically a simulation of human actions by machines, especially computer systems.

Blockchain: A blockchain is generally a database that links together encrypted data blocks to create a continuous single source of truth for the data. We can also refer to it as online ledger.

Blockchain Mining: It is a peer-to-peer computer process by which the blockchain transactions are validated on the network and added to the blockchain ledger. It is basically used to secure and verify the blockchain transactions.

Consensus: A general agreement between two or more parties.

Cryptography: A mechanism of securing the transactions by encrypting the data using different algorithm which can only be decoded by the intended user.

Digital Wallets: Software used to store cryptocurrency.

Gas Fees: A cryptocurrency transaction fee that is charged to users when performing crypto transactions.

Metaverse: It is an evolution in the internet by evolving it as a single, universal and immersive virtual world which will be facilitated by using virtual augmented reality headsets. Simply it's a virtual world.

NFT Auction: A process of selling NFT without freezing a fixed price, during an auction the price of NFT depends on its popularity.

NFT Minting: It refers to the process of converting a digital file into crypto collection or a digital asset that can be stored on the blockchain.

Peer-to-Peer: Computing or networking is a distributed application architecture that partitions tasks or workloads between peers.

Proof-of-Stake: These proofs are a class of consensus mechanisms for blockchains that work by selecting validators in proportion to their quantity of holdings in the associated cryptocurrency.

Proof-of-Work: A form of cryptographic proof in which one party proves to others that a certain amount of a specific computational effort has been expended.

Quantum Cryptography: A method of encrypting the data by making use of both mathematical cryptography and the laws of quantum physics in order to make transaction secure and transmit the data in such a way that it cannot be hacked.

Quantum Entanglement: When two particles, such as a pair of photons or electrons, become entangled, they remain connected even when separated by vast distances.

Smart Contracts: A piece of code return to perform a desired work automatically for example, smart contract might establish the conditions for transferring corporate bonds, the terms of payment for travel insurance, and many other things.

Conclusion

While going through the different chapters of the book we realize that quantum computing and blockchain are not contenders of each other rather they complement and supplement each other. We believe that while blockchain technology will continue forming a strong backbone for transparent and responsible tech-driven societies and businesses the quantum computing will provide revolutionary computing solutions that would help solving both cryptographic and real-world problems for a safer and secure computing. At this juncture it is too early to predict the future of the blockchain and quantum computing; and the kind of effect that quantum computing will have on blockchain world. The integration of both the emerging technologies, quantum computing and blockchain technology, will help world to be more secure, transparent, and democratized. This book provides a systematic study of different industries, businesses and operations that are using blockchain technology and how they are evolving themselves for a quantum proof world.

Chapter 1, "Quantum Blockchain: A Systematic Review," suggests that the interest of the community and researchers is continuously increasing for the post quantum blockchain. It also very clearly states the differences between the classical blockchain and post quantum blockchain. It thoroughly discusses various concepts like quantum key distribution, Quantum Resistant Ledger, qubits and many more. It explains various mechanisms and algorithms for quantum proofing the blockchain systems. It suggests the future work, for a specific case of blockchain based land management, will be to develop and implement a low-level framework of the blockchain for land management and administration to make the whole process of land identification, verification, and acquisition transparent for the parties involved, in this case, the landowners and those purchasing the lands. This will resolve a major problem in Ghana and Africa. A quantum dimension of this blockchain for land management and administration is of great interest amongst researchers.

Chapter 2, "Introduction to Quantum-Resistant Blockchain," indicates that the threat that quantum computers pose to blockchain networks is mostly related to the insecure digital signatures of blockchain activities and the poor key-exchange protocols used for peer-to-peer communication over the network. It advocates that future blockchain applications should be able to handle several cryptographic algorithms in the PQC era in order to process both quantum and classical ciphers. New apps should be able to defend themselves against quantum threats while upholding the conventional standards by using hybrid key methods. Organizations will eventually need to get ready for new encryption standards. It also suggests that the field of post-quantum cryptography is finally catching up, and four different types of cryptosystems - elliptic curves, lattices, isogenies, and hash-based signatures—are gaining popularity. The security of blockchain is facilitated by post-quantum cryptography and quantum key distribution. Blockchain communities that aggressively search for new and effective ways to construct a Quantum-Resistant Blockchain are always developing innovative techniques to combat quantum computing processing power.

Chapter 3, "Emerging Blockchain Technology vis-à-vis Limitations and Issues: Emphasizing the Indian Context," states that Blockchain technology has significant impact in financial segment and in this regard not only private organization but also Government bodies, establishments and ministries playing leading role for the improvement of the Blockchain technology infrastructure. It draws attention towards the fact that, Foreign Direct Investment in India has increased in the areas of Computing and IT industry to 26.14 billion USD in the year 2020-2021 though in the year 2019-20 it was just 7.67 billion US Dollar.

Chapter 4, "Design of a Blockchain-Powered Biometric Template Security Framework Using Augmented Sharding," explains how sharding is used in order to reduce overall delay and energy consumption of biometric storage system via effective blockchain splitting. This splitting allows the blockchain to reduce number of computations needed in order to add, update, search and access internal blocks. Shards when combined can further improve upon the overall system performance by reducing delay and number of computations needed for hashing. Due to this combination, the proposed model is able to obtain over 20% reduction in communication delay, over 25% reduction in energy consumption, and over 20% improvement in overall storage throughput. Due to faster storage performance across fewer number of blocks, the probability of packet dropping is also reduced, this results in increasing the packet delivery ratio by 10% and reducing overall delay jitter by over 15% when compared with other sidechaining algorithms. i.e., also suggest that in future, researchers can further extend the performance of this algorithm by using better block truncation algorithms, and by utilizing improved machine learning models for shard creation. Moreover, the truncated data parts can be given moderate level of security in order to reduce chances of modification due to external and internal attacks, which will further strengthen network security.

Chapter 5, "Green Currency Based on Blockchain Technology for Sustainable Development," stresses that there is a need to establish value in the environmental assets that are utterly overlooked by society owing to ignorance. It advocates that the new virtual green currency based on blockchain technology has the potential to play a key role in the development of a market for green currency based on environmental green assets. This paper suggests one technology-based method to evaluate green assets and establish a market for green currencies. There are various other technologies also available to verify data captured and asset valuation. i.e. GPS. If this happens, it will certainly have a long-term impact on individual and societal behaviour when it comes to the proper use of natural resources. It stresses that in fact by not assigning a monetary value to green assets, we are undervaluing the efforts of people who are devoted to preserving them for a long-ago, particularly the primitives.

Chapter 6, "Blockchain in Gaming," explains how blockchain is being used in the gaming industry. Blockchain (BC) technology has revolutionised numerous fields, including no-prerequisite trading. Bitcoin used BC developments in 2009, and BC development ambitions increased. Electronic currency systems with an all-trades database were important applications. These deals use cryptographic hashes and key matching. The trade history preserves a chain of events so that adjusting or changing a past trade requires recalculating all subsequent blocks of trades. BC technology is in its early phases but depends on cryptographic rules and data storage. Many proposed algorithms use the development as of now. The advancement will likely evaporate as BC development becomes another tool. Through dispersion, a BC uses already-built association, cryptographic, and recording innovations. Innovation that examines the benefits and risks of new technologies will be crucial. Once a BC is done and accepted, it may be hard to change. When data is stored in a BC, it's permanent whenever there's a raise. BC development is still fresh; thus we should use it only when necessary.

Chapter 7, "A Scrutiny Review of CPS 4.0-Based Blockchain With Quantum Resistance," depicts a very vivid review of the CPS based Blockchain. Certainly, the concept is just an idea and the required approach with the CPS 4.0. The article sheds light on basics of blockchain, quantum computing and quantum effects on blockchain and quantum resistant blockchain. The ideas are linked with one another sequentially in this article. This article does open many new problems about the implementation of the ideas by giving them an expression. This article can be referenced as a material for understanding all the prerequisites required to implement the systems.

Chapter 8, "Quantum and Blockchain for Computing Paradigms: Vision and Advancements," described the blockchain strategies alongside the quantum strategies. In conclusion, the authors described blockchain strategies alongside quantum strategies. How Blockchain is being used in various industries as technology advances. A blockchain protocol with information-theoretically consistent authentication that is completely based on a community to which every pair of nodes is linked via a QKD link. Through a three-birthday birthday celebration city fibre community QKD, we tested our protocol experimentally. In addition to using QKD for authentication, it has significantly redefined the protocol of adding new blocks in a manner that is markedly different from current cryptocurrencies. Rather than concentrating the development of new blocks in the hands of individual miners, we use the information-theoretically consistent broadcast protocol, in which all nodes reach an agreement on a brand-new block on the same terms. One significant advantage of our blockchain protocol is its ability to maintain transaction transparency and integrity in the face of quantum algorithm attacks. As a result, our findings open up new avenues for understanding scalable quantum-secure blockchain structures. If realised, any such blockchain platform could limit the financial and social risks posed by upcoming breakthroughs in quantum computation technology. The typical key technology costs of currently available QKD technology are sufficient for running large-scale blockchain structures entirely based on our protocol. Furthermore, fantastic advancements in the theory and practise of quantum communications, such as current experiments on ground-to-satellite tv for pc QKD and quantum repeaters, may want to open the door to growing a public international QKD community ("the quantum Internet") and expanding quantum-secure blockchain structures to a global scale. The advancement of the "quantum Internet" will allow our protocol to maintain the anonymity of all community members. A member may be able to connect to the global QKD community from any location, authenticate themselves to different parties utilising their personal seed keys, and carry out a desired transaction. The quantum and blockchain paradigms will lead to advancements in a wide range of fields.

Chapter 9, "Quantum Blockchain for Smart Society: Applications, Challenges, and Opportunities," discusses that Blockchain-based smart cities are a pivotal step that must be protected from future quantum assaults since they include sensitive information and data about users and their various components. This article provides a broad overview of the potential future risks of a Blockchain-based smart society. The study examined the quantum Blockchain-based smart cities' facts, challenges, and opportunities and presented some of the most interesting post-Quantum solutions. Consumer, civilian, military and government activities can benefit from Blockchain. However, this is a very fast-paced and flexible environment. As a result, keeping up with and understanding the most recent breakthroughs in the expansion and implementation of Blockchain, which is the subject of this thorough analysis, is critical. The work conducted a rigorous literature analysis on blockchain applications in notable intelligent city applications and attempted real-world case studies of how blockchain technology was successfully used to provide dependable and secure services in smart metropolises. The study also examined the open research problems impeding Blockchain's adoption as a critical technology for creating smart cities.

Chapter 10, "Advancements in Blockchain Technology With the Use of Quantum Blockchain and Non-Fungible Tokens," suggests that the blockchain is growing and even have the potential to push all the limits but as with the great power comes greater responsibility, it is our first and foremost responsibility to maintain the blockchain, we cannot rely on the buggy system for our future hence we always have to overcome the faults with powerful solutions.

Glossary

Advanced Encryption Standard (AES): The United States government selected the symmetric block cipher known as Advanced Encryption Standard (AES) to safeguard sensitive data.

Algorithm: An algorithm is a step-by-step procedure to solve any problem or a task which does not depend on a particular programming language, above chapter has used a layered architecture where computer games use blockchain safely.

Application Programming Interface (API): It simplify software development and innovation by enabling applications to exchange data and functionality easily and securely.

Artificial Intelligence: Artificial intelligence is basically a simulation of human actions by machines, especially computer systems.

Asymmetric Encryption: Also known as public-key cryptography is a method of encrypting and decrypting data.

Asynchronous Blockchain: It is the blockchain network that can be designed whether to prioritize consistency or availability. If the network wants to prioritize availability, all transactions are added without any downtime. If the network wants to prioritize consistency, some transactions might not be processed or halted until all the previous transactions are confirmed.

Authentication: Is used by a client to verify that the server is what it purports to be.

Binary Computers: Arc computers that express messages, computer processor commands, and other types of data using a two-symbol system based on numbers, "0s" and "1s."

Bitcoin: Bitcoin uses a particular technology which is not using any bank or government authority as maintaining and managing all transaction is done over a network which is completely safe. It is an open source no one owns or controls it as anyone can participate in it. It does not require any prior payments.

Bits: Is a commonly used subdivision or unit of a single Bitcoin.

Block: Block is a place in a blockchain where information is stored and encrypted.

Blockchain: A blockchain is a distributed database or ledger that is shared among the nodes of a computer network. As a database, a blockchain stores information electronically in digital format. Blockchains are best known for their crucial role in cryptocurrency systems, such as Bitcoin, for maintaining a secure and decentralized record of transactions. The innovation with a blockchain is that it guarantees the fidelity and security of a record of data and generates trust without the need for a trusted third party.

Blockchain Applications: Blockchain technology utilizations are rising gradually and applicable in diverse areas like Financial and Banking Services, Education and Research, Healthcare and Medical Systems, Government and Administration, Travel and Hospitality, and so on.

Blockchain Mining: It is a peer-to-peer computer process by which the blockchain transactions are validated on the network and added to the blockchain ledger. It is basically used to secure and verify the blockchain transactions.

Blockchain Systems: Is a method of storing data that makes it difficult or impossible to alter, tamper with, or trick the system.

Blockchain Technology: Blockchain technology is the encrypted and distributed database connected with the transaction, contract, and depends on different independent record. Blockchain is the digital ledger and a particular place is being used to store data. Blockchain is strengthening the financial segment and activities for proper digital currency like bitcoin transactions.

Classical Blockchain: Is a traditional blockchain, the most basic level, a digital log of transactions kept on numerous computers (referred to as nodes) connected by a network.

Consensus: A general agreement between two or more parties.

Convolutional Neural Network (CNN): A convolutional neural network (CNN) is a type of artificial neural network used in image recognition and processing.

Cryptocurrency: Cryptocurrency is the encrypted data and which are denotes a unit of currency. Here peer-to-peer network play important role which is called blockchain. This is helpful in securing ledger based digital transactions for the things viz. buying, selling, and transferring.

Cryptography: Is the technique of securing information and communications through use of codes so that only those persons for whom the information is intended can understand it and process it, thus preventing unauthorized access to information.

Data Integrity: Today's era is of big data, but it is equally important to maintain that data safely in reference to any currency data integrity must be managed properly.

Decentralized Application: A decentralized application (dApp) is a type of distributed open-source software application that runs on a peer-to-peer (P2P) blockchain network rather than on a single computer. DApps are visibly like other software applications that are supported on a website or mobile device but are P2P supported.

Decentralized Database: Is a hybrid of a regular database and a distributed database, supported by many layers of blockchains and using a database interface or compute interface for data recording and transactions.

Deposit and Refund System: A system that imposes an upfront charge to pay for potential pollution damages that are returned for positive action, such as returning a product for proper disposal or recycling.

Digital Wallets: Software used to store cryptocurrency.

Environmental/Ecological Parity: Green currency market generates demand for and supply of green assets globally. Nations and persons with rich green assets get rewarded and nations having low green assets have to check development or purchase GA. That's how the global green assets parity is maintained.

Ethereum: Ethereum is the community-run technology powering the cryptocurrency ether (ETH) and thousands of decentralized applications. Ethereum is used in all industries, and it uses smart contracts.

Euclid's Division Formula: Or lemma can be used to determine the HCF of two numbers. It says that if there are two integers a and b , then q and r must exist such that they satisfy the formula a = bq + r, where O £ r < b .

Externalities: A cost or benefit arising from any activity which does not accrual to the person or organization directly involved but extends to a third party outside the market. Externalities are positive or negative. Environment degradation creates negative externality as it generates costs to the third party. The environment is a public common good so those who are responsible for the damage need not pay for the damage as property rights are not well defined.

Financial Engineering: Financial Engineering is a branch of Interdisciplinary Engineering concentrated on designing, development and management of the financial systems, applications, machines, and automation systems.

Gas Fees: A cryptocurrency transaction fee that is charged to users when performing crypto transactions.

Goppa's Code: Is a general kind of linear code created by utilizing an algebraic curve X over a finite field, which is an algebraic geometric code.

Green Assets: A green asset is an asset that generates more energy than it consumes. This creates a positive impact on the environment, as well as provides a net positive benefit to the economy. Green assets cover all-natural assets that facilitate our lives on this planet and protect us from the ills of global warming due to the rapid environmental degradation of the forest. These assets are particularly protected and possessed by primitives. An asset possessed by individuals, government, NGOs, industries, and institutions that has a positive environmental impact such as forests, open space, trees, water bodies, waste recycling plants, water treatment plants, grazing land, farms, etc. It includes Natural Assets, Environmental Assets as well as Soft Assets.

Green Assets Valuation: Green assets are becoming more popular and as a result, new valuation techniques have been developed to measure their value. These techniques take into account the environmental benefits of green assets, such as reduced air pollution and greenhouse gas emissions, and this can translate into higher returns. We can assign value to any green asset according to its CO_2 sequestration capacity or O_2 generation capacity.

Green Currency Based on GAV: On the basis of green asset valuation a value could be assigned to green assets and green currency could be launched based on or operated globally through blockchain technology. This GC will be not centrally controlled like the current money market and also global currency in the true sense and will control or check the development process considering the potential of the environment and pressure on it. Apart from this Green Currency has intrinsic value.

Green Currency Market: The market developed and is based on the global transaction of green currency through blockchain technology. This market will motivate all those who preserve the environment and also checks pressure on natural resources. GCM generates demand for and supply of green assets globally.

Green Subsidy: A payment or tax concession that provides financial assistance for pollution reductions or plans to abate in the future using environment-friendly techniques of production.

Green Tax/Pollution Charges: A fee charged to the polluter that varies with the number of pollutants released.

Grover's Algorithm: In quantum computing, Grover's algorithm, also known as the quantum search algorithm, refers to a quantum algorithm for unstructured search that finds with high probability the unique input to a black box function that produces a particular output value, using just evaluations of the function, where N is the size of the function's domain. It was devised by Lov Grover in 1996.

Hacker: Is someone who utilizes computers to obtain data without authorization or one who steals from a vulnerable entity.

Hash: A cryptographic hash function is an algorithm that takes an arbitrary amount of data input credential and produces a fixed-size output of enciphered text called a hash value, or just hash. That enciphered text can then be stored instead of the password itself, and later used to verify the user.

Identity Management: Is the organizational process for ensuring individuals have the appropriate access to technology resources. This includes the identification, authentication and authorization of a person, or persons, to have access to applications, systems, or networks.

Individual and Social Behavior: Individual behavior can be defined as a mix of responses to external and internal stimuli. It is the way a person reacts in different situations and the way someone expresses different emotions like anger, happiness, love, etc. Social behavior is behavior among two or more organisms within the same species and encompasses any behavior in which one member affects the other. This is due to interaction among those members. In the case of humans, social behavior can be determined by both the individual characteristics of the person, and the situation they are in.

Internet of Things (IoT): Describes physical objects (or groups of such objects) with sensors, processing ability, software, and other technologies that connect and exchange data with other devices and systems over the Internet or other communications networks.

Interoperability: Blockchain interoperability is not a set rule book. It refers to a broad range of techniques that allow different blockchains to listen to each other, transfer digital assets and data between one another and enable better collaboration.

Intrusion: Is the occurrence of an unauthorized user obtaining data or access permission that they are prohibited from.

Jitter: Is the variation in the time between packets arriving, caused by network congestion, timing drift, or route changes.

Lattice Cryptosystem: Is a generic term for construction of cryptographic primitives or scheme consisting of a set of algorithms that involve lattices and is used to convert plaintext to ciphertext to encode or decode messages securely.

League Championship Algorithm (LCA): Is a population-based algorithm framework for global optimization over a continuous search space.

Logic Computations: Blockchain transactions can be linked to computational logic which is, in essence, programs due to the ledger's digital character, so users may create formulas and guidelines that initiate transactions between nodes automatically.

Malicious Transactions: Include any type of fraud, identity theft, or hacking done with the purpose of gaining an unfair advantage or benefiting from deceit.

Man in the Middle (MITM) Attack: A man in the middle (MITM) attack is a general term for when a perpetrator positions himself in a conversation between a user and an application.

McEliece Code: Robert McEliece first suggested the McEliece code as a code-based public key cryptosystem in 1978.

Metaverse: It is an evolution in the internet by evolving it as a single, universal and immersive virtual world which will be facilitated by using virtual augmented reality headsets. Simply it's a virtual world.

NFT: Non-fungible token are tokens which cannot be replicated and are being used in blockchain. They could be anything representing a real-world entity just like real estate or an artwork. Selling or buying these tokens is called tokenizing which reduces the probability of fraud.

NFT Auction: A process of selling NFT without freezing a fixed price, during an auction the price of NFT depends on its popularity.

NFT Minting: It refers to the process of converting a digital file into crypto collection or a digital asset that can be stored on the blockchain.

Node: Is one of the machines running the blockchain's software to verify and preserve the whole history of transactions on the network is referred to as a node.

Peer-to-Peer: Computing or networking is a distributed application architecture that partitions tasks or workloads between peers.

Permissioned Blockchain: Is a distributed ledger that is not publicly accessible. It can only be accessed by users with permissions. The users can only perform specific actions granted to them by the ledger administrators and are required to identify themselves through certificates or other digital means.

Permissionless Blockchain: Also known as trustless or public blockchains, are open networks available to everyone to participate in the consensus process that blockchains use to validate transactions and data. They are fully decentralized across unknown parties.

Pollution Permits Trading System: The establishment of a market for rights to pollute, using either credits or allowances.

Post-Quantum Cryptography: Post-quantum cryptography refers to cryptographic algorithms (usually public-key algorithms) that are thought to be secure against an attack by a quantum computer. These complex mathematical equations take traditional computers months or even years to break. However, quantum computers running Shor's algorithm will be able to break math-based systems in moments.

Potential for Development: Nature can meet our needs but not greed. Nature nurtures naturally all living beings, but it has its own limitations. Unless and until it revies which takes too much time resources are limited. The introduction of green asset valuation and the green currency market presents a guiding principle to control unsustain growth. As the growth of a country depends upon the use of natural resources globally the current economic models have no checks on the growth and development process as all models never take into account the capacity or the potential of growth.

Private Key: Like a password, is a secret number that is used in cryptography. In cryptocurrencies, they are also employed to verify transactions and establish who owns a blockchain address.

Proof of Authority (PoA): Is an algorithm used with blockchains that delivers comparatively fast transactions through a consensus mechanism based on identity as a stake.

Proof of Work (PoW): By making the process of mining, or recording transactions, challenging, Proof of Work is the mechanism that enables the Bitcoin network to remain stable. It is the blockchain network's initial consensus algorithm.

Proof-of-Stake (PoS): Is a cryptocurrency consensus mechanism for processing transactions and creating new blocks in a blockchain. A consensus mechanism is a method for validating entries into a distributed database and keeping the database secure.

Property Rights: The rights of an owner over the property. As property rights of the environment, green assets, and public goods or common goods are not well defined it hinders economic efficiency. So, to enhance economic efficiency green assets possessed by individuals, firms, governments, or organizations must be calculated and an asset value must be assigned to the owner. Due to negative externality, too much of the good will be produced as the market price does not reflect external costs.

Protocols: Protocols are crucial components of Blockchain technologies that enable information to be shared automatically across cryptocurrency networks securely and reliably. In the field of computing, protocols are essentially rules that define how data is allowed to be transferred between different computer systems.

Public Key Crytography (PKC): Public key cryptography involves a pair of keys known as a public key and a private key (a public key pair), which are associated with an entity that needs to authenticate its identity electronically or to sign or encrypt data.

Public Keys: Make it possible for cryptocurrency transaction execution. It is paired with a private key and a cryptographic code and employed to transfer cryptocurrency to a wallet.

Quality of Service (QoS): It is the use of mechanisms or technologies that work on a network to control traffic and ensure the performance of critical applications with limited network capacity.

Quantum: Quantum is the smallest parcels into which are normally having many forms of energy, and which are subdivided. Therefore, quantum is the quantized physical magnitude like magnetic moment.

Quantum Bitcoin: Quantum computers will eventually break much of today's encryption, and that includes the signing algorithm of Bitcoin and other cryptocurrencies.

Quantum Blockchain: Quantum blockchain is helps in proper security management using proper principles of quantum computers, the conventional blockchains is dedicated in collecting records and the same is connecting with the cryptography with the chronological order. Here records of blocks basically encoded (here records are encoded into a series) with photons which are entangled with each other.

Quantum Computing: It is a Technology that uses laws of quantum mechanics to solve difficult and classical problems.

Quantum Cryptography: Quantum cryptography is a method of encryption that uses the naturally occurring properties of quantum mechanics to secure and transmit data in a way that cannot be hacked. Cryptography is the process of encrypting and protecting data so that only the person who has the right secret key can decrypt it.

Quantum Entanglement: When two particles, such as a pair of photons or electrons, become entangled, they remain connected even when separated by vast distances.

Quantum Key Distribution: Is a secure communication method which implements a cryptographic protocol involving components of quantum mechanics. It enables two parties to produce a shared random secret key known only to them, which can then be used to encrypt and decrypt messages.

Quantum Secure Direct Communication (QSDC): Is a significant quantum communication protocol, that uses a direct conversation between communicating parties rather than the production of secret keys beforehand to send confidential information. Without the use of a private key, confidential information can be sent directly through a quantum channel.

Quantum Technologies: Quantum technologies are improving and rising its applications in different places. Among the Quantum segment Quantum Mechanics, Quantum Computing, Quantum Informatics considered as worthy.

Quantum-Resistant Blockchain: Is immune to attacks from quantum computers. It uses encryption and quantum mechanics to allow two parties to communicate safe data while also detecting and defending against outsiders.

Quantum-Resistant Ledger: Is a decentralized communication layer and post-quantum value storage that addresses the threat that quantum computing will bring to cryptocurrencies in the future.

Radio Frequency Identification (RFID): It is a type of passive wireless technology that allows for tracking or matching of an item or individual.

Ripple: Ripple is the company that is behind XRP, the cryptocurrency where XRP is a technology that is mainly known for its digital payment network and protocol. Many major banks use the XRP payment system. Bitcoin transaction confirmations may take many minutes with high transaction costs, while XRP transactions are confirmed in seconds with little cost.

Secure Hashing Algorithm (SHA): Is used for hashing data and certificates, designed to safeguard data.

Secure Hashing Algorithm in 256-Bit Mode (SHA256): SHA-256 is a patented cryptographic hash function that outputs a value that is 256 bits long.

Shor's Algorithm: Is a practical polynomial quantum technique for the factorization of integers that is tuned for finding prime factors in a hypothetical quantum computer.

Signature Scheme: Is a technique to assure an entity's acknowledgment of having seen a certain digital message.

Smart Contract: Smart contract can be defined as set of instructions being stored on a blockchain system which gets executed over a particular condition which is already defined earlier in a proper manner. Smart contacts get executed automatically which helps in reducing time wastage and this done over an agreement.

Superposition: Is one of the characteristics that set a quantum computer apart from a conventional computer. Users can tokenize, trade, and profit from their potential future income using this decentralized fixed income protocol.

Supply Chain: Is a network of individuals and companies who are involved in creating a product and delivering it to the consumer.

Sustainable Development: Sustainable development is an organizing principle for meeting human development goals while also sustaining the ability of natural systems to provide the natural resources and ecosystem services on which the economy and society depend.

Threshold Cryptosystem: The basis for the field of threshold cryptography, is a cryptosystem that protects information by encrypting it and distributing it among a cluster of fault-tolerant computers.

Time Stamp: A time stamp is input of signing authority which is a piece of data or information at specific time it uses protocol which checks or certifies all timestamps using X.509 certificates and public key infrastructure.

Tokenization: Is the process of exchanging sensitive data for nonsensitive data called "tokens" that can be used in a database or internal system without bringing it into scope.

Transparency: Transparency, as used in science, engineering, business, the humanities and in other social contexts, is operating in such a way that it is easy for others to see what actions are performed. Transparency implies openness, communication, and accountability.

Compilation of References

Ablayev, F. M., Bulychkov, D. A., Sapaev, D. A., Vasiliev, A. V., & Ziatdinov, M. T. (2018). Quantum-Assisted Blockchain. *Lobachevskii Journal of Mathematics*, *39*(7), 957–960. doi:10.1134/S1995080218070028

Abou, J., & Saade, R. G. (2019). Blockchain applications–usage in different domains. *IEEE Access: Practical Innovations, Open Solutions*, *7*, 45360–45381. doi:10.1109/ACCESS.2019.2902501

Abulkasim, Mashatan, & Ghose. (2021). *Quantum-based privacy-preserving sealed-bid auction on the blockchain.* . doi:10.1016/j.ijleo.2021.167039

Acheampong, P., Zhiwen, L., Hiran, K. K., Serwaa, O. E., Boateng, F., & Bediako, I. A. (2018). Examining the Intervening Role of Age and Gender on mobile payment Acceptance in Ghana: UTAUT Model. *Canadian Journal of Applied Science and Technology*, *5*(2).

Acquah, M. A., Chen, N., Pan, J. S., Yang, H. M., & Yan, B. (2020). Securing Fingerprint Template Using Blockchain and Distributed Storage System. *Symmetry*, *12*(6), 951. doi:10.3390ym12060951

Aditya, U. S. P. S., Singh, R., Singh, P. K., & Kalla, A. (2021). A Survey on Blockchain in Robotics: Issues, Opportunities, Challenges, and Future Directions. *Journal of Network and Computer Applications, 196*. doi:10.1016/j.jnca.2021.103245

AdjeiFrempong, M., & Kant Hiran, K. (2014). Awareness and Understanding of Computer Forensics in the Ghana Legal System. *International Journal of Computers and Applications*, *89*(20), 54–59. Advance online publication. doi:10.5120/15752-4640

Agarap, A. (2018). *Deep learning using rectified linear units (relu).* arXiv preprint arXiv:1803.08375.

Agbesi, S. (2020). Institutional Drivers of Internet Voting Adoption in Ghana : A Qualitative Exploratory Studies. *Centre for Communication, Media & Information Technology*, *1*, 53–76. doi:10.13052/nbjict1902-097X.2020.003

Aggarwal, D., Brennen, G., Lee, T., Santha, M., & Tomamichel, M. (2017). *Quantum attacks on Bitcoin, and how to protect against them.* arXiv preprint arXiv:1710.10377.

Aggarwal, D., Brennen, G., Lee, T., Santha, M., & Tomamichel, M. (2018). Quantum Attacks on Bitcoin, and How to Protect Against Them. *Ledger*, *3*, 1–21. doi:10.5195/ledger.2018.127

Aggarwal, S., Chaudhary, R., Aujla, G. S., Kumar, N., Choo, K. K. R., & Zomaya, A. Y. (2019). Blockchain for smart communities: Applications, challenges and opportunities. *Journal of Network and Computer Applications*, *144*, 13–48. doi:10.1016/j.jnca.2019.06.018

Agrawal, T. K., Kumar, V., Pal, R., Wang, L., & Chen, Y. TK. (2021). Blockchain-based framework for supply chain traceability: A case example of textile and clothing industry. *Computers & Industrial Engineering*, *154*, 107130. doi:10.1016/j.cie.2021.107130

Aguida, M., Ouchani, S., & Benmalek, M. (2020). A Review on Cyber-Physical Systems: Models and Architectures. In *2020 IEEE 29th International Conference on Enabling Technologies: Infrastructure for Collaborative Enterprises (WETICE)* (pp. 275-278). IEEE.

Ahl, A., Yarime, M., Goto, M., Chopra, S. S., Kumar, N. M., Tanaka, K., & Sagawa, D. (2020). Exploring blockchain for the energy transition: Opportunities and challenges based on a case study in Japan. *Renewable and Sustainable Energy Reviews, 117*(September), 109488. doi:10.1016/j.rser.2019.109488

al Baqari, M., & Barka, E. (2020). *Biometric-Based Blockchain EHR System (BBEHR). In 2020 International Wireless Communications and Mobile Computing.* IWCMC. doi:10.1109/IWCMC48107.2020.9148357

Alam, T. (2021). Blockchain cities: The futuristic cities driven by Blockchain, big data and internet of things. *GeoJournal*, *1*, 1–10. doi:10.100710708-021-10508-0

Alasbali, N., Azzuhri, S. R., Salleh, R. B., Kiah, M. L. M., Shariffuddin, A. A. A. S. A., Kamel, N. M. I. N. M., & Ismail, L. (2022). Rules of Smart IoT Networks within Smart Cities towards Blockchain Standardization. *Mobile Information Systems*, *2022*, 1–11. Advance online publication. doi:10.1155/2022/9109300

Albawi, S., Mohammed, T., & Al-Zawi, S. (2017). Understanding of a convolutional neural network. In *2017 International Conference on Engineering and Technology (ICET)* (pp. 1-6). Academic Press.

Alharthi, A., Ni, Q., & Jiang, R. (2021). A Privacy-Preservation Framework Based on Biometrics Blockchain (BBC) to Prevent Attacks in VANET. *IEEE Access: Practical Innovations, Open Solutions*, *9*, 87299–87309. doi:10.1109/ACCESS.2021.3086225

Al-Housni, N. (2019). An Exploratory Study in Blockchain Technology. *PQDT - Global*, 89. https://www.proquest.com/dissertations-theses/exploratory-study-blockchain-technology/docview/2199337101/se-2?accountid=27931

Ali, W. A., Sahib, N. M., & Waleed, J. (2019). Preservation Authentication and Authorization on Blockchain. *2019 2nd International Conference on Engineering Technology and Its Applications (IICETA)*. 10.1109/IICETA47481.2019.9012996

Allende Lopez, M., Lopez Leon, D., Ceron, S., Leal Batista, A., Pareja, A., Da Silva, M., Pardo, A., Jones, D., Worrall, D., Merriman, B., Gilmore, J., Kitchener, N., Venegas-Andraca, S.E. (2021). *Quantum-Resistance in Blockchain Networks*. doi:10.18235/0003313

Compilation of References

Allende, M., Leon, D., Ceron, S., Leal, A., Pareja, A., Da Silva, M., Pardo, A., Jones, D., Worrall, D., & Merriman, B. (2021). *Quantum-resistance in blockchain networks*. arXiv preprint arXiv:2106.06640.

Allende, M., López, D., Cerón, S., Leal, A., Pareja, A., Da, M., Pardo, S. A., Jones, D., Worrall, D., Merriman, B., Gilmore, J., Kitchener, N., & Venegas-Andraca, S. E. (2021). *Quantum-Resistance in Blockchain Networks*. ITE Department IDB Lab. http://www.iadb.org

Almohammadi, K., Hagras, H., Alghazzawi, D., & Aldabbagh, G. (2017). *A survey of artificial intelligence techniques employed for adaptive educational systems within e-learning platforms*. doi:10.1515/jaiscr-2017-0004

Alpaydin, E. (2020). *Introduction to machine learning*. MIT Press.

Al-Zubaidie, M., Zhang, Z., & Zhang, J. (2019). *Efficient and secure ECDSA algorithm and its applications: a survey*. arXiv preprint arXiv:1902.10313.

An, H., & Kim, K. (2018). QChain: Quantum-resistant and Decentralized PKI using Blockchain. *2018 Symposium on Cryptography and Information Security*.

Anjum, A., Sporny, M., & Sill, A. (2017). Blockchain standards for compliance and trust. *IEEE Cloud Computing*, *4*(4), 84–90. doi:10.1109/MCC.2017.3791019

Anschuetz, E., Olson, J., Aspuru-Guzik, A., & Cao, Y. (2018). *Variational quantum factoring*. arXiv preprint arXiv:1808.08927.

Ansom, H. H. (1982). Strategic Intelligence. *Proceedings of the Academy of Political Science, 34*(4), 153. doi:10.2307/3700977

Antonucci, F., Figorilli, S., Costa, C., Pallottino, F., Raso, L., & Menesatti, P. (2019). A Review on blockchain applications in the agri. *Journal of the Science of Food and Agriculture*, *99*(14), 6129–6138. doi:10.1002/jsfa.9912 PMID:31273793

Arulprakash, M., & Jebakumar, R. (2022). *Towards developing a Block Chain based Advanced Data Security-Reward Model (DSecCS) in mobile crowd sensing networks. Egyptian Informatics Journal*. doi:10.1016/j.eij.2022.03.002

arXiv. (2019). How a quantum computer could break 2048-bit RSA encryption in 8 hours. *MIT Technology Review*. https://www.technologyreview.com/2019/05/30/65724/how-a-quantum-computer-could-break-2048-bit-rsa-encryption-in-8-hours/

Asri, A., Le Masson, V., Montalescot, V., Lim, P. E., Nor, A. M., Hussin, H., & Shaxson, L. (2021). The role of migrants in the Malaysian seaweed value-chain. *Marine Policy*, *134*, 104812. Advance online publication. doi:10.1016/j.marpol.2021.104812

Azhar, M. T., Khan, M. B., & Khan, A. U. R. (2019). Blockchain based secure crypto-currency system with quantum key distribution protocol. *8th International Conference on Information and Communication Technologies, ICICT 2019*, 31–35. 10.1109/ICICT47744.2019.9001979

Băcescu-Cărbunaru, A. (2018). Global Demographic Pressures and Management of Natural Resources – Foresights about the Future of Mankind. *Review of International Comparative Management*, *19*(1), 40–53. doi:10.24818/RMCI.2018.1.40

Banafa, A. (2020). *12 Quantum Computing and Blockchain: Facts and Myths. In Blockchain Technology and Applications*. River Publishers.

Banerjee, S., Mukherjee, A., & Panigrahi, P. K. (2020). Quantum blockchain using weighted hypergraph states. *Physical Review Research*, *2*(1), 1–7. doi:10.1103/PhysRevResearch.2.013322

BardD. A.KearneyJ. J.Perez-DelgadoC. A. (2021). Quantum Advantage on Proof of Work. doi:10.2139/ssrn.3979439

Barker, W., & Polk, W. (2021). *Getting Ready for Post-Quantum Cryptography*. Academic Press.

Barua, T., Doshi, R., & Hiran, K. K. (2020). *Mobile Application Development*. De Gruyter.

Barua, T., Doshi, R., & Hiran, K. K. (2020). Mobile Applications Development. In *Mobile Applications Development*. De Gruyter.

Barua, T., Doshi, R., & Hiran, K. K. (2020). *Mobile Applications Development*. Mobile Applications Development. doi:10.1515/9783110689488

Bathen, L. A. D., Flores, G. H., & Jadav, D. (2020). RiderS: Towards a Privacy-Aware Decentralized Self-Driving Ride-Sharing Ecosystem. *2020 IEEE International Conference on Decentralized Applications and Infrastructures (DAPPS)*. 10.1109/DAPPS49028.2020.00004

Bavdekar, R., Chopde, E., Bhatia, A., Tiwari, K., & Daniel, S. (2022). *Post Quantum Cryptography: Techniques, Challenges, Standardization, and Directions for Future Research*. arXiv preprint arXiv:2202.02826.

Bendechache, M., Saber, T., Muntean, G.-M., & Tal, I. (2021). *Application of blockchain technology to 5G-enabled vehicular networks: survey and future directions*. In *18th International Symposium on High Performance Mobile Computing & Wireless Networks for HPC (MCWN 2020)*, Barcelona, Spain.

Bennet, A. J., & Daryanoosh, S. (2019). Energy-Efficient Mining on a Quantum-Enabled Blockchain Using Light. *Ledger*, *4*. Advance online publication. doi:10.5195/ledger.2019.143

Bennett, C. H., Bernstein, E., Brassard, G., & Vazirani, U. (1997). Strengths and weaknesses of quantum computing. *SIAM Journal on Computing*, *26*(5), 1510–1523. https://doi.org/10.1137/S0097539796300933

Ben, W., Ben, I., Kondrateva, G., & Hikkerova, L. (2021). The role of trust in intention to use the IoT in eHealth : Application of the modified UTAUT in a consumer context. *Technological Forecasting and Social Change*, *167*(February), 120688. doi:10.1016/j.techfore.2021.120688

Berck, P., & Helfand, G. E. (2005). The case of markets versus standards for pollution policy. *Natural Resources Journal*, *45*(2), 345–367.

Berman, G. P., Kamenev, D. I., & Tsifrinovich, V. I. (2005). Collective decoherence of the superpositional entangled states in the quantum Shor algorithm. *Physical Review A*, *71*(3), 032346. Advance online publication. doi:10.1103/PhysRevA.71.032346

Bernstein, Hopwood, Hulsing, Lange, Niederhagen, Papachristodoulou, Schwabe, & Wilcox-O'Hearn (2014). SPHINCS: Practical Stateless Hash-Based Signatures. *IACR Cryptol. ePrint Arch., 2014*, 795.

Besançon, L., Da Silva, C. F., & Ghodous, P. (2019, May). Towards blockchain interoperability: Improving video games data exchange. In *2019 IEEE international conference on blockchain and cryptocurrency (ICBC)* (pp. 81-85). IEEE.

Besançon, L., Ghodous, P., Gelas, J. P., & Da Silva, C. F. (2021, March). Modelling of Decentralised Blockchain Applications Development. *The 2020 International Conference on High Performance Computing & Simulation (HPCS 2020)*.

Bharti, K., Cervera-Lierta, A., Kyaw, T., Haug, T., Alperin-Lea, S., Anand, A., Degroote, M., Heimonen, H., Kottmann, J., Menke, T., Mok, W.-K., Sim, S., Kwek, L.-C., & Aspuru-Guzik, A. (2022). Noisy intermediate-scale quantum algorithms. *Reviews of Modern Physics*, *94*(1), 015004. doi:10.1103/RevModPhys.94.015004

Bhatt, H., & Gautam, S. (2019). Quantum Computing: A New Era of Computer Science. In *2019 6th International Conference on Computing for Sustainable Global Development (INDIACom)* (pp. 558-561). Academic Press.

Bhavin, M., Tanwar, S., Sharma, N., Tyagi, S., & Kumar, N. (2021). Blockchain and quantum blind signature-based hybrid scheme for healthcare 5.0 applications. *Journal of Information Security and Applications*, *56*, 1–15. doi:10.1016/j.jisa.2020.102673

Bi, W., Jia, X., & Zheng, M. (2018). *A secure multiple elliptic curves digital signature algorithm for blockchain*. arXiv preprint arXiv:1808.02988.

Birda, R. K. (2019). Study of ICT and E-Governance Facilities in Tribal District of Rajasthan. *Kamal*, *9*(7), 39–49.

Blockchain for industry 4.0: A comprehensive review. (n.d.). *IEEE Access, 8*, 79764–79800. doi:10.1109/ACCESS

Bochkovskiy, A., Wang, C. Y., & Liao, H. Y. (2020). *Yolov4: Optimal speed and accuracy of object detection*. arXiv preprint arXiv:2004.10934.

Bohr, N. (2020). *Global Future Council on Quantum Computing Frequently Asked Questions*. Academic Press.

Bolya, D., Zhou, C., Xiao, F., & Lee, Y. (2019). Yolact: Real-time instance segmentation. In *Proceedings of the IEEE/CVF international conference on computer vision* (pp. 9157–9166). IEEE.

Bolya, D., Zhou, C., Xiao, F., & Lee, Y. (2020). Yolact++: Better real-time instance segmentation. *IEEE Transactions on Pattern Analysis and Machine Intelligence*. PMID:32755851

Bowen, W. M., Park, S., & Elvery, J. A. (2013). Empirical Estimates of the Influence of Renewable Energy Portfolio Standards on the Green Economies of States. *Economic Development Quarterly*, *27*(4), 338–351. doi:10.1177/0891242413491316

Breiman, L. (1996). Bagging predictors. *Machine Learning*, *24*(2), 123–140. doi:10.1007/BF00058655

Breiman, L. (2001). Random forests. *Machine Learning*, *45*(1), 5–32. doi:10.1023/A:1010933404324

Brotsis, S., Limniotis, K., Bendiab, G., Kolokotronis, N., & Shiaeles, S. (2021). On the suitability of blockchain platforms for IoT applications: Architectures, security, privacy, and performance. *Computer Networks*, *191*, 1–29. doi:10.1016/j.comnet.2021.108005

Buchmann, J. A., Butin, D., Göpfert, F., & Petzoldt, A. (n.d.). *Post-Quantum Cryptography: State of the Art*. Academic Press.

Buchmann, J., Dahmen, E., & Hülsing, A. (2011). XMSS – A practical forward secure signature scheme based on minimal security assumptions. In Proceedings of the 4th International Conference on Post-Quantum Cryptography, PQCRYPTO'11 (pp. 117–129). Springer. doi:10.1007/978-3-642-25405-5_8

Budd, J., Miller, B. S., Manning, E. M., Lampos, V., Zhuang, M., Edelstein, M., Rees, G., Emery, V. C., Stevens, M. M., Keegan, N., Short, M. J., Pillay, D., Manley, E., Cox, I. J., Heymann, D., Johnson, A. M., & McKendry, R. A. (2020). Digital technologies in the public-health response to COVID-19. In Nature Medicine (Vol. 26, Issue 8). doi:10.103841591-020-1011-4

Bünz, B., Bootle, J., Boneh, D., Poelstra, A., Wuille, P., & Maxwell, G. 2018. Bulletproofs: Short proofs for confidential transactions and more. In *Proceedings of the IEEE Symposium on Security and Privacy (SP'18)*. IEEE. 10.1109/SP.2018.00020

Casino, F., Dasaklis, T. K., & Patsakis, C. (2019). A systematic literature review of blockchain-based applications: Current status, classification and open issues. *Telematics and Informatics*, *36*, 55–81. doi:10.1016/j.tele.2018.11.006

Chattu, V. K., Nanda, A., Chattu, S. K., Kadri, S. M., & Knight, A. W. (2019). The emerging role of blockchain technology applications in routine disease surveillance systems to strengthen global health security. *Big Data and Cognitive Computing*, *3*(2), 25–35. doi:10.3390/bdcc3020025

Chen, Jordan, Liu, & Moody. (2016). Report on Post-Quantum Cryptography. *Huabei Gongxueyuan Xuebao/Journal of North China Institute of Technology, 22*(3).

Chen, G., Xu, B., Lu, M., & Chen, N. S. (2018). Exploring blockchain technology and its potential applications for education. *Smart Learning Environments*, *5*(1), 1–10. doi:10.118640561-017-0050-x

Chen, H. (2020). Quantum relay blockchain and its applications in key service. *ACM International Conference Proceeding Series*, 95–99. 10.1145/3377644.3377657

Chen, J., Gan, W., Hu, M., & Chen, C. M. (2021). On the construction of a post-quantum blockchain for smart city. *Journal of Information Security and Applications, 58,* 102780. Advance online publication. doi:10.1016/j.jisa.2021.102780

Chen, T., & Guestrin, C. (2016). Xgboost: A scalable tree boosting system. In *Proceedings of the 22nd acm sigkdd international conference on knowledge discovery and data mining* (pp. 785–794). 10.1145/2939672.2939785

Cheon, J. H., Han, K., Kim, J., Lee, C., & Son, Y. (2017). A practical post-quantum public-key cryptosystem based on spLWE. *Lecture Notes in Computer Science, 10157,* 51–74. doi:10.1007/978-3-319-53177-9_3

Cho, K., Van Merrienboer, B., Gulcehre, C., Bahdanau, D., Bougares, F., Schwenk, H., & Bengio, Y. (2014). *Learning phrase representations using RNN encoder-decoder for statistical machine translation.* arXiv preprint arXiv:1406.1078.

Choi, M. K., Yeun, C. Y., & Seong, P. H. (2020). A Novel Monitoring System for the Data Integrity of Reactor Protection System Using Blockchain Technology. *IEEE Access: Practical Innovations, Open Solutions, 8,* 118732–118740. doi:10.1109/ACCESS.2020.3005134

Choubisa, M., & Doshi, R. (2022). Crop Protection Using Cyber Physical Systems and Machine Learning for Smart Agriculture. In *Real-Time Application of Machine Learning in Cyber-Physical Systems* (pp. 134–147). IGI Global.

Choubisa, M., & Doshi, R. (2022). Crop Protection Using Cyber Physical Systems and Machine Learning for Smart Agriculture. In *Real-Time Applications of Machine Learning in Cyber-Physical Systems* (pp. 134–147). IGI Global.

Choubisa, M., Doshi, R., Khatri, N., & Hiran, K. K. (2022, May). A Simple and Robust Approach of Random Forest for Intrusion Detection System in Cyber Security. In *2022 International Conference on IoT and Blockchain Technology (ICIBT)* (pp. 1-5). IEEE. 10.1109/ICIBT52874.2022.9807766

Christ, K. L., & Helliar, C. V. (2021). Blockchain technology and modern slavery: Reducing deceptive recruitment in migrant worker populations. *Journal of Business Research, 131,* 112–120. doi:10.1016/j.jbusres.2021.03.065

Cormack, R. M. (1971). A Review of Classification. *Journal of the Royal Statistical Society. Series A (General), 134*(3), 321–367. doi:10.2307/2344237

Costa, D. G., & Peixoto, J. P. J. (2020). COVID-19 pandemic: A review of smart cities initiatives to face new outbreaks. *IET Smart Cities, 2*(2), 64–73. doi:10.1049/iet-smc.2020.0044

Cui, Z., Ke, R., Pu, Z., & Wang, Y. (2018). *Deep bidirectional and unidirectional LSTM recurrent neural network for network-wide traffic speed prediction.* arXiv preprint arXiv:1801.02143.

Cunningham, P., & Delany, S. (2021). k-Nearest neighbour classifiers-A Tutorial. *ACM Computing Surveys, 54*(6), 1–25. doi:10.1145/3459665

Dadhich & Pahwa. (2021). Analytical Study of Financial Wellbeing of Selected Public and Private Sector Banks: A CAMEL Approach. *IEEE Explore, Emerging Trends in Industry 4.0 (ETI 4.0)*, 1–6. . doi:10.1109/ETI4.051663.2021.9619424

Dadhich, M., Rao, S. S., Sethy, S., & Sharma, R. (2021). Determining the Factors Influencing Cloud Computing Implementation in Library Management System (LMS): A High Order PLS-ANN Approach. *Library Philosophy and Practice*, 6281.

Dadhich, S., Pathak, V., Mittal, R., & Doshi, R. (2021). Machine learning for weather forecasting. Machine Learning for Sustainable Development. doi:10.1515/9783110702514-010

Dadhich, M. (2016). A Comparative Study of Investment Portfolio of Life fund of LIC of India and ICICI Prudential Life Insurers. *International Journal of Research in Economics and Social Sciences*, 6(10), 229–238.

Dadhich, M. (2017). Impact of Demonetization on Indian Economy. *International Journal of Research in Social Sciences*, 7(8), 208–215.

Dadhich, M. (2019). Stochastic pattern of major indices of Bombay stock exchange. *International Journal of Recent Technology and Engineering*, 8(3), 6774–6779. doi:10.35940/ijrte.C6068.098319

Dadhich, M., Hiran, K. K., Rao, S. S., & Sharma, R. (2022). Impact of Covid-19 on Teaching-Learning Perception of Faculties and Students of Higher Education in Indian Purview. *Journal of Mobile Multimedia*, 18(4), 957–980. doi:10.13052/jmm1550-4646.1841

Dadhich, M., Pahwa, M. S., & Rao, S. S. (2018). Factor Influencing to Users Acceptance of Digital Payment System. *International Journal on Computer Science and Engineering*, 06(09), 46–50. doi:10.26438/ijcse/v6si9.4650

Dadhich, M., Purohit, H., & Bhasker, A. A. (2021). Determinants of green initiatives and operational performance for manufacturing SMEs. *Materials Today: Proceedings*, 46(20), 10870–10874. doi:10.1016/j.matpr.2021.01.889

Daniels, A. (2019). *Information Security in an Internet of Things Network Based on Blockchains and User Participation*. Academic Press.

De Ryck, T., Lanthaler, S., & Mishra, S. (2021). On the approximation of functions by tanh neural networks. *Neural Networks*, 143, 732–750. doi:10.1016/j.neunet.2021.08.015 PMID:34482172

de Villiers, C., Chen, S., jin, C., & Zhu, Y. (2014). Carbon sequestered in the trees on a university campus: A case study. *Sustainability Accounting. Management and Policy Journal*, 5(2), 149–171. doi:10.1108/SAMPJ-11-2013-0048

Deepa, Pham, Nguyen, Bhattacharya, Prabadevi, Gadekallu, Maddikunta, Fang, & Pathirana. (2021). *A Survey on Blockchain for Big Data: Approaches, Opportunities, and Future Directions*. https://arxiv.org/pdf/2009.00858.pdf

Delgado-Mohatar, O., Fierrez, J., Tolosana, R., & Vera-Rodriguez, R. (2019). Biometric Template Storage With Blockchain: A First Look Into Cost and Performance Tradeoffs. *2019 IEEE/CVF Conference on Computer Vision and Pattern Recognition Workshops (CVPRW)*. 10.1109/CVPRW.2019.00342

Deshpande, A., Stewart, K., Lepetit, L., & Gunashekar, S. (2017). *Distributed Ledger Technologies/Blockchain: Challenges, opportunities and the prospects for standards. Overview report. The British Standards Institution*. BSI.

Devlin, J., Chang, M. W., Lee, K., & Toutanova, K. (2018). *Bert: Pre-training of deep bidirectional transformers for language understanding*. arXiv preprint arXiv:1810.04805.

Dinesh, A. D., Durga Prasad Reddy, C., Gopi, G. V., Jain, R., & Shankar, T. N. (2021). A Durable Biometric Authentication Scheme via Blockchain. *2021 International Conference on Advances in Electrical, Computing, Communication and Sustainable Technologies (ICAECT)*. 10.1109/ICAECT49130.2021.9392415

Dolev, S., & Wang, Z. (2020). SodsBC: Stream of Distributed Secrets for Quantum-safe Blockchain. *Proceedings - 2020 IEEE International Conference on Blockchain, Blockchain 2020*, 247–256. 10.1109/Blockchain50366.2020.00038

Doshi, R. (2018, June). An Institutional Adoption Framework of the Cloud Computing in Higher Education: Case of Sub-Saharan Africa. *International Journal of Research in Engineering, IT and Social Sciences*, *8*(6), 51–56.

Duchi, J., Hazan, E., & Singer, Y. (2011). Adaptive Subgradient Methods for Online Learning and Stochastic Optimization. *Journal of Machine Learning Research*, *12*(61), 2121–2159.

Durneva, P., Cousins, K., & Chen, M. (2020). The Current State of Research, Challenges, and Future Research Directions of Blockchain Technology in Patient Care: Systematic Review. *Journal of Medical Internet Research*, *22*(7), e18619. doi:10.2196/18619 PMID:32706668

Easwaran, B., Hiran, K. K., Krishnan, S., & Doshi, R. (Eds.). (2022). *Real-Time Applications of Machine Learning in Cyber-Physical Systems*. doi:10.4018/978-1-7998-9308-0

Elgendy, N., & Elragal, A. (2014). Big data analytics: a literature review paper. In Industrial conference on data mining (pp. 214–227). doi:10.1007/978-3-319-08976-8_16

English, M., Auer, S., & Domingue, J. (2016). *Block Chain Technologies & The Semantic Web : A Framework for Symbiotic Development*. Computer Science Conference for University of Bonn Students.

Esgin, M. F., Zhao, R. K., Steinfeld, R., Liu, J. K., & Liu, D. (2019). Matrict: Efficient, scalable and post-quantum blockchain confidential transactions protocol. *Proceedings of the ACM Conference on Computer and Communications Security*, 567–584. 10.1145/3319535.3354200

Espitau, T., Fouque, P.-A., Gérard, B., & Tibouchi, M. (2017). Side-Channel Attacks on BLISS Lattice-Based Signatures: Exploiting Branch Tracing against strongSwan and Electromagnetic Emanations in Microcontrollers. *Proceedings of the 2017 ACM SIGSAC Conference on Computer and Communications Security*. 10.1145/3133956.3134028

Farell, R. (2015). *An Analysis of the Cryptocurrency Industry.* Academic Press.

Fernandez-Carames, T. M., & Fraga-Lamas, P. (2020). Towards Post-Quantum Blockchain: A Review on Blockchain Cryptography Resistant to Quantum Computing Attacks. *IEEE Access: Practical Innovations, Open Solutions*, 8, 21091–21116. doi:10.1109/ACCESS.2020.2968985

Fingerhuth, M., Babej, T., & Wittek, P. (2018). Open source software in quantum computing. In PLoS ONE (Vol. 13, Issue 12). doi:10.1371/journal.pone.0208561

Fluhrer, S. R. (2017). Reassessing Grover's Algorithm. *IACR Cryptology EPrint Archive, 2017*.

Foley, C. P., Scientist, C., Gambetta, J., Rao, J. R., Dixon, W., & Head, G. (2021). *Is your cybersecurity ready to take the quantum leap?* https://www.weforum.org/agenda/2021/05/cybersecurity-quantum-computing-algorithms/

Forson, I. K., & Vuopala, E. (2019). Online learning readiness: Perspective of students enrolled in distance education in Ghana. *The Online Journal of Distance Education and E-Learning*, 7(4), 277–294.

Frauenthaler, P., Sigwart, M., Spanring, C., Sober, M., & Schulte, S. (2020, November). ETH relay: A cost-efficient relay for ethereum-based blockchains. In *2020 IEEE International Conference on Blockchain (Blockchain)* (pp. 204-213). IEEE. 10.1109/Blockchain50366.2020.00032

Freund, Y., & Schapire, R. E. (1999). A Short Introduction to Boosting. Academic Press.

Gabison, G. (2016). Policy considerations for the blockchain technology public and private applications. *SMU Sci. & Tech. L. Rev.*, *19*(1), 327–334.

Gamage, H. T. M., Weerasinghe, H. D., & Dias, N. G. J. (2020). A survey on blockchain technology concepts, applications, and issues. *SN Computer Science*, *1*(2), 1–15. doi:10.100742979-020-00123-0

Gao, Y. L., Chen, X. B., Chen, Y. L., Sun, Y., Niu, X. X., & Yang, Y. X. (2018). A Secure Cryptocurrency Scheme Based on Post-Quantum Blockchain. *IEEE Access, 6*(2), 27205–27213. doi:10.1109/ACCESS.2018.2827203

Gao, S., Zheng, D., Guo, R., Jing, C., & Hu, C. (2019). An anti-quantum e-voting protocol in blockchain with audit function. *IEEE Access: Practical Innovations, Open Solutions, 7*, 115304–115316. doi:10.1109/ACCESS.2019.2935895

Gao, Y. L., Chen, X. B., Xu, G., Yuan, K. G., Liu, W., & Yang, Y. X. (2020). A novel quantum blockchain scheme base on quantum entanglement and DPoS. *Quantum Information Processing*, *19*(12), 420. Advance online publication. doi:10.100711128-020-02915-y

Garcia, P. (2018). Biometrics on the blockchain. *Biometric Technology Today*, *1*(5), 5–7. doi:10.1016/S0969-4765(18)30067-5

Gereffi, G., Wadhwa, V., Rissing, B., & Ong, R. (2008). Getting the numbers right: International engineering education in the United States, China, and India. *Journal of Engineering Education*, *97*(1), 13–25. doi:10.1002/j.2168-9830.2008.tb00950.x

Gill, S. S., Tuli, S., Xu, M., Singh, I., Singh, K. V., Lindsay, D., Tuli, S., Smirnova, D., Singh, M., Jain, U., Pervaiz, H., Sehgal, B., Kaila, S. S., Misra, S., Aslanpour, M. S., Mehta, H., Stankovski, V., & Garraghan, P. (2019). Transformative effects of IoT, Blockchain and Artificial Intelligence on cloud computing: Evolution, vision, trends and open challenges. *Internet of Things (Netherlands)*, *8*, 1–26. doi:10.1016/j.iot.2019.100118

Girshick, R. (2015). Fast r-cnn. In *Proceedings of the IEEE international conference on computer vision* (pp. 1440–1448). IEEE.

Girshick, R., Donahue, J., Darrell, T., & Malik, J. (2014). Rich feature hierarchies for accurate object detection and semantic segmentation. In *Proceedings of the IEEE conference on computer vision and pattern recognition* (pp. 580–587). 10.1109/CVPR.2014.81

Goel, A., Agarwal, A., Vatsa, M., Singh, R., & Ratha, N. (2019). Securing CNN Model and Biometric Template using Blockchain. *2019 IEEE 10th International Conference on Biometrics Theory, Applications and Systems (BTAS)*. 10.1109/BTAS46853.2019.9185999

Goel, U., Sonanis, R., Rastogi, I., Lal, S., & De, A. (2020). Criticality Aware Orderer for Heterogeneous Transactions in Blockchain. *2020 IEEE International Conference on Blockchain and Cryptocurrency (ICBC)*. 10.1109/ICBC48266.2020.9169439

Golosova, J., & Romanovs, A. (2018, November). The advantages and disadvantages of the blockchain technology. In *2018 IEEE 6th workshop on advances in information, electronic and electrical engineering (AIEEE)* (pp. 1-6). IEEE.

Goodfellow, I., Bengio, Y., & Courville, A. (2016). *Deep learning*. MIT Press.

Gordon, W. J., & Catalini, C. (2018). Blockchain technology for healthcare: Facilitating the transition to patient-driven interoperability. *Computational and Structural Biotechnology Journal*, *16*, 224–230. doi:10.1016/j.csbj.2018.06.003 PMID:30069284

Green Assets. (n.d.). Local Govt and Municipal Knowledge Base Australia. http://lgam.wikidot.com/green-asset

Gregory, M. (2015). *Confidential Transactions*. Retrieved from: https://people.xiph.org/ greg/confidential_ values.txt

Grover, L. (1996). A fast quantum mechanical algorithm for database search. In *Proceedings of the twenty-eighth annual ACM symposium on Theory of computing* (pp. 212–219). 10.1145/237814.237866

Grover, L. K. (1997). Quantum mechanics helps in searching for a needle in a haystack. *Physical Review Letters*, 79(2), 325–328. https://doi.org/10.1103/PhysRevLett.79.325

Grover, M., Reinicke, B., & Cummings, J. (2016). How secure is education in Information Technology? A method for evaluating security education in IT. *Information Systems Education Journal*, 14(3), 29–37.

Gulati, H., & Huang, C. T. (2019). Self-Sovereign Dynamic Digital Identities based on lockchain Technology. *2019 SoutheastCon*. doi:10.1109/SoutheastCon42311.2019.9020518

Gupta, A., Joshi, R., Tambe, S., Laban, R., Tandlekar, G., & Chitre, V. (2022). Optimization Effects for Word Representations with L2-Regularized Non-Parametric Model for Contrasting Epochs. In *2022 3rd International Conference for Emerging Technology (INCET)* (pp. 1–6). 10.1109/INCET54531.2022.9824562

Gupta, A., Nair, S., Joshi, R., & Chitre, V. (2022). Residual-Concatenate Neural Network with Deep Regularization Layers for Binary Classification. In *2022 6th International Conference on Intelligent Computing and Control Systems (ICICCS)* (pp. 1018–1022). 10.1109/ICICCS53718.2022.9788437

Gupta, A., Shetty, S., Joshi, R., & Laban, R. (2021). Succinct differentiation of disparate boosting ensemble learning methods for prognostication of polycystic ovary syndrome diagnosis. In *2021 International Conference on Advances in Computing, Communication, and Control (ICAC3)* (pp. 1–5). 10.1109/ICAC353642.2021.9697163

Gupta, A., Soni, H., Joshi, R., & Laban, R. (2022). *Discriminant Analysis in Contrasting Dimensions for Polycystic Ovary Syndrome Prognostication.* arXiv preprint arXiv:2201.03029.

Gupta, A., Thustu, S., Thakor, R., Patil, S., Joshi, R., & Laban, R. (2022). *Prediction of Maneuvering Status for Aerial Vehicles using Supervised Learning Methods.* arXiv preprint arXiv:2206.10303.

Gupta, A., Joshi, R., & Laban, R. (2022). *Detection of Tool based Edited Images from Error Level Analysis and Convolutional Neural Network.* arXiv preprint arXiv:2204.09075.

Gupta, H., & Patel, M. (2021, March). Method Of Text Summarization Using Lsa And Sentence Based Topic Modelling With Bert. In *2021 International Conference on Artificial Intelligence and Smart Systems (ICAIS)* (pp. 511-517). IEEE. 10.1109/ICAIS50930.2021.9395976

Haji, K. (2021). E-commerce development in rural and remote areas of BRICS countries. *Journal of Integrative Agriculture*, 20(4), 979–997. doi:10.1016/S2095-3119(20)63451-7

Haney Seamus Brain. (2020). *Blockchain: Post-quantum security & legal economics.* Author.

Hardjono, T., Lipton, A., & Pentland, A. (2018). *Towards a design philosophy for interoperable blockchain systems.* arXiv preprint arXiv:1805.05934.

Hearst, M., Dumais, S., Osuna, E., Platt, J., & Scholkopf, B. (1998). Support vector machines. *IEEE Intelligent Systems & their Applications*, 13(4), 18–28. doi:10.1109/5254.708428

Hebert, C., & Di Cerbo, F. (2019). Secure blockchain in the enterprise: A methodology. *Pervasive and Mobile Computing*, *59*, 1–14. doi:10.1016/j.pmcj.2019.101038

Heilman, E., Kendler, A., Zohar, A., & Goldberg, S. (2015). Eclipse Attacks on Bitcoin's Peer-to-Peer Network. *USENIX Security Symposium*.

He, K., Zhang, X., Ren, S., & Sun, J. (2016). Deep residual learning for image recognition. In *Proceedings of the IEEE conference on computer vision and pattern recognition* (pp. 770–778). IEEE.

Helbing. (2014). A better financial system for the future. *ETH Zurich - Swiss Federal Institute of Technology*, 1–14.

Hilal, A. M., Hassine, S. B. H., Larabi-Marie-Sainte, S., Nemri, N., Nour, M. K., Motwakel, A., Zamani, A. S., & al Duhayyim, M. (2022). Malware Detection Using Decision Tree Based SVM Classifier for IoT. *Computers. Materials and Continua*, *72*(1). Advance online publication. doi:10.32604/cmc.2022.024501

Hiran, K. K., & Doshi, R. (2013). Robust & secure digital image watermarking technique using concatenation process. *International Journal of ICT and Management*.

Hiran, K. K., Jain, R. K., Hiran, K., & Paliwal, G. (2012). Quantum cryptography: A new generation of information security system. *International Journal of Computers and Distributed Systems,* Error! Hyperlink reference not valid.2. https://www.researchgate.net/publication/320404164

Hiran, K. K., Khazanchi, D., Vyas, A. K., & Padmanaban, S. (2021). Machine learning for sustainable development. *Machine Learning for Sustainable Development*. doi:10.1515/9783110702514

Hiran, K. (2021). Investigating Factors Influencing the Adoption of IT Cloud Computing Platforms in Higher Education: Case of Sub-Saharan Africa With IT Professionals. *International Journal of Human Capital and Information Technology Professionals*, *12*(3), 21–36. doi:10.4018/IJHCITP.2021070102

Hiran, K. K. (2021). Impact of Driving Factors on Cloud Computing Adoption in the Higher Education. *IOP Conference Series. Materials Science and Engineering*, *1131*(1), 012016. Advance online publication. doi:10.1088/1757-899X/1131/1/012016

Hiran, K. K., & Doshi, R. (2013). An artificial neural network approach for brain tumor detection using digital image segmentation. *Brain*, *2*(5), 227–231.

Hiran, K. K., Doshi, R., & Rathi, R. (2014). Security & privacy issues of cloud & grid computing networks. *International Journal on Computational Sciences & Applications*, *4*(1), 83–91. doi:10.5121/ijcsa.2014.4108

Hiran, K. K., Doshi, R., & Rathi, R. (2014). Security & Privacy issues of cloud & grid computing networks. *International Journal on Computertational Science & Applications*, *4*(1), 83–91.

Hiran, K. K., & Henten, A. (2020). An integrated TOE–DoI framework for cloud computing adoption in the higher education sector: Case study of Sub-Saharan Africa, Ethiopia. *International Journal of System Assurance Engineering and Management*, *11*(2), 441–449. doi:10.100713198-019-00872-z

Hiran, K. K., Jain, R. K., Lakhwani, K., & Doshi, R. (2021). *Machine Learning: Master Supervised and Unsupervised Learning Algorithms with Real Examples (English Edition)*. BPB Publications.

Holcomb, A., Pereira, G., Das, B., & Mosca, M. (2021). PQFabric: A Permissioned Blockchain Secure from Both Classical and Quantum Attacks. *2021 IEEE International Conference on Blockchain and Cryptocurrency (ICBC)*, 1-9. 10.1109/ICBC51069.2021.9461070

Hongqing, G., Peiyong, S., Wenzhong, G., & Kun, G. (2018). Component-based Assembling Tool and Runtime Engine for the Machine Learning Process. *2018 International Conference on Cloud Computing, Big Data and Blockchain (ICCBB)*. 10.1109/ICCBB.2018.8756448

Huberty, C. J. (1975). Discriminant Analysis. *Review of Educational Research*, *45*(4), 543–598. doi:10.3102/00346543045004543

Hülsing. (2017). *WOTS+ – Shorter Signatures for Hash-Based Signature Schemes*. Academic Press.

Huo, R., Zeng, S., Wang, Z., Shang, J., Chen, W., Huang, T., Wang, S., Yu, F. R., & Liu, Y. (2022). A comprehensive survey on blockchain in industrial internet of things: Motivations, research progresses, and future challenges. *IEEE Communications Surveys and Tutorials*, *24*(1), 88–122. doi:10.1109/COMST.2022.3141490

Ibrahim, M., Ravindran, K., Lee, H., Farooqui, O., & Mahmoud, Q. H. (2021). ElectionBlock: An Electronic Voting System using Blockchain and Fingerprint Authentication. *2021 IEEE 18th International Conference on Software Architecture Companion (ICSA-C)*. 10.1109/ICSA-C52384.2021.00033

Ikeda, K. (2018). qBitcoin: A Peer-to-Peer Quantum Cash System. *Intelligent Computing*, 763–771. . doi:10.1007/978-3-030-01174-1_58

Ioannou, A., Tussyadiah, I., & Lu, Y. (2020). Privacy concerns and disclosure of biometric and behavioral data for travel. *International Journal of Information Management*, *54*(January), 102122. doi:10.1016/j.ijinfomgt.2020.102122

Iovane, G. (2021a). Computational quantum key distribution (CQKD) on decentralized ledger and blockchain. *Journal of Discrete Mathematical Sciences and Cryptography*, *24*(4), 1021–1042. doi:10.1080/09720529.2020.1820691

Iovane, G. (2021b). MuReQua Chain: Multiscale Relativistic Quantum Blockchain. *IEEE Access: Practical Innovations, Open Solutions*, *9*, 39827–39838. doi:10.1109/ACCESS.2021.3064297

Iovane, G., Bisogni, C., de Maio, L., & Nappi, M. (2020). An Encryption Approach Using Information Fusion Techniques Involving Prime Numbers and Face Biometrics. *IEEE Transactions on Sustainable Computing*, *5*(2), 260–267. doi:10.1109/TSUSC.2018.2793466

Iovane, G., Nappi, M., Chinnici, M., Petrosino, A., Castiglione, A., & Barra, S. (2019). A Novel Blockchain Scheme Combining Prime Numbers and Iris for Encrypting Coding. *2019 IEEE Intl Conf on Dependable, Autonomic and Secure Computing, Intl Conf on Pervasive Intelligence and Computing, Intl Conf on Cloud and Big Data Computing, Intl Conf on Cyber Science and Technology Congress(DASC/PiCom/CBDCom/CyberSciTech).* 10.1109/DASC/PiCom/CBDCom/CyberSciTech.2019.00117

Jaffer, S. A., Pandey, S., Mehta, R., & Bhavathankar, P. (2020). Blockchain Based Direct Benefit Transfer System For Subsidy Delivery. *2020 International Conference for Emerging Technology (INCET).* 10.1109/INCET49848.2020.9154178

Jain, R. K., Hiran, K., & Paliwal, G. (2012). Quantum Cryptography: A New Generation Of Information Security System. *Proceedings of International Journal of Computers and Distributed Systems.*

Jain, R. K., Hiran, K., & Paliwal, G. (2012). Quantum Cryptography: A New Generation of Information Security System. *Proceedings of International Journal of Computers and Distributed Systems.* doi:10.1109/ICOIN.2018.8343163

Jain, R.K., Hiran, K., Raliwal, G. (2012) Quantum Cryptography: A new Generation of information security system. *Proceedings of Information Journal of Computers & Distributed Systems.*

Jain, R. K., Hiran, K., & Paliwal, G. (2012). Quantum Cryptography: A New Generation Of Information Security System. *Proceedings of International Journal of Computers and Distributed Systems, 2*(1), 42–45.

Jakh-u, R. S. (2019). Independent Review of the Remote Sensing Space Systems Act. *SSRN Electronic Journal.* doi:10.2139/ssrn.3397158

Jangid, P. S., & Bharadi, V. A. (2020). Evolving Authentication Design Consideration and BaaS Architecture for Internet of Biometric things. *2020 International Conference on Convergence to Digital World - Quo Vadis (ICCDW).* 10.1109/ICCDW45521.2020.9318664

Jansen, S. (2021). *Quantum-resistant platform solves scalability and bandwidth bottlenecks present on the blockchain.* https://cointelegraph.com/news/quantum-resistant-platform-solves-scalability-and-bandwidth-bottlenecks-present-on-the-blockchain

Jazaeri, F., Beckers, A., Tajalli, A., & Sallese, J. M. (2019). A review on quantum computing: From qubits to front-end electronics and cryogenic MOSFET physics. In *2019 MIXDES-26th International Conference "Mixed Design of Integrated Circuits and Systems"* (pp. 15–25). Academic Press.

Jazdi, N. (2014). Cyber physical systems in the context of Industry 4.0. *2014 IEEE International Conference on Automation, Quality and Testing, Robotics*, 1-4. 10.1109/AQTR.2014.6857843

Jin, H., Dai, X., & Xiao, J. (2018, July). Towards a novel architecture for enabling interoperability amongst multiple blockchains. In *2018 IEEE 38th International Conference on Distributed Computing Systems (ICDCS)* (pp. 1203-1211). IEEE. 10.1109/ICDCS.2018.00120

Jirgensons, M., & Kapenieks, J. (2018). Blockchain and the future of digital learning credential assessment and management. *Journal of Teacher Education for Sustainability, 20*(1), 145-156.

Joshi, R., & Gupta, A. (2022). *Performance Comparison of Simple Transformer and Res-CNN-BiLSTM for Cyberbullying Classification.* arXiv preprint arXiv:2206.02206.

Joshi, R., Gupta, A., & Kanvinde, N. (2022). *Res-CNN-BiLSTM Network for overcoming Mental Health Disturbances caused due to Cyberbullying through Social Media.* arXiv preprint arXiv:2204.09738.

Jun, Z., Yong, Y., Xiao, W., & Fei-Yue, W. (2019). Quantum blockchain:can blockchain integrated with quantum information technology resist quantum supremacy? *Chinese Journal of Intelligent Science and Technology, 1*(4), 409–414.

Kailashi Punit, D., & Kamal Hiran, I. S. (2021). *Essence of life Divide By Zero.* Notion Press.

Kanvinde, N., Gupta, A., & Joshi, R. (2022). *Binary Classification for High Dimensional Data using Supervised Non-Parametric Ensemble Method.* arXiv preprint arXiv:2202.07779.

Kappert, N., Karger, E., & Kureljusic, M. (2021). Quantum Computing – The Impending End for the Blockchain? *PACIS 2021 Proceedings,* 1–14.

Kappert, N., Karger, E., & Kureljusic, M. (2021). Quantum Computing – The Impending End for the Blockchain? *PACIS 2021 Proceedings.* https://aisel.aisnet.org/pacis2021/114

Kapur, D., & Mehta, P. B. (2004). Indian higher education reform: From half-baked socialism to half-baked capitalism. *Center for International Development Working Paper, 103.*

Karbasi, A. H., & Shahpasand, S. (2020). A post-quantum end-to-end encryption over smart contract-based blockchain for defeating man-in-the-middle and interception attacks. *Peer-to-Peer Networking and Applications, 13*(5), 1423–1441. doi:10.100712083-020-00901-w

Kasotia. (n.d.). The Health Effects Of Global Warming: Developing Countries Are The Most Vulnerable. *UN Chronicle.* https://www.un.org/en/chronicle/article/health-effects-global-warming-developing-countries-are-most-vulnerable

Kathuria, A., Mann, A., Khuntia, J., Saldanha, T. J. V., Kauffman, J., Kathuria, A., Mann, A., Khuntia, J., & Saldanha, T. J. V. (2018). A Strategic Value Appropriation Path for Cloud Computing A Strategic Value Appropriation Path for Cloud Computing. *Journal of Management Information Systems, 35*(3), 740–775. doi:10.1080/07421222.2018.1481635

Kaur, A., Nayyar, A., & Singh, P. (2020). BlockChain. *Cryptocurrencies and Blockchain Technology Applications,* 25–42. doi:10.1002/9781119621201.ch2

Kearney, J. J., & Perez-Delgado, C. A. (2021). Vulnerability of blockchain technologies to quantum attacks. *Array, 10*(November), 100065. doi:10.1016/j.array.2021.100065

Kefford, M. (2021). *4 Ways Blockchain Is Revolutionizing FinTech.* https://www.businessbecause.com/news/insights/7534/blockchain-fintech?sponsored

Khalid, Z. M., & Askar, S. (2021). Resistant blockchain cryptography to quantum computing attacks. *International Journal of Science and Business*, *5*(3), 116–125.

Khalid, Z. M., & Askar, S. (2021). Resistant Blockchain Cryptography to Quantum Computing Attacks. *International Journal of Science and Business*, *5*(3), 116–125. doi:10.5281/zenodo.4497732

Khan, S. N., Loukil, F., Ghedira-Guegan, C., Benkhelifa, E., & Bani-Hani, A. (2021). Blockchain smart contracts: Applications, challenges, and future trends. *Peer-to-Peer Networking and Applications*, *14*(5), 2901–2925. doi:10.100712083-021-01127-0 PMID:33897937

Khazanchi, D., Vyas, A. K., Hiran, K. K., & Padmanaban, S. (2021). Blockchain 3.0 for sustainable development. *Blockchain 3.0 for Sustainable Development*. doi:10.1515/9783110702507/EPUB

Khazanchi, D., Vyas, A. K., Hiran, K. K., & Padmanaban, S. (Eds.). (2021). *Blockchain 3.0 for sustainable development* (Vol. 10). Walter de Gruyter GmbH & Co KG.

Khazanchi, D., Vyas, K., & Ajay, K. H. (2021). *Kamal and Padmanaban, Sanjeevikumar. Blockchain 3.0 for Sustainable Development*. De Gruyter. doi:10.1515/9783110702507

Khezr, S., Moniruzzaman, M., Yassine, A., & Benlamri, R. (2019). Blockchain technology in healthcare: A comprehensive review and directions for future research. *Applied Sciences (Basel, Switzerland)*, *9*(9), 1736–1745. doi:10.3390/app9091736

Kiktenko, E. O., Pozhar, N. O., Anufriev, M. N., Trushechkin, A. S., Yunusov, R. R., Kurochkin, Y. V., Lvovsky, A. I., & Fedorov, A. K. (2018a). Quantum-secured blockchain. *Quantum Science and Technology*, *3*(3), 1–6. doi:10.1088/2058-9565/aabc6b

Kingma, D., & Ba, J. (2014). *Adam: A method for stochastic optimization*. arXiv preprint arXiv:1412.6980.

Klarin, A. (2020). The decade-long cryptocurrencies and the blockchain rollercoaster: Mapping the intellectual structure and charting future directions. *Research in International Business and Finance*, *51*, 101067. doi:10.1016/j.ribaf.2019.101067

Kolb, J., AbdelBaky, M., Katz, R. H., & Culler, D. E. (2020). Core Concepts, Challenges, and Future Directions in Blockchain. *ACM Computing Surveys*, *53*(1), 1–39. doi:10.1145/3366370

Kolstad, C. D. (2011). Intermediate Environmental Economics (2nd ed.). Oxford University Press.

Kothari, D., Patel, M., & Sharma, A. K. (2021, January). Implementation of Grey Scale Normalization in Machine Learning & Artificial Intelligence for Bioinformatics using Convolutional Neural Networks. In *2021 6th International Conference on Inventive Computation Technologies (ICICT)* (pp. 10711074). IEEE. 10.1109/ICICT50816.2021.9358549

Kothari, R., Choudhary, N., & Jain, K. (2021). CP-ABE Scheme with Decryption Keys of Constant Size Using ECC with Expressive Threshold Access Structure. In *Emerging Trends in Data Driven Computing and Communications* (pp. 15–36). Springer. doi:10.1007/978-981-16-3915-9_2

Kotsiantis, S. (2007). Supervised Machine Learning: A Review of Classification Techniques. In *Proceedings of the 2007 Conference on Emerging Artificial Intelligence Applications in Computer Engineering: Real Word AI Systems with Applications in EHealth, HCI, Information Retrieval and Pervasive Technologies* (pp. 3–24). IOS Press.

Krishnapriya, S., & Sarath, G. (2020). Securing Land Registration using Blockchain. *Procedia Computer Science, 171*(2019), 1708–1715. doi:10.1016/j.procs.2020.04.183

Krishnaswamy, D. (2020). Quantum blockchain networks. *Proceedings of the International Symposium on Mobile Ad Hoc Networking and Computing (MobiHoc), 2*, 327–332. 10.1145/3397166.3412802

Krizhevsky, A., Sutskever, I., & Hinton, G. (2012). Imagenet classification with deep convolutional neural networks. *Advances in Neural Information Processing Systems, 25*.

Küfner, P., Nestmann, U., Rickmann, C., Küfner, P., Nestmann, U., Rickmann, C., & Verification, F. (2017). Formal Verification of Distributed Algorithms. *7th International Conference on Theoretical Computer Science (TCS), 209*–224.

Kumar, M., & Dadhich, N. (2015). An Analysis of Factors Affecting to Entrepreneur Development in Rajasthan. *International Journal of Management, IT and Engineering, 5*(12), 41–48.

Kumari, R., & Kr, S. (2017). Machine Learning: A Review on Binary Classification. *International Journal of Computers and Applications, 160*(7), 11–15. doi:10.5120/ijca2017913083

Kumar, N. M., & Mallick, P. K. (2018). Blockchain technology for security issues and challenges in IoT. *Procedia Computer Science, 132*(1), 1815–1823. doi:10.1016/j.procs.2018.05.140

Kumar, N., & Dadhich, M. (2014). Risk Management for Investors in Stock Market. *EXCEL International Journal of Multidisciplinary Management Studies, 4*(3), 103–108.

Kumar, R. L., Pham, Q. V., Khan, F., Piran, M. J., & Dev, K. (2021). Blockchain for securing aerial communications: Potentials, solutions, and research directions. *Physical Communication, 47*, 1–19. doi:10.1016/j.phycom.2021.101390

Kumar, S., Tiwari, P., & Zymbler, M. (2019). Internet of Things is a revolutionary approach for future technology enhancement: A review. *Journal of Big Data, 6*(1), 1–21. doi:10.118640537-019-0268-2

Kuperberg, M. (2020, November). Towards enabling deletion in append-only blockchains to support data growth management and GDPR Compliance. In *2020 IEEE International Conference on Blockchain (Blockchain)* (pp. 393-400). IEEE. 10.1109/Blockchain50366.2020.00057

Kursh, S. R., & Gold, N. A. (2016). Adding fintech and blockchain to your curriculum. *Business Education Innovation Journal, 8*(2), 6–12.

Ladd, T., Jelezko, F., Laflamme, R., Nakamura, Y., Monroe, C., & O'Brien, J. (2010). Quantum computers. *Nature, 464*(7285), 45–53.

Lakhwani, K., Gianey, H. K., Wireko, J. K., & Hiran, K. K. (2020). *Internet of Things (IoT): Principles, Paradigms and Applications of IoT (English Edition).* https://www.amazon.in/Internet-Things-IoT-Principles-Applications-ebook/dp/B085DQ919Z

Lakhwani, K., Gianey, H. K., Wireko, J., & Hiran, K. K. (2020). *Internet of Things (IoT): Principles, Paradigms and applications of IoT.* BPB Publications.

Lakhwani, K., Gianey, H., Wireko, J., & Hiran, K. (2020). *Internet of Things (IoT): Principles, paradigms and applications of IoT.* BPB Publications.

Lal, C., & Marijan, D. (2020). *Blockchain for Healthcare: Opportunities, Challenges, and Future Directions.* Simula Research Laboratory. https://www.simula.no/publications/blockchain-healthcare-opportunities-challenges-and-future-directions

Lamarque, M., & Master. (2016). *The Blockchain Revolution: New Opportunities in Equity Markets.* https://dspace.mit.edu/handle/1721.1/104522

Lambertini. (2018). *Technology can help us save the planet. But more than anything, we must learn to value nature.* World Economic Forum.

Längkvist, M., Karlsson, L., & Loutfi, A. (2014). A review of unsupervised feature learning and deep learning for time-series modeling. *Pattern Recognition Letters, 42,* 11–24. doi:10.1016/j.patrec.2014.01.008

LaPierre, R. (2021). *Shor Algorithm.* doi:10.1007/978-3-030-69318-3_13

Latifi, S., Zhang, Y., & Cheng, L. C. (2019, July). Blockchain-based real estate market: One method for applying blockchain technology in commercial real estate market. In *2019 IEEE International Conference on Blockchain (Blockchain)* (pp. 528-535). IEEE. 10.1109/Blockchain.2019.00002

Latif, S., Idrees, Z., Huma, Z., & Ahmad, J. (2021). Blockchain technology for the industrial Internet of Things: A comprehensive survey on security challenges, architectures, applications, and future research directions. *Transactions on Emerging Telecommunications Technologies, 32*(11). Advance online publication. doi:10.1002/ett.4337

LeCun, Y., Bengio, Y., & Hinton, G. (2015). Deep learning. *Nature, 521*(7553), 436–444.

LeCun, Y., Bottou, L., Bengio, Y., & Haffner, P. (1998). Gradient-based learning applied to document recognition. *Proceedings of the IEEE, 86*(11), 2278–2324. doi:10.1109/5.726791

Li, B., & Wu, F. (2021). Post Quantum Blockchain with Segregation Witness. *2021 IEEE 6th International Conference on Computer and Communication Systems (ICCCS),* 522-527. 10.1109/ICCCS52626.2021.9449309

Li, S., & Tso, G. (2018). *Bottleneck supervised u-net for pixel-wise liver and tumor segmentation.* arXiv preprint arXiv:1810.10331.

Li, C. Y., Chen, X. B., Chen, Y. L., Hou, Y. Y., & Li, J. (2019). A New Lattice-Based Signature Scheme in Post-Quantum Blockchain Network. *IEEE Access: Practical Innovations, Open Solutions, 7*, 2026–2033. doi:10.1109/ACCESS.2018.2886554

Li, C., Tian, Y., Chen, X., & Li, J. (2021). An efficient anti-quantum lattice-based blind signature for blockchain-enabled systems. *Information Sciences, 546*, 253–264. doi:10.1016/j.ins.2020.08.032

Li, C., Xu, Y., Tang, J., & Liu, W. (2019). Quantum Blockchain: A Decentralized, Encrypted and Distributed Database Based on Quantum Mechanics. *Journal of Quantum Computing, 1*(2), 49–63. https://doi.org/10.32604/jqc.2019.06715

Li, D., Luo, Z., & Cao, B. (2021a). Blockchain-based federated learning methodologies in smart environments. *Cluster Computing*. Advance online publication. doi:10.100710586-021-03424-y PMID:34744493

Li, J., Sun, A., Han, J., & Li, C. (2020). A survey on deep learning for named entity recognition. *IEEE Transactions on Knowledge and Data Engineering, 34*(1), 50–70. doi:10.1109/TKDE.2020.2981314

Lin, W., Huang, X., Fang, H., Wang, V., Hua, Y., Wang, J., Yin, H., Yi, D., & Yau, L. (2020). Blockchain technology in current agricultural systems: From techniques to applications. *IEEE Access: Practical Innovations, Open Solutions, 8*, 143920–143937. doi:10.1109/ACCESS.2020.3014522

Li, T., & Yin, Z. Q. (2016). Quantum superposition, entanglement, and state teleportation of a microorganism on an electromechanical oscillator. *Science Bulletin, 61*(2), 163–171. doi:10.100711434-015-0990-x

Liu, Y., Sun, G., & Schuckers, S. (2019). Enabling Secure and Privacy Preserving Identity Management via Smart Contract. *2019 IEEE Conference on Communications and Network Security (CNS)*. 10.1109/CNS.2019.8802771

Li, W., Wu, J., Cao, J., Chen, N., Zhang, Q., & Buyya, R. (2021). Blockchain-based trust management in cloud computing systems: A taxonomy, review and future directions. *Journal of Cloud Computing, 10*(1), 35. Advance online publication. doi:10.118613677-021-00247-5

López-Incera, A., Hartmann, A., & Dür, W. (2020). Encrypt me! A game-based approach to Bell inequalities and quantum cryptography. *European Journal of Physics, 41*(6), 065702. Advance online publication. doi:10.1088/1361-6404/ab9a67

Lunesu, M. I., Tonelli, R., & Ioini, N. E. (2022). *Blockchain solutions for IoT*. https://www.frontiersin.org/research-topics/25758/blockchain-solutions-for-iot#overview

Macrinici, D., Cartofeanu, C., & Gao, S. (2018). Smart contract applications within blockchain technology: A systematic mapping study. *Telematics and Informatics, 35*(8), 2337–2354. doi:10.1016/j.tele.2018.10.004

Madakam, S., Lake, V., Lake, V., Lake, V., & ... (2015). Internet of Things (IoT): A literature review. *Journal of Computer and Communications, 3*(05), 164–173. doi:10.4236/jcc.2015.35021

Madine, M., Salah, K., Jayaraman, R., Al-Hammadi, Y., Arshad, J., & Yaqoob, I. (2021). appXchain: Application-Level Interoperability for Blockchain Networks. *IEEE Access: Practical Innovations, Open Solutions*, *9*, 87777–87791. doi:10.1109/ACCESS.2021.3089603

Mahrishi, M., Hiran, K. K., Meena, G., & Sharma, P. (2020). *Machine Learning and Deep Learning in Real-Time Applications*. IGI Global. https://www.igi-global.com/book/machine-learning-deep-learning-real/240152

Mahrishi, M., Hiran, K. K., Meena, G., & Sharma, P. (Eds.). (2020). Machine Learning and Deep Learning in Real-Time Applications. IGI Global.

Mahrishi, M., Hiran, K., Meena, G., & Sharma, P. (2020). *Machine Learning and Deep Learning in Real-Time Applications*. IGI Global. doi:10.4018/978-1-7998-3095-5

Makridakis, S., Polemitis, A., Giaglis, G., & Louca, S. (2018). *Blockchain: The Next Breakthrough in the Rapid Progress of AI*. Artificial Intelligence - Emerging Trends and Applications. doi:10.5772/intechopen.75668

Malik, S., Dedeoglu, V., Kanhere, S. S., & Jurdak, R. (2019, July). Trustchain: Trust management in blockchain and iot supported supply chains. In *2019 IEEE International Conference on Blockchain (Blockchain)* (pp. 184-193). IEEE. 10.1109/Blockchain.2019.00032

Mandal, S., Bera, B., Sutrala, A. K., Das, A. K., Choo, K. K. R., & Park, Y. (2020). Certificateless-Signcryption-Based Three-Factor User Access Control Scheme for IoT Environment. *IEEE Internet of Things Journal*, *7*(4), 3184–3197. doi:10.1109/JIOT.2020.2966242

Marsal-Llacuna, M. L. (2020). The people's smart city dashboard (PSCD): Delivering on community-led governance with blockchain. *Technological Forecasting and Social Change*, *158*, 1–11. doi:10.1016/j.techfore.2020.120150

Martin, G., & Chang, H. (2001). System-on-Chip design. In *ASICON 2001. 2001 4th International Conference on ASIC Proceedings* (Cat. No.01TH8549) (pp. 12-17). 10.1109/ICASIC.2001.982487

Mastronardi, G., & Tato, S. I. (2020). HoSè: Hospital Security - How to make the surgical site safer using RFID blockchain and biometric techniques. *2020 IEEE International Symposium on Medical Measurements and Applications (MeMeA)*. 10.1109/MeMeA49120.2020.9137348

Mathew, S., Gulia, S., Singh, V. P., & Sachin Dev, V. (2017). A Review Paper on Cloud Computing and Its Security Concerns. RICE. doi:10.15439/2017R70

Maulud, D., & Abdulazeez, A. (2020). A Review on Linear Regression Comprehensive in Machine Learning. *Journal of Applied Science and Technology Trends*, *1*(4), 140–147. doi:10.38094/jastt1457

Menaria, H. K., Nagar, P., & Patel, M. (2020). Tweet sentiment classification by semantic and frequency base features using hybrid classifier. In *First International Conference on Sustainable Technologies for Computational Intelligence* (pp. 107-123). Springer. 10.1007/978-981-15-0029-9_9

Mesnager, S., Sınak, A., & Yayla, O. (2020). Threshold-based post-quantum secure verifiable multi-secret sharing for distributed storage blockchain. *Mathematics*, *8*(12), 1–15. doi:10.3390/math8122218

Mijwil, M. M., Aggarwal, K., Doshi, R., Kant Hiran, K., Sundaravadivazhagan, B., & Mussanah, A. (2022). Deep Learning Techniques for COVID-19 Detection Based on Chest X-ray and CT-scan Images: A Short Review and Future Perspective Solving Traveling Salesman Problem (TSP) View project Digital Image Processing View project Deep Learning Techniques for COVID-19 Detection Based on Chest X-ray and CT-scan Images: A Short Review and Future Perspective. *Asian Journal of Applied Sciences*, *10*(3), 2321–0893. doi:10.24203/ajas.v10i3.6998

Milovanova, M. M., Markova, T. S., Mushrub, V., Ordynskaya, M. E., & Plaksa, J. V. (2020). Business education: Training in the use of blockchain technology for business development. *Revista Inclusiones*, 408-420.

Min, T., & Cai, W. (2019, June). A security case study for blockchain games. In *2019 IEEE Games, Entertainment, Media Conference (GEM)* (pp. 1-8). IEEE.

Mohamed, K. S. (2020). Cryptography Concepts: Integrity, Authentication, Availability, Access Control, and Non-repudiation. New Frontiers in Cryptography. doi:10.1007/978-3-030-58996-7_3

Monz, T., Nigg, D., Martinez, E. A., Brandl, M. F., Schindler, P., Rines, R., Wang, S. X., Chuang, I. L., & Blatt, R. (2016). Realization of a scalable Shor algorithm. *Science*, *351*(6277), 1068–1070. Advance online publication. doi:10.1126cience.aad9480 PMID:26941315

Morano, F., Ferretti, C., Leporati, A., Napoletano, P., & Schettini, R. (2019). A blockchain technology for protection and probative value preservation of vehicle driver data. *2019 IEEE 23rd International Symposium on Consumer Technologies (ISCT)*. 10.1109/ISCE.2019.8900982

Mosca, M. (2011). *Cybersecurity in an era with quantum computers: Will we be ready?* Academic Press.

Mosteanu, N. R., & Faccia, A. (2021). Fintech frontiers in quantum computing, fractals, and blockchain distributed ledger: Paradigm shifts and open innovation. *Journal of Open Innovation*, *7*(1), 19. Advance online publication. doi:10.3390/joitmc7010019

Motlagh, N. H., Mohammadrezaei, M., Hunt, J., & Zakeri, B. (2020). Internet of things (IoT) and the energy sector. *Energies*, *13*(2), 1–27. doi:10.3390/en13020494

Musale, M., & Joshi, R. (2021). Compendious Comparison of Capsule Network and Convolutional Neural Network through end-to-end Digit Classification Application. In *International Journal of Intelligent Communication*. Computing and Networks.

Naganuma, K., Suzuki, T., Yoshino, M., Takahashi, K., Kaga, Y., & Kunihiro, N. (2020). New Secret Key Management Technology for Blockchains from Biometrics Fuzzy Signature. *2020 15th Asia Joint Conference on Information Security (AsiaJCIS)*. 10.1109/AsiaJCIS50894.2020.00020

Nair, S., Gupta, A., Joshi, R., & Chitre, V. (2022). *Combining Varied Learners for Binary Classification using Stacked Generalization*. arXiv preprint arXiv:2202.08910.

Nakamoto, S. (2009). Bitcoin: A Peer-to-Peer Electronic Cash System. Academic Press.

Nakamoto, S. (2016). *Bitcoin: A Peer-to-Peer Electronic Cash System.* Available: https://bitcoin.org/bitcoin.pdf

Natekin, A., & Knoll, A. (2013). Gradient boosting machines, a tutorial. *Frontiers in Neurorobotics, 7.* PMID:24409142

Niemi, H. (2021). AI in learning: Preparing grounds for future learning. *Journal of Pacific Rim Psychology, 15.* Advance online publication. doi:10.1177/18344909211038105

Nieto-Chaupis, H. (2019). Description of Processes of Blockchain and Cryptocurrency with Quantum Mechanics Theory. *IEEE CHILEAN Conference on Electrical, Electronics Engineering, Information and Communication Technologies, CHILECON 2019, 7,* 31–34. 10.1109/CHILECON47746.2019.8988006

Noether, S., Mackenzie, A., & Research Lab, T. M. (2016). Ring Confidential Transactions. *Ledger, 1,* 1–18. doi:10.5195/ledger.2016.34

O'Neill, J. (2001). Markets and the environment: Domesday scenario. *Economic and Political Weekly, 411*(8954), 1865–1873.

Omar, I. A., Jayaraman, R., Salah, K., Yaqoob, I., & Ellahham, S. (2021). Applications of blockchain technology in clinical trials: Review and open challenges. *Arabian Journal for Science and Engineering, 46*(4), 3001–3015. doi:10.100713369-020-04989-3

Oord, A., Dieleman, S., Zen, H., Simonyan, K., Vinyals, O., Graves, A., Kalchbrenner, N., Senior, A., & Kavukcuoglu, K. (2016). *Wavenet: A generative model for raw audio.* arXiv preprint arXiv:1609.03499.

Opitz, D., & Maclin, R. (1999). Popular ensemble methods: An empirical study. *Journal of Artificial Intelligence Research, 11,* 169–198. doi:10.1613/jair.614

Othman, A., & Callahan, J. (2018). The Horcrux Protocol: A Method for Decentralized Biometric-based Self-sovereign Identity. *2018 International Joint Conference on Neural Networks (IJCNN).* 10.1109/IJCNN.2018.8489316

Pamecha, S., & Sharma, P. (2022). Waste Management Under Swachh Bharat Mission With Reference to National Green Tribunal's Guidelines in Smart City Udaipur. *Sanshodhan, 11*(1), 12. doi:10.53957anshodhan/2022/v11i1/169814

Pane, J., Verhamme, K. M., Shrum, L., Rebollo, I., & Sturkenboom, M. C. (2020). Blockchain technology applications to postmarket surveillance of medical devices. *Expert Review of Medical Devices, 17*(10), 1123–1132. doi:10.1080/17434440.2020.1825073 PMID:32954855

Parry, I. (2019). Putting a price on pollution. *Finance & Development, 56*(4), 16–19.

Patel, S., Vyas, A. K., & Hiran, K. K. (2022). *Infrastructure Health Monitoring Using Signal Processing Based on an Industry 4.0 System, Cyber-physical Systems and Industry 4.0: Practical Applications and Security Management*. Academic Press.

Patel, S., Vyas, A. K., & Hiran, K. K. (2022). Infrastructure Health Monitoring Using Signal Processing Based on an Industry 4.0 System. *Cyber-Physical Systems and Industry 4.0: Practical Applications and Security Management*, 249-260.

Patel, S., Vyas, A., & Hiran, K. (2022). Infrastructure Health Monitoring Using Signal Processing Based on an Industry 4.0 System. *Cyber-Physical Systems and Industry 4.0: Practical Applications and Security Management*, 249–260.

Paul, P. K., Aithal, P. S., Bhuimali, A., & Kumar, K. (2017). Emerging Degrees and Collaboration: The Context of Engineering Sciences in Computing & IT—An Analysis for Enhanced Policy Formulation in India. *International Journal on Recent Researches In Science. Engineering & Technology*, 5(12), 13–27.

Paul, P. K., Bhuimali, A., & Chatterjee, D. (2016). Retail Informatics: Basics and emerging scenario with special reference to Design and Development of Proposed MSc-Information Science (Retail Informatics) in Indian Scenario. *International Journal of Information Dissemination and Technology*, 6(2), 140–144.

Peng, C.-Y. J., Lee, K. L., & Ingersoll, G. M. (2002). An Introduction to Logistic Regression Analysis and Reporting. *The Journal of Educational Research*, 96(1), 3–14. doi:10.1080/00220670209598786

Permenkes. (2018). Performance Analysis of Blockchain Platforms. *Master Thesis, 10*(2), 1–15.

Pillai, B., Biswas, K., & Muthukkumarasamy, V. (2020). Cross-chain interoperability among blockchain-based systems using transactions. *The Knowledge Engineering Review*, 35, 35. doi:10.1017/S0269888920000314

Politi, A., Matthews, J., & O'brien, J. (2009). Shor's quantum factoring algorithm on a photonic chip. *Science*, 325(5945), 1221–1221. doi:10.1126cience.1173731 PMID:19729649

Pólvora, A., Nascimento, S., Lourenço, J. S., & Scapolo, F. (2020). Blockchain for industrial transformations: A forward-looking approach with multi-stakeholder engagement for policy advice. *Technological Forecasting and Social Change*, 157, 1–18. doi:10.1016/j.techfore.2020.120091

Priyadarshi, N., Padmanaban, S., Hiran, K. K., Holm-Nielsen, K. B., & Bansal, R. C. (Eds.). (2021). *Artificial Intelligence and Internet of Things for Renewable Energy Systems* (Vol. 12). Walter de Gruyter GmbH&Co KG.

Prokhorenkova, L., Gusev, G., Vorobev, A., Dorogush, A., & Gulin, A. (2018). CatBoost: Unbiased boosting with categorical features. *Advances in Neural Information Processing Systems*, 31.

Proos, J., & Zalka, C. (2003). *Shor's discrete logarithm quantum algorithm for elliptic curves*. arXiv preprint quant-ph/0301141.

Putz, B., & Pernul, G. (2020, November). Detecting blockchain security threats. In *2020 IEEE International Conference on Blockchain (Blockchain)* (pp. 313-320). IEEE. 10.1109/Blockchain50366.2020.00046

QRL. (2022). *Quantum Resistant Ledger. The Future of Post-Quantum Resistant Blockchain.* https://www.theqrl.org/the-future-of-post-quantum-resistant-blockchains/

Quantum Blockchain. (2020). doi:10.1142/9781786348210_0006

Quantum Cryptography vs Post-Quantum Cryptography. (n.d.). *FedTech Magazine.*

Quarmby, B. (2022). *JPMorgan unveils research on quantum resistant blockchain network.* https://cointelegraph.com/news/jpmorgan-unveils-research-on-quantum-resistant-blockchain-network

Quinlan, J. (1986). Induction of Decision Trees. *Machine Learning, 1*(1), 81–106. doi:10.1007/BF00116251

Radanović, I., & Likić, R. (2018). Opportunities for use of blockchain technology in medicine. *Applied Health Economics and Health Policy, 16*(5), 583–590. doi:10.100740258-018-0412-8 PMID:30022440

Rajan, D., & Visser, M. (2019). Quantum blockchain using entanglement in time. *Quantum Reports, 1*(1), 1–9. doi:10.3390/quantum1010002

Ramayah, T., Ahmad, N. H., Halim, H. A., Siti, R. M. Z., & Lo, M.-C. (2010). Discriminant analysis: An illustrated example. *African Journal of Business Management, 4,* 1654–1667.

Rawung, R., & Putrada, A. (2014). Cyber physical system: Paper survey. In *2014 International Conference on ICT For Smart Society (ICISS)* (pp. 273-278). Academic Press.

Redmon, J., Divvala, S., Girshick, R., & Farhadi, A. (2016). You only look once: Unified, real-time object detection. In *Proceedings of the IEEE conference on computer vision and pattern recognition* (pp. 779–788). 10.1109/CVPR.2016.91

Regoniel, P. (2020). *Environmental and Natural Resources: 3 Key Differences.* https://simplyeducate.me/2020/09/28/environmental-and-natural-resources/

Rehman, H., Asif, M., & Ahmad, M. (2017). Future applications and research challenges of IOT. In *2017 International Conference on Information and Communication Technologies (ICICT)* (pp. 68-74). 10.1109/ICICT.2017.8320166

Ren, S., He, K., Girshick, R., & Sun, J. (2015). Faster r-cnn: Towards real-time object detection with region proposal networks. *Advances in Neural Information Processing Systems, 28.*

Rivest, R., Shamir, A., & Adleman, L. (1978). A Method for Obtaining Digital Signatures and Public-Key Cryptosystems. *Communications of the ACM, 21*(2), 120–126. doi:10.1145/359340.359342

Rodenburg, B., & Pappas, S. P. (2017). *Blockchain and Quantum Computing.* Mitre Technical Report. https://www.mitre.org/sites/default/files/publications/17-4039-blockchain-and-quantum-computing.pdf

Roetteler, M., Naehrig, M., Svore, K., & Lauter, K. (2017). Quantum resource estimates for computing elliptic curve discrete logarithms. In *International Conference on the Theory and Application of Cryptology and Information Security* (pp. 241–270). 10.1007/978-3-319-70697-9_9

Roman, J., Estes, J. A., Morissette, L., Smith, C., Costa, D., McCarthy, J., Nation, J. B., Nicol, S., Pershing, A., & Smetacek, V. (2014). Whales as marine ecosystem engineers. *Frontiers in Ecology and the Environment, 12*(7), 377–385. doi:10.1890/130220

Ronneberger, O., Fischer, P., & Brox, T. (2015). U-net: Convolutional networks for biomedical image segmentation. In *International Conference on Medical image computing and computer-assisted intervention* (pp. 234–241). 10.1007/978-3-319-24574-4_28

Ruder, S. (2016). *An overview of gradient descent optimization algorithms.* arXiv preprint arXiv:1609.04747.

Russakovsky, O., Deng, J., Su, H., Krause, J., Satheesh, S., Ma, S., Huang, Z., Karpathy, A., Khosla, A., Bernstein, M., Berg, A. C., & Fei-Fei, L. (2015). Imagenet large scale visual recognition challenge. *International Journal of Computer Vision, 115*(3), 211–252. doi:10.100711263-015-0816-y

Saini, H. K., Jain, K. L., Hiran, K. K., & Bhati, A. (2021). Paradigms to make smart city using blockchain. *Blockchain 3.0 for Sustainable Development, 10*, 21.

Saini, H. K., Jain, K. L., Hiran, K. K., & Bhati, A. (2021). Paradigms to make smart city using blockchain. Blockchain 3.0 for Sustainable Development.

Sakhipov, A. A., & Baygozhanova, D. S. (2020). Blockchain Technology in Education. *Scientific Evolution*, (1), 36–39.

Salman, T., Jain, R., & Gupta, L. (2019, July). A reputation management framework for knowledge-based and probabilistic blockchains. In *2019 IEEE International Conference on Blockchain (Blockchain)* (pp. 520-527). IEEE. 10.1109/Blockchain.2019.00078

Sang, Z., & Li, K. (2019). ITU-T standardization activities on smart sustainable cities. *IET Smart Cities, 1*(1), 3–9. doi:10.1049/iet-smc.2019.0023

Sarker, I. (2021). Machine learning: Algorithms, real-world applications and research directions. *SN Computer Science, 2*(3), 1–21. doi:10.100742979-021-00592-x PMID:33778771

Sarmah, S. S. (2019). Application of block chain in cloud computing. *International Journal of Innovative Technology and Exploring Engineering, 8*(12), 4698–4704. Advance online publication. doi:10.35940/ijitee.L3585.1081219

Sattath, O. (2020). On the insecurity of quantum Bitcoin mining. *International Journal of Information Security, 19*(3), 291–302. https://doi.org/10.1007/s10207-020-00493-9

Sawant, G., & Bharadi, V. (2020). Permission Blockchain based Smart Contract Utilizing Biometric Authentication as a Service: A Future Trend. *2020 International Conference on Convergence to Digital World - Quo Vadis (ICCDW)*. 10.1109/ICCDW45521.2020.9318715

Schapire, R. (1999). A Brief Introduction to Boosting. In *Proceedings of the 16th International Joint Conference on Artificial Intelligence* - Volume 2 (pp. 1401–1406). Morgan Kaufmann Publishers Inc.

SchlapkohlK. (2020). The future of blockchain. https://www.ibm.com/blogs/blockchain/2020/04/the-future-of-blockchain/

Schulz, K., & Feist, M. (2021). Leveraging blockchain technology for innovative climate finance under the Green Climate Fund. *Earth System Governance*, 7, 1–10. doi:10.1016/j.esg.2020.100084

Selvaraj, S., & Sundaravaradhan, S. (2020). Challenges and opportunities in IoT healthcare systems : A systematic review. *SN Applied Sciences*, 2(1), 1–8. doi:10.100742452-019-1925-y

Sengupta, J., Ruj, S., & Das Bit, S. (2020). A Comprehensive Survey on Attacks, Security Issues and Blockchain Solutions for IoT and IIoT. *Journal of Network and Computer Applications*, 149, 1–20. doi:10.1016/j.jnca.2019.102481

Seon, C. (2021). Blockchain for IoT-based smart cities : Recent advances, requirements, and future challenges. *Journal of Network and Computer Applications*, 181(February), 103007. doi:10.1016/j.jnca.2021.103007

Shahriar, M. A., Bappy, F. H., Hossain, A. K. M. F., Saikat, D. D., Ferdous, M. S., Chowdhury, M. J. M., & Bhuiyan, M. Z. A. (2020). Modelling attacks in blockchain systems using petri nets. *Proceedings - 2020 IEEE 19th International Conference on Trust, Security and Privacy in Computing and Communications, TrustCom 2020*, 1069–1078. doi:10.1109/TrustCom50675.2020.00142

Shalendra Singh Rao, M. D. (n.d.). Impact of Foreign Direct Investment in Indian Capital Market. *International Journal of Research in Economics and Social Sciences*, 7(6), 172–178.

Shankar, T. N., Rakesh, P., Bhargawa Rao, T., Hari Bharadwaj, L., Rakesh, C., & Lakshmi Madhuri, M. (2021). Providing Security to Land Record with the computation of Iris, Blockchain, and One Time Password. *2021 International Conference on Computing, Communication, and Intelligent Systems (ICCCIS)*. 10.1109/ICCCIS51004.2021.9397176

Shan, Z., Zhang, Y., Zhang, Y., Tang, S., & Wang, W. (2021). A review of recent progress and developments in China smart cities. *IET Smart Cities*, 3(4), 189–200. doi:10.1049mc2.12020

Sharma, T. K. (2022). *Blockchain Operating System_A Complete Overview*. Blockchain Counsil. https://www.blockchain-council.org/blockchain/blockchain-operating-system-a-complete-overview/

Sharma, P., Bhatia, V., & Prakash, S. (2021). Securing Optical Networks using Quantum-secured Blockchain: An Overview. *IEEE Journal of Quantum Electronics*, 1–7. https://arxiv.org/abs/2105.10663

Sharma, P., Jindal, R., & Borah, M. D. (2022). A review of smart contract-based platforms, applications, and challenges. *Cluster Computing*, 1, 1–27. doi:10.100710586-021-03491-1

Sharma, R., Kamble, S. S., Gunasekaran, A., Kumar, V., & Kumar, A. (2020). A systematic literature review on machine learning applications for sustainable agriculture supply chain performance. *Computers & Operations Research, 119*, 1–12. doi:10.1016/j.cor.2020.104926

Sheikh, R., Patel, M., & Sinhal, A. (2020). Recognizing MNIST handwritten data set using PCA and LDA. In *International Conference on Artificial Intelligence: Advances and Applications 2019* (pp. 169177). Springer. 10.1007/978-981-15-1059-5_20

Shinde, P., & Shah, S. (2018). A Review of Machine Learning and Deep Learning Applications. In *2018 Fourth International Conference on Computing Communication Control and Automation (ICCUBEA)* (pp. 1-6). 10.1109/ICCUBEA.2018.8697857

Shor, P. (1999). Polynomial-time algorithms for prime factorization and discrete logarithms on a quantum computer. *SIAM Review, 41*(2), 303–332. doi:10.1137/S0036144598347011

Shor, P. W. (1997). Polynomial-time algorithms for prime factorization and discrete logarithms on a quantum computer. *SIAM Journal on Computing, 26*(5), 1484–1509. https://doi.org/10.1137/S0097539795293172

Sigurdsson, G., Giaretta, A., & Dragoni, N. (2020). Vulnerabilities and Security Breaches in Cryptocurrencies. *Advances in Intelligent Systems and Computing, 925*(March), 288–299. doi:10.1007/978-3-030-14687-0_26

Simonyan, K., & Zisserman, A. (2014). *Very deep convolutional networks for large-scale image recognition*. arXiv preprint arXiv:1409.1556.

Siyal, A. A., Junejo, A. Z., Zawish, M., Ahmed, K., Khalil, A., & Soursou, G. (2019). Applications of blockchain technology in medicine and healthcare: Challenges and future perspectives. *Cryptography, 3*(1), 3. doi:10.3390/cryptography3010003

Solaiman, E., Wike, T., & Sfyrakis, I. (2021). Implementation and evaluation of smart contracts using a hybrid on- and off-blockchain architecture. *Concurrency and Computation, 33*(1), 1–17. doi:10.1002/cpe.5811

Somy, N. B., Kannan, K., Arya, V., Hans, S., Singh, A., Lohia, P., & Mehta, S. (2019, July). Ownership preserving AI market places using blockchain. In *2019 IEEE International Conference on Blockchain (Blockchain)* (pp. 156-165). IEEE. 10.1109/Blockchain.2019.00029

Sonnino, A., & Sonnino, G. (2016). *Elliptic-Curves Cryptography on High-Dimensional Surfaces*. arXiv preprint arXiv:1610.01518.

Staudemeyer, R., & Morris, E. (2019). *Understanding LSTM–a tutorial into long short-term memory recurrent neural networks*. arXiv preprint arXiv:1909.09586.

Stewart, I., Ilie, D. I., Zamyatin, A., Werner, S. M., Torshizi, M. F., & Knottenbelt, W. J. (2018). Committing to quantum resistance: A slow defence for Bitcoin against a fast quantum computing attack. *Royal Society Open Science, 5*(6), 5. doi:10.1098/rsos.180410 PMID:30110420

Sun, X., Wang, Q., Kulicki, P., & Zhao, X. (2018). Quantum-enhanced Logic-based Blockchain I: Quantum Honest-success Byzantine Agreement and Qulogicoin. https://arxiv.org/abs/1805.06768

Sun, J., Yan, J., & Zhang, K. Z. (2016). Blockchain-based sharing services: What blockchain technology can contribute to smart cities. *Financial Innovation*, 2(1), 1–9. doi:10.118640854-016-0040-y

Sun, X., Kulicki, P., & Sopek, M. (2020). Lottery and auction on quantum blockchain. *Entropy (Basel, Switzerland)*, 22(12), 1–9. doi:10.3390/e22121377 PMID:33279922

Sun, X., Sopek, M., Wang, Q., & Kulicki, P. (2019). Towards quantum-secured permissioned blockchain: Signature, consensus, and logic. *Entropy (Basel, Switzerland)*, 21(9), 1–15. doi:10.3390/e21090887

Sun, X., Wang, Q., Kulicki, P., & Sopek, M. (2019). A Simple Voting Protocol on Quantum Blockchain. *International Journal of Theoretical Physics*, 58(1), 275–281. doi:10.100710773-018-3929-6

Szegedy, C., Liu, W., Jia, Y., Sermanet, P., Reed, S., Anguelov, D., Erhan, D., Vanhoucke, V., & Rabinovich, A. (2015). Going deeper with convolutions. In *Proceedings of the IEEE conference on computer vision and pattern recognition* (pp. 1–9). IEEE.

Tambe, S., Joshi, R., Gupta, A., Kanvinde, N., & Chitre, V. (2022). *Effects of Parametric and Non-Parametric Methods on High Dimensional Sparse Matrix Representations*. arXiv preprint arXiv:2202.02894.

Tasatanattakool, P., & Techapanupreeda, C. (2018, January). Blockchain: Challenges and applications. In *2018 International Conference on Information Networking (ICOIN)* (pp. 473-475). IEEE.

Teskey, R. O., Saveyn, A., Steppe, K., & McGuire, M. A. (2008). Origin, fate and significance of CO_2 in tree stems. *The New Phytologist*, 177(1), 17–32. doi:10.1111/j.1469-8137.2007.02286.x PMID:18028298

Tezel, A., Papadonikolaki, E., Yitmen, I., & Hilletofth, P. (2020). Preparing construction supply chains for blockchain technology: An investigation of its potential and future directions. *Frontiers of Engineering Management*, 7(4), 547–563. doi:10.100742524-020-0110-8

The Paris Agreement. (n.d.). https://unfccc.int/process-and-meetings/the-paris-agreement/the-paris-agreement

Thompson, D. (2021). *Why Quantum Resistance Is the Next Blockchain Frontier*. https://www.techtimes.com/articles/264625/20210826/why-quantum-resistance-is-the-next-blockchain-frontier.htm

Thuraisingham, B. (2020, October). Blockchain technologies and their applications in data science and cyber security. In *2020 3rd international conference on smart blockchain (SmartBlock)* (pp. 1-4). IEEE. 10.1109/SmartBlock52591.2020.00008

Tie-xiong, S. U., Shi-wen, Y., Zhi-qin, G., Xiao-lei, L. I., Bao-cheng, Z., & Yi, Z. (2001). Review on dynamic. Simulation model of complex structural joints. *Huabei Gongxueyuan Xuebao/ Journal of North China Institute of Technology, 22*(3), 221–222.

Torino, P. (2019). *Introduction to Post-Quantum Cryptography*. Academic Press.

Toutara, F., & Spathoulas, G. (2020). A distributed biometric authentication scheme based on blockchain. *2020 IEEE International Conference on Blockchain (Blockchain)*. 10.1109/Blockchain50366.2020.00068

Tribis, Y., El Bouchti, A., & Bouayad, H. (2018). Supply chain management based on blockchain: A systematic mapping study. *MATEC Web of Conferences, 200*. 10.1051/matecconf/201820000020

Trichni, S., Omary, F., & Bougrine, M. (2022). New Blockchain Protocol for Partial Confidentiality and Transparency (PPCT). *International Journal of Advanced Computer Science and Applications, 13*(2). Advance online publication. doi:10.14569/IJACSA.2022.0130273

Tyagi, S. K. S., Mukherjee, A., Pokhrel, S. R., & Hiran, K. (2020a). An Intelligent and Optimal Resource Allocation Approach in Sensor Networks for Smart Agri-IoT. *Smart Agri-IoT. IEEE Sensors Journal, 21*(16), 17439–17446. https://doi.org/10.1109/JSEN.2020.3020889

UN News. (2021). *Sustainability solution or climate calamity? The dangers and promise of cryptocurrency technology*. https://news.un.org/en/story/2021/06/1094362

V., S., Sarkar, A., Paul, A., & Mishra, S. (2019). Block Chain Based Cloud Computing Model on EVM Transactions for Secure Voting. *2019 3rd International Conference on Computing Methodologies and Communication (ICCMC)*. doi:10.1109/ICCMC.2019.8819649

Van Den Bosch, H. (2020). Humane by choice, smart by default: 39 building blocks for cities of the future. *IET Smart Cities, 2*(3), 111–121. doi:10.1049/iet-smc.2020.0030

Van Hijfte, S. (2020). Blockchain and Other Emerging Technologies. In *Decoding Blockchain for Business*. Apress. doi:10.1007/978-1-4842-6137-8_2

Van Trinh, T. (2020). *Quantum-safe Bitcoin How to protect blockchain systems from quantum-computer attacks*. University of Oslo.

Vaswani, A., Shazeer, N., Parmar, N., Uszkoreit, J., Jones, L., Gomez, A. K., & Polosukhin, I. (2017). Attention is all you need. Advances in neural information processing systems, 30.

Vigliotti, M. G., & Jones, H. (2020). The Future of the Blockchain. In *The Executive Guide to Blockchain*. Palgrave Macmillan. doi:10.1007/978-3-030-21107-3_10

Vignesh, V., Gopalan, S. H., Mohan, M., Ramya, R. S., & Ananthakumar, R. (2021). A Quantum-Based Blockchain Approach to Voting Protocol Using Hyperledger Sawtooth. *Journal of Physics: Conference Series, 1916*(1), 012088. Advance online publication. doi:10.1088/1742-6596/1916/1/012088

Viriyasitavat, W., Da Xu, L., Bi, Z., & Hoonsopon, D. (2019). Blockchain technology for applications in internet of things—Mapping from system design perspective. *IEEE Internet of Things Journal*, *6*(5), 8155–8168. doi:10.1109/JIOT.2019.2925825

Vujicic, D., Jagodic, D., & Randic, S. (2018). Blockchain technology, bitcoin, and Ethereum: A brief overview. *2018 17th International Symposium INFOTEH-JAHORINA (INFOTEH)*, 1-6.

Vyas, A. K., Dhiman, H., & Hiran, K. K. (2021). Modelling of symmetrical quadrature optical ring resonator with four different topologies and performance analysis using machine learning approach. *Journal of Optical Communications*. doi:10.1515/joc-2020-0270

Waheed, A., & Venkata Krishna, P. (2020). Comparing Biometric and Blockchain Security Mechanisms in Smart Parking System. *2020 International Conference on Inventive Computation Technologies (ICICT)*. 10.1109/ICICT48043.2020.9112483

Wang, Q., Li, R., Wang, Q., & Chen, S. (2021). *Non-fungible token (NFT): Overview, evaluation, opportunities and challenges.* arXiv preprint arXiv:2105.07447.

Wang, L. J., Zhang, K. Y., Wang, J. Y., Cheng, J., Yang, Y. H., Tang, S. B., Yan, D., Tang, Y. L., Liu, Z., Yu, Y., Zhang, Q., & Pan, J. W. (2021). Experimental authentication of quantum key distribution with post-quantum cryptography. *NPJ Quantum Information*, *7*(1), 67. Advance online publication. doi:10.103841534-021-00400-7

Wang, L., & Wang, Y. (2022). Supply chain financial service management system based on block chain IoT data sharing and edge computing. *Alexandria Engineering Journal*, *61*(1), 147–158. Advance online publication. doi:10.1016/j.aej.2021.04.079

Wang, P., Chen, X., & Jiang, G. (2022). Quantum Demiric-Selcuk Meet-in-the-Middle Attacks on Reduced-Round AES. *International Journal of Theoretical Physics*, *61*(1), 5. Advance online publication. doi:10.100710773-022-05003-2

Wan, L., Eyers, D., & Zhang, H. (2019, July). Evaluating the impact of network latency on the safety of blockchain transactions. In *2019 IEEE International Conference on Blockchain (Blockchain)* (pp. 194-201). IEEE. 10.1109/Blockchain.2019.00033

We must address the security risks posed by quantum computers. (n.d.). *World Economic Forum.* https://www.weforum.org/agenda/2020/06/quantum-computers-security-challenges/

Weking, J., Mandalenakis, M., Hein, A., Hermes, S., Böhm, M., & Krcmar, H. (2020). The impact of blockchain technology on business models – a taxonomy and archetypal patterns. *Electronic Markets*, *30*(2), 285–305. doi:10.100712525-019-00386-3

Wen, Chen, Fan, Yi, Jiang, & Fang. (2021). Quantum blockchain system. *Modern Physics Letters B, 35*(20). doi:10.1142/S0217984921503437

Williams, P. (2019). Does competency-based education with blockchain signal a new mission for universities? *Journal of Higher Education Policy and Management*, *41*(1), 104–117. doi:10.1080/1360080X.2018.1520491

Wireko, J. K., Hiran, K. K., & Doshi, R. (2018). Culturally based User Resistance to New Technologies in the Age of IoT in Developing Countries: Perspectives from Ethiopia. *International Journal of Emerging Technology and Advanced Engineering.* https://vbn.aau.dk/en/publications/culturally-based-user-resistance-to-new-technologies-in-the-age-o

Wireko, J. K., Brenya, B., & Doshi, R. (2021). Financial Impact of Internet Access Infrastructure of Online Learning Mode on Tertiary Students in Covid-19 Era in Ghana. *2021 International Conference on Computing, Communication and Green Engineering, CCGE 2021.* 10.1109/CCGE50943.2021.9776422

Wireko, J. K., Hiran, K. K., & Doshi, R. (2018). Culturally Based User Resistance to New Technologies in the Age of IoT In Developing Countries: Perspectives From Ethiopia. *International Journal of Emerging Technology and Advanced Engineering, 8*(4), 96–105.

Wolpert, D. H. (1992). Stacked generalization. *Neural Networks, 5*(2), 241–259. doi:10.1016/S0893-6080(05)80023-1

World Economic Forum. (2021). *Is your cybersecurity ready to take the quantum leap?* World Economic Forum. https://www.weforum.org/agenda/2021/05/cybersecurity-quantum-computing-algorithms/

Wu, C., Ke, L., & Du, Y. (2021). Quantum resistant key-exposure free chameleon hash and applications in redactable blockchain. *Information Sciences, 548,* 438–449. doi:10.1016/j.ins.2020.10.008

Xiang, X., Wang, M., & Fan, W. (2020). A Permissioned Blockchain-Based Identity Management and User Authentication Scheme for E-Health Systems. *IEEE Access: Practical Innovations, Open Solutions, 8,* 171771–171783. doi:10.1109/ACCESS.2020.3022429

Xiang, X., & Zhao, X. (2022). Blockchain-assisted searchable attribute-based encryption for e-health systems. *Journal of Systems Architecture, 124,* 1–15. doi:10.1016/j.sysarc.2022.102417

Xie, G., Liu, Y., Xin, G., & Yang, Q. (2021). Blockchain-Based Cloud Data Integrity Verification Scheme with High Efficiency. *Security and Communication Networks, 2021,* 1–15. Advance online publication. doi:10.1155/2021/9921209

Xu, M., Zhao, F., Zou, Y., Liu, C., Cheng, X., & Dressler, F. (2022). BLOWN: A Blockchain Protocol for Single-Hop Wireless Networks under Adversarial SINR. *IEEE Transactions on Mobile Computing,* 1. Advance online publication. doi:10.1109/TMC.2022.3162117

Xu, X., Weber, I., & Staples, M. (2019). Blockchain in Software Architecture. In *Architecture for Blockchain Applications* (pp. 83–92). Springer. doi:10.1007/978-3-030-03035-3_5

Yamashita, R., Nishio, M., Do, R., & Togashi, K. (2018). Convolutional neural networks: An overview and application in radiology. *Insights Into Imaging, 9*(4), 611–629. doi:10.100713244-018-0639-9 PMID:29934920

Yang, X. M., Li, X., Wu, H. Q., & Zhao, K. Y. (2017). The application model and challenges of blockchain technology in education. *Modern Distance Education Research, 2,* 34-45.

Yang, C. S. (2019). Maritime shipping digitalization: Blockchain-based technology applications, future improvements, and intention to use. *Transportation Research Part E, Logistics and Transportation Review*, *131*, 108–117. doi:10.1016/j.tre.2019.09.020

Yapa, C., de Alwis, C., Liyanage, M., & Ekanayake, J. (2021). Survey on blockchain for future smart grids: Technical aspects, applications, integration challenges and future research. *Energy Reports*, *7*, 6530–6564. doi:10.1016/j.egyr.2021.09.112

Yaqin, A., Dahlan, A., & Hermawan, R. (2019). Implementation of Algorithm Rabin-Karp for Thematic Determination of Thesis. In *2019 4th International Conference on Information Technology, Information Systems and Electrical Engineering (ICITISEE)* (pp. 395-400). Academic Press.

Yazdinejad, A., Srivastava, G., Parizi, R. M., Dehghantanha, A., Choo, K. K. R., & Aledhari, M. (2020). Decentralized Authentication of Distributed Patients in Hospital Networks Using Blockchain. *IEEE Journal of Biomedical and Health Informatics*, *24*(8), 2146–2156. doi:10.1109/JBHI.2020.2969648 PMID:31995507

Yi, H. (2022, May 1). Secure Social Internet of Things Based on Post-Quantum Blockchain. *IEEE Transactions on Network Science and Engineering*, *9*(3), 950–957. Advance online publication. doi:10.1109/TNSE.2021.3095192

Yin, W., Wen, Q., Li, W., Zhang, H., & Jin, Z. (2017). An anti-quantum transaction authentication approach in blockchain. *IEEE Access: Practical Innovations, Open Solutions*, *6*, 5393–5401. doi:10.1109/ACCESS.2017.2788411

Yu, S., Lv, K., Shao, Z., Guo, Y., Zou, J., & Zhang, B. (2018, August). A high performance blockchain platform for intelligent devices. In *2018 1st IEEE international conference on hot information-centric networking (HotICN)* (pp. 260-261). IEEE. 10.1109/HOTICN.2018.8606017

Yuan, B., Wu, F., Qiu, W., Wang, W., Zhu, H., & Zhou, D. (2021). Blockchain-Based Infrastructure for Artificial Intelligence with Quantum Resistant. *2021 4th International Conference on Artificial Intelligence and Big Data (ICAIBD)*, 627-631. 10.1109/ICAIBD51990.2021.9458982

Zhang, P., Wang, L., Wang, W., Fu, K., & Wang, J. (2021). A Blockchain System Based on Quantum-Resistant Digital Signature. *Security and Communication Networks, 2021*(2). doi:10.1155/2021/6671648

Zhang, P., Wang, L., Wang, W., Fu, K., Wang, J., & He, D. (2021). A Blockchain System Based on Quantum-Resistant Digital Signature. *Sec. and Commun. Netw., 2021*.

Zhang, H., Ji, Z., Wang, H., & Wu, W. (2019). Survey on quantum information security. *China Communications*, *16*(10), 1–36. Advance online publication. doi:10.23919/JCC.2019.10.001

Zhang, P. (2022). Quantum Attacks on Sum of Even–Mansour Construction with Linear Key Schedules. *Entropy (Basel, Switzerland)*, *24*(2), 153. Advance online publication. doi:10.3390/e24020153 PMID:35205449

Zhang, S., & Lee, J. H. (2020). Analysis of the main consensus protocols of blockchain. *ICT Express*, *6*(2), 93–97. Advance online publication. doi:10.1016/j.icte.2019.08.001

Zhang, Y., Jin, R., & Zhou, Z. H. (2010). Understanding bag-of-words model: A statistical framework. *International Journal of Machine Learning and Cybernetics*, *1*(1), 43–52. doi:10.100713042-010-0001-0

Zhao, G., Liu, S., Lopez, C., Lu, H., Elgueta, S., Chen, H., & Boshkoska, B. M. (2019). Blockchain technology in agri-food value chain management: A synthesis of applications, challenges and future research directions. *Computers in Industry*, *109*, 83–99. doi:10.1016/j.compind.2019.04.002

Zheng, W., & Ren, Z. (2010). Field Programmable Gate Array Design and Implementation for Fast Fourior Transform Processor. In *2010 International Conference on E-Business and E-Government* (pp. 4039-4042). 10.1109/ICEE.2010.1014

Zhu, H., Wang, X., Chen, C. M., & Kumari, S. (2020). Two novel semi-quantum-reflection protocols applied in connected vehicle systems with blockchain. *Computers & Electrical Engineering*, *86*, 106714. doi:10.1016/j.compeleceng.2020.106714

Related References

To continue our tradition of advancing information science and technology research, we have compiled a list of recommended IGI Global readings. These references will provide additional information and guidance to further enrich your knowledge and assist you with your own research and future publications.

Aasi, P., Rusu, L., & Vieru, D. (2017). The Role of Culture in IT Governance Five Focus Areas: A Literature Review. *International Journal of IT/Business Alignment and Governance, 8*(2), 42-61. https://doi.org/ doi:10.4018/IJITBAG.2017070103

Abdrabo, A. A. (2018). Egypt's Knowledge-Based Development: Opportunities, Challenges, and Future Possibilities. In A. Alraouf (Ed.), *Knowledge-Based Urban Development in the Middle East* (pp. 80–101). Hershey, PA: IGI Global. doi:10.4018/978-1-5225-3734-2.ch005

Abu Doush, I., & Alhami, I. (2018). Evaluating the Accessibility of Computer Laboratories, Libraries, and Websites in Jordanian Universities and Colleges. *International Journal of Information Systems and Social Change, 9*(2), 44–60. doi:10.4018/IJISSC.2018040104

Adegbore, A. M., Quadri, M. O., & Oyewo, O. R. (2018). A Theoretical Approach to the Adoption of Electronic Resource Management Systems (ERMS) in Nigerian University Libraries. In A. Tella & T. Kwanya (Eds.), *Handbook of Research on Managing Intellectual Property in Digital Libraries* (pp. 292–311). Hershey, PA: IGI Global. doi:10.4018/978-1-5225-3093-0.ch015

Afolabi, O. A. (2018). Myths and Challenges of Building an Effective Digital Library in Developing Nations: An African Perspective. In A. Tella & T. Kwanya (Eds.), *Handbook of Research on Managing Intellectual Property in Digital Libraries* (pp. 51–79). Hershey, PA: IGI Global. doi:10.4018/978-1-5225-3093-0.ch004

Agarwal, P., Kurian, R., & Gupta, R. K. (2022). Additive Manufacturing Feature Taxonomy and Placement of Parts in AM Enclosure. In S. Salunkhe, H. Hussein, & J. Davim (Eds.), *Applications of Artificial Intelligence in Additive Manufacturing* (pp. 138–176). IGI Global. https://doi.org/10.4018/978-1-7998-8516-0.ch007

Al-Alawi, A. I., Al-Hammam, A. H., Al-Alawi, S. S., & AlAlawi, E. I. (2021). The Adoption of E-Wallets: Current Trends and Future Outlook. In Y. Albastaki, A. Razzaque, & A. Sarea (Eds.), *Innovative Strategies for Implementing FinTech in Banking* (pp. 242–262). IGI Global. https://doi.org/10.4018/978-1-7998-3257-7.ch015

Alsharo, M. (2017). Attitudes Towards Cloud Computing Adoption in Emerging Economies. *International Journal of Cloud Applications and Computing*, 7(3), 44–58. doi:10.4018/IJCAC.2017070102

Amer, T. S., & Johnson, T. L. (2017). Information Technology Progress Indicators: Research Employing Psychological Frameworks. In A. Mesquita (Ed.), *Research Paradigms and Contemporary Perspectives on Human-Technology Interaction* (pp. 168–186). Hershey, PA: IGI Global. doi:10.4018/978-1-5225-1868-6.ch008

Andreeva, A., & Yolova, G. (2021). Liability in Labor Legislation: New Challenges Related to the Use of Artificial Intelligence. In B. Vassileva & M. Zwilling (Eds.), *Responsible AI and Ethical Issues for Businesses and Governments* (pp. 214–232). IGI Global. https://doi.org/10.4018/978-1-7998-4285-9.ch012

Anohah, E. (2017). Paradigm and Architecture of Computing Augmented Learning Management System for Computer Science Education. *International Journal of Online Pedagogy and Course Design*, 7(2), 60–70. doi:10.4018/IJOPCD.2017040105

Anohah, E., & Suhonen, J. (2017). Trends of Mobile Learning in Computing Education from 2006 to 2014: A Systematic Review of Research Publications. *International Journal of Mobile and Blended Learning*, 9(1), 16–33. doi:10.4018/IJMBL.2017010102

Arbaiza, C. S., Huerta, H. V., & Rodriguez, C. R. (2021). Contributions to the Technological Adoption Model for the Peruvian Agro-Export Sector. *International Journal of E-Adoption*, 13(1), 1–17. https://doi.org/10.4018/IJEA.2021010101

Bailey, E. K. (2017). Applying Learning Theories to Computer Technology Supported Instruction. In M. Grassetti & S. Brookby (Eds.), *Advancing Next-Generation Teacher Education through Digital Tools and Applications* (pp. 61–81). Hershey, PA: IGI Global. doi:10.4018/978-1-5225-0965-3.ch004

Baker, J. D. (2021). Introduction to Machine Learning as a New Methodological Framework for Performance Assessment. In M. Bocarnea, B. Winston, & D. Dean (Eds.), *Handbook of Research on Advancements in Organizational Data Collection and Measurements: Strategies for Addressing Attitudes, Beliefs, and Behaviors* (pp. 326–342). IGI Global. https://doi.org/10.4018/978-1-7998-7665-6.ch021

Banerjee, S., Sing, T. Y., Chowdhury, A. R., & Anwar, H. (2018). Let's Go Green: Towards a Taxonomy of Green Computing Enablers for Business Sustainability. In M. Khosrow-Pour (Ed.), *Green Computing Strategies for Competitive Advantage and Business Sustainability* (pp. 89–109). Hershey, PA: IGI Global. doi:10.4018/978-1-5225-5017-4.ch005

Basham, R. (2018). Information Science and Technology in Crisis Response and Management. In M. Khosrow-Pour, D.B.A. (Ed.), Encyclopedia of Information Science and Technology, Fourth Edition (pp. 1407-1418). Hershey, PA: IGI Global. doi:10.4018/978-1-5225-2255-3.ch121

Batyashe, T., & Iyamu, T. (2018). Architectural Framework for the Implementation of Information Technology Governance in Organisations. In M. Khosrow-Pour, D.B.A. (Ed.), Encyclopedia of Information Science and Technology, Fourth Edition (pp. 810-819). Hershey, PA: IGI Global. doi:10.4018/978-1-5225-2255-3.ch070

Bekleyen, N., & Çelik, S. (2017). Attitudes of Adult EFL Learners towards Preparing for a Language Test via CALL. In D. Tafazoli & M. Romero (Eds.), *Multiculturalism and Technology-Enhanced Language Learning* (pp. 214–229). Hershey, PA: IGI Global. doi:10.4018/978-1-5225-1882-2.ch013

Bergeron, F., Croteau, A., Uwizeyemungu, S., & Raymond, L. (2017). A Framework for Research on Information Technology Governance in SMEs. In S. De Haes & W. Van Grembergen (Eds.), *Strategic IT Governance and Alignment in Business Settings* (pp. 53–81). Hershey, PA: IGI Global. doi:10.4018/978-1-5225-0861-8.ch003

Bhardwaj, M., Shukla, N., & Sharma, A. (2021). Improvement and Reduction of Clustering Overhead in Mobile Ad Hoc Network With Optimum Stable Bunching Algorithm. In S. Kumar, M. Trivedi, P. Ranjan, & A. Punhani (Eds.), *Evolution of Software-Defined Networking Foundations for IoT and 5G Mobile Networks* (pp. 139–158). IGI Global. https://doi.org/10.4018/978-1-7998-4685-7.ch008

Bhatt, G. D., Wang, Z., & Rodger, J. A. (2017). Information Systems Capabilities and Their Effects on Competitive Advantages: A Study of Chinese Companies. *Information Resources Management Journal, 30*(3), 41–57. doi:10.4018/IRMJ.2017070103

Bhattacharya, A. (2021). Blockchain, Cybersecurity, and Industry 4.0. In A. Tyagi, G. Rekha, & N. Sreenath (Eds.), *Opportunities and Challenges for Blockchain Technology in Autonomous Vehicles* (pp. 210–244). IGI Global. https://doi.org/10.4018/978-1-7998-3295-9.ch013

Bhyan, P., Shrivastava, B., & Kumar, N. (2022). Requisite Sustainable Development Contemplating Buildings: Economic and Environmental Sustainability. In A. Hussain, K. Tiwari, & A. Gupta (Eds.), *Addressing Environmental Challenges Through Spatial Planning* (pp. 269–288). IGI Global. https://doi.org/10.4018/978-1-7998-8331-9.ch014

Boido, C., Davico, P., & Spallone, R. (2021). Digital Tools Aimed to Represent Urban Survey. In M. Khosrow-Pour D.B.A. (Ed.), *Encyclopedia of Information Science and Technology, Fifth Edition* (pp. 1181-1195). IGI Global. https://doi.org/10.4018/978-1-7998-3479-3.ch082

Borkar, P. S., Chanana, P. U., Atwal, S. K., Londe, T. G., & Dalal, Y. D. (2021). The Replacement of HMI (Human-Machine Interface) in Industry Using Single Interface Through IoT. In R. Raut & A. Mihovska (Eds.), *Examining the Impact of Deep Learning and IoT on Multi-Industry Applications* (pp. 195–208). IGI Global. https://doi.org/10.4018/978-1-7998-7511-6.ch011

Brahmane, A. V., & Krishna, C. B. (2021). Rider Chaotic Biography Optimization-driven Deep Stacked Auto-encoder for Big Data Classification Using Spark Architecture: Rider Chaotic Biography Optimization. *International Journal of Web Services Research*, *18*(3), 42–62. https://doi.org/10.4018/ijwsr.2021070103

Burcoff, A., & Shamir, L. (2017). Computer Analysis of Pablo Picasso's Artistic Style. *International Journal of Art, Culture and Design Technologies*, *6*(1), 1–18. doi:10.4018/IJACDT.2017010101

Byker, E. J. (2017). I Play I Learn: Introducing Technological Play Theory. In C. Martin & D. Polly (Eds.), *Handbook of Research on Teacher Education and Professional Development* (pp. 297–306). Hershey, PA: IGI Global. doi:10.4018/978-1-5225-1067-3.ch016

Calongne, C. M., Stricker, A. G., Truman, B., & Arenas, F. J. (2017). Cognitive Apprenticeship and Computer Science Education in Cyberspace: Reimagining the Past. In A. Stricker, C. Calongne, B. Truman, & F. Arenas (Eds.), *Integrating an Awareness of Selfhood and Society into Virtual Learning* (pp. 180–197). Hershey, PA: IGI Global. doi:10.4018/978-1-5225-2182-2.ch013

Carneiro, A. D. (2017). Defending Information Networks in Cyberspace: Some Notes on Security Needs. In M. Dawson, D. Kisku, P. Gupta, J. Sing, & W. Li (Eds.), Developing Next-Generation Countermeasures for Homeland Security Threat Prevention (pp. 354-375). Hershey, PA: IGI Global. https://doi.org/ doi:10.4018/978-1-5225-0703-1.ch016

Carvalho, W. F., & Zarate, L. (2021). Causal Feature Selection. In A. Azevedo & M. Santos (Eds.), *Integration Challenges for Analytics, Business Intelligence, and Data Mining* (pp. 145-160). IGI Global. https://doi.org/10.4018/978-1-7998-5781-5.ch007

Chase, J. P., & Yan, Z. (2017). Affect in Statistics Cognition. In *Assessing and Measuring Statistics Cognition in Higher Education Online Environments: Emerging Research and Opportunities* (pp. 144–187). Hershey, PA: IGI Global. doi:10.4018/978-1-5225-2420-5.ch005

Chatterjee, A., Roy, S., & Shrivastava, R. (2021). A Machine Learning Approach to Prevent Cancer. In G. Rani & P. Tiwari (Eds.), *Handbook of Research on Disease Prediction Through Data Analytics and Machine Learning* (pp. 112–141). IGI Global. https://doi.org/10.4018/978-1-7998-2742-9.ch007

Cifci, M. A. (2021). Optimizing WSNs for CPS Using Machine Learning Techniques. In A. Luhach & A. Elçi (Eds.), *Artificial Intelligence Paradigms for Smart Cyber-Physical Systems* (pp. 204–228). IGI Global. https://doi.org/10.4018/978-1-7998-5101-1.ch010

Cimermanova, I. (2017). Computer-Assisted Learning in Slovakia. In D. Tafazoli & M. Romero (Eds.), *Multiculturalism and Technology-Enhanced Language Learning* (pp. 252–270). Hershey, PA: IGI Global. doi:10.4018/978-1-5225-1882-2.ch015

Cipolla-Ficarra, F. V., & Cipolla-Ficarra, M. (2018). Computer Animation for Ingenious Revival. In F. Cipolla-Ficarra, M. Ficarra, M. Cipolla-Ficarra, A. Quiroga, J. Alma, & J. Carré (Eds.), *Technology-Enhanced Human Interaction in Modern Society* (pp. 159–181). Hershey, PA: IGI Global. doi:10.4018/978-1-5225-3437-2.ch008

Cockrell, S., Damron, T. S., Melton, A. M., & Smith, A. D. (2018). Offshoring IT. In M. Khosrow-Pour, D.B.A. (Ed.), Encyclopedia of Information Science and Technology, Fourth Edition (pp. 5476-5489). Hershey, PA: IGI Global. https://doi.org/ doi:10.4018/978-1-5225-2255-3.ch476

Coffey, J. W. (2018). Logic and Proof in Computer Science: Categories and Limits of Proof Techniques. In J. Horne (Ed.), *Philosophical Perceptions on Logic and Order* (pp. 218–240). Hershey, PA: IGI Global. doi:10.4018/978-1-5225-2443-4.ch007

Dale, M. (2017). Re-Thinking the Challenges of Enterprise Architecture Implementation. In M. Tavana (Ed.), *Enterprise Information Systems and the Digitalization of Business Functions* (pp. 205–221). Hershey, PA: IGI Global. doi:10.4018/978-1-5225-2382-6.ch009

Das, A., & Mohanty, M. N. (2021). An Useful Review on Optical Character Recognition for Smart Era Generation. In A. Tyagi (Ed.), *Multimedia and Sensory Input for Augmented, Mixed, and Virtual Reality* (pp. 1–41). IGI Global. https://doi.org/10.4018/978-1-7998-4703-8.ch001

Dash, A. K., & Mohapatra, P. (2021). A Survey on Prematurity Detection of Diabetic Retinopathy Based on Fundus Images Using Deep Learning Techniques. In S. Saxena & S. Paul (Eds.), *Deep Learning Applications in Medical Imaging* (pp. 140–155). IGI Global. https://doi.org/10.4018/978-1-7998-5071-7.ch006

De Maere, K., De Haes, S., & von Kutzschenbach, M. (2017). CIO Perspectives on Organizational Learning within the Context of IT Governance. *International Journal of IT/Business Alignment and Governance, 8*(1), 32-47. https://doi.org/doi:10.4018/IJITBAG.2017010103

Demir, K., Çaka, C., Yaman, N. D., İslamoğlu, H., & Kuzu, A. (2018). Examining the Current Definitions of Computational Thinking. In H. Ozcinar, G. Wong, & H. Ozturk (Eds.), *Teaching Computational Thinking in Primary Education* (pp. 36–64). Hershey, PA: IGI Global. doi:10.4018/978-1-5225-3200-2.ch003

Deng, X., Hung, Y., & Lin, C. D. (2017). Design and Analysis of Computer Experiments. In S. Saha, A. Mandal, A. Narasimhamurthy, S. V, & S. Sangam (Eds.), *Handbook of Research on Applied Cybernetics and Systems Science* (pp. 264-279). Hershey, PA: IGI Global. doi:10.4018/978-1-5225-2498-4.ch013

Denner, J., Martinez, J., & Thiry, H. (2017). Strategies for Engaging Hispanic/Latino Youth in the US in Computer Science. In Y. Rankin & J. Thomas (Eds.), *Moving Students of Color from Consumers to Producers of Technology* (pp. 24–48). Hershey, PA: IGI Global. doi:10.4018/978-1-5225-2005-4.ch002

Devi, A. (2017). Cyber Crime and Cyber Security: A Quick Glance. In R. Kumar, P. Pattnaik, & P. Pandey (Eds.), *Detecting and Mitigating Robotic Cyber Security Risks* (pp. 160–171). Hershey, PA: IGI Global. doi:10.4018/978-1-5225-2154-9.ch011

Dhaya, R., & Kanthavel, R. (2022). Futuristic Research Perspectives of IoT Platforms. In D. Jeya Mala (Ed.), *Integrating AI in IoT Analytics on the Cloud for Healthcare Applications* (pp. 258–275). IGI Global. doi:10.4018/978-1-7998-9132-1.ch015

Doyle, D. J., & Fahy, P. J. (2018). Interactivity in Distance Education and Computer-Aided Learning, With Medical Education Examples. In M. Khosrow-Pour, D.B.A. (Ed.), Encyclopedia of Information Science and Technology, Fourth Edition (pp. 5829-5840). Hershey, PA: IGI Global. https://doi.org/ doi:10.4018/978-1-5225-2255-3.ch507

Eklund, P. (2021). Reinforcement Learning in Social Media Marketing. In B. Christiansen & T. Škrinjarić (Eds.), *Handbook of Research on Applied AI for International Business and Marketing Applications* (pp. 30–48). IGI Global. https://doi.org/10.4018/978-1-7998-5077-9.ch003

El Ghandour, N., Benaissa, M., & Lebbah, Y. (2021). An Integer Linear Programming-Based Method for the Extraction of Ontology Alignment. *International Journal of Information Technology and Web Engineering*, *16*(2), 25–44. https://doi.org/10.4018/IJITWE.2021040102

Elias, N. I., & Walker, T. W. (2017). Factors that Contribute to Continued Use of E-Training among Healthcare Professionals. In F. Topor (Ed.), *Handbook of Research on Individualism and Identity in the Globalized Digital Age* (pp. 403–429). Hershey, PA: IGI Global. doi:10.4018/978-1-5225-0522-8.ch018

Fisher, R. L. (2018). Computer-Assisted Indian Matrimonial Services. In M. Khosrow-Pour, D.B.A. (Ed.), Encyclopedia of Information Science and Technology, Fourth Edition (pp. 4136-4145). Hershey, PA: IGI Global. doi:10.4018/978-1-5225-2255-3.ch358

Galiautdinov, R. (2021). Nonlinear Filtering in Artificial Neural Network Applications in Business and Engineering. In Q. Do (Ed.), *Artificial Neural Network Applications in Business and Engineering* (pp. 1–23). IGI Global. https://doi.org/10.4018/978-1-7998-3238-6.ch001

Gardner-McCune, C., & Jimenez, Y. (2017). Historical App Developers: Integrating CS into K-12 through Cross-Disciplinary Projects. In Y. Rankin & J. Thomas (Eds.), *Moving Students of Color from Consumers to Producers of Technology* (pp. 85–112). Hershey, PA: IGI Global. doi:10.4018/978-1-5225-2005-4.ch005

Garg, P. K. (2021). The Internet of Things-Based Technologies. In S. Kumar, M. Trivedi, P. Ranjan, & A. Punhani (Eds.), *Evolution of Software-Defined Networking Foundations for IoT and 5G Mobile Networks* (pp. 37–65). IGI Global. https://doi.org/10.4018/978-1-7998-4685-7.ch003

Garg, T., & Bharti, M. (2021). Congestion Control Protocols for UWSNs. In N. Goyal, L. Sapra, & J. Sandhu (Eds.), *Energy-Efficient Underwater Wireless Communications and Networking* (pp. 85–100). IGI Global. https://doi.org/10.4018/978-1-7998-3640-7.ch006

Gauttier, S. (2021). A Primer on Q-Method and the Study of Technology. In M. Khosrow-Pour D.B.A. (Eds.), *Encyclopedia of Information Science and Technology, Fifth Edition* (pp. 1746-1756). IGI Global. https://doi.org/10.4018/978-1-7998-3479-3.ch120

Ghafele, R., & Gibert, B. (2018). Open Growth: The Economic Impact of Open Source Software in the USA. In M. Khosrow-Pour (Ed.), *Optimizing Contemporary Application and Processes in Open Source Software* (pp. 164–197). Hershey, PA: IGI Global. doi:10.4018/978-1-5225-5314-4.ch007

Ghobakhloo, M., & Azar, A. (2018). Information Technology Resources, the Organizational Capability of Lean-Agile Manufacturing, and Business Performance. *Information Resources Management Journal*, *31*(2), 47–74. doi:10.4018/IRMJ.2018040103

Gikandi, J. W. (2017). Computer-Supported Collaborative Learning and Assessment: A Strategy for Developing Online Learning Communities in Continuing Education. In J. Keengwe & G. Onchwari (Eds.), *Handbook of Research on Learner-Centered Pedagogy in Teacher Education and Professional Development* (pp. 309–333). Hershey, PA: IGI Global. doi:10.4018/978-1-5225-0892-2.ch017

Gokhale, A. A., & Machina, K. F. (2017). Development of a Scale to Measure Attitudes toward Information Technology. In L. Tomei (Ed.), *Exploring the New Era of Technology-Infused Education* (pp. 49–64). Hershey, PA: IGI Global. doi:10.4018/978-1-5225-1709-2.ch004

Goswami, J. K., Jalal, S., Negi, C. S., & Jalal, A. S. (2022). A Texture Features-Based Robust Facial Expression Recognition. *International Journal of Computer Vision and Image Processing*, *12*(1), 1–15. https://doi.org/10.4018/IJCVIP.2022010103

Hafeez-Baig, A., Gururajan, R., & Wickramasinghe, N. (2017). Readiness as a Novel Construct of Readiness Acceptance Model (RAM) for the Wireless Handheld Technology. In N. Wickramasinghe (Ed.), *Handbook of Research on Healthcare Administration and Management* (pp. 578–595). Hershey, PA: IGI Global. doi:10.4018/978-1-5225-0920-2.ch035

Hanafizadeh, P., Ghandchi, S., & Asgarimehr, M. (2017). Impact of Information Technology on Lifestyle: A Literature Review and Classification. *International Journal of Virtual Communities and Social Networking*, *9*(2), 1–23. doi:10.4018/IJVCSN.2017040101

Haseski, H. İ., Ilic, U., & Tuğtekin, U. (2018). Computational Thinking in Educational Digital Games: An Assessment Tool Proposal. In H. Ozcinar, G. Wong, & H. Ozturk (Eds.), *Teaching Computational Thinking in Primary Education* (pp. 256–287). Hershey, PA: IGI Global. doi:10.4018/978-1-5225-3200-2.ch013

Hee, W. J., Jalleh, G., Lai, H., & Lin, C. (2017). E-Commerce and IT Projects: Evaluation and Management Issues in Australian and Taiwanese Hospitals. *International Journal of Public Health Management and Ethics*, *2*(1), 69–90. doi:10.4018/IJPHME.2017010104

Hernandez, A. A. (2017). Green Information Technology Usage: Awareness and Practices of Philippine IT Professionals. *International Journal of Enterprise Information Systems*, *13*(4), 90–103. doi:10.4018/IJEIS.2017100106

Hernandez, M. A., Marin, E. C., Garcia-Rodriguez, J., Azorin-Lopez, J., & Cazorla, M. (2017). Automatic Learning Improves Human-Robot Interaction in Productive Environments: A Review. *International Journal of Computer Vision and Image Processing*, *7*(3), 65–75. doi:10.4018/IJCVIP.2017070106

Hirota, A. (2021). Design of Narrative Creation in Innovation: "Signature Story" and Two Types of Pivots. In T. Ogata & J. Ono (Eds.), *Bridging the Gap Between AI, Cognitive Science, and Narratology With Narrative Generation* (pp. 363–376). IGI Global. https://doi.org/10.4018/978-1-7998-4864-6.ch012

Hond, D., Asgari, H., Jeffery, D., & Newman, M. (2021). An Integrated Process for Verifying Deep Learning Classifiers Using Dataset Dissimilarity Measures. *International Journal of Artificial Intelligence and Machine Learning*, *11*(2), 1–21. https://doi.org/10.4018/IJAIML.289536

Horne-Popp, L. M., Tessone, E. B., & Welker, J. (2018). If You Build It, They Will Come: Creating a Library Statistics Dashboard for Decision-Making. In L. Costello & M. Powers (Eds.), *Developing In-House Digital Tools in Library Spaces* (pp. 177–203). Hershey, PA: IGI Global. doi:10.4018/978-1-5225-2676-6.ch009

Hu, H., Hu, P. J., & Al-Gahtani, S. S. (2017). User Acceptance of Computer Technology at Work in Arabian Culture: A Model Comparison Approach. In M. Khosrow-Pour (Ed.), *Handbook of Research on Technology Adoption, Social Policy, and Global Integration* (pp. 205–228). Hershey, PA: IGI Global. doi:10.4018/978-1-5225-2668-1.ch011

Huang, C., Sun, Y., & Fuh, C. (2022). Vehicle License Plate Recognition With Deep Learning. In C. Chen, W. Yang, & L. Chen (Eds.), *Technologies to Advance Automation in Forensic Science and Criminal Investigation* (pp. 161-219). IGI Global. https://doi.org/10.4018/978-1-7998-8386-9.ch009

Ifinedo, P. (2017). Using an Extended Theory of Planned Behavior to Study Nurses' Adoption of Healthcare Information Systems in Nova Scotia. *International Journal of Technology Diffusion*, 8(1), 1–17. doi:10.4018/IJTD.2017010101

Ilie, V., & Sneha, S. (2018). A Three Country Study for Understanding Physicians' Engagement With Electronic Information Resources Pre and Post System Implementation. *Journal of Global Information Management*, 26(2), 48–73. doi:10.4018/JGIM.2018040103

Ilo, P. I., Nkiko, C., Ugwu, C. I., Ekere, J. N., Izuagbe, R., & Fagbohun, M. O. (2021). Prospects and Challenges of Web 3.0 Technologies Application in the Provision of Library Services. In M. Khosrow-Pour D.B.A. (Ed.), *Encyclopedia of Information Science and Technology, Fifth Edition* (pp. 1767-1781). IGI Global. https://doi.org/10.4018/978-1-7998-3479-3.ch122

Inoue-Smith, Y. (2017). Perceived Ease in Using Technology Predicts Teacher Candidates' Preferences for Online Resources. *International Journal of Online Pedagogy and Course Design*, 7(3), 17–28. doi:10.4018/IJOPCD.2017070102

Islam, A. Y. (2017). Technology Satisfaction in an Academic Context: Moderating Effect of Gender. In A. Mesquita (Ed.), *Research Paradigms and Contemporary Perspectives on Human-Technology Interaction* (pp. 187–211). Hershey, PA: IGI Global. doi:10.4018/978-1-5225-1868-6.ch009

Jagdale, S. C., Hable, A. A., & Chabukswar, A. R. (2021). Protocol Development in Clinical Trials for Healthcare Management. In M. Khosrow-Pour D.B.A. (Ed.), *Encyclopedia of Information Science and Technology, Fifth Edition* (pp. 1797-1814). IGI Global. https://doi.org/10.4018/978-1-7998-3479-3.ch124

Jamil, G. L., & Jamil, C. C. (2017). Information and Knowledge Management Perspective Contributions for Fashion Studies: Observing Logistics and Supply Chain Management Processes. In G. Jamil, A. Soares, & C. Pessoa (Eds.), *Handbook of Research on Information Management for Effective Logistics and Supply Chains* (pp. 199–221). Hershey, PA: IGI Global. doi:10.4018/978-1-5225-0973-8.ch011

Jamil, M. I., & Almunawar, M. N. (2021). Importance of Digital Literacy and Hindrance Brought About by Digital Divide. In M. Khosrow-Pour D.B.A. (Ed.), *Encyclopedia of Information Science and Technology, Fifth Edition* (pp. 1683-1698). IGI Global. https://doi.org/10.4018/978-1-7998-3479-3.ch116

Janakova, M. (2018). Big Data and Simulations for the Solution of Controversies in Small Businesses. In M. Khosrow-Pour, D.B.A. (Ed.), Encyclopedia of Information Science and Technology, Fourth Edition (pp. 6907-6915). Hershey, PA: IGI Global. doi:10.4018/978-1-5225-2255-3.ch598

Jhawar, A., & Garg, S. K. (2018). Logistics Improvement by Investment in Information Technology Using System Dynamics. In A. Azar & S. Vaidyanathan (Eds.), *Advances in System Dynamics and Control* (pp. 528–567). Hershey, PA: IGI Global. doi:10.4018/978-1-5225-4077-9.ch017

Kalelioğlu, F., Gülbahar, Y., & Doğan, D. (2018). Teaching How to Think Like a Programmer: Emerging Insights. In H. Ozcinar, G. Wong, & H. Ozturk (Eds.), *Teaching Computational Thinking in Primary Education* (pp. 18–35). Hershey, PA: IGI Global. doi:10.4018/978-1-5225-3200-2.ch002

Kamberi, S. (2017). A Girls-Only Online Virtual World Environment and its Implications for Game-Based Learning. In A. Stricker, C. Calongne, B. Truman, & F. Arenas (Eds.), *Integrating an Awareness of Selfhood and Society into Virtual Learning* (pp. 74–95). Hershey, PA: IGI Global. doi:10.4018/978-1-5225-2182-2.ch006

Kamel, S., & Rizk, N. (2017). ICT Strategy Development: From Design to Implementation – Case of Egypt. In C. Howard & K. Hargiss (Eds.), *Strategic Information Systems and Technologies in Modern Organizations* (pp. 239–257). Hershey, PA: IGI Global. doi:10.4018/978-1-5225-1680-4.ch010

Kamel, S. H. (2018). The Potential Role of the Software Industry in Supporting Economic Development. In M. Khosrow-Pour, D.B.A. (Ed.), Encyclopedia of Information Science and Technology, Fourth Edition (pp. 7259-7269). Hershey, PA: IGI Global. doi:10.4018/978-1-5225-2255-3.ch631

Kang, H., Kang, Y., & Kim, J. (2022). Improved Fall Detection Model on GRU Using PoseNet. *International Journal of Software Innovation*, 10(2), 1–11. https://doi.org/10.4018/IJSI.289600

Kankam, P. K. (2021). Employing Case Study and Survey Designs in Information Research. *Journal of Information Technology Research*, 14(1), 167–177. https://doi.org/10.4018/JITR.2021010110

Karas, V., & Schuller, B. W. (2021). Deep Learning for Sentiment Analysis: An Overview and Perspectives. In F. Pinarbasi & M. Taskiran (Eds.), *Natural Language Processing for Global and Local Business* (pp. 97–132). IGI Global. https://doi.org/10.4018/978-1-7998-4240-8.ch005

Kaufman, L. M. (2022). Reimagining the Magic of the Workshop Model. In T. Driscoll III, (Ed.), *Designing Effective Distance and Blended Learning Environments in K-12* (pp. 89–109). IGI Global. https://doi.org/10.4018/978-1-7998-6829-3.ch007

Kawata, S. (2018). Computer-Assisted Parallel Program Generation. In M. Khosrow-Pour, D.B.A. (Ed.), Encyclopedia of Information Science and Technology, Fourth Edition (pp. 4583-4593). Hershey, PA: IGI Global. doi:10.4018/978-1-5225-2255-3.ch398

Kharb, L., & Singh, P. (2021). Role of Machine Learning in Modern Education and Teaching. In S. Verma & P. Tomar (Ed.), *Impact of AI Technologies on Teaching, Learning, and Research in Higher Education* (pp. 99-123). IGI Global. https://doi.org/10.4018/978-1-7998-4763-2.ch006

Khari, M., Shrivastava, G., Gupta, S., & Gupta, R. (2017). Role of Cyber Security in Today's Scenario. In R. Kumar, P. Pattnaik, & P. Pandey (Eds.), *Detecting and Mitigating Robotic Cyber Security Risks* (pp. 177–191). Hershey, PA: IGI Global. doi:10.4018/978-1-5225-2154-9.ch013

Khekare, G., & Sheikh, S. (2021). Autonomous Navigation Using Deep Reinforcement Learning in ROS. *International Journal of Artificial Intelligence and Machine Learning, 11*(2), 63–70. https://doi.org/10.4018/IJAIML.20210701.oa4

Khouja, M., Rodriguez, I. B., Ben Halima, Y., & Moalla, S. (2018). IT Governance in Higher Education Institutions: A Systematic Literature Review. *International Journal of Human Capital and Information Technology Professionals, 9*(2), 52–67. doi:10.4018/IJHCITP.2018040104

Kiourt, C., Pavlidis, G., Koutsoudis, A., & Kalles, D. (2017). Realistic Simulation of Cultural Heritage. *International Journal of Computational Methods in Heritage Science, 1*(1), 10–40. doi:10.4018/IJCMHS.2017010102

Köse, U. (2017). An Augmented-Reality-Based Intelligent Mobile Application for Open Computer Education. In G. Kurubacak & H. Altinpulluk (Eds.), *Mobile Technologies and Augmented Reality in Open Education* (pp. 154–174). Hershey, PA: IGI Global. doi:10.4018/978-1-5225-2110-5.ch008

Lahmiri, S. (2018). Information Technology Outsourcing Risk Factors and Provider Selection. In M. Gupta, R. Sharman, J. Walp, & P. Mulgund (Eds.), *Information Technology Risk Management and Compliance in Modern Organizations* (pp. 214–228). Hershey, PA: IGI Global. doi:10.4018/978-1-5225-2604-9.ch008

Lakkad, A. K., Bhadaniya, R. D., Shah, V. N., & Lavanya, K. (2021). Complex Events Processing on Live News Events Using Apache Kafka and Clustering Techniques. *International Journal of Intelligent Information Technologies*, *17*(1), 39–52. https://doi.org/10.4018/IJIIT.2021010103

Landriscina, F. (2017). Computer-Supported Imagination: The Interplay Between Computer and Mental Simulation in Understanding Scientific Concepts. In I. Levin & D. Tsybulsky (Eds.), *Digital Tools and Solutions for Inquiry-Based STEM Learning* (pp. 33–60). Hershey, PA: IGI Global. doi:10.4018/978-1-5225-2525-7.ch002

Lara López, G. (2021). Virtual Reality in Object Location. In A. Negrón & M. Muñoz (Eds.), *Latin American Women and Research Contributions to the IT Field* (pp. 307–324). IGI Global. https://doi.org/10.4018/978-1-7998-7552-9.ch014

Lee, W. W. (2018). Ethical Computing Continues From Problem to Solution. In M. Khosrow-Pour, D.B.A. (Ed.), Encyclopedia of Information Science and Technology, Fourth Edition (pp. 4884-4897). Hershey, PA: IGI Global. doi:10.4018/978-1-5225-2255-3.ch423

Lin, S., Chen, S., & Chuang, S. (2017). Perceived Innovation and Quick Response Codes in an Online-to-Offline E-Commerce Service Model. *International Journal of E-Adoption*, *9*(2), 1–16. doi:10.4018/IJEA.2017070101

Liu, M., Wang, Y., Xu, W., & Liu, L. (2017). Automated Scoring of Chinese Engineering Students' English Essays. *International Journal of Distance Education Technologies*, *15*(1), 52–68. doi:10.4018/IJDET.2017010104

Ma, X., Li, X., Zhong, B., Huang, Y., Gu, Y., Wu, M., Liu, Y., & Zhang, M. (2021). A Detector and Evaluation Framework of Abnormal Bidding Behavior Based on Supplier Portrait. *International Journal of Information Technology and Web Engineering*, *16*(2), 58–74. https://doi.org/10.4018/IJITWE.2021040104

Mabe, L. K., & Oladele, O. I. (2017). Application of Information Communication Technologies for Agricultural Development through Extension Services: A Review. In T. Tossy (Ed.), *Information Technology Integration for Socio-Economic Development* (pp. 52–101). Hershey, PA: IGI Global. doi:10.4018/978-1-5225-0539-6.ch003

Mahboub, S. A., Sayed Ali Ahmed, E., & Saeed, R. A. (2021). Smart IDS and IPS for Cyber-Physical Systems. In A. Luhach & A. Elçi (Eds.), *Artificial Intelligence Paradigms for Smart Cyber-Physical Systems* (pp. 109–136). IGI Global. https://doi.org/10.4018/978-1-7998-5101-1.ch006

Manogaran, G., Thota, C., & Lopez, D. (2018). Human-Computer Interaction With Big Data Analytics. In D. Lopez & M. Durai (Eds.), *HCI Challenges and Privacy Preservation in Big Data Security* (pp. 1–22). Hershey, PA: IGI Global. doi:10.4018/978-1-5225-2863-0.ch001

Margolis, J., Goode, J., & Flapan, J. (2017). A Critical Crossroads for Computer Science for All: "Identifying Talent" or "Building Talent," and What Difference Does It Make? In Y. Rankin & J. Thomas (Eds.), *Moving Students of Color from Consumers to Producers of Technology* (pp. 1–23). Hershey, PA: IGI Global. doi:10.4018/978-1-5225-2005-4.ch001

Mazzù, M. F., Benetton, A., Baccelloni, A., & Lavini, L. (2022). A Milk Blockchain-Enabled Supply Chain: Evidence From Leading Italian Farms. In P. De Giovanni (Ed.), *Blockchain Technology Applications in Businesses and Organizations* (pp. 73–98). IGI Global. https://doi.org/10.4018/978-1-7998-8014-1.ch004

Mbale, J. (2018). Computer Centres Resource Cloud Elasticity-Scalability (CRECES): Copperbelt University Case Study. In S. Aljawarneh & M. Malhotra (Eds.), *Critical Research on Scalability and Security Issues in Virtual Cloud Environments* (pp. 48–70). Hershey, PA: IGI Global. doi:10.4018/978-1-5225-3029-9.ch003

McKee, J. (2018). The Right Information: The Key to Effective Business Planning. In *Business Architectures for Risk Assessment and Strategic Planning: Emerging Research and Opportunities* (pp. 38–52). Hershey, PA: IGI Global. doi:10.4018/978-1-5225-3392-4.ch003

Meddah, I. H., Remil, N. E., & Meddah, H. N. (2021). Novel Approach for Mining Patterns. *International Journal of Applied Evolutionary Computation, 12*(1), 27–42. https://doi.org/10.4018/IJAEC.2021010103

Mensah, I. K., & Mi, J. (2018). Determinants of Intention to Use Local E-Government Services in Ghana: The Perspective of Local Government Workers. *International Journal of Technology Diffusion, 9*(2), 41–60. doi:10.4018/IJTD.2018040103

Mohamed, J. H. (2018). Scientograph-Based Visualization of Computer Forensics Research Literature. In J. Jeyasekar & P. Saravanan (Eds.), *Innovations in Measuring and Evaluating Scientific Information* (pp. 148–162). Hershey, PA: IGI Global. doi:10.4018/978-1-5225-3457-0.ch010

Montañés-Del Río, M. Á., Cornejo, V. R., Rodríguez, M. R., & Ortiz, J. S. (2021). Gamification of University Subjects: A Case Study for Operations Management. *Journal of Information Technology Research, 14*(2), 1–29. https://doi.org/10.4018/JITR.2021040101

Moore, R. L., & Johnson, N. (2017). Earning a Seat at the Table: How IT Departments Can Partner in Organizational Change and Innovation. *International Journal of Knowledge-Based Organizations*, 7(2), 1–12. doi:10.4018/IJKBO.2017040101

Mukul, M. K., & Bhattaharyya, S. (2017). Brain-Machine Interface: Human-Computer Interaction. In E. Noughabi, B. Raahemi, A. Albadvi, & B. Far (Eds.), *Handbook of Research on Data Science for Effective Healthcare Practice and Administration* (pp. 417–443). Hershey, PA: IGI Global. doi:10.4018/978-1-5225-2515-8.ch018

Na, L. (2017). Library and Information Science Education and Graduate Programs in Academic Libraries. In L. Ruan, Q. Zhu, & Y. Ye (Eds.), *Academic Library Development and Administration in China* (pp. 218–229). Hershey, PA: IGI Global. doi:10.4018/978-1-5225-0550-1.ch013

Nagpal, G., Bishnoi, G. K., Dhami, H. S., & Vijayvargia, A. (2021). Use of Data Analytics to Increase the Efficiency of Last Mile Logistics for Ecommerce Deliveries. In B. Patil & M. Vohra (Eds.), *Handbook of Research on Engineering, Business, and Healthcare Applications of Data Science and Analytics* (pp. 167–180). IGI Global. https://doi.org/10.4018/978-1-7998-3053-5.ch009

Nair, S. M., Ramesh, V., & Tyagi, A. K. (2021). Issues and Challenges (Privacy, Security, and Trust) in Blockchain-Based Applications. In A. Tyagi, G. Rekha, & N. Sreenath (Eds.), *Opportunities and Challenges for Blockchain Technology in Autonomous Vehicles* (pp. 196–209). IGI Global. https://doi.org/10.4018/978-1-7998-3295-9.ch012

Naomi, J. F. M., K., & V., S. (2021). Machine and Deep Learning Techniques in IoT and Cloud. In S. Velayutham (Ed.), *Challenges and Opportunities for the Convergence of IoT, Big Data, and Cloud Computing* (pp. 225-247). IGI Global. https://doi.org/10.4018/978-1-7998-3111-2.ch013

Nath, R., & Murthy, V. N. (2018). What Accounts for the Differences in Internet Diffusion Rates Around the World? In M. Khosrow-Pour, D.B.A. (Ed.), Encyclopedia of Information Science and Technology, Fourth Edition (pp. 8095-8104). Hershey, PA: IGI Global. https://doi.org/ doi:10.4018/978-1-5225-2255-3.ch705

Nedelko, Z., & Potocan, V. (2018). The Role of Emerging Information Technologies for Supporting Supply Chain Management. In M. Khosrow-Pour, D.B.A. (Ed.), Encyclopedia of Information Science and Technology, Fourth Edition (pp. 5559-5569). Hershey, PA: IGI Global. doi:10.4018/978-1-5225-2255-3.ch483

Negrini, L., Giang, C., & Bonnet, E. (2022). Designing Tools and Activities for Educational Robotics in Online Learning. In N. Eteokleous & E. Nisiforou (Eds.), *Designing, Constructing, and Programming Robots for Learning* (pp. 202–222). IGI Global. https://doi.org/10.4018/978-1-7998-7443-0.ch010

Ngafeeson, M. N. (2018). User Resistance to Health Information Technology. In M. Khosrow-Pour, D.B.A. (Ed.), Encyclopedia of Information Science and Technology, Fourth Edition (pp. 3816-3825). Hershey, PA: IGI Global. doi:10.4018/978-1-5225-2255-3.ch331

Nguyen, T. T., Giang, N. L., Tran, D. T., Nguyen, T. T., Nguyen, H. Q., Pham, A. V., & Vu, T. D. (2021). A Novel Filter-Wrapper Algorithm on Intuitionistic Fuzzy Set for Attribute Reduction From Decision Tables. *International Journal of Data Warehousing and Mining*, *17*(4), 67–100. https://doi.org/10.4018/IJDWM.2021100104

Nigam, A., & Dewani, P. P. (2022). Consumer Engagement Through Conditional Promotions: An Exploratory Study. *Journal of Global Information Management*, *30*(5), 1–19. https://doi.org/10.4018/JGIM.290364

Odagiri, K. (2017). Introduction of Individual Technology to Constitute the Current Internet. In *Strategic Policy-Based Network Management in Contemporary Organizations* (pp. 20–96). Hershey, PA: IGI Global. doi:10.4018/978-1-68318-003-6.ch003

Odia, J. O., & Akpata, O. T. (2021). Role of Data Science and Data Analytics in Forensic Accounting and Fraud Detection. In B. Patil & M. Vohra (Eds.), *Handbook of Research on Engineering, Business, and Healthcare Applications of Data Science and Analytics* (pp. 203–227). IGI Global. https://doi.org/10.4018/978-1-7998-3053-5.ch011

Okike, E. U. (2018). Computer Science and Prison Education. In I. Biao (Ed.), *Strategic Learning Ideologies in Prison Education Programs* (pp. 246–264). Hershey, PA: IGI Global. doi:10.4018/978-1-5225-2909-5.ch012

Olelewe, C. J., & Nwafor, I. P. (2017). Level of Computer Appreciation Skills Acquired for Sustainable Development by Secondary School Students in Nsukka LGA of Enugu State, Nigeria. In C. Ayo & V. Mbarika (Eds.), *Sustainable ICT Adoption and Integration for Socio-Economic Development* (pp. 214–233). Hershey, PA: IGI Global. doi:10.4018/978-1-5225-2565-3.ch010

Oliveira, M., Maçada, A. C., Curado, C., & Nodari, F. (2017). Infrastructure Profiles and Knowledge Sharing. *International Journal of Technology and Human Interaction*, *13*(3), 1–12. doi:10.4018/IJTHI.2017070101

Otarkhani, A., Shokouhyar, S., & Pour, S. S. (2017). Analyzing the Impact of Governance of Enterprise IT on Hospital Performance: Tehran's (Iran) Hospitals – A Case Study. *International Journal of Healthcare Information Systems and Informatics*, *12*(3), 1–20. doi:10.4018/IJHISI.2017070101

Otunla, A. O., & Amuda, C. O. (2018). Nigerian Undergraduate Students' Computer Competencies and Use of Information Technology Tools and Resources for Study Skills and Habits' Enhancement. In M. Khosrow-Pour, D.B.A. (Ed.), Encyclopedia of Information Science and Technology, Fourth Edition (pp. 2303-2313). Hershey, PA: IGI Global. https://doi.org/ doi:10.4018/978-1-5225-2255-3.ch200

Özçınar, H. (2018). A Brief Discussion on Incentives and Barriers to Computational Thinking Education. In H. Ozcinar, G. Wong, & H. Ozturk (Eds.), *Teaching Computational Thinking in Primary Education* (pp. 1–17). Hershey, PA: IGI Global. doi:10.4018/978-1-5225-3200-2.ch001

Pandey, J. M., Garg, S., Mishra, P., & Mishra, B. P. (2017). Computer Based Psychological Interventions: Subject to the Efficacy of Psychological Services. *International Journal of Computers in Clinical Practice*, *2*(1), 25–33. doi:10.4018/ IJCCP.2017010102

Pandkar, S. D., & Paatil, S. D. (2021). Big Data and Knowledge Resource Centre. In S. Dhamdhere (Ed.), *Big Data Applications for Improving Library Services* (pp. 90–106). IGI Global. https://doi.org/10.4018/978-1-7998-3049-8.ch007

Patro, C. (2017). Impulsion of Information Technology on Human Resource Practices. In P. Ordóñez de Pablos (Ed.), *Managerial Strategies and Solutions for Business Success in Asia* (pp. 231–254). Hershey, PA: IGI Global. doi:10.4018/978-1-5225-1886-0.ch013

Patro, C. S., & Raghunath, K. M. (2017). Information Technology Paraphernalia for Supply Chain Management Decisions. In M. Tavana (Ed.), *Enterprise Information Systems and the Digitalization of Business Functions* (pp. 294–320). Hershey, PA: IGI Global. doi:10.4018/978-1-5225-2382-6.ch014

Paul, P. K. (2018). The Context of IST for Solid Information Retrieval and Infrastructure Building: Study of Developing Country. *International Journal of Information Retrieval Research*, *8*(1), 86–100. doi:10.4018/IJIRR.2018010106

Paul, P. K., & Chatterjee, D. (2018). iSchools Promoting "Information Science and Technology" (IST) Domain Towards Community, Business, and Society With Contemporary Worldwide Trend and Emerging Potentialities in India. In M. Khosrow-Pour, D.B.A. (Ed.), Encyclopedia of Information Science and Technology, Fourth Edition (pp. 4723-4735). Hershey, PA: IGI Global. https://doi.org/ doi:10.4018/978-1-5225-2255-3.ch410

Pessoa, C. R., & Marques, M. E. (2017). Information Technology and Communication Management in Supply Chain Management. In G. Jamil, A. Soares, & C. Pessoa (Eds.), *Handbook of Research on Information Management for Effective Logistics and Supply Chains* (pp. 23–33). Hershey, PA: IGI Global. doi:10.4018/978-1-5225-0973-8.ch002

Pineda, R. G. (2018). Remediating Interaction: Towards a Philosophy of Human-Computer Relationship. In M. Khosrow-Pour (Ed.), *Enhancing Art, Culture, and Design With Technological Integration* (pp. 75–98). Hershey, PA: IGI Global. doi:10.4018/978-1-5225-5023-5.ch004

Prabha, V. D., & R., R. (2021). Clinical Decision Support Systems: Decision-Making System for Clinical Data. In G. Rani & P. Tiwari (Eds.), *Handbook of Research on Disease Prediction Through Data Analytics and Machine Learning* (pp. 268-280). IGI Global. https://doi.org/10.4018/978-1-7998-2742-9.ch014

Pushpa, R., & Siddappa, M. (2021). An Optimal Way of VM Placement Strategy in Cloud Computing Platform Using ABCS Algorithm. *International Journal of Ambient Computing and Intelligence*, *12*(3), 16–38. https://doi.org/10.4018/ IJACI.2021070102

Qian, Y. (2017). Computer Simulation in Higher Education: Affordances, Opportunities, and Outcomes. In P. Vu, S. Fredrickson, & C. Moore (Eds.), *Handbook of Research on Innovative Pedagogies and Technologies for Online Learning in Higher Education* (pp. 236–262). Hershey, PA: IGI Global. doi:10.4018/978-1-5225-1851-8.ch011

Rahman, N. (2017). Lessons from a Successful Data Warehousing Project Management. *International Journal of Information Technology Project Management*, *8*(4), 30–45. doi:10.4018/IJITPM.2017100103

Rahman, N. (2018). Environmental Sustainability in the Computer Industry for Competitive Advantage. In M. Khosrow-Pour (Ed.), *Green Computing Strategies for Competitive Advantage and Business Sustainability* (pp. 110–130). Hershey, PA: IGI Global. doi:10.4018/978-1-5225-5017-4.ch006

Rajh, A., & Pavetic, T. (2017). Computer Generated Description as the Required Digital Competence in Archival Profession. *International Journal of Digital Literacy and Digital Competence, 8*(1), 36–49. doi:10.4018/IJDLDC.2017010103

Raman, A., & Goyal, D. P. (2017). Extending IMPLEMENT Framework for Enterprise Information Systems Implementation to Information System Innovation. In M. Tavana (Ed.), *Enterprise Information Systems and the Digitalization of Business Functions* (pp. 137–177). Hershey, PA: IGI Global. doi:10.4018/978-1-5225-2382-6.ch007

Rao, A. P., & Reddy, K. S. (2021). Automated Soil Residue Levels Detecting Device With IoT Interface. In V. Sathiyamoorthi & A. Elci (Eds.), *Challenges and Applications of Data Analytics in Social Perspectives* (Vol. S, pp. 123–135). IGI Global. https://doi.org/10.4018/978-1-7998-2566-1.ch007

Rao, Y. S., Rauta, A. K., Saini, H., & Panda, T. C. (2017). Mathematical Model for Cyber Attack in Computer Network. *International Journal of Business Data Communications and Networking, 13*(1), 58–65. doi:10.4018/IJBDCN.2017010105

Rapaport, W. J. (2018). Syntactic Semantics and the Proper Treatment of Computationalism. In M. Danesi (Ed.), *Empirical Research on Semiotics and Visual Rhetoric* (pp. 128–176). Hershey, PA: IGI Global. doi:10.4018/978-1-5225-5622-0.ch007

Raut, R., Priyadarshinee, P., & Jha, M. (2017). Understanding the Mediation Effect of Cloud Computing Adoption in Indian Organization: Integrating TAM-TOE- Risk Model. *International Journal of Service Science, Management, Engineering, and Technology, 8*(3), 40–59. doi:10.4018/IJSSMET.2017070103

Rezaie, S., Mirabedini, S. J., & Abtahi, A. (2018). Designing a Model for Implementation of Business Intelligence in the Banking Industry. *International Journal of Enterprise Information Systems, 14*(1), 77–103. doi:10.4018/IJEIS.2018010105

Rezende, D. A. (2018). Strategic Digital City Projects: Innovative Information and Public Services Offered by Chicago (USA) and Curitiba (Brazil). In M. Lytras, L. Daniela, & A. Visvizi (Eds.), *Enhancing Knowledge Discovery and Innovation in the Digital Era* (pp. 204–223). Hershey, PA: IGI Global. doi:10.4018/978-1-5225-4191-2.ch012

Rodriguez, A., Rico-Diaz, A. J., Rabuñal, J. R., & Gestal, M. (2017). Fish Tracking with Computer Vision Techniques: An Application to Vertical Slot Fishways. In M. S., & V. V. (Eds.), Multi-Core Computer Vision and Image Processing for Intelligent Applications (pp. 74-104). Hershey, PA: IGI Global. https://doi.org/doi:10.4018/978-1-5225-0889-2.ch003

Romero, J. A. (2018). Sustainable Advantages of Business Value of Information Technology. In M. Khosrow-Pour, D.B.A. (Ed.), Encyclopedia of Information Science and Technology, Fourth Edition (pp. 923-929). Hershey, PA: IGI Global. doi:10.4018/978-1-5225-2255-3.ch079

Romero, J. A. (2018). The Always-On Business Model and Competitive Advantage. In N. Bajgoric (Ed.), *Always-On Enterprise Information Systems for Modern Organizations* (pp. 23–40). Hershey, PA: IGI Global. doi:10.4018/978-1-5225-3704-5.ch002

Rosen, Y. (2018). Computer Agent Technologies in Collaborative Learning and Assessment. In M. Khosrow-Pour, D.B.A. (Ed.), Encyclopedia of Information Science and Technology, Fourth Edition (pp. 2402-2410). Hershey, PA: IGI Global. doi:10.4018/978-1-5225-2255-3.ch209

Roy, D. (2018). Success Factors of Adoption of Mobile Applications in Rural India: Effect of Service Characteristics on Conceptual Model. In M. Khosrow-Pour (Ed.), *Green Computing Strategies for Competitive Advantage and Business Sustainability* (pp. 211–238). Hershey, PA: IGI Global. doi:10.4018/978-1-5225-5017-4.ch010

Ruffin, T. R., & Hawkins, D. P. (2018). Trends in Health Care Information Technology and Informatics. In M. Khosrow-Pour, D.B.A. (Ed.), Encyclopedia of Information Science and Technology, Fourth Edition (pp. 3805-3815). Hershey, PA: IGI Global. doi:10.4018/978-1-5225-2255-3.ch330

Sadasivam, U. M., & Ganesan, N. (2021). Detecting Fake News Using Deep Learning and NLP. In S. Misra, C. Arumugam, S. Jaganathan, & S. S. (Eds.), *Confluence of AI, Machine, and Deep Learning in Cyber Forensics* (pp. 117-133). IGI Global. https://doi.org/10.4018/978-1-7998-4900-1.ch007

Safari, M. R., & Jiang, Q. (2018). The Theory and Practice of IT Governance Maturity and Strategies Alignment: Evidence From Banking Industry. *Journal of Global Information Management, 26*(2), 127–146. doi:10.4018/JGIM.2018040106

Sahin, H. B., & Anagun, S. S. (2018). Educational Computer Games in Math Teaching: A Learning Culture. In E. Toprak & E. Kumtepe (Eds.), *Supporting Multiculturalism in Open and Distance Learning Spaces* (pp. 249–280). Hershey, PA: IGI Global. doi:10.4018/978-1-5225-3076-3.ch013

Sakalle, A., Tomar, P., Bhardwaj, H., & Sharma, U. (2021). Impact and Latest Trends of Intelligent Learning With Artificial Intelligence. In S. Verma & P. Tomar (Eds.), *Impact of AI Technologies on Teaching, Learning, and Research in Higher Education* (pp. 172-189). IGI Global. https://doi.org/10.4018/978-1-7998-4763-2.ch011

Sala, N. (2021). Virtual Reality, Augmented Reality, and Mixed Reality in Education: A Brief Overview. In D. Choi, A. Dailey-Hebert, & J. Estes (Eds.), *Current and Prospective Applications of Virtual Reality in Higher Education* (pp. 48–73). IGI Global. https://doi.org/10.4018/978-1-7998-4960-5.ch003

Salunkhe, S., Kanagachidambaresan, G., Rajkumar, C., & Jayanthi, K. (2022). Online Detection and Prediction of Fused Deposition Modelled Parts Using Artificial Intelligence. In S. Salunkhe, H. Hussein, & J. Davim (Eds.), *Applications of Artificial Intelligence in Additive Manufacturing* (pp. 194–209). IGI Global. https://doi.org/10.4018/978-1-7998-8516-0.ch009

Samy, V. S., Pramanick, K., Thenkanidiyoor, V., & Victor, J. (2021). Data Analysis and Visualization in Python for Polar Meteorological Data. *International Journal of Data Analytics*, *2*(1), 32–60. https://doi.org/10.4018/IJDA.2021010102

Sanna, A., & Valpreda, F. (2017). An Assessment of the Impact of a Collaborative Didactic Approach and Students' Background in Teaching Computer Animation. *International Journal of Information and Communication Technology Education*, *13*(4), 1–16. doi:10.4018/IJICTE.2017100101

Sarivougioukas, J., & Vagelatos, A. (2022). Fused Contextual Data With Threading Technology to Accelerate Processing in Home UbiHealth. *International Journal of Software Science and Computational Intelligence*, *14*(1), 1–14. https://doi.org/10.4018/IJSSCI.285590

Scott, A., Martin, A., & McAlear, F. (2017). Enhancing Participation in Computer Science among Girls of Color: An Examination of a Preparatory AP Computer Science Intervention. In Y. Rankin & J. Thomas (Eds.), *Moving Students of Color from Consumers to Producers of Technology* (pp. 62–84). Hershey, PA: IGI Global. doi:10.4018/978-1-5225-2005-4.ch004

Shanmugam, M., Ibrahim, N., Gorment, N. Z., Sugu, R., Dandarawi, T. N., & Ahmad, N. A. (2022). Towards an Integrated Omni-Channel Strategy Framework for Improved Customer Interaction. In P. Lai (Ed.), *Handbook of Research on Social Impacts of E-Payment and Blockchain Technology* (pp. 409–427). IGI Global. https://doi.org/10.4018/978-1-7998-9035-5.ch022

Sharma, A., & Kumar, S. (2021). Network Slicing and the Role of 5G in IoT Applications. In S. Kumar, M. Trivedi, P. Ranjan, & A. Punhani (Eds.), *Evolution of Software-Defined Networking Foundations for IoT and 5G Mobile Networks* (pp. 172–190). IGI Global. https://doi.org/10.4018/978-1-7998-4685-7.ch010

Siddoo, V., & Wongsai, N. (2017). Factors Influencing the Adoption of ISO/IEC 29110 in Thai Government Projects: A Case Study. *International Journal of Information Technologies and Systems Approach*, *10*(1), 22–44. doi:10.4018/IJITSA.2017010102

Silveira, C., Hir, M. E., & Chaves, H. K. (2022). An Approach to Information Management as a Subsidy of Global Health Actions: A Case Study of Big Data in Health for Dengue, Zika, and Chikungunya. In J. Lima de Magalhães, Z. Hartz, G. Jamil, H. Silveira, & L. Jamil (Eds.), *Handbook of Research on Essential Information Approaches to Aiding Global Health in the One Health Context* (pp. 219–234). IGI Global. https://doi.org/10.4018/978-1-7998-8011-0.ch012

Simões, A. (2017). Using Game Frameworks to Teach Computer Programming. In R. Alexandre Peixoto de Queirós & M. Pinto (Eds.), *Gamification-Based E-Learning Strategies for Computer Programming Education* (pp. 221–236). Hershey, PA: IGI Global. doi:10.4018/978-1-5225-1034-5.ch010

Simões de Almeida, R., & da Silva, T. (2022). AI Chatbots in Mental Health: Are We There Yet? In A. Marques & R. Queirós (Eds.), *Digital Therapies in Psychosocial Rehabilitation and Mental Health* (pp. 226–243). IGI Global. https://doi.org/10.4018/978-1-7998-8634-1.ch011

Singh, L. K., Khanna, M., Thawkar, S., & Gopal, J. (2021). Robustness for Authentication of the Human Using Face, Ear, and Gait Multimodal Biometric System. *International Journal of Information System Modeling and Design*, *12*(1), 39–72. https://doi.org/10.4018/IJISMD.2021010103

Sllame, A. M. (2017). Integrating LAB Work With Classes in Computer Network Courses. In H. Alphin Jr, R. Chan, & J. Lavine (Eds.), *The Future of Accessibility in International Higher Education* (pp. 253–275). Hershey, PA: IGI Global. doi:10.4018/978-1-5225-2560-8.ch015

Smirnov, A., Ponomarev, A., Shilov, N., Kashevnik, A., & Teslya, N. (2018). Ontology-Based Human-Computer Cloud for Decision Support: Architecture and Applications in Tourism. *International Journal of Embedded and Real-Time Communication Systems*, *9*(1), 1–19. doi:10.4018/IJERTCS.2018010101

Smith-Ditizio, A. A., & Smith, A. D. (2018). Computer Fraud Challenges and Its Legal Implications. In M. Khosrow-Pour, D.B.A. (Ed.), Encyclopedia of Information Science and Technology, Fourth Edition (pp. 4837-4848). Hershey, PA: IGI Global. doi:10.4018/978-1-5225-2255-3.ch419

Sosnin, P. (2018). Figuratively Semantic Support of Human-Computer Interactions. In *Experience-Based Human-Computer Interactions: Emerging Research and Opportunities* (pp. 244–272). Hershey, PA: IGI Global. doi:10.4018/978-1-5225-2987-3.ch008

Srilakshmi, R., & Jaya Bhaskar, M. (2021). An Adaptable Secure Scheme in Mobile Ad hoc Network to Protect the Communication Channel From Malicious Behaviours. *International Journal of Information Technology and Web Engineering*, *16*(3), 54–73. https://doi.org/10.4018/IJITWE.2021070104

Sukhwani, N., Kagita, V. R., Kumar, V., & Panda, S. K. (2021). Efficient Computation of Top-K Skyline Objects in Data Set With Uncertain Preferences. *International Journal of Data Warehousing and Mining*, *17*(3), 68–80. https://doi.org/10.4018/IJDWM.2021070104

Susanto, H., Yie, L. F., Setiana, D., Asih, Y., Yoganingrum, A., Riyanto, S., & Saputra, F. A. (2021). Digital Ecosystem Security Issues for Organizations and Governments: Digital Ethics and Privacy. In Z. Mahmood (Ed.), *Web 2.0 and Cloud Technologies for Implementing Connected Government* (pp. 204–228). IGI Global. https://doi.org/10.4018/978-1-7998-4570-6.ch010

Syväjärvi, A., Leinonen, J., Kivivirta, V., & Kesti, M. (2017). The Latitude of Information Management in Local Government: Views of Local Government Managers. *International Journal of Electronic Government Research*, *13*(1), 69–85. doi:10.4018/IJEGR.2017010105

Tanque, M., & Foxwell, H. J. (2018). Big Data and Cloud Computing: A Review of Supply Chain Capabilities and Challenges. In A. Prasad (Ed.), *Exploring the Convergence of Big Data and the Internet of Things* (pp. 1–28). Hershey, PA: IGI Global. doi:10.4018/978-1-5225-2947-7.ch001

Teixeira, A., Gomes, A., & Orvalho, J. G. (2017). Auditory Feedback in a Computer Game for Blind People. In T. Issa, P. Kommers, T. Issa, P. Isaías, & T. Issa (Eds.), *Smart Technology Applications in Business Environments* (pp. 134–158). Hershey, PA: IGI Global. doi:10.4018/978-1-5225-2492-2.ch007

Tewari, P., Tiwari, P., & Goel, R. (2022). Information Technology in Supply Chain Management. In V. Garg & R. Goel (Eds.), *Handbook of Research on Innovative Management Using AI in Industry 5.0* (pp. 165–178). IGI Global. https://doi.org/10.4018/978-1-7998-8497-2.ch011

Thompson, N., McGill, T., & Murray, D. (2018). Affect-Sensitive Computer Systems. In M. Khosrow-Pour, D.B.A. (Ed.), Encyclopedia of Information Science and Technology, Fourth Edition (pp. 4124-4135). Hershey, PA: IGI Global. doi:10.4018/978-1-5225-2255-3.ch357

Triberti, S., Brivio, E., & Galimberti, C. (2018). On Social Presence: Theories, Methodologies, and Guidelines for the Innovative Contexts of Computer-Mediated Learning. In M. Marmon (Ed.), *Enhancing Social Presence in Online Learning Environments* (pp. 20–41). Hershey, PA: IGI Global. doi:10.4018/978-1-5225-3229-3.ch002

Tripathy, B. K. T. R., S., & Mohanty, R. K. (2018). Memetic Algorithms and Their Applications in Computer Science. In S. Dash, B. Tripathy, & A. Rahman (Eds.), Handbook of Research on Modeling, Analysis, and Application of Nature-Inspired Metaheuristic Algorithms (pp. 73-93). Hershey, PA: IGI Global. https://doi.org/doi:10.4018/978-1-5225-2857-9.ch004

Turulja, L., & Bajgoric, N. (2017). Human Resource Management IT and Global Economy Perspective: Global Human Resource Information Systems. In M. Khosrow-Pour (Ed.), *Handbook of Research on Technology Adoption, Social Policy, and Global Integration* (pp. 377–394). Hershey, PA: IGI Global. doi:10.4018/978-1-5225-2668-1.ch018

Unwin, D. W., Sanzogni, L., & Sandhu, K. (2017). Developing and Measuring the Business Case for Health Information Technology. In K. Moahi, K. Bwalya, & P. Sebina (Eds.), *Health Information Systems and the Advancement of Medical Practice in Developing Countries* (pp. 262–290). Hershey, PA: IGI Global. doi:10.4018/978-1-5225-2262-1.ch015

Usharani, B. (2022). House Plant Leaf Disease Detection and Classification Using Machine Learning. In M. Mundada, S. Seema, S. K.G., & M. Shilpa (Eds.), *Deep Learning Applications for Cyber-Physical Systems* (pp. 17-26). IGI Global. https://doi.org/10.4018/978-1-7998-8161-2.ch002

Vadhanam, B. R. S., M., Sugumaran, V., V., V., & Ramalingam, V. V. (2017). Computer Vision Based Classification on Commercial Videos. In M. S., & V. V. (Eds.), Multi-Core Computer Vision and Image Processing for Intelligent Applications (pp. 105-135). Hershey, PA: IGI Global. https://doi.org/ doi:10.4018/978-1-5225-0889-2.ch004

Vairinho, S. (2022). Innovation Dynamics Through the Encouragement of Knowledge Spin-Off From Touristic Destinations. In C. Ramos, S. Quinteiro, & A. Gonçalves (Eds.), *ICT as Innovator Between Tourism and Culture* (pp. 170–190). IGI Global. https://doi.org/10.4018/978-1-7998-8165-0.ch011

Valverde, R., Torres, B., & Motaghi, H. (2018). A Quantum NeuroIS Data Analytics Architecture for the Usability Evaluation of Learning Management Systems. In S. Bhattacharyya (Ed.), *Quantum-Inspired Intelligent Systems for Multimedia Data Analysis* (pp. 277–299). Hershey, PA: IGI Global. doi:10.4018/978-1-5225-5219-2.ch009

Vassilis, E. (2018). Learning and Teaching Methodology: "1:1 Educational Computing. In K. Koutsopoulos, K. Doukas, & Y. Kotsanis (Eds.), *Handbook of Research on Educational Design and Cloud Computing in Modern Classroom Settings* (pp. 122–155). Hershey, PA: IGI Global. doi:10.4018/978-1-5225-3053-4.ch007

Verma, S., & Jain, A. K. (2022). A Survey on Sentiment Analysis Techniques for Twitter. In B. Gupta, D. Peraković, A. Abd El-Latif, & D. Gupta (Eds.), *Data Mining Approaches for Big Data and Sentiment Analysis in Social Media* (pp. 57–90). IGI Global. https://doi.org/10.4018/978-1-7998-8413-2.ch003

Wang, H., Huang, P., & Chen, X. (2021). Research and Application of a Multidimensional Association Rules Mining Method Based on OLAP. *International Journal of Information Technology and Web Engineering*, *16*(1), 75–94. https://doi.org/10.4018/IJITWE.2021010104

Wexler, B. E. (2017). Computer-Presented and Physical Brain-Training Exercises for School Children: Improving Executive Functions and Learning. In B. Dubbels (Ed.), *Transforming Gaming and Computer Simulation Technologies across Industries* (pp. 206–224). Hershey, PA: IGI Global. doi:10.4018/978-1-5225-1817-4.ch012

Wimble, M., Singh, H., & Phillips, B. (2018). Understanding Cross-Level Interactions of Firm-Level Information Technology and Industry Environment: A Multilevel Model of Business Value. *Information Resources Management Journal*, *31*(1), 1–20. doi:10.4018/IRMJ.2018010101

Wimmer, H., Powell, L., Kilgus, L., & Force, C. (2017). Improving Course Assessment via Web-based Homework. *International Journal of Online Pedagogy and Course Design*, *7*(2), 1–19. doi:10.4018/IJOPCD.2017040101

Wong, S. (2021). Gendering Information and Communication Technologies in Climate Change. In M. Khosrow-Pour D.B.A. (Eds.), *Encyclopedia of Information Science and Technology, Fifth Edition* (pp. 1408-1422). IGI Global. https://doi.org/10.4018/978-1-7998-3479-3.ch096

Wong, Y. L., & Siu, K. W. (2018). Assessing Computer-Aided Design Skills. In M. Khosrow-Pour, D.B.A. (Ed.), Encyclopedia of Information Science and Technology, Fourth Edition (pp. 7382-7391). Hershey, PA: IGI Global. doi:10.4018/978-1-5225-2255-3.ch642

Wongsurawat, W., & Shrestha, V. (2018). Information Technology, Globalization, and Local Conditions: Implications for Entrepreneurs in Southeast Asia. In P. Ordóñez de Pablos (Ed.), *Management Strategies and Technology Fluidity in the Asian Business Sector* (pp. 163–176). Hershey, PA: IGI Global. doi:10.4018/978-1-5225-4056-4.ch010

Yamada, H. (2021). Homogenization of Japanese Industrial Technology From the Perspective of R&D Expenses. *International Journal of Systems and Service-Oriented Engineering, 11*(2), 24–51. doi:10.4018/IJSSOE.2021070102

Yang, Y., Zhu, X., Jin, C., & Li, J.J. (2018). Reforming Classroom Education Through a QQ Group: A Pilot Experiment at a Primary School in Shanghai. In H. Spires (Ed.), *Digital Transformation and Innovation in Chinese Education* (pp. 211–231). Hershey, PA: IGI Global. doi:10.4018/978-1-5225-2924-8.ch012

Yilmaz, R., Sezgin, A., Kurnaz, S., & Arslan, Y. Z. (2018). Object-Oriented Programming in Computer Science. In M. Khosrow-Pour, D.B.A. (Ed.), Encyclopedia of Information Science and Technology, Fourth Edition (pp. 7470-7480). Hershey, PA: IGI Global. doi:10.4018/978-1-5225-2255-3.ch650

Yu, L. (2018). From Teaching Software Engineering Locally and Globally to Devising an Internationalized Computer Science Curriculum. In S. Dikli, B. Etheridge, & R. Rawls (Eds.), *Curriculum Internationalization and the Future of Education* (pp. 293–320). Hershey, PA: IGI Global. doi:10.4018/978-1-5225-2791-6.ch016

Yuhua, F. (2018). Computer Information Library Clusters. In M. Khosrow-Pour, D.B.A. (Ed.), Encyclopedia of Information Science and Technology, Fourth Edition (pp. 4399-4403). Hershey, PA: IGI Global. doi:10.4018/978-1-5225-2255-3.ch382

Zakaria, R. B., Zainuddin, M. N., & Mohamad, A. H. (2022). Distilling Blockchain: Complexity, Barriers, and Opportunities. In P. Lai (Ed.), *Handbook of Research on Social Impacts of E-Payment and Blockchain Technology* (pp. 89–114). IGI Global. https://doi.org/10.4018/978-1-7998-9035-5.ch007

Zhang, Z., Ma, J., & Cui, X. (2021). Genetic Algorithm With Three-Dimensional Population Dominance Strategy for University Course Timetabling Problem. *International Journal of Grid and High Performance Computing, 13*(2), 56–69. https://doi.org/10.4018/IJGHPC.2021040104

About the Contributors

Mahendra Kumar Shrivas is heading various smart governance projects as a Project Lead at the Centre for Smart Governance (CSG), Department of Personnel and Administrative Reforms (E-Governance), Government of Karnataka, Bangalore, India and is a senior member of IEEE with over fifteen years of experience in Academics, Industries, and Research work in Asia, the Middle East, and Africa. He holds a Doctorate of Philosophy (Ph.D.) degree in Computer Science (Blockchain Technologies) from the Central University of Nicaragua. He has proven experience in large-scale enterprise software architecture, development, and high-performance developer team management as a team lead. He has been supervising research projects of graduate, post-graduate and doctoral scholars and giving lectures on the UK, American, African, and Indian-based university curriculums to research scholars. He is a Microsoft certified technology specialist and certified Java programmer along with NIIT & HCL certified technical trainer. His area of research interests includes but is not limited to Blockchain Technologies, Quantum Blockchains, Cybersecurity, Quantum Cryptography, Cloud Computing, AI/ML, and Database Technologies. He has published remarkable research papers in various peer-reviewed international journals and conferences. He is also contributing as a reviewer, technical program committee & editorial board member of various reputed International Journals/Conferences such as IEEE, IGI Global, etc. He has got prestigious awards for notable services and contributions towards the advancement of IEEE and the Engineering Professions in 2018 & 2020 by the IEEE Ghana Section, along with best trainer and faculty awards from NIIT and Sikkim Manipal University respectively. He has trained more than 8000 Computer Science and Information Technology Engineers in the advanced software engineering practices, technologies and tools in India and Abroad.

Kamal Kant Hiran is having more than 17 years of academic and research experience in Asia, Africa, Europe, and North America. He has published 15 International books with repute publishers like BPB Publications, IGI Global, De Gruyter from India, Germany, USA, UK. His book titled "Cloud Computing: Master the

Concepts, Architecture and Applications with Real-World Examples and Case Studies" is popular among Indian and overseas market and got the best seller category in the emerging technology trends books. He has made significant contributions to our society's technological transformation. He has several awards to his credit such as International travel grant for attending the IEEE Region 8 Committee Meeting at Warsaw, Poland; International travel grant for Germany from ITS Europe, Passau, Germany; Best Research Paper Award at the University of Gondar, Ethiopia; IEEE Liberia Subsection Founder Award; Gold Medal Award in MTech (Hons.); IEEE Ghana Section Award-Technical and Professional Activity Chair; IEEE Senior Member Recognition, Best IEEE Student Branch Award, Elsevier Reviewer Recognition Award. He has published 45 scientific research papers in SCI/Scopus/ Web of Science and IEEE Transactions Journal, conferences, 2 Indian Patents, 1 Australian Patent Grants. He has made several international visits to Denmark, Sweden, Germany, Norway, Ghana, Liberia, Ethiopia, Russia, Dubai, Mexico, and Jordan for research exposures. His research interests focus on Cloud computing, Machine-deep learning and Intelligent IoT. His research work is appreciated by several media and renowned bodies across the world - ITS Europe, IEEE USA, Springer, Rajasthan Patrika and Danik Bhaskar.

Ashok Bhansali is currently serving as Professor and Dean, Department of Computer Engineering and Applications at GLA University, Mathura, India. He possesses approximately 25 years of amalgamated experience of industry and academia, during which he has worked with top MNCs and Universities like Tech-Mahindra, NELCO, Symbiosis University, and OP Jindal University. Dr. Ashok is an active IEEE volunteer and has been general chair for many IEEE conferences. He has delivered many keynote sessions and lectures at FICCI, CII and national/ international conferences and workshops. He has published more than 40 papers in different journals/conferences on different topics including social network mining, eLearning, ad-hoc networks, IoT, Blockchain etc. He has a special interest in Education 4.0 and implementing and promoting eLearning. He was an advisor to Govt of Chhattisgarh for the virtual education project of MHRD, Govt. of India.

Ruchi Doshi has more than 16 years of academic, research and software development experience in Asia, Europe, and Africa. Currently she is working as Research Supervisor and Associate Professor at the Azteca University, Mexico and Adjunct Professor at the Jyoti Vidyapeeth Women's University, Rajasthan, India. She worked at the BlueCrest University College, Liberia, Africa; BlueCrest University College, Ghana, Africa; Amity University, India; Trimax IT Infrastructure & Services, India. She is interested in the field of Machine Learning and Cloud computing framework development. She has published research papers in peer-reviewed international journals and conferences; 3 Indian Patents; 3 books on Cloud Computing, Machine Learning, Mobile Cloud computing, Intelligent IoT Systems for Big Data Analysis and Mobile application development. She is Reviewer, Advisor, Ambassador and Editorial board member of various reputed International Journals and Conferences with IEEE, Springer, and Elsevier. She is an active member in organizing many international seminars, workshops, and conferences. She is nominated from by IEEE Headquarter, USA for the Chair, Women in Engineering (WIE) position in Liberia, West Africa.

* * *

Adebayo Felix Adekoya is a Chartered Information Technology Professional (CITP) and an alumnus of the DAAD-DIES International Deans' Course. He is an Associate Professor of Computer Science in the Department of Computer Science and Informatics and expert in artificial intelligence, software engineering, learning analytics and information systems.

Emmanuel Adjei Domfeh is currently a Senior Research Assistant in the Department of Computer Science and Informatics at the University of Energy and Natural Resources. He is keenly noted for his roles in championing hands-on practical workshops to equip the youth with relevant tech skills for the job market He has a Bachelor of Science as well as Masters of Philosophy in Computer Science from the University of Energy and Natural Resources. As a young academic, he has taught a lot of relevant Computer Science and IT courses ranging from Artificial Intelligence, Software Engineering, Information Systems, web engineering, IT project management and a list of others. His research interest spans from Quantum Computing, Human Centered AI, Machine Learning and HCI.

Chitra Bhole is an Assistant Professor in department of Computer engineering and pursuing PH.D from Sir Padampat Singhania University,Udaipur. She has total 17 years of experiance. She likes teaching profession that is why she in this profession. She always ensures the things that have been taught in the lectures and/ or practical have been understood by the students from merit holders to average ones. She plans her lecture in advance and cover the syllabus from both examination point of view and knowledge point of view. She utilizes entire lecture time to impart the knowledge. She has good subject knowledge and is satisfied both a lecture well organized. As a teacher, she always have the strived for see the overall development of the students. She wants her students to be good and responsible citizens. To build rapport with the students, she believes in strong subject knowledge, good communication skill, actually clarity and convincing power, transparency in all issues mainly assessment in term-work/papers. Honesty, dedication towards work, understanding of problems of students and colleagues and helpful nature keeps the relationships healthy. She has published & presented around 18 papers at national and in international conference. She is good at job and home. She wishes to devote sometime for some social work but could not manage till now. But in future she will definitely serve for society. Her parents and teachers have played an important role in nurturing her life. Her hobbies are spending time with her daughter, touring and traveling & reading. She has done BE in Computers from Pune University & M.E from VIT, Wadala, Mumbai. Her role model is her mother who taught her to value change, respecting others and to be patient. She appreciates honesty, truthfulness and accountability.. She has taught the different subjects like Computer Programming-I, Computer Networks, Advanced Computer Networks, Web Engineering, Object Oriented Software Engineering, Web Technology, Theory of Computer Science, Distributed Computing Her fields of interest are Image Processing Artificial Intelligence, Deep Learning .and Web Technology in computer engineering branch. She has reviewed and published the book of the Software Engineering, Semester V, Computer Engineering branch in 2021-22.As well as reviewed and published the book of the Software Engineering, Semester V, Electronics and Computer Science branch in 2022-23. She is working for IET (Institution of Engineering and Technology), International Professional body.

Manish Dadhich is Ph.D. from the Department of Commerce, EAFM, University of Rajasthan, M. Com, UGC-NET (Commerce); MBA-FM, UGC-NET (Management), RPSC-SET (Management). He has 12+ years of teaching experience in various colleges, universities, and corporate sectors, a rare blend of academia, industry, corporate consultancy, and research. He is presently working as Assistant Professor in School of Management, Sir Padampat Singhania University, Udaipur. He has published more than 62 research papers in reputed international & national journals, including 18 papers in Scopus/SCI/IEEE/WoS. He also presented more than 52 research papers at national and international conferences. He is a reviewer, advisor, and editorial board member of various reputed International Journals and Conferences of IEEE, Springer, and Elsevier. He was awarded two gold medals in National Seminar for the best research paper. He authored one textbook and an edited book. He is a regular invitee for FDP, research workshops, orientation, and refresher course lectures. He is also awarded one Australian patent. Further, his main research focuses on Finance, Banking, AI-ML, Econometrics, and Statistics.

Ritesh Kumar Jain works as an Assistant Professor, at the Geetanjali Institute of Technical Studies, (GITS), Udaipur, Rajasthan, India. He has more than 16 years of teaching and research experience. He has completed his BE and MTech. He worked as an Assistant Professor & Head of Department at S. S. College of Engineering. Udaipur; Assistant Professor at Sobhasaria Engineering College, Sikar; Lecturer at the Institute of Technology & Management, Bhilwara. He is a reviewer of international peer-review journals. He is author of several research papers in peer reviewed international journals and conferences.

Sarika Khandelwal is working as Associate Professor in CSE dept. of G H Raisoni College of Engineering, Nagpur. She has more than 21 years of teaching experience. Her domain of interest includes biometric template security.

Jacob Mensah has both a BSc and MPhil in Computer Science from the University of Energy and Natural Resources. He is a Senior Research Assistant in the Department of Computer Science and Informatics at the University of Energy and Natural Resources. He received his BSc degree in Computer Science and MPhil in Computer Science from University of Energy and Natural Resources, Sunyani Ghana. His research interest includes Machine Learning, Data Analysis and Quantum Computing.

Maad M. Mijwil is an Iraqi Academician; he is born in Baghdad, Iraq, in 1987. He received his B.Sc. degree in software engineering from Baghdad college of economic sciences university, Iraq, in 2009. He received a M.Sc. degree in 2015 from the computer science department, university of Baghdad in the field of wireless sensor networks, Iraq. Currently, he is working as a Lecturer and an academic member of staff in the computer techniques engineering department at Baghdad college of economic sciences university, Iraq. He has over ten years of experience in teaching and guiding projects for undergraduates. He has authored more than 80 publications, including papers/ chapters (published 39 peer reviewed papers in national/international conferences and journals), preprints, presentations, and posters. He is also an editor in more than 10 international/national journals and a reviewer in more than 70 international/national journals. He has served on technical program committees for many prestigious conferences. Also, he graduated from Publons academy as a peer reviewer. His Google citations are over 200 mark. His research interests include artificial intelligence, machine learning, deep learning, wireless sensor networks, genetic algorithm.

Peter Nimbe is a Lecturer in the Department of Computer Science and Informatics at the University of Energy and Natural Resources (UENR) in Ghana. His specialty is in Quantum Computing and Information Security. He is a Quantum Researcher. He is a member of IEEE Quantum Technical Community, IEEE Nanotechnology Council, IEEE Sensors Council, IEEE Computer Society Technical Committee, and

IEEE Collabratec. He belongs to the following organizations; Stanford Quantum Computing Association, Institute of ICT Professionals Ghana (IIPGH), Python Ghana, European Alliance for Innovation (EAI), International Computer Science and Engineering Society (ICSES), Institute of Research Engineers and Doctors (IRED), Ghana Science Association (GSA), University Teachers Association of Ghana (UTAG), International Association of Engineers (IAENG), and International Association of Computer Science and IT (IACSIT).

Prantosh Kumar Paul is working as an Executive Director (PG CIS Program) & Asst. Professor (IST), Head/ Coordinator, Dept. of Computer & Information Sciences, and Information Scientist Position at Raiganj University, West Bengal India. Additionally he is also holding the Position of Honorary Professor, Logos University International, Louisiana, USA, Chief Advisor (Innovative Program & Research Planning), Srinivas University, India holds Ph.D. in IST from India's premier & oldest Public Engineering Institute IIEST Shibpur (An Institute of National Importance), M.Tech. (By Research) in IST, MS by Research in Information Assurance & IT Management, M.Sc. (Double) and MBA in InfoSys. He is actively engaged in the research and academic activities in the field of IST. He is also CEO and VP of IST Foundation. Virtually he is among the few Indian Information Science professional who holds Post Graduate Qualification in almost all the dimensions of Information Sciences; ranging from Computer Sciences, Management Science, Information Science and Information Technology. He is in favor on starting programs and specialization in emerging IT & Computing subjects that are applied and having social and business touch. He is also mastermind for designing interdisciplinary Masters (MSc) program on computing i.e. MSc-Computer & Information Science based on principles of interaction of information-technology-people. He has credited over 25 Authored & Edited Books in diverse areas and focused on emerging and interdisciplinary Information Science. Further He has about 200+ research/ policy paper on Cloud Computing Applications in Information Science, Green Computing or Green IT in Information Field, I-Schools aspects/ Usability Engineering/ Information Science Educational aspects etc. He is Chief Editor of IJASE, New Delhi, India and Chief Editor, IRA International Journal of Management and Social Sciences, Chief Editor of IJISC, New Delhi, India. He is also involved as Editorial Board Member of more than 130 National and International Journals in diverse field He has completed many Invited Talk viz. SRM University, Sikkim University, VIT University, Srinivas University, Mangalore University, TCG Digital, CloudNet India. He has the track record of associating more than 200 International Conferences as TPC, Advisory Committee, Speakers and in Organizing Body. Among his Awards few important are Best Researcher Award in Information Sciences (from IARA, Trichy), Best Faculty Award from IARA, David Clark Blair Young Scientist Award in Computer

& Information Science (from BSS, India), International Young Scientist Award (from ISROSET) in Health Informatics, Citation Award (from Sri Sai University) Distinguished Young Information Science & Computing Academician in Asia from IRDP, Asian Information Science and Technology Ambassador Award-19, International Social Informatics and Digital Society Think Tank Award-2020, etc.

Omega John Unogwu holds a Bachelor of Science degree in Geography and Education from the Ahmadu Bello University, Zaria - Nigeria; a Post Graduate and Master of Science degrees from the National Open University of Nigeria, and Sikkim Manipal University, Accra - Ghana respectively. He is currently undertaking a PhD in Computer Science at the Universidad Azteca, Mexico. He is a Chief Scientist with over 13 years of research experience in Space Science and Technology at the Centre for Geodesy and Geodynamics, National Space Research and Development Agency, Nigeria, with keen interest in Computing, (AI, Blockchain, IoT and Machine Learning); Interferometric Synthetic Aperture Radar (InSAR) as well as Global Navigation Satellite Systems (GNSS). He holds membership in IEEE, NAG, Nigeria Computer Society and has participated in various national and international conferences and workshops.

Benjamin Asubam Weyori received his Ph. D. and M. Phil. in Computer Engineering from the Kwame Nkrumah University of Science and Technology (KNUST), Ghana in 2016 and 2011, respectively. He obtained his Bachelor of Science in Computer Science from the University for Development Studies (UDS), Tamale, Ghana in 2006. He is a Senior Lecturer and currently the Acting Director of Center for Distance Education and E-Learning. He was the Former Acting Head of the Department of Computer Science and Informatics, the University of Energy and Natural Resources (UENR) in Ghana. His main research interest includes artificial intelligence, computer visions (image processing), machine learning and web engineering.

Index

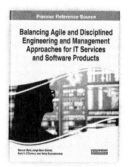

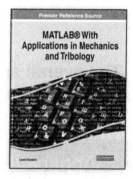

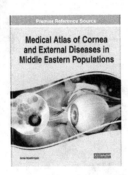
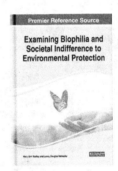
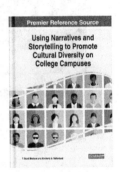

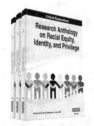

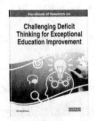

Printed in the United States
by Baker & Taylor Publisher Services